DEMOCRACY AND POLICING

The Policy Studies Institute (PSI) is Britain's leading independent research organisation undertaking studies of economic, industrial and social policy, and the workings of political institutions.

PSI is a registered charity, run on a non-profit basis, and is not associated with any political party, pressure group or commercial interest.

PSI attaches great importance to covering a wide range of subject areas with its multi-disciplinary approach. The Institute's 40+ researchers are organised in teams which currently cover the following programmes:

Family Finances – *Employment* – *Information Policy* – *Social Justice and Social Order* – *Health Studies and Social Care* – *Education* – *Industrial Policy and Futures* – *Arts and the Cultural Industries* – *Environment and Quality of Life*

This publication arises from the Social Justice and Social Order programme and is one of over 30 publications made available by the Institute each year.

Information about the work of PSI, and a catalogue of available books can be obtained from:

Marketing Department, PSI
100 Park Village East, London NW1 3SR

Democracy and Policing

Trevor Jones, Tim Newburn and David J. Smith

POLICY STUDIES INSTITUTE
London

The publishing imprint of the independent
POLICY STUDIES INSTITUTE
100 Park Village East, London NW1 3SR
Telephone: 071-387 2171 Fax: 071-388 0914

© Policy Studies Institute 1994.

ISBN 0 85374 579 X

PSI Research Report 784

A CIP catalogue record of this book is available from the British Library.

1 2 3 4 5 6 7 8 9

PSI publications are available from
BEBC Distribution Ltd
P O Box 1496, Poole, Dorset, BH12 3YD

Books will normally be despatched within 24 hours. Cheques should be made payable to BEBC Distribution Ltd.

Credit card and telephone/fax orders may be placed on the following freephone numbers:

FREEPHONE: 0800 262260
FREEFAX: 0800 262266

Booktrade representation (UK & Eire):
Book Representation and Distribution Ltd (BRAD)
244a London Road, Hadleigh, Essex SS7 2DE

PSI subscriptions are available from PSI's subscription agent
Carfax Publishing Company Ltd
P O Box 25, Abingdon, Oxford OX14 3UE

Laserset by Policy Studies Institute
Printed in Great Britain by BPC Books and Journals, Ltd Exeter

Contents

Preface and acknowledgements

This book is the first in a series that examines the making of policing policy. It looks at how and why policing policy in England has changed over recent years, and what this tells us about the relationship between policing and democracy in Britain today. Subsequent books in the series will cover the making of policing policy in France, and in the Netherlands. The English part of the study was funded jointly by the Leverhulme Trust and the Economic and Social Research Council. The Leverhulme Trust provided additional funds for the studies of policing policy in France and the Netherlands.

The original proposal for a study of the making of policing policy was developed by Christine Horton, then a research fellow at PSI. She played a leading role in the initial stages of the English study, and later carried out the research on the making of policing policy in France whilst based in Paris.

The research in England was carried out between 1990 and 1992. The overall aim was to describe and analyse how the various actors involved in the policy-making process interact to produce changes in the style, organisation and operation of policing on the ground. A central part of the research involved detailed case studies of four provincial police forces, and relevant organistions in the four areas. We would particularly like to thank the chief constables, officers and civilian staff of the participating forces. They not only welcomed PSI researchers, but in many cases provided a very high degree of extra help, far above what had been expected. Without the time and effort given by the police officers and civilians from these forces, it goes without saying, this study would not have been possible. We also would like to record our thanks to Home Office officials for supporting the project, and for the information, advice and general help given throughout.

A number of other people made important contributions to the study. Julie Humphreys, Kate Joyce and Ann Welsh, on placement at PSI from the University of Surrey, carried out a number of important interviews with women's organisations and representatives of the media. We would also like to thank Dr Michael Freeden who made helpful comments on drafts of the first chapter. Finally, we would like to thank our colleagues at PSI, particularly Sue Johnson, for advice and support given throughout the project.

1 Exploring Democracy

Introduction

This book explores democracy by analysing how and why policing policy has changed in recent years. Most research and writing on democracy focuses on explicitly 'political' institutions: on parliaments, political parties, cabinets, electoral systems, and suchlike. However, in the modern service delivery state, it can be argued that the way in which public services impinge on the lives of citizens may be more important, as the embodiment or negation of the democratic ideal, than parliament or central government. The protection of liberty, social and economic opportunities, and the ability of individuals to shape and develop their lives are crucially affected by a range of public services.

The police are arguably the central public service in a modern state. They are there to protect our essential freedoms, and to do so have a monopoly over the legitimate use of force. In the words of David Bayley (1991), 'Because the police are the most visibly coercive instrument of government, their actions powerfully influence whether government is perceived to be legitimate'. Yet differences in policing structures and styles exist across societies that are all described as democratic. The explicitly political set of national institutional arrangements has only an indirect influence on what the public services actually do.

This study therefore approaches democracy by an unorthodox route. Instead of starting from explicitly political institutions, it focuses on a public service that has a unique relationship with the institutions of democracy and their legitimacy. The central objective is to establish what shapes policing policy, principally by considering how and why it changes. An equally important task is to test the actual process of policy formation against touchstones of democracy, so as to establish how far and in what ways the developments in policing policy in England conform to a democratic ideal.

As Reiner (1992) has pointed out, policing has emerged from the shadows to the forefront of public debate in the 1980s and 1990s. This new-found interest reached a climax in 1993 with the publication of three major reports and sets of proposals: the report of the Royal Commission on Criminal Justice, which had been set up in response to a series of miscarriages of justice, many of them involving police misconduct; the report of the Sheehy Committee (Sheehy, 1993), established by the Home Secretary to develop proposals on rank structure, pay, and measures of police performance; and the government White Paper on police reform (Home Office, 1993b), which led in 1994 to the Police and Magistrates' Courts Bill (Home Office, 1993a). The reasons for this rash of reports and proposals are complex, but they include the increasing salience, from 1979 onwards, of the Conservative Party's promise of better 'law and order'; their continuing failure to deliver, as crime rates have continued to rise; the realisation that increasing expenditure on the police was producing no tangible results, at least in terms that the electorate would recognise; and a perceived collapse of public confidence in the police, associated with the riots of 1981 and 1985, and the police misconduct highlighted by well-publicised miscarriages of justice. In fact, there has been no general collapse in confidence, although opinion polls did show some decline, from a very high level, in public approval during the 1980s.[1] However, the perception of such a collapse, combined with the other factors, has projected the police to the top of the list of priorities for reform by a government still looking for ways to be radical.

Among the proposals of the White Paper were ones that would affect the governance of the police by changing the structure, funding, and powers of police authorities, and by generating more information about what the police do and achieve. These proposals have met with a chorus of criticism from many organisations involved with policing. The spokespersons of the opposition parties, of the local authority associations, of police authorities, and of the police staff associations have been united in their condemnation. Where those bodies have led, the House of Lords has duly followed. Whereas a number of specific criticisms have surfaced, it is the perceived threat to the accountability of the police service that appears to have caused the most upset. At a conference organised by the local authority associations (under the ominous banner *Democracy at Risk*), the Labour spokesperson on Home Affairs described the proposals as 'an attack on local democracy'. His Liberal Democrat counterpart argued that the proposals would undermine a system of accountability and control that was the envy of other countries. The President of the Association of Chief Police Officers (ACPO) said the proposals were a threat to 'policing by consent'. Numerous representatives of local authorities argued that the proposed reforms would jeopardise our 'democratic' system of policing (ACC & AMA, 1993).

Two things in particular are striking about the terms of the debate over the White Paper and the subsequent Bill. First, the unlikely partners forming the coalition of opposition to the proposals. Is it really only ten years ago that chief constables clashed with radical Labour metropolitan police authorities, and raised concerns about the local political control of operational policing? Second, it is striking that terms like 'democracy', 'democratic policing' and 'local accountability' are waved like flags, as if their meaning were beyond doubt, and their virtues beyond question. Even the most cursory glance at writings on the theory of democracy reveals fundamental disagreements about what democracy is, and about whether it should be accepted uncritically as a 'Good Thing'. Corcoran (1983:15) describes democracy as 'the world's new universal religion', and reminds us that the term has not always been used by political thinkers to imply praise. In order to make progress, it is necessary to clarify what is meant by democracy, and how these ideas can be related to policing. More specifically, it is important to isolate a number of criteria against which the actual structures that determine the pattern of policing can be tested. Since in modern times democracy is a positive ideal, and therefore demands approval, it is also important to consider why democratic policing, on some proposed definition, is preferable to other arrangements.

The core of this book (Chapters 2-5) consists of an analysis of the making of policing policy within four English police forces during the 1980s and early 1990s. This chapter establishes the framework of analysis within which the findings on the making of policing policy will be located. The following section shows how this work grows out of a recent tradition of research and writing on the police, discusses the idea of policing policy, which is central to this inquiry, and describes the scope and methods of the study. Subsequent sections describe the structure and powers of the institutions concerned with the governance of the police, and distil from a discussion of the concept of democracy a set of criteria for judging in what ways a system might be considered to be 'democratic'. This prepares the way for the later chapters, which set out the evidence on how and why certain major changes of policy have come about.

Two traditions of research on policing

Broadly speaking, two traditions of research and writing on the police can be identified. One is concerned with the governance of the police, and therefore concentrates on legal and political institutions and their relationships with the police service. In this tradition there are writers who approach the subject from the standpoint of constitutional theory, such as Geoffrey Marshall (1965, 1978), from that of social history and law, such as Lawrence Lustgarten (1986), and from a broader sociological perspective, such as Robert Reiner (1992). The second tradition, which started in the 1970s and gained force throughout the 1980s, is concerned with what police officers actually do, how they do it, and what shapes policing behaviour and the pattern of policing from day to day. Until relatively recently, there has been little linkage between these two streams of work. At the extremes, practitioners in each of the traditions simply assumed that their own set of problems were the only important ones. For example, Marshall (1965, 1978) never considered whether the constitutional arrangements that he wrote about actually influenced the style or pattern or policing in a significant way. At the other extreme, the team of PSI researchers, when they embarked on the unprecedented programme of research on the Metropolitan Police in 1980, explicitly decided not to study constitutional arrangements on the assumption that they would be largely irrelevant to policing on the ground. In a long review article commenting on *Police and People in London*, Lustgarten (1984) complained that it was the wrong study, because it was not about policy-making by chief constables and how that was influenced by the wider political and constitutional framework.

This present programme of research[2] can be seen as a bridge between the two traditions. In fact, although *Police and People in London* (Small, 1983; Smith, 1983a,b; Smith & Gray, 1983) was primarily concerned with policing on the ground, the analysis of the findings pushed towards making links with legal and political institutions. That earlier programme of research consisted of four main elements, which together provided a number of different perspectives on interactions between the police and the public and on the processes, external constraints, and organisational structures that shape policing behaviour. These elements were, first, a survey of Londoners, which provided a detailed account of people's contacts with the police from their perspective, their attitudes towards the police, their policing policy preferences, and their experience as victims of crime. Although half of the sample of Londoners in the survey were members of ethnic minority groups, there was a danger that the experience and attitudes of young black men would not be adequately tapped by a formal survey method. The second element filled that gap through participant observation by a young black researcher of a group of young unemployed men in a self-help hostel. The third element was a large-scale survey of police officers up to the rank of Inspector, which collected systematic information about their deployment, pattern of work, use of time, interactions with the public from the police perspective, career patterns, and attitudes towards police work. The final element, published as *The Police in Action* (Smith & Gray, 1983), was based on extensive observation by two researchers of police work in 12 London divisions and within a number of specialist groups; the results of these observations were interpreted in the light of the organisational structure and dynamics of the police force and of the constraints and rewards originating from outside the police organisation.

It was clear that the law and its wider constitutional framework influenced the pattern of policing and the behaviour of individual police officers at best in only an indirect way. The clearest message from the 1983 reports was that in seeking to control or influence policing behaviour a due process model was hopelessly inadequate. Those who aimed to reform policing through further legal regulation ignored the fact, well established by this programme of research, that existing regulations were frequently ignored, and could even be counter-productive. There might be conditions in which regulation could work, but those who were interested in changing the pattern of policing would have to take an interest in the police organisation, the way it was managed, the satisfactions and frustrations of police officers, and the dynamics of their interactions with the public.

Although the PSI authors considered that the relationship between police behaviour and externally imposed constraints was indirect, they also considered that the task of understanding the nature of that relationship was the most important one for researchers in the field. Within the scope of the research carried out at the time, it was possible only to start to address the problem. Smith & Gray (1983:169-72) approached this subject by observing that 'People inside and outside the Force generally think of policing behaviour as being shaped chiefly by the application of rules and set procedure'. While it was true that a complex network of rules and set procedures was a central feature of the way the force was organised, there would be dangers in taking too superficial a view of the way the rules function. 'It is important to recognise that these rules are almost purely negative in their effect: that is, police officers may be disciplined, prosecuted, or otherwise get into difficulties if they are seen to break the rules, but they will not necessarily be praised, enjoy their work or achieve their career objectives if they keep to them.' It was argued that because positive objectives were at least as influential as rules, the view that policing behaviour was chiefly shaped by rules might well be wrong.

Observing that 'Because a rule exists, it does not follow that it automatically and rigidly governs day-to-day policing behaviour', Smith & Gray (1983:171) we;.t on to make a distinction between three types of rules. This analysis was offered more as an aid to discovery in future research than as a summary of existing findings.

> *Working rules* are those that are internalised by police officers to become guiding principles of their conduct. *Inhibitory rules* are those which are not internalised, but which police officers take into account when

deciding how to act and which tend to discourage them from behaving in certain ways in case they should be caught and the rule invoked against them. *Presentational rules* are ones that exist to give an acceptable appearance to the way that police work is carried out. It is important to realise that it is not only or even mainly the police who seek to put this gloss in the reality of policing behaviour and interactions between the police and the public. Most of the presentational rules derive from the law and are part of a (successful) attempt by the wider society to deceive itself about the realities of policing.

The argument that many rules are presentational resonates with McBarnet's (1981) contention that many of the principles that are said to underlie criminal justice (for example, that every citizen is equal under the law) are largely rhetorical, and have little influence on actual outcomes.

Although this analysis needs to be taken further, it suggests that one part of the framework that is supposed to influence policing and is external to it – the framework of law – has an important effect in some instances, and not in others. The same will probably apply to other external influences, such as police authorities, or Home Office circulars. The purpose of the present programme of research is to trace these relationships between external influences and the pattern of policing in more detail. It therefore occupies an intermediate position between the analysis of constitutional structures and the description of the culture and behaviour of working groups of police officers, and aims to form a bridge between these two traditions. Policing policy is the appropriate level of analysis for a study of this kind.

Policing policy
Allen (1976:97) argued that 'We do not say to the police: "Here is the problem. Deal with it." We say: "Here is a detailed code. Enforce it."' That view would tend to exclude the possibility of policing policy, but it has become increasingly discredited in recent years. As argued, for example, by Lustgarten (1986), Smith (1986), and Reiner (1992), although the police have a duty to enforce the law, this does not impose any particular pattern of policing, because policing resources are limited, whereas the opportunities for law enforcement are limitless. Decisions must be taken about priorities. Some of these are made at a high level, and expressed by organisational structure and staffing allocation (for example, the creation of a specialist squad). Others are taken by individual officers from day to day, although their individual use of discretion is influenced by assumptions and perceptions stemming from the police organisation and beyond. Apart from deciding which laws to enforce, it is also necessary to decide how to enforce them, and different decisions on methods of enforcement may lead

to entirely opposite patterns of policing (for example, uniform patrol, plainclothes surveillance, or targeting of offenders through collated intelligence may all be used to tackle street crime).

A further objection to Allen's model is that much policing is not directly concerned with law enforcement, but with containing incidents that might lead to lawbreaking ('keeping the peace'); and some is concerned with crime prevention. In addition, a number of offences (such as 'obstructing a police officer in the execution of his duty') are deliberately framed vaguely, so as to provide the police with a flexible resource in seeking to achieve some other objective (such as 'keeping the peace'). Hence it would not make sense to say that enforcing the law against 'obstructing a police officer in the execution of his duty' was a statement about what the police are actually supposed to do.

It follows that even if the police always acted in accordance with the law, this would only set broad limits to possible patterns of policing, and would not determine any actual pattern in a positive way. Whatever does determine the pattern of policing within those broad limits can be called policing policy. This is a conclusion that used to be resisted by senior police officers up to about 15 years ago. It was commonly said that the task of the police was to 'enforce the law without fear or favour' with the implication that any attempt to identify a policy and discuss whether it should be changed would be an infringement of constabulary independence. Yet over the past 15 years, senior police officers have moved from the posture of defending their autonomy to the last ditch to one of seeking to consult with elements of the wider society before taking decisions. (Perhaps more accurately, chief constables who defended their autonomy to the last ditch have retired and have been replaced by younger men with a different approach.) Hence the idea that there is and must be such a thing as policing policy, and that it is a legitimate subject of public debate, has increasingly gained acceptance.

This definition of policing policy is deliberately a broad one. It includes many features or consequences of the police organisation and of policing behaviour that have not been explicitly discussed or decided upon. Hence the practice, before the 1980s, of routinely disbelieving women's allegations that they had been raped (Chambers & Millar, 1983) can rightly be described as a policy, even though no-one inside or outside the police force had ever explicitly or formally resolved that rape allegations should be dealt with in that way. A policy can be deduced from a pattern of behaviour. Also, where a stated policy is contradicted by the actual pattern of policing, the real policy is likely to be that inherent in behaviour: to the extent that a policy is not carried through, it is merely rhetorical.

The present programme of research, therefore, is concerned with the middle range indexed by the term policing policy, and how that policy is shaped by the institutional framework that surrounds the police and links them to the other institutions of a democracy. It is not concerned with the fine grain of policing on the ground, but it is not limited to statements of policy either, since policy is interpreted as that which is inherent in the actual pattern of policing.

Scope and methods of the study

The overall aim of this study is to analyse what democracy means in practice by examining policy change in a key public service. Thus the objective is to describe and analyse how the various actors involved in the policy-making process interact to produce changes in the style, organisation or operation of policing on the ground. In England, these key actors include the Home Office, Her Majesty's Inspectorate of Constabulary, the Home Secretary, the police authorities, pressure and community groups, political parties, the media, and the police service itself. In particular, the study seeks to assess how the present police policy-making process fits in with the 1964 Police Act, and the nature and extent of democratic involvement in that process.

The plan was to identify a few specific policy areas in which there had been substantial and concrete changes in recent years, and to use an intensive study of policy change in these areas as the basis for wider generalisation about the democratic input into policy-making. A limitation of this approach is that it looks at why certain policies *have* changed, but not at why other features of policing have remained constant. This approach to analysing the policy-making process has been criticised on the ground that its notion of political power is one-dimensional. Bachrach and Baratz (1962) have drawn attention to a second dimension of political power. On this view, there are important issues that do not reach the decision-making process, because they are manipulated off the agenda. The 'mobilisation of bias' (where 'bias' is a set of predominant values, beliefs, rituals and institutional procedures) can be used to confine the decision-making process to relatively 'safe' issues. These 'non-decisions' are of central importance as an exercise of political power, but are not apparent from the observation of key political decisions. What is required is a deeper examination of the policy-making process to seek out suppressed grievances and unarticulated policy preferences that would challenge the established order. The crucial exercise of power, on this view, is that which prevents such challenges from surfacing. Lukes (1974) took this argument one step further, when he maintained that the 'two-dimensional' notion of power is itself too limited. He argued that there is a third dimension of power that also involves the mobilisation of bias to keep certain issues from the agenda of politics, However, the third dimension, unlike the second, does not necessarily involve a conscious exercise of power, but arises through people's wants being manipulated by socialisation processes. As a consequence, people's articulated policy preferences may conflict with their 'real' interests.

It is not clear how the existence or nature of Lukes's third dimension of power could be revealed by any kind of research or analysis (although Lukes claimed that it could be). The practice of ascribing 'real interests' to people on the basis of a political ideology, where these conflict with their expressed preferences, seems anti-democratic on any reasonable interpretation of democracy. Nevertheless, these criticisms do underline the problem that the chosen research method focuses on change rather than continuity. For two reasons, however, that limitation is less important than it may at first appear.

First, the last twenty years have been a period of remarkable change in the police service. If the period under consideration had been the 1930s or the 1950s, it would indeed have been perverse to focus on change, because these were periods of stability or even stasis in the police service. Since the period under consideration is one of considerable turbulence, it is appropriate and illuminating to focus on the reasons for change. Of course, even in a period of substantial change, there are still enormously important continuities, so an investigation of change cannot tell us everything about the influences on policing policy, but provided that we remain aware of the continuities, that is not a crippling limitation.

Second, the examination of actual policy change proves to be far more revealing than Lukes (1974) would have expected. It shows that issues that formerly did not reach the decision-making process have moved onto the agenda for various reasons. In practice, therefore, the apparently hidden dimensions of power can be studied by observing the change in policies over time.

Choice of policy areas

The areas of policy were chosen so as to provide contrasting illustrations of decision-making about policing matters. The eventual choice was made after analysis of recent Home Office circulars and discussions with key people in organisations involved with policing. The chosen areas were as follows.

- The development of crime prevention policy. There was a sharp increase in the rate of crime, whether measured by victimisation surveys or by recorded crime, across nearly all western countries over the 1980s (see Smith, in press). This has led to an upsurge of interest in crime prevention in many countries, and Britain was no exception. For many years, crime prevention was seen as primarily the task of the police, whose main strategy involved visible patrol. More recently, there has been a growing doubt about the effectiveness of the police role in crime prevention. Many sources question whether the police are a suitable agency to take the leading role in developing some of the newer environmental and community-based forms of crime prevention.

- New policing responses to rape, domestic violence, and child abuse. Recent years have seen a rapid increase in the awareness of family violence, and of the sexual abuse of women and children. This has led to demands for major changes in the way that the police deal with the investigation of sexual assault and domestic violence, and the support that they offer to victims.

- Civilianisation. During the 1980s there has been a substantial increase in the number and proportion of civilians employed in the police service. While the majority of civilians have traditionally been employed in lower clerical positions, there has been a recent trend towards increasing the civilian representation in more senior positions in the police organisation.

One of the three policy areas – civilianisation – is of great importance for efficiency and effectiveness, but is not salient in public debate. It was deliberately chosen so as to test the democratic input into important policy changes that are internal to the police service, and which the public tend to know little about.

An obvious area left out of the study is the policing of major 'public order events' such as the miners' strike of 1984-5 or the riots of 1985. Major changes in policing policy, having far-reaching implications, occurred in this field over the 1980s.[3] However, partly because of the fall-out from *Police and People in London*, PSI had substantial difficulty in gaining acceptance for this research project within the police service, and in fact the approval of ACPO was never granted. In those circumstances, we judged that it would not be practicable to include the sensitive topic of public order policing among those under detailed consideration.

The research carried out

Research was carried out within four police force areas in England, and at the national level. The choice of possible forces was made after discussions with Home Office officials and other experts. When ACPO approval was withheld, the procedure was to write to individual chief constables in the first instance. In the event, four chief constables agreed, after a total of ten had been approached. The choice of possible police force areas was informed by a number of considerations. A key requirement was to include forces that differed in terms of the institutional arrangements for the democratic involvement in policy-making. The four police forces that agreed to participate did cover an appropriate mix of police authority types. Two were single county forces, where the police authority was a committee of the county council. One of the forces covered two administrative counties, and thus had a joint police authority made up of equal proportions of county councillors and magistrates from each geographical area. The fourth was a metropolitan police force with a joint board police authority. Two of the areas were in the North of England, one in the Midlands, and one in the South.

Within the police forces themselves, the research involved informal interviews with senior officers, and with other officers and civilian staff at force headquarters dealing with the policy issues under consideration. A substantial body of internal documents and statistics was collected from each participating force. In addition to the research carried out at headquarters, the researchers visited two sub-divisions within each force to find out about the implementation of policy at the level of the basic management units. In each sub-division informal interviews were carried out with the sub-divisional commander and with a range of other officers and civilian staff.

A second focus of research was the four police authorities within the chosen force areas. Informal interviews were conducted with leading members and the secretariat, and records of police authority meetings over the six to ten years before the visit were analysed. Relevant information was extracted from the minutes, and in three forces, a police authority meeting was attended by a researcher.

In each force area research was carried out within a number of organisations concerned with the chosen policy issues, or which come into contact with the police in some other way. These included local police consultative committees (some of whose meetings we attended), crime prevention panels and other organisations concerned with crime prevention, victim support schemes, voluntary groups concerned with women's issues and child abuse, and representatives of social services departments.

Research was also carried out within central government, Parliament, and other national organisations. A large number of informal interviews were carried out with Home Office officials responsible for the chosen policy areas. In addition, interviews were conducted with representatives of the Association of Metropolitan Authorities and the Association of County Councils; each of these bodies also made available documentary evidence concerning policy change. A senior representative of the Police Federation was interviewed, and gave access to documentary evidence from the Federation's files. Interviews were conducted with some Members of Parliament, with journalists, and with national organisations having an interest in the chosen policy issues. For example, interviews were carried out with national representatives of a number of organisations concerned with women's issues, with the main trade union representing civilian staff in the police service, and with the Audit Commission. The published reports of Her Majesty's Inspectorate of Constabulary were reviewed, and press coverage of policing issues was monitored over a period of two years. Finally, we carried out an analysis of policy-related circulars and guidelines issued by the Home Office over a number of years.

THE PRESENT ARRANGEMENTS FOR THE GOVERNANCE OF THE POLICE

There are currently 43 police forces in England and Wales (including the Metropolitan Police and City of London Police). For the 41 provincial forces, the 1964 Police Act reconfirmed what is usually described as a 'tripartite structure'. This divides formal responsibility for the police between chief constables, the Home Secretary and local police authorities. This section considers the powers and responsibilities of each of these under the Act, and examines how their roles have developed in practice.

Chief constables and constabulary independence

The view that has been orthodox until recently is that chief constables must be independent of political pressures because the job of the police is to enforce the law impartially. However, this view dates only from around 1930. Marshall (1965; 1978) pointed out that during the nineteenth century there was never any challenge to the right of the Home Secretary to issue instructions in matters of law enforcement. Lustgarten (1986) showed that the Metropolitan Police were directed in detail by the Home Secretary for roughly the first hundred years of their existence and that borough forces were directed by their watch committees. The level of control was least in the counties where the justices (the responsible authority) were disinclined to meet often and felt that they could rely on the chief constable as being 'one of them', but even there the model of the independent chief constable had not developed by 1914. It was the enfranchisement of the working class and the fear of socialism and trade union militancy that made it dangerous to leave the police under local control. It is no accident that the doctrine of the independence of the police became established at the time of the depression.

The case that is most often quoted as establishing the model of constabulary independence is that of *Fisher v. Oldham Corporation* ([1930] 2 KB 364). Fisher sued the corporation and the watch committee for wrongful imprisonment. He lost on the ground that there could be no master/servant relationship between the corporation or watch committee and a police officer. This case has been repeatedly cited as having far-reaching implications for the status of a police constable. In the judgement, reference was made to *Stanbury v. Exeter Corporation* ([1905] 2KB 838), where the judge had made a comparison with the police. The argument was that if an official was mandated to perform public and national functions, local government should not be made liable for his actions. *Stanbury* concerned an inspector of sheep disease, yet as Lustgarten (1986) has persuasively pointed out, nobody imagined the decision meant that such inspectors have a unique constitutional status. A second strand of the argument in *Fisher v. Oldham Corporation* was that constables have authority conferred directly on them and are not subject to the control of those who pay for them. Yet power is conferred directly on many other public officials (such as tax inspectors) but the same conclusion is not drawn for them. More generally, the argument incorporates an over-simplified view of police discretion, which *is* limited by the structure of the police organisation, and by advice and instructions received through it.

The conclusions wrongly reached in *Fisher v. Oldham Corporation* have been expanded and confirmed in further judgements. The independence doctrine received the final seal of judicial approval in *R v Metropolitan Police Commissioner, ex p Blackburn* ([1968] 2QB 118). Lord Denning concluded his judgement (shown by Lustgarten to be full of simple errors) by saying:

> I hold it to be the duty of the Commissioner of Police, as it is of every chief constable, to enforce the law of the land... No Minister of the Crown can tell him that he must, or must not, keep observation on this place or on that; or that he must, or must not, prosecute this man or that one. Nor can any police authority tell him so. The responsibility for law enforcement lies on him. He is answerable to law and to the law alone.

Yet, as argued earlier in this chapter, the law does not even pretend to control the pattern of policing. The effect of Lord Denning's ringing judgement, therefore, was to distance the police from control by anyone.

The Police Act 1964 is the basis for the present structure of policing in England and Wales, although it may soon be superseded by the current Police and Magistrates' Courts Bill. In some ways the 1964 Act codified the doctrine of constabulary independence, whereas in others it balanced this against the powers of the Home Office and the police authorities. In any case, the Act contained much studied ambiguity. Indeed, Morgan (1986:86) has described it as 'a gentlemen's agreement to gloss over the ambiguities and contradictions concerning the responsibilities for framing, monitoring and financing policing policy'. Section 5.1 stated that the police force in any area is subject to the direction and control of the chief constable. In the light of the judicial judgements analysed above, this was widely interpreted as meaning that the chief constable had independent responsibility for all 'operational matters', and 'operational matters' were widely interpreted to include patterns and policies of policing as well as decisions in specific cases. Whether that is what the legislators meant is unclear, but it is in principle possible for other bodies to have an influence on policy without seeking to interfere with decisions in individual cases. Indeed, it was increasingly accepted during the 1970s and 1980s that the Home Office should have an influence on the pattern of policing and the policies followed by chief constables, at a time when any such influence by police authorities was widely interpreted as 'political interference' and 'a threat to constabulary independence and impartiality'.

Shortly after the passage of the Police Act 1964, Marshall (1965) argued that it should have included provision for the police to receive direction in policy matters from local politicians, but by 1978 he had changed his view:

> The long-run interests and rights of citizens may well be furthered by the construction of buttresses against some kinds of overt political pressures, even when exerted honestly and in the name of democratic majorities. The occasional frustration of such majority pressures may be required by the need to protect civil liberties and secure the impartial treatment of individuals... If therefore in the field of law enforcement we have to give a calculated and impartial answer in 1977 to the question whether civil liberties and impartial justice are more to be expected from chief constables than from elected politicians... many liberal democrats would feel justified in placing more trust in the former than in the latter. [1978: 61]

This was put forward as a practical justification for the doctrine of constabulary independence. Marshall himself admitted that the legal justification was much less clear. The individual constable could not be directed to act in a certain way in a particular case; he must use his discretion as an independent officer under the Crown. However, as Marshall admitted, there was no legal principle that ruled out the issue of instructions on prosecution matters framed in general terms; and there was certainly no legal principle forbidding the intervention of police authorities in matters of general law enforcement policy outside the area of prosecution.

It was Denning's judgement in *R v Metropolitan Police Commissioner, ex p Blackburn* that began to extend the doctrine of independence beyond the constable's discretion in individual cases. A series of further judgements in the 1980s confirmed the weak position of police authorities under the Act. From 1981, a number of Labour-controlled police authorities attempted to gain influence over general policy matters in the metropolitan areas. The chief constables, backed by the courts, successfully resisted all these attempts. The distinction between 'operational' and 'policy' matters became totally blurred, so that in practice the chief constables were able to exert strong control over general policy matters as well as individual cases of law enforcement.

Of course, advocates of the independence of chief constables did not argue that they should not be subject to any controls at all. Marshall (1978) suggested a style of accountability that he called the 'explanatory and cooperative' mode, in contrast to the 'subordinate and obedient' mode. This meant that police authorities should not be able to issue orders, but should be able to request information and explanations that could subsequently be analysed and debated in public.

It was generally accepted that individual police officers would from time to time exceed their powers or commit malpractice. The 1964 Act laid down provisions for a complaints mechanism to deal with such cases. Section 49 of the Act gave the police the duty to record and investigate all complaints against themselves. In the case of more serious complaints, the investigation was to be handled by officers from another division, or even from another force. This system was criticised on the grounds that it lacked any independent element and left the police open to accusations that they were biased judges in their own cause. The system has subsequently been reformed, but without requiring complaints investigations to be *conducted* by an independent body, as now advocated by the Police Federation.

There is only one view on which the doctrine of constabulary independence (and the role of the chief constables in the tripartite structure) could be seen as democratic. It is one that emphasises that the police are established, governed and regulated by statute. The body of law, approved by an elected parliament, in some way represents the collective will of the people. It is the responsibility of the police to uphold and enforce these laws, and in this they play a central role in the democratic order. The will of the people is embodied in a detailed legal code, and the straightforward task of the police is to enforce this code. The danger to the smooth operation of this process comes from partisan interference with police decision-making. This could come from corrupt officials or politicians, manipulating the system for their own ends, or even from politicians directed by poorly-informed or irrational public opinion. In either case, the protection of the system lies with the professionalism and judgement of the police force, the head of which must be given the legal powers to resist any such interventions.

As was shown above, the fatal flaw in that view is the false assumption that the rules and regulations laid down by statute largely determine the pattern of policing. Once it is recognised that they do not and cannot, it becomes difficult to resist the argument that elected representatives and others should have an influence on the making of policing policy.

Police authorities

Discussions about the role of local elected representatives in policing lie at the heart of the debate about the 1993 White Paper and subsequent Police and Magistrates' Courts Bill. It is the Government's proposal to change the status and composition of local police authorities that has incensed local government in particular, and has also been attacked by those more recent converts to local democratic control, ACPO and the Police Federation.

Under the present arrangements each of the 41 provincial police forces in England and Wales is administered by a police authority consisting of two-thirds elected councillors, and one-third magistrates from the force area. There are three kinds of police authority, all of which were covered by this study. In single-county police forces ('shire forces') the police authorities function as a committee of the county council. In the former metropolitan areas, the police authorities are 'joint boards' made up of district councillors and magistrates from the metropolitan districts. In police forces covering more than one administrative county, there are 'combined police authorities' consisting of councillors and magistrates in equal proportions from each of the constituent areas.

Under the Act, police authorities have a general duty to 'secure an adequate and efficient police force for the area'. The Act lays down that the authority should concern itself with local standards of policing and offer advice and guidance to the chief constable. Although the police authority appoints the chief constable (along with the deputy and assistant chief constables) these appointments are, crucially, subject to the approval of the Home Secretary, who in 1991 exercised his veto in the case of Derbyshire. The police authority can call upon the chief constable to report on any aspect of policing of the local area (although the chief constable can refuse to do so if the Home Secretary agrees that such a report would be against the public interest). The police authority must approve all expenditure on policing, although this power was circumscribed by the Court of Appeal judgement in *R v Secretary of State for the Home Department, ex p*

Northumbria Police Authority ([1988] 2 WLR 590). The Northumbria Police Authority had sought a judicial review of a Home Office circular which offered to supply CS gas or plastic bullets from a central store to chief constables not permitted by their police authorities to purchase them. The Court of Appeal rejected the argument that the Home Secretary was acting beyond his powers on the ground that he had the power to do what was necessary to preserve the Queen's Peace, and on the basis of an interpretation of his statutory power to supply common services and promote general police efficiency. Reiner (1992: 240) has argued that this case 'seems to underline the impotence of local police authorities... making them a fig leaf of local influence'. However, the case was implicitly concerned with possible public disorder that would transcend local police boundaries; it is less clear that the budgetary power of police authorities is limited by the judgement with regard to purely local matters.

A central part of the debate about the accountability and control of the police in recent years has concerned the way that police authorities have exercised their functions under the Police Act 1964. Before 1980, there was a remarkable political consensus over policing, and examples of conflict between chief constables and their police authorities were rare. As noted earlier, during the early and mid 1980s a number of Labour-controlled police authorities (particularly in the metropolitan areas) came into conflict with their chief constables. The mining dispute of 1984-85 brought these conflicts to a head. Under the 'mutual aid' arrangements, the National Reporting Centre at New Scotland Yard coordinated a national anti-picket operation that moved large numbers of police officers away from their home areas to control picket lines in other parts of the country. The problem with such a system was that the funding for a national operation came from the budgets of local police authorities, many of whom had no striking miners in their own areas. Some police authorities challenged these arrangements, and argued that they prevented them from fulfilling their statutory duty of providing an adequate and efficient police force. In all such cases, the Home Secretary or the courts ruled in favour of the chief constables (Lloyd, 1985). In 1988, this culminated in the case involving the Northumbria Police Authority referred to above.

It has frequently been argued in recent years, especially by Reiner (1991; 1992) that police authorities are impotent, but this is from an analysis of leading cases, and not from detailed research on relations between police authorities and chief constables from day to day. Commentators have disagreed about whether the impotence that they ascribe to police authorities is due to a lack of sufficient statutory powers or to the way that the authorities have defined their own roles.

Morgan and Swift (1987) and Day and Klein (1987) reported on research conducted among police authorities in the 1980s. Both studies found that police authorities were rather inactive, but that this was partly because members were unaware of their legal powers and responsibilities, or did not wish to exercise them. The Audit Commission (1990) has argued that police authorities could do more within the present statutory arrangements to contribute towards policing policy, and has called them 'passive receivers of information'.

Reiner (1991) found that most chief constables went to some lengths to develop good working relationships with their police authorities; such relationships would suggest that policing policy was largely in tune with elected members' wishes. However, Reiner also argued from a few cases considered to be crucial, such as the dispute about plastic bullets and CS gas in Northumbria, that the chief constable can always get his way on a matter of consequence. On that view the apparent influence of police authorities is a fiction, because it is only an influence that the chief constable and the Home Office allows them to exert as long as this is not inconvenient.

Those who advocate the strengthening of the role of local police authorities appear to see their 'democratic' properties in several ways. The first democratic property flows from the fact of election: police authorities are supposed to represent local opinion. Second, they are intended to provide some check on the powers of the other two parties in the tripartite system. This assumes that to concentrate the power over policing is undemocratic, and stresses the importance of pluralism in the democratic system. Third, there are those who argue that an active contribution of local police authorities is essential for *effective* policing:

> The immediate future for local elected police authorities and local responsibility which has traditionally characterised policing in England and Wales would... appear to look bleak. This must be a matter of concern as direct involvement in locally run services encourages responsive management and greater police commitment. [Loveday, 1993: 68-69]

A central purpose of the present study is to collect more detailed information about the activities and influence of police authorities, and to analyse it in more depth. The conclusions drawn by earlier writers were not always based on very extensive information. Further, the argument that the outcome of key cases demonstrates that police authorities are impotent needs to be analysed in greater depth. From the fact that chief constables and the Home Office have won some battles with police authorities it does not necessarily follow that they could choose to fight any battle and still win it.

The Home Office

There are few who would argue against the proposition that the Home Office is now the most powerful party in the tripartite structure. Under the 1964 Act, the Home Secretary has a number of specific powers. He forms the police authority for the country's largest and most influential police force, the Metropolitan Police. With respect to provincial forces the Home Secretary has a number of powers: he can require a chief constable to resign in the interests of efficiency; he can call for reports into any aspect of policing an area, set up a local enquiry into a policing matter, and has a number of powers of approval over police authority appointments. Most important though, is the influence of the Home Secretary on the funding of the police.

Funding of the police

In formal terms, the Home Office pays 51 per cent of the police budgets for each force, whereas the police authority pays 49 per cent. In practice, however, the central government share is much higher, because much of the expenditure of local government rather than coming from local taxation (now the Council Tax and Business Rate) comes from central government in the form of Revenue Support Grant paid to local authorities by the Department of the Environment. Consequently, whereas the Home Office contribution to local policing budgets amounts to 51 per cent, the total central government contribution amounts to 76 per cent.

Local expenditure on the police has not historically been subject to cash limits. Once the local police authority had set the police budget, the Home Office was therefore obliged to pay its share, and the contribution by the Department of the Environment was determined by a complex formula, which took account (among many other things) of the number of police officers, but not of the number of civilians, within the local police service.

In theory, the Home Office can refuse to pay its share of the police budget if the force has not been certified as efficient by Her Majesty's Inspectorate of Constabulary. Until recently, there was no case of a refusal to certify a force as efficient. In 1992, then again in 1993, the Inspectorate refused to certify Derbyshire police force as efficient, following a long-running dispute between the police authority and the Home Office. However, in practice the police grant has continued to be paid. The only effective kinds of financial control available to the Home Office have been through the use of its power to approve police officer establishment, through control of police pay by means of nationally negotiated agreements, and through controls on capital expenditure. Police authorities could not increase the police officer establishment without Home Office approval, and therefore they could not increase the number of police officers employed once the establishment had been reached. There was no parallel control by the Home Office of the numbers of civilians employed within the police service. Consequently, as outlined in Chapter 5, the Home Office had to use bargaining over police establishment as a means of increasing the number of posts filled by civilians.

Other controls
In recent years the Home Office has explicitly sought to strengthen the role of Her Majesty's Inspectorate of Constabulary (HMIC). One sign of this is the appointment of some relatively young chief constables to the Inspectorate, whereas nearly all inspectors in the past were chief constables who had passed the normal age of retirement. Another indication is the increasingly systematic approach adopted by HMIC towards the development of indicators of police force performance and the collection and analysis of relevant information. A further indication was the decision in 1989 to publish the reports on individual forces that had hitherto remained private.

The increasing influence of HMIC is linked with the recent policy of developing national criteria of police performance. The Audit Commission has been given the task of defining measures of performance that could be routinely applied at the force level.

It has been argued (Reiner, 1991) that the Home Office exerts substantial influence over senior police officers, including chief constables, by controlling their career opportunities. The Home Affairs Committee of the House of Commons argued in its report on higher police training (Home Affairs Committee, 1989) that the career paths of senior officers should explicitly be controlled by the Home Office on a national basis.

An important development over recent years has been the increasing incidence of policy-related circulars from the Home Office. In theory, such circulars are only advisory, but a number of authors have pointed out that they tend to be treated as instructions. For example, a circular on consultation between the police and local communities (Home Office, 1982) led to the creation of police consultative committees in most force areas on a common pattern before consultative arrangements were required by statute in the Police and Criminal Evidence Act 1984.

Other developments that have increased the influence of the Home Office over policing are the growth of the common police services budget, and the creation of a National Criminal Intelligence Service (NCIS).

The measures in the Police and Magistrates' Courts Bill

At the time of writing, the Police and Magistrates' Courts Bill seems likely to be heavily amended in its passage through Parliament. In its original form, it would have given the Home Office substantial power over the composition of police authorities, through the right to appoint the chairs and some of the members of authorities limited to a total size of 16. The Bill also provides for the introduction of a national set of measures of police performance, and would give the Home Office the power to enforce them through budgetary controls. However, the Home Office power to appoint chairs and the limits upon total size of membership were subsequently dropped, as was the proposal that appointments of non-elected people should be made directly by the Home Secretary.

The analysis in this report will concentrate on the system operating before the passage of the new Bill. An important issue is whether the degree of Home Office power within the pre-1994 structure was consistent with the plurality of power inherent in the democratic ideal. That issue will be addressed in later chapters. The final chapter will also evaluate the proposals in the current Bill in the light of what has been established about the working of the existing arrangements.

Further developments

Although the three elements of the tripartite structure have remained in place in the 1980s, the structure has come under increasing strain. In response to these new stresses, there have been three key developments in the relationships between policing and democratic institutions: the introduction of police-community consultative committees; the enhanced legal regulation of police powers through the Police and Criminal Evidence Act (1984) (PACE) codes of practice: and the application of the government's Financial Management Initiative (FMI) to the police service. These were adjuncts to the existing arrangements rather than attempts to overhaul the tripartite structure.

Responsiveness to the community: consultative committees

Following the inner city disturbances of the early 1980s, it was increasingly accepted that, at least in certain localities, the police had become distanced from sections of the community. However, it was not deemed necessary to reform the Police Act, but rather to introduce forums in which the police could consult with representatives of local people in areas much smaller than are covered by police authorities. A key recommendation of the Scarman Report into the Brixton disturbances (Scarman, 1982) was that the police should make arrangements to obtain the views of the community. A Home Office circular 54/82 advised that such arrangements should be put in place, and set out a model structure of local consultative committees. These were already in place in most force areas by the time that a statutory duty was imposed on police authorities to set up consultative arrangements under section 106 of PACE. In most force areas, one police-community liaison committee was established per sub-division, although there was one notable exception within a force area covered by the present study (see Chapter 5). There has since been much discussion surrounding the functions, powers and effects of such committees. Morgan (1989) argued that in introducing the police-community liaison committees, the government had four explicit objectives:

- improved articulation of the consumer's viewpoint;

- improved education of the consumers about the nature of policing;

- the tackling of conflicts between police and particular community groups;

- encouraging of community crime prevention initiatives.

This formed an exercise in participation; it involved keeping the basic structure of policing the same at the national and police authority levels, but trying to encourage more community participation at a level below the police authority. In his research on consultative committees in 1987-88, Morgan (1989) found that they had been moderately successful at gathering the consumers' viewpoint from groups that are not hostile to the police but would like more attention from them. They had similarly had some limited success in educating consumers who were already well-disposed towards the police about the limitations on what the police could achieve. They had played no role in resolving conflicts between the police and particular community groups, and their role in promoting crime prevention initiatives was unclear. Stratta's (1990) findings from case studies of the workings of two police-community liaison committees in one force area supported Morgan's conclusions. She found that in terms of social status and where they lived, the members of the committees were in no way representative of small neighbourhood localities. A central finding was that committees tended to be composed of members whose social characteristics, in terms of age, sex, socio-economic group, ethnic background, and income, were totally atypical of the victims and offenders with whom the police have most contact. Members lacked a basic knowledge about the practicalities of policing, and could be of little help in advising the local police in setting substantive objectives. Stratta also found a generally uncritical approach to the police from the committees she examined, confirming the findings of other research (for example, Morgan and Maggs, 1985).

Thus previous research suggests that the aim of increasing participation in decision-making about policing policy has yet to be achieved by consultative groups. There seem to be a number of underlying difficulties. While consultative committees may help to attain one more modest aim of democratic process – the opportunity to participate should the need arise – it is questionable how meaningful this opportunity is. Critics would emphasise that these committees lack not only the necessary expertise to affect policy, but also sufficient powers. Also, even where the local police commander is open to influence from a sufficiently informed and powerful committee, the constraints imposed by central management of police forces, and upon the forces by central government, may limit flexibility of response at the local level.

Existing information does not allow a firm choice between a number of competing accounts of the effects of consultative committees. Some would argue that the real decision-making process is simply unaffected. Others would argue that there are limited effects in terms of providing information about policing, and articulating community wishes, and that there is the potential to make more progress. From a radical perspective, the police-community consultative committees are neither neutral nor potentially positive in their effects, but actually negative. They are used by the police to put a sheen of legitimacy on their actions, without ever posing a serious threat to their decision-making autonomy. They increase the support of the establishment for tough policing of minorities, who are excluded from the agenda. Some (for example, Nelken, 1985) would even argue that consultative committees are a means of increasing state control, by encouraging people to spy on the local population. Later chapters will provide further evidence against which to test these competing accounts.

Enhanced legal regulation of police powers
PACE instituted a framework of regulations designed to provide a tighter regulation of police powers. The Act introduced new provisions for the admissibility of documentary evidence, new controls on the treatment of suspects held at police stations, rationalised the law relating to evidence in criminal proceedings, and rationalised and consolidated police powers to stop and search persons and vehicles, to set up road checks, to search premises, and to arrest suspects. One important change was that the

prescribed codes of practice were henceforth approved by Parliament, whereas previously most of the matters covered by the codes had been regulated by the 'Judges' Rules' as interpreted by the judiciary and expressed by case law. Police officers became liable to disciplinary proceedings for failure to comply with any provision of a code of practice, unless proceedings were precluded by the Act.

One of the central aims of the Act was an attempt to balance police powers with protections for those people arrested. Representative police bodies criticised the Act for reducing the powers of the police to prove a case against a guilty person, whereas the civil liberties lobby criticised it for extending police powers. These contradictory stances were possible because PACE both extended police powers and attempted to regulate police behaviour more effectively through the four codes of practice. Furthermore, where police powers were extended this was in many cases a codification and legitimation of practices that had been widespread or universal: such changes could be regarded either as the abolition of ancient rights that had too long been dormant or as the introduction of new controls, depending on one's point of view.

The considerable research on the impact of PACE has recently been summarised by Reiner (1992). In broad terms, controls on treatment of suspects inside the police station have been much more effective than on police behaviour outside the police station. There is some evidence that outlawed behaviour may be shifted to zones that are not subject to close control (for example, the real interrogation may not take place in the police station). There is evidence that the judiciary have adopted stricter attitudes to violations of PACE codes than they did towards the old Judges' Rules (Feldman, 1990). Nevertheless, Sanders (1993) has argued that the codes of practice have changed the way that police officers account for their exercise of discretion, but without changing the way they actually exercise it.

Increased responsiveness to consumer pressure

A third important development during the 1980s was the increased emphasis, largely driven by central government, on improved management of policing and the efficient use of resources. For a time, the police service largely escaped the organisational restructuring and expenditure restrictions that Conservative governments introduced across the public sector during the 1980s. In fact, real expenditure on the police grew at a substantially higher rate than was experienced by any other public service. Pay, conditions and equipment were significantly improved during the early 1980s, and the number of police officers grew.

After 1982, the government developed its 'Financial Management Initiative' in the public sector. This was intended to promote cost savings and efficiency by introducing business management methods to government departments. In 1983, this initiative was extended to the police with the publication of the Home Office circular 114/83, *Manpower, Effectiveness and Efficiency in the Police Service*. From the late 1980s onwards, the Audit Commission published a series of papers that applied private sector management principles to police work. The Home Office began to develop work on performance indicators for the police service (Sinclair & Miller, 1984), work that was later developed by the Audit Commission and HMIC. This work has taken on a new importance recently with the Citizens' Charter requirements that local authorities publish key indicators concerning public service provision. Local authorities will be required to publish indicators of police force effectiveness from 1995 onwards. As mentioned above, under the proposals laid out in the Police and Magistrates' Courts Bill, the Home Office would take on the key role of setting national standards against which police performance will be measured.

The most important pressure contributing to these changes was the continued rise in crime rates and decline in detection rates throughout the 1980s, despite substantial increases in public expenditure on policing. In addition, the late 1980s and early 1990s saw a number of miscarriages of justice come to light. Police malpractice was a major factor in all of them, and this contributed to what some commentators called a crisis of confidence in the police service. The appointment of Kenneth Clarke as Home Secretary in April 1992 was seen as highly significant given the key role he had played in the Government's reforms of the health and education services in his previous cabinet posts. Not long after his appointment, the new Home Secretary announced an inquiry into working practices, pay and rank structure in the police service. In May 1993, the Sheehy Inquiry recommended substantial changes in the internal organisation and management of the police service, including a rationalisation of the rank structure, fixed-term contracts for police officers, and performance-related pay. The report met with a chorus of criticism from all levels of the police service; indeed, a number of senior chief constables, including the Metropolitan Police Commissioner, stated that they would consider resigning if the proposals were implemented in full. The Home Secretary was later to drop some of the most controversial recommendations of the Sheehy report.

However, the proposals outlined in the White Paper, and later in the Bill, also underline a commitment to 'consumer responsiveness'. The 'purchaser-provider' split is to be extended to the police service, chief constables are to be given greater control over their budgets with cash-limited grants replacing the old staffing-related grant, and forces will be required to devolve resources to the local level. As stated earlier, the Home Office will set performance targets, and chief constables will be held accountable for the performance of their forces. Police authorities will be required to carry out public satisfaction surveys to gauge local people's view on policing.

The stresses in the tripartite structure

The Royal Commission established in 1960, whose report in 1962 led to the Police Act of 1964, had been a response to a number of developments that have found an echo in more recent years. The famous case in Nottingham in 1959 of Captain Popkess[4] had raised concerns about who was ultimately responsible for local policing policy. As in the 1980s and 1990s, there had been a number of well-publicised cases of police malpractice leading to concerns about control of the police and investigation of complaints against officers. As in later years, there was rising public concern about increasing crime rates and changes in the types of criminal activity. Thus three concerns lay behind the Royal Commission that led to the 1964 Act: accountability (who is responsible), redress (complaints against individual officers), and effectiveness (the police's ability to address rising crime rates and new kinds of crime). As outlined above, the Act tried to address each of these issues.

Parallel concerns have again brought the police service to the forefront of public debate in the 1990s. Developments of the tripartite system in the 1980s attempted to enhance local responsiveness through police consultative committees, to improve police accountability to the law through PACE, and most crucially for the present Government, to improve the efficiency and effectiveness of the police service. The Government has, however, concluded that these developments were not enough, and that a more radical change in the arrangements for the governance of the police is needed in order to deal with the increasing strains in the system.

PROPOSALS FOR REFORM

The public debate about policing in recent years has created a climate of opinion in which it is assumed that major reforms of the arrangements for the governance of the police are necessary. Many proposals have been put forward to address the perceived problems of the present system. Three broad types of proposal will be considered here, together with the notions of 'democratic policing' that underpin them.

Stronger police authorities

Proposals for strengthening police authorities have come mainly from the moderate Left. These proposals spring from a number of criticisms of the existing system. First, it is not at all clear who is ultimately responsible for policing. It is argued that the division of responsibility between police authorities, chief constables, and the Home Office is a deliberate fudge which has the effect of hiding decision-making from view, so that the real power structure is disguised. A second impetus for these proposals is the view that there has been a major shift in the balance of power towards the Home Office and chief constables (Reiner, 1991; 1992; 1993). Because of the combined effect of these two factors – the lack of transparency, and the shift of power to chief constables and central government – it is argued that there are few effective checks and balances in the system. Elected representatives lack the formal powers they would need in order to exert an influence on policing policy; and this lack of power is compounded by their lack of information about the organisation and outputs of policing. Consequently, the participation of local people in decision-making about policing is confined to taking part in elections of local councillors who have little say in policing matters. Not surprisingly, issues of policing policy seldom or never feature in local election campaigns. Police consultative committees are held to be unrepresentative and marginal. Hence, it is argued that there is little effective consultation about policing policy with interested groups and individuals.

Another criticism of the current arrangements concerns effectiveness. It is argued that, because the structures of local accountability are weak, it is difficult for policing to be in tune with the needs of local communities. This is said to undermine the efforts of the police to deliver an effective service.

In the early 1980s, the Labour MP Jack Straw proposed (in a Private Member's Bill) that the 1964 Act be reformed so as to give police authorities new powers to direct policy. On these proposals, police authorities would determine 'general policing policies' for their areas, and would appoint senior officers down to the level of superintendent. This proposal relies on making a distinction between matters of general policy and law enforcement decisions in particular cases; chief officers would remain in control of the latter. Mr Straw also proposed that the magistrate members be removed from police authorities, which would then consist entirely of elected local councillors. The proposals included a number of checks on the powers of police authorities; for example the Home Secretary was to adjudicate in the event of disputes between police authorities and chief constables.

Although Jack Straw's proposals did not make progress in Parliament, this kind of programme is still on the agenda of the moderate Left. Recent recommendations from the Institute of Public Policy Research (IPPR), which is independent yet linked with the Labour Party, include making police authorities entirely elected bodies, and giving them more statutory powers (Reiner and Spencer, 1993). As will be clear from earlier sections, this can be interpreted as a return to the relationships between watch committees and police forces that existed in the nineteenth century.

The impetus for these proposals is a belief in the value and importance of local democracy. On this view, the low turnout in local elections is largely a function of the relative powerlessness of local government in general, particularly apparent in the field of policing. Democracy on this view flows primarily from the fact of election. A concern with effective service delivery is present, but is not clearly defined. There are vague references to the need for responsiveness to the community, but exactly how this is achieved is not elucidated. The main concerns are therefore with the nature of the decision-making process and the lack of effective checks in the system.

Community democracy: new structures of participation

A more radical alternative to the present tripartite system has been suggested by Jefferson and Grimshaw (1984). In their view, the present system both incorporates and disguises an imbalance of power more fundamental than can be addressed by giving police authorities more formal influence. In particular, the present arrangements fail to guarantee representation of the weak, the unorganised, or minority groups. The unequal power structure hides the true nature of the process of decision-making. Furthermore, it does not ensure that representatives will be controlled by those they represent. So even if the police are brought under closer control by elected representatives, this will not guarantee 'democratic policing'. It may even result in the harnessing of the support of the respectable majority for the oppressive policing of marginal groups.

Jefferson and Grimshaw developed a model of what they called 'democratic, just policing'. The starting point is an acceptance that police officers have a general duty to uphold the law. This duty is not delegated, but is inherent in the office of constable. However, the model attempts to distinguish between the kinds of decision that are to be left to the discretion of the police officer, and those that may be subject to guidance by a democratic body. The former category is much narrower than in other models. It consists of decisions about cases where the law is a clear guide to action, and where there is an identified complainant. Even within this category, Jefferson and Grimshaw (1984) argue for more control over what the police do, for example by new forms of prosecution authority, by new methods of safeguarding suspects' rights and testing evidence, and by a strengthened and fully independent complaints system.

Since the law offers little or no guidance on matters of general policy, it is argued that such guidance must be provided by a democratic authority. The authors advocated a new kind of democratic body called 'police commissions', that would be charged with the duty of upholding the law and concerned with interpreting the general legal duty of the police. Police commissioners would be directly elected as such, and would be able to issue instructions to local police chiefs on matters of policy. The territorial areas that these police commissions would cover was not made clear, but they would apparently be smaller than those covered by the current police authorities, and might perhaps cover a town, or a current police sub-division. The authors saw no potential problem arising from a lack of policing expertise on the part of the police commissioners:

> With the best legal advice available, there seems no reason why elected laypeople could not undertake the tasks of determining the scope of the general task of upholding the law and of issuing policy instructions to the chief officers in respect of that task. [Jefferson & Grimshaw, 1984:176]

The material responsibility for providing the police with buildings, funds and equipment would stay with the police authority (minus the magistrate members), and the Home Secretary. The commissions would appoint chief officers subject to the Home Secretary's approval. They would be obliged to send regular reports to Parliament about the policing of their area.

The authors argued that the apparent apathy that exists under the present system is due to the lack of structures for enabling people to articulate their real interests. They proposed, therefore, that decision-making take place at 'natural points' of collective assembly, such as schools, offices, community centres, and factories.

Central to this model of democracy is the idea of equality: 'At the heart of the democratic state is the idea of the equality of citizens: a democratic state is obliged to respect all citizens equally' (Jefferson & Grimshaw, 1984:170). Most theories of democracy place some emphasis on equality on some definition or other. However, Jefferson and Grimshaw argued that the notion of equality should take the form of a statutory obligation on police commissions to treat all citizens equally in respect of their legal rights and duties. Commissioners would be legally required to make clear their definition of public justice, and to respond to the definitions of justice held by their constituents. Groups that feel they are treated unequally in policing should have the opportunity to make their case heard to the commissioners, who, it was argued, will thus have to pursue equality in some 'definite sense'.

The conception of equality put forward is implicitly one deriving from the *group justice model* rather than from the *individual justice model* (McCrudden *et al.,* 1991: 5-6). The individual justice model concentrates on cleansing the process of decision making, and is not concerned with the result except as an indicator of a flawed process: it concentrates on securing fairness for the individual. By contrast, the group justice model is concerned with outcomes rather than with the decision-making process; it is redistributive, and is concerned with the relative position of groups rather than individuals. The group justice model has most commonly been applied in the field of the regulation of racial and sexual discrimination, although many have criticised the model even in that field. Jefferson and Grimshaw did not consider that the application of the group justice model in the field of criminal justice might have some unintended consequences. For example, if the objective is to achieve equal outcomes, then it must follow that the arrest rate of women and men must be equalised, even though men commit about ten times as many offences, on average, as women do.

However, Jefferson and Grimshaw did not quote that kind of example. Instead, they used their conception of equality to argue that the police should prioritise offences that 'bear hard on those least able to fend for themselves'. For example, they held that higher priority should be given to offences like rape, because of the social impact of the offence on women. The police should also attempt to reduce arrest rates in those offence categories for which a high proportion of convicted persons are disadvantaged. For such offences, the police interventions should be preventive rather than leading to detection and prosecution.

What underlies these proposals is a model of direct 'community democracy' that seeks to incorporate the views of minority groups, and interests that are marginalised by existing formal mechanisms. It is held that the occasional casting of a vote in national and local elections is not sufficient to articulate the suppressed interests of disadvantaged groups. What is required is continuous participation in new forms of participative democracy at workplaces, crèches, and so on. The model lays a particular stress on democratic outcomes, and in particular on equality interpreted uncompromisingly in terms of outcomes for groups rather than fairness for individuals.

However, the model is vague about exactly how the new participatory structures will be designed and how they will work. The vision of well-informed workers gathering at tea breaks to discuss the policing policies for their area is clearly utopian; long experience of many sorts of community initiatives shows that continuous participation of that kind, even when there are immediate benefits for the people concerned, has so far proved impossible to achieve. The model ignores the fact, strongly highlighted by the 'New Realist' criminology, that many of the most common kinds of crime impact most heavily on marginal and dispossessed groups as victims. Reducing arrest rates among groups that are normal targets of police activity would be extremely unpopular among the similar, dispossessed groups that are the usual victims of crime. The model offers no prospect of resolving this conflict. In any case, there is no definition of what are to count as disadvantaged groups. There is no discussion of how to safeguard the control of policing from partisan interests: indeed, some aspects of the model may increase the potential for this to happen.

Most important, Jefferson and Grimshaw took one of the ideas associated with democracy – equality of outcome – and elevated it above the rest. If the logic of this position were consistently followed, it would lead, as argued above, to results that could not be acceptable to anyone. This valuably illustrates the point that the democratic ideal contains within it a number of values that have to be carefully balanced against one another. Absurd results are produced if any one of these values is given an unchecked ascendancy.

The citizen as consumer: market solutions

Central to Conservative policy since 1979 has been the idea of applying 'market disciplines' to public service provision so as to obtain better 'value for money'. The Government has started to apply these principles to the police service much later than to other public services, but the proposals outlined in the Sheehy report, the White Paper, and the Police and Magistrates' Courts Bill are a determined attempt to find market-oriented solutions. It is therefore important to consider the 'market critique' of the current arrangements and the alternative models it suggests, and to examine the notion of democracy behind such thinking.

Much of the 'New Right' thinking about the police service echoes criticisms of public service provision generally. The argument is that the police, like other public bureaucracies, have no pecuniary incentives towards economically efficient behaviour. Because they are monopoly suppliers, the bargaining power of their customers is negligible, and competition is non-existent. The bureaucracy has tended to retain a monopoly of information about the costs of providing policing services and the effects of policing activity. Because of the lack of external constraints, the police are largely able to determine and pursue their own goals. As with other public bureaucracies, their overriding objective is to obtain more resources from government. Police authorities have shown little interest in improving efficiency of service, and have been content to follow the police line that declining levels of service are due to lack of sufficient resourcing from central government. The police themselves have clung to outdated management methods and restrictive work practices. Evans (1991) has summarised the New Right critique of the police service in a recent paper published by the Adam Smith Institute:

> Removed from the constant need to maintain a competitive edge which spurs the private sector, the police service has found itself undermined by the same problems of other state monopolies; high and rising costs, top-heavy bureaucracy, a lack of flexibility, and a propensity to favour ever-greater increments in police manpower. New working practices and methods are slow to be implemented because of the inherent conservatism of the structure: the Service's monopoly status removes the incentive to respond to the new challenges and demands made by society. [Evans, 1991:12]

Of course, free market thinking cannot be applied to policing in a simple and direct way. In classical economic theory, the perfectly competitive market is one in which many buyers and sellers come together to bargain over a standardised good. The price mechanism conveys information to sellers about the wants of consumers, and to consumers about the quality and availability of the good. Competition between producers provides choice for the consumer, and encourages efficiency in production. If one producer tries to charge an artificially high price for a good, consumers will simply go elsewhere. In the knowledge of this, producers (as profit maximisers) have every incentive to innovate and maximise productive efficiency. The concept of 'perfect competition' is a theoretical model, built on a number of assumptions that are strictly inapplicable to most markets (perfect information, many buyers, many sellers). Nevertheless, many economists have held that with suitable qualifications the model is close enough to many real-life economic systems for it to say something useful about them.

Policing, in so far as it is a *public good*, is a classic example of one of the kinds of 'market failure' listed in economics textbooks. In economic theory, a pure public good is one that must be made equally available to all members of the community. Public goods are characterised by jointness of supply; it is difficult or impossible to exclude individuals or groups from their benefits. When the police maintain order or enforce the law, they are supposed to do so for the benefit of all, not in the interests of some private consumers. The free market would never provide 'public policing' in this sense, as there is no incentive for an individual consumer to pay for it, as he or she cannot exclude other people from the benefits of the good. It is just as rational for the consumer to wait until another individual pays for such a good, when he or she can reap the benefits without paying anything (the 'free rider' situation).

Furthermore, policing is not a standardised good. As Horton and Smith (1988) have argued, a key feature of policing (along with a number of public services) is the difficulty of specifying output and measuring performance. The goals of policing are many and varied, and may conflict with each other. The relationship between policing 'inputs' and 'outputs' is tenuous and uncertain, whether the outputs are conceived of as the delivery of services (for example, to victims of crime) or as change in the wider society (for example, reduction of crime rates).

A further difficulty with applying market principles in a straightforward way is that policing is free at the point of delivery, so that the level of demand for policing services takes no account of the cost of meeting that demand. Moreover, the idea of a consumer or customer often has no meaning in the context of policing. Where interactions between the police and members of the public are conflictual rather than consensual, there is no specific customer, but the police action is carried out on behalf of the community at large.

For these reasons, and others, there cannot be a market for policing on the model of a corn exchange. However, what the New Right have in mind seems to be a more limited application of market principles. In parallel with the reforms of the National Health Service, the functions of purchasers and providers could be split. On one model, the fund-holders could be new-style police authorities, and a market would be created by alternative suppliers bidding for contracts let by the fund-holders. A development of this could involve devolution of budgetary control within the police organisation, which might create conditions reminiscent of markets. Local police commanders would hold budgets and would be required to demonstrate that agreed objectives were being met, as assessed by measures of performance. Their chances of holding onto or increasing their budgets would depend on their success on these criteria.

These suggestions for the application of market principles are vague and speculative. However, there are two valuable elements in this line of thinking: the emphasis on finding out what people want from policing, and on effectively delivering it. These are important elements of the democratic ideal. They are emphasised by the New Right in contrast with the emphasis among thinkers of the moderate Left on the mechanism of decision making.

Another strand of thinking among the New Right seeks to apply the programme of privatisation to the police service. There are few who would argue that the core activities of policing should be hived off wholesale to the private sector. But there are organisations, such as private security firms, whose functions overlap with police activities. When policing is seen in its broad symbolic sense, it is much easier to portray it as a public good which must be provided by the state. But when it is broken down into its constituent functions, it is possible to identify tasks which could be, and sometimes already are, undertaken by organisations other than the police. Hiving off these functions to private organisations would arguably allow the police to concentrate on their core activities without undermining their position. In support of this argument, social order is in any case largely maintained by informal controls, or by formal controls administered by private organisations (banks, employers etc.). Shifting the boundaries between what the police do and what private organisations do will not necessarily undermine the police.

Heald and Morris (1984) have presented a typology of four kinds of privatisation applied by successive Conservative governments in Britain. The four types they are identify are:

- *denationalisation*, which involves selling off nationalised industries to the private sector, or gradual withdrawal from comprehensive public provision in areas where this was previously the norm;

- *liberalisation*, or the introduction of competition into public monopolies;

- *substitution* of customer fees for tax finance (for example NHS charges); and

- *contracting out*, in which public authorities continue to be responsible for provision and quality of service, but the actual service is delivered by private firms.

So far, the first and fourth of these have been applied in a limited way to the police service. The police staff associations have argued that restrictions on staffing and resources constitute 'gradual withdrawal', and the government is actively encouraging the contracting out of some services previously the preserve of the police (prisoner escort, security at Ministry of Defence properties).

A number of internal reforms already introduced or planned are designed to imitate the conditions of a market in a very loose sense. For example, the performance measures that are now being emphasised are a substitute for information conveyed by the multitude of individual transactions in a perfect market. The Audit Commission and the HMIC have developed a considerable array of performance measures, and in doing so have tried to show that, in spite of the many difficulties, many of the outputs of policing can be assessed, even if the outcomes of police activity in the wider world cannot routinely be measured. The White Paper and the Bill propose that the Home Secretary should set national standards against which forces' performance will be measured. The requirement on police authorities to publish a range of information about the performance of their forces after 1995, and the proposal that they should commission regular surveys of public satisfaction should, in theory, provide information to consumers about how their police force is doing.

Market-based approaches, then, have the virtue of emphasising the need to find out what people want and supply it effectively, but because of conflicts with other objectives, they only have limited application in the field of policing. The public good argument is not defeated by simply breaking down the police task into its constituent functions, because many of these specific functions still carry public good characteristics. This applies, for example, to uniform preventive patrol. Because of the free-rider effect, a universal system of uniform patrol could probably never be financed by private subscriptions. At best, private patrols can be organised in wealthy housing estates (where burglary and violent crime tends to be low in any case). This private solution to a public problem cannot work. The overall effect is probably to displace crime to high-crime areas that cannot afford to pay for protection. This is inefficient, even for those paying for protection, whose peace and safety will eventually be threatened by events in unpoliced areas nearby. It is also inequitable: and in fact a general argument for public service provision (Ascher, 1987) is that unlike the market it uses equitable criteria for allocating the service between end users.

Privatisation depends on the assumption that certain policing functions can be hived off without any detriment to remaining functions, but this may be unrealistic in many instances. The different activities of a single organisation may feed into each other. For example, it has often been suggested that there is no need for the police to control traffic or enforce road regulations, and that specialist traffic functions could be performed by some other organisation. Against that, a large proportion of crime is theft of or from motor vehicles, and people engaged in other sorts of crime generally move about in motor vehicles. Hence, there is a substantial interaction between traffic policing and the prevention and detection of crime. It follows that there would be substantial losses in efficiency and effectiveness if the traffic police were hived off to a separate organisation.

Hiving off the consensual policing functions also carries with it a further danger. If the police are just left with the adversarial functions, the public will only come into contact with them in situations of confrontation, which will tend to erode their legitimacy and to reduce public cooperation.

A point that clearly emerges from this analysis is that different values that may well be counted democratic often conflict to some degree. For example, a key concern of those advocating these 'market-based' changes is with cost-effectiveness in service delivery. As already emphasised, delivering the service that people want more cheaply and effectively may well be counted democratic. Other interpretations of democracy emphasise, instead, the need to ensure that the decision-making process itself reproduces the wishes of the people. The priorities of effective service delivery and cleansing decision-making probably conflict. Lengthy decision-making processes, insistence on consulting as many people as possible, allowing minority interests to block and delay: all of these can be seen as democratic but may well undermine effectiveness.

Another potential conflict is between the democratic values of choice and equity. Of course, the Right often argues that markets are the fairest as well as the most efficient of systems, because they offer everyone the maximum opportunity to choose. For example, Enoch Powell (1969:33) has written that 'In this great and continuous general election of the free economy, nobody, not even the poorest, is disenfranchised: we are all voting all of the time'. Again, in a critique of local government, the Adam Smith Institute (1983:3) has used the same analogy: 'In this sense, the market sector is more genuinely democratic than the public sector, involving the decisions of far more individuals and at much more frequent intervals'. In fact, however, free choice conflicts with equity, so that this attempt to appropriate democratic rhetoric for economic liberalism is much too glib. In the 'general election' of the free market, the wealthy can vote more often than the poor, and each of their votes has a higher value.

Conclusion

Each of the various proposals for reform of police governance highlights different weaknesses in the existing system, and each places a different order of priority on the various values inherent in the idea of democracy. In order to resolve these contradictions, it is necessary to examine the democratic ideal more deeply. The aim in doing so will be to distil a set of criteria of democracy against which present and future systems of police governance can be judged.

THE CONCEPT OF DEMOCRACY

Democracy is, of course, a growth industry. While the early 1990s saw large parts of the developed world fall back into economic recession, the demand for democracy showed no sign of diminishing. In fact, there was an expansion into new markets facilitated by the fall of communism in the former Warsaw pact countries, and so pervasive was this transformation felt to be that one analyst (Fukuyama, 1989) referred to the process as 'the end of history'. In the West, thoughts of the inevitable economic hardship and instability arising from restructuring and adaptation to a new political and economic order were initially set aside in the general euphoria surrounding the triumph of democracy over dictatorship. At the present time, the term 'democratic' is used not only to denote a particular set of political institutions or processes, but also as a gesture of approval. As Hirst (1988) has put it, democracy has become the 'dominant idiom' in much political discourse. Corcoran (1983:15) has gone further in describing democracy as 'the world's new universal religion'. He reminds us that for much of the history of political thought, democracy did not occupy such an elevated position in the minds of theorists:

> It is a fact, now routinely ignored by the democratic faithful as a position beneath contempt, that the great preponderance of political thinkers for two-and-a-half millennia have insisted upon the perversity of democratic constitutions, the disorderliness of democratic politics, and the moral depravity of the democratic character. [Corcoran, 1983:15]

Although much of the debate about the meaning of democracy has tended in the past to focus on explicitly 'political' institutions at the national level such as parliaments, executives, electoral systems, and political parties, more recent developments have tended to emphasise the importance of both larger and smaller units than the state. Because of the long-term trend towards European integration, political decisions taken at the supra-national level will be of increasing importance in future years. At the same time, a strong body of opinion across a number of European Community countries speaks in favour of increased local autonomy and the devolution of power to regional (or lower) levels. Although these trends are particularly evident in the 1990s, interest in extending the political sphere beyond national government is far from new. A number of writers (for example, Wolin, 1960) have stressed the importance of other social groups and organisations in the political lives of citizens.

Democracy in political thought

Most textbook discussions of democracy start from the literal translation of the Greek word, which meant 'rule of (or by) the people'. The term was first used to describe a form of government found in some of the ancient Greek city states, characterised by the sharing of the right to participate in public affairs amongst 'the people'. Plato, in *The Republic* (Book VIII) described the ends of democracy as liberty, equality, and variety. From that approach to the subject, it is clear that almost from the beginning 'the word "democracy" was associated with a set of ideals as well as with a form of government' (Raphael, 1976:144). Equally, it was heavily criticised in the ancient world. Plato rejected democracy precisely because he rejected the ideals of liberty, equality, and variety that he believed were at the heart of it.

The modern revival and rehabilitation of the democratic ideal was begun in the eighteenth century. In the development of the concept of democracy since then, there have been wide differences and disagreements between writers on basic points such as the priority to be accorded to different values or objectives, and the appropriate role of 'the people' in a democratic system.

One fundamental division is between writers who see democracy as a set of social ideals, and those who see it as denoting a set of political institutions. The analytic approach adopted in the present study is based on Plato's view that democracy is essentially a set of ideals, and that particular institutions must be judged by their capacity to meet or embody those ideals.

There has been a long-running debate on this question between those who have been termed 'classical theorists' such as Rousseau, James Mill, J. S. Mill, Bentham, and others in that tradition, who analyse democracy in terms of ideal values and the worth of the individual; and twentieth century writers, starting with Joseph Schumpeter, who developed 'empirical' theories in which democracy is conceived solely as a political method. Some authors have questioned the simplicity of such a division. Pateman (1970) has argued that the notion of one 'classical theory of democracy' is a myth, and has stressed the diversity of the set of theorists concerned. However, as Pateman herself admitted, the notion of a classical theory of democracy has been an enduring one, and still has a strong influence today, particularly on politicians' rhetoric (as Joseph Schumpeter points out, politicians like a rhetoric that flatters the masses). Hence, although there are important differences between theorists described as classical, it seems reasonable to consider the common elements of democratic theory that writers in the mid twentieth century thought they were challenging.

The classical theories and their contemporary offspring emphasised participation, the importance of self-development of the individual, and democracy as an ideal in itself. Consideration of the hypothetical situation of a perfect benevolent dictator brings out the contrast between conceiving democracy as having value in itself, and democracy as purely a kind of political method. J. S Mill wrote in *Representative Government* that a necessary condition of good government was the promotion of the right kind of individual character, and without the opportunities for participation, beyond the mere fact of voting, in public functions and decision making 'the sphere of action of human beings is artificially circumscribed, their sentiments are narrowed and dwarfed'. It is only within the context of these popular and participatory institutions that the right kind of public-spirited character is developed. This of course implies an optimistic view of human nature, as essentially rational and improvable, and that it is possible to develop the kinds of institutions in which active political participation can occur.

The view that a vibrant representative democracy, in which electors with definite beliefs about policy would periodically vote freely for parties who would try to implement these policies, was increasingly challenged during the first half of the twentieth century. The work of the élite theorists was based on the premise that the mass of people were a threat to political stability and inherently incompetent: at best the mass of people were passive and pliable, at worst, unruly and threatening to the established order (Pareto, 1939; Mosca, 1935). Gustave Le Bon's (1960 [1895]) work on crowd psychology had already undermined optimistic assumptions about human nature. Roberto Michels (1958) argued that true democracy was in practice unattainable. From a study of European party systems and of various bureaucracies he deduced that all social organisations were subject to 'the iron law of oligarchy': an inevitable and irreversible trend to domination of the many by an élite leadership.

The mid twentieth century saw the appearance of a very different kind of democratic theory, one which adopted a narrower, and in the views of its supporters, a more realistic view of what democracy is. Joseph Schumpeter was one of the first proponents of this kind of theory (later characterised by Bachrach (1969) as 'democratic élitism') which saw democracy as simply a procedure for arriving at political decisions. Democracy, in Schumpeter's words, is no more than 'that institutional arrangement for arriving at political decisions in which individuals acquire the power to decide by means of a competitive struggle for the peoples' vote' (1961:269). These ideas were advanced as 'scientific' or 'positive' theories of democracy, because they were based upon observations of actual political practice and disassociated from ideals or ultimate values. Such theories saw little potential for mass participation in public affairs; they held that the energies and capacities of most people are absorbed primarily in their personal lives, and that participation in politics (unless under highly unusual conditions) is of marginal interest. Findings gathered by American political scientists supported the view that most people participate in politics to only a limited extent. For example, Berelson's (1954) study of voting behaviour found that the majority of people lack motivation, interest and knowledge about politics and the political system. Schumpeter and associated theorists did not see such findings as a threat to democracy; they assumed instead that an inactive and demotivated electorate was essential to the democratic system.

On this view, the mass of people are not a source of ideas or initiatives, but they still play an important role by choosing between competing élites. Writers like Dahl (1961) believed that the essence and safeguard of the democratic system lies in the dynamics of competitive behaviour between a plurality of élites. Downs (1957) and later Tullock (1976) developed an analogy between democracy and the market economy: they maintained that political parties and also individuals in the political sphere make rational choices with the object of maximising 'utility' for themselves, as assumed in classical economics. Just as in economic theory individual actions determined by self-interest produce output and employment for society at large, so in the economic theory of democracy, self-interested individual actions in the form of votes produce parties and administrations.

From this perspective, democracy denotes a set of political institutions. What makes a system democratic is competition for votes between leadership élites at periodic free elections. Elections are the principal way in which people exert influence over their leaders, who are influenced in their behaviour by the threat of being removed from office. Political equality means the right to vote, and a chance to join the leadership élite by running for election. Participation in political decisions means participation in the choice of those who are to take the decisions.

The re-emergence of a participatory theory
These 'empirical' theories of democracy gained widespread support during the 1950s and 1960s. The emphasis had moved away from looking for ways to extend participation, and towards stabilising the established system. Writers like Sartori saw the more idealistic participatory theories as verging on the dangerous:

> Democracy is terribly difficult. It is so difficult that only expert and accountable elites can save it from the excesses of perfectionism, from the vortex of demagogy, and from the degeneration of the *lex majoris partis*. [1962:64]

A major difficulty for those who believed that there was more to democracy than the occasional choice between élite decision-makers was that these 'democratic élitist' theories seemed to provide the best fit to modern industrial society. Even where there was the opportunity for more widespread political participation, it was argued, the evidence was that people simply would not be not interested. Politics was the interest of some, the hobby of a few, and the passion of even fewer.

Theorists who believed that more participation was possible responded by emphasising the potential importance of two settings for political participation outside the arena of national politics: the workplace, and local government. They argued that confining the sphere of politics to national institutions and processes made it inevitable that participation would be limited. But if the conception of 'the political' was extended to other social organisations and contexts, then the possibilities of participation would be expanded. It was the lack of such possibilities that had stifled interest in national politics and had fostered ignorance and apathy. The focus of most authors who took this line was upon extending the notion of democracy to the workplace (Bachrach, 1969; Pateman, 1970; Hodgson, 1984). The idea was that people will participate in decision-making about matters that affect them directly from day to day, whereas they may have little sense of involvement in matters debated in a national election, which generally seem far removed from their daily lives. Another potential arena for participation in democracy is of course local government. In fact, earlier theorists had not concentrated exclusively on national state institutions in their discussions of democracy. J.S Mill had argued strongly for an active local democracy, as a means of improving both administrative efficiency and the 'public education' of citizens.

The evidence from studies of workplace participation and industrial democracy is somewhat mixed. Much of the literature shares theoretical considerations with wider discussions about democracy. Fox (1974) distinguished between low- and high-trust principles of management control. Low-trust organisations are characterised by the strict division of labour, the separation of planning from execution, the breaking down of work into small separate tasks, the predominance of prescriptive rules, tight supervision and inspection, and the importance of management control. The costs of such a structure could be to alienate the workforce from the goals of the organisation, personal exclusion, low productivity and workplace conflict. In contrast, high-trust principles stress higher order worker needs over and above material gain, and try to develop ways of increasing worker commitment and motivation. The workforce are integrated into the organisation and given 'responsible autonomy'. This should reduce supervision costs, but more importantly, give the workforce the chance to participate in decisions immediately affecting their working lives. The concepts of shared goals, personal development, and moral involvement with the social structure of which one is a part, echo those found in participatory theories of democracy. This 'high-trust' approach inspired an influential movement in personnel management away from traditional structures of collective bargaining and towards more individualistic attempts to enhance employee involvement. As the popularity of what became known as 'human resource management' (HRM) grew during the 1980s, there was increasing evidence that employers were adopting new measures designed to seek the active commitment and cooperation of employees. Such developments included team briefings, task participation groups such as quality circles, joint consultative committees, and incentive schemes designed to encourage identification with site, divisional or corporate objectives. The evidence from a number of studies, however, shows only a marginal effect of these developments. Marginson *et al.* (1988) found little evidence of a new integrated approach to employee relations, with few firms able to give detailed accounts of their policies, and those changes which had occurred being concentrated at higher management levels. Dale and Hayward (1984) found that the introduction of quality circles into British manufacturing firms had only a marginal effect. A more recent study of the Workplace Industrial Relations Survey (Millward, 1994:127) found that in terms of a shift towards HRM there was 'rather modest change and development, rather than a sea change'. Employment research evidence therefore tends to suggest that hopes for developing a vibrant participatory democracy at the workplace have yet to be realised.

With regard to local government, the experience of post-war Britain bears little resemblance to the vision of J.S Mill. Low turnouts in local elections provided further support for the democratic élitist notion that lack of interest and involvement in politics was the norm even at the local level: in fact, turnout is much lower in local than in national elections. After the 1960s there was a growing tendency for nationally-determined party priorities to be imposed on local government, with the result that local issues took on less importance. The style of local representation also provided good reasons for scepticism about local government. Cumbersome committee structures and slow decision-making processes made it difficult to see how citizens could influence local developments even if they did vote in larger numbers. It appeared that the democratic élitist model applied to local as well as to national politics. The welfare state had in effect delegated most of the responsibility for running public services to an élite who, according to critics, were largely insulated from the demands of the public. Increasing concern with the participation of the public in service provision surfaced in the late 1960s with the publication of Lord Seebohm's (1968) Report on social services, which singled out participation as an important goal. Richardson (1983) outlined some of the main problems that were confronted by attempts to enhance consumer and employee participation across a number of public services during the 1970s. Most practical proposals focused upon direct consumers rather than the public in general, and gave the new participants only limited consultative powers. The central problem was the representativeness of participants because of the uneven distribution of the opportunity and the willingness to participate.

Concern with local participation was to reappear during the 1980s, when political radicalism in local government reached a peak, and tensions between radical left-wing councils and a radical Conservative central government broke out into open hostilities. Very different models of local democracy were developed by radicals of the Left and of the Right, but each, in its own way, claimed that it emphasised the increased participation of people in the system. Community theories of democracy stressed direct participation of suppressed interest groups, whereas market-based theories advocated the participation of citizens through individual consumer decisions (as discussed in an earlier section).

Conclusion

Discussions about democracy are ultimately concerned with values. Even though the development of 'empirical' theories of democracy attempted to separate the meaning of democracy from ideals, such theories themselves can in many ways be considered normative. As Pateman (1970) has argued, such theories do not simply describe how democratic systems function, but provide a set of criteria by which a system may be judged, and strongly imply that such criteria define a system we should value. For example, these theories not only describe the practical difficulty of attaining more wide-spread participation in political decisions, but also imply that it would be dangerous to attempt to develop this. They place value on leadership and stability, on a pluralistic competition between élites, and on the effectiveness of the system in producing political decisions. Thus, there are a number of ideals associated with democracy which need to be balanced. Different models of democracy involve an explicit or implicit value-judgement about the relative importance of these ideals.

Criteria of democracy: towards a framework of analysis

The preceding discussion has established that democracy is a set of ideals as well as a set of ideas. It has also shown that there have been many interpretations of democratic ideas, and that these differ in the emphasis they give to the various values inherent in them. The largest area of disagreement is over the emphasis that should be given to participation.

Of course, these ideas about democracy have largely been developed in the context of debate about national political systems. A central argument of this book is that the governance of organisations like the police force, which form a vital part of the social fabric, is at least as important in its implications for democracy as Parliament or the institutions of central government. In order to test in what ways the system of policing is democratic, it is necessary to adapt ideas about democracy that were largely developed to describe and evaluate national political systems.

The task in this final section is to propose a set of criteria for the purpose of testing how far the arrangements for making policing policy follow democratic principles. The following are the main candidates that have emerged from the preceding review.

Equity. In so far as the police are delivering services, these should be distributed fairly between groups and individuals. In so far as the police are enforcing the law in their adversarial role, the pattern of enforcement should be fair.

Delivery of service. The police should deliver the appropriate services (as determined on other criteria) effectively and efficiently.

Responsiveness. In determining the order of priorities, the allocation of resources between different activities and objectives, and the choice of policing methods, the police should be responsive to the views of a representative body.

Distribution of power. Power to determine policing policy should not be concentrated but distributed between a number of different bodies.

Information should be regularly published on funding, expenditure, activity, and outputs. A representative body should be able to engage in a continuing dialogue with the professional managers of the police force so as to become better informed and to elicit relevant information through a sequence of interactions.

Redress. It should be possible for a representative body to dismiss an incompetent or corrupt chief officer, or one who exceeds his powers. There should be means of redress for unlawful or unreasonable treatment by individual officers.

Participation. As far as possible, citizens should participate in discussion of policing policy with police managers.

Participation
Following the above discussion, there is a need to set these criteria of democracy in a suggested order of priority. This is not to suggest that those criteria coming lower down the list are unimportant – simply that there are 'democratic criteria' which, as regards policing, are *more* important. The

most important feature of this suggested order is that participation appears last. The wide disagreements between theorists as to the importance of participation as a principle of democracy have been set out above. There are two reasons for suggesting that it should be given a lower priority here: one general, the other particular to policing. The general point is that an emphasis on participation as something of value in itself to the self-development of the citizen only seems possible in a highly stratified society in which political activity is confined to a small élite. It would be unwise to overlook the fact that the idea of active participation in democratic government developed in the ancient world in small societies where the great majority of people were slaves or women, and were consequently excluded from the political process. J.S. Mill, now often considered the great proponent of participatory democracy, was writing at a time when only about five per cent of the population in England had the right to vote. In the highly stratified societies of the ancient world or the early nineteenth century, it was practicable to recommend that everyone who had the right to vote should take some part in politics at some level. In an industrial or post-industrial society with universal education, universal adult suffrage, and the mass media of communication, this no longer seems practicable, because it is not the case that every literate and sane person expects or wishes to actively participate in public policy-making. Indeed, it has been argued that 'freedom from politics' – the right *not* to participate – is a central element of contemporary democracy (Arendt, 1963).

The particular reason for placing participation last is that experience has shown, on the evidence summarised earlier in this chapter, that getting together groups of people to discuss policing policy is an uphill struggle. Most of the time, the issues are not salient enough to stimulate a continuing concern and commitment among a large number of people. The conclusion earlier reached by Schumpeter and others about participation in national politics also seems to apply to making policy about a local public service.

Of course, any kind of democratic process requires the participation of members of the public in some sense, whether it be as representatives, or in a broader sense. However, widening that participation beyond a fairly narrow circle may not always be possible or necessary, and other democratic objectives are substantially more important, because they can have a greater impact on the quality of life of the majority.

Equity

The idea of equity runs through all democratic theory. It is placed first in the order of priority here, because in practice other elements of democracy derive from it. For example, the argument for universal suffrage is that it is fair for every adult to have an equal vote.

Although equity is here chosen as the first criterion of democracy, the application of the concept to policing policy is difficult, as was illustrated by the earlier discussion of Jefferson and Grimshaw's (1984) proposals. There is a serious conceptual deficit here, because the idea that there have to be policing policies is relatively new, so that how to decide whether particular policies are fair and just has been very little discussed. The best that can be done at this stage is to give a few pointers to the analysis of the problem.

First, it will be important to make a clear distinction between the police as providers of a service (for example, uniform patrol, security advice, help to victims of crime) and the police in their adversarial relationships with offenders or suspects. Where the police are providers of services, principles of distributive justice apply, which probably means in this case that services should be allocated fairly in relation to needs. Where the police are enforcing the law on offenders or suspects, equity dictates that the level of enforcement should be proportionate to the number and severity of the offences. If this principle is not qualified, it will lead to relatively high levels of enforcement among certain groups and in certain areas, the outcome that Jefferson and Grimshaw (1984) particularly wanted to avoid. How that can be mitigated is an important subject for discussion. Perhaps the most promising option is to require that different methods of enforcement should be reviewed, and that methods that are more even in their impact (for example on different ethnic groups) should be preferred so long as that is consistent with adequate law enforcement.

In any case, the application of the general principle of equity to policing policy is not something that could or should be decided in advance. There have to be institutional structures through which the general principles of equity can be applied to policing policy as part of a democratic process of decision making.

Delivery of service

Because policing is a public good, every citizen benefits if the service is delivered effectively and efficiently. Because a well-policed society is more just than a badly-policed one, the principle of effective service delivery flows from the principle of equity. Service delivery is given a higher priority than, for example, responsiveness or information because even citizens who know nothing about policing and do not wish to express a view will benefit if policing is effectively and efficiently delivered.

Responsiveness

The idea that policing policy should be responsive to some expression of the views of the public derives from the democratic principle that government should reflect the wishes of the people. This principle has to be placed lower than the general principle of equity or justice, however. For example, it would be undemocratic for the police to adopt a highly discriminatory policy of law enforcement, even if a local majority favoured such a policy.

What is the most appropriate method of testing the views of the public is open to debate. One method is through elected or nominated representatives. However, there is also an argument for using surveys of the general public, of people who have been in contact with the police. One approach could be to adopt a combination of different methods. One of the forces in the study supplemented the formal local representative mechanisms with a specially-designed public attitudes survey.

Distribution of power

The idea that power should not be too much concentrated among a few individuals or groups is one that runs through democratic theory. In any social structure, that individuals and groups will have different interests so that some conflict of interests is inevitable. An important feature of democracy is the provision of mechanisms to achieve stable compromises in the case of such conflict. Some concentration of political power in the decision-making structure is a necessary condition for effective administration, but it is important that there are sources of countervailing power and that no single group always prevails. Most criticisms of the current arrangements for police governance have identified the concentration of power in some sense as the problem. For example, critics on the Left have argued that the power balance excludes the interests of the dispossessed and disadvantaged. Other critics on the Left see the power balance as having shifted too far to the centre. Free market critics have argued that the monopoly supplier has too much power in the sense of being insulated from the demands of the consumer. Hence there is agreement across the political spectrum that power should be more evenly distributed. The need to prevent undue concentration of power flows from the prior democratic principle of equity.

Information

Good information is crucial for the achievement of all of the other democratic objectives. There is, again, wide agreement on this point across the political spectrum. It is notable, for example, that the Conservative

Government's policy of developing better measures of police performance, and publishing information based on those measures, is capable of providing material that will be useful to critics on the Left. However, the framework of any set of measures of performance springs from a set of political objectives. The democratic criterion cannot therefore be met by the provision of routine information alone. It is important, in addition, that some body should be able to interrogate the police service and find out more through a sequence of interactions.

Redress

The notion of redress is strongest in the theory of democracy as competition between élites, in which the ultimate sanction of the electorate is to remove an incompetent or malevolent administration from office. By extension of this idea, it should be possible to remove an incompetent or malevolent police management.

If certain groups are unfairly targeted by policing policies, it should also be possible for those groups to have the policy reversed. Finally, it should be possible for individuals who have been wronged by the police to have their complaints investigated, and to gain compensation if they are upheld.

Notes

1. There are differences of opinion as to how public opinion poll ratings of confidence in the police should be interpreted. For some, it is perceived as a significant falling off of public support (Kinsey, Lea and Young, 1986) and for others merely a slight decline from a position of extremely high public confidence (ACPO, 1993).

2. Smaller studies of the making of policing policy in France and the Netherlands will also be published by PSI.

3. These are discussed in considerable detail, from differing viewpoints, in T. Jefferson (1990) and P.A.J. Waddington (1991).

4. The Home Secretary intervened to prevent the watch committee from dismissing their chief constable who was investigating a number of councillors.

2 The Growth of Crime Prevention

The story of policy change in the field of crime prevention is considerably more complex than in either of the other two cases considered in this study. That is because crime prevention is potentially a large and varied activity which, although it is one of the primary functions of the police, also involves a wide range of other agencies. Police activity in crime prevention must be seen in the context of crime prevention as a whole. As the level of crime prevention activity increases, and as the different agencies involved proliferate, there is an increasing need to decide what should be the role of the police in crime prevention. Through all the policy developments of the 1980s, that question remained unresolved.

In 1829, the founders of the Metropolitan Police named preventing crime as one of the three basic functions of the new organisation, along with maintaining public tranquillity and upholding the law. They believed that the new police could achieve the objective of preventing crime by patrolling in uniform and on foot. That may have been a reasonable assumption at a time when working class people lived much of their lives on the streets of the rapidly expanding cities, and when the focus of public concern was the disorder, danger, and crime on those streets. Probably foot patrol always had a limited effect as a method of crime prevention, but in any case many of the developments of the twentieth century have made it still less effective: most notably, the telephone, the motor car, and the retreat to private and protected places, such as comfortable and well-equipped houses and flats, shopping precincts, workplaces, and sports and leisure centres. The period since the Second World War during which these developments have gathered pace has also seen an unprecedented rise in crime. Clarke and Hough (1984) convincingly argued that police patrols could not conceivably be an effective method of preventing or detecting most of this crime; and they were able to cite a considerable body of American research to show that increasing the number of police patrols or their speed of response had little or no effect on the crime rate.

The perception that police patrols were bound to be an ineffective way of dealing with the alarming rise in crime led to the growth of other approaches to crime prevention in the 1980s. The problem for the police service was to find a new role for itself in these changing circumstances, and it seems that the solution has not yet been found.

THE DEVELOPMENT OF CRIME PREVENTION WITHIN THE POLICE SERVICE

Mollie Weatheritt in her (1986) summary of the development of crime prevention work within the police has argued that two histories can be written. The first is a police-oriented conventional history which consists of little more than rhetorical assertions of the importance and effectiveness of crime prevention initiatives. The critical history by contrast, highlights the marginal position of the specialism, the rudimentary arrangements for the identification and dissemination of good practice in this area, and the virtual absence up to that point of any thoroughgoing analysis of the work of crime prevention officers.

It was made clear in the first instruction book of the Metropolitan Police that 'every effort' was to be directed towards the prevention of crime (Emsley, 1983). The manual went on:

> The security of person and property, the preservation of the public tranquility, and all other objects of a police establishment will thus be better effected than by the detection and punishment of the offender after he has succeeded in committing the crime. This should constantly be kept in mind by every member of the police force, as the guide for his own conduct. Officers and police constables should endeavour to distinguish themselves by such vigilance and activity as may render it impossible for any one to commit a crime within that portion of the town under their charge.

At the heart of the new force was the uniformed constable – the bobby on the beat – who not only formed the bedrock of the police in the nineteenth century, but who remains central, if only on an ideological level, to modern philosophies of policing (Reiner, 1992:98). The visible presence of the police on the street was seen as the key to crime prevention. More recent evaluations have, however, found that although increased patrols may reduce the fear of crime, crime levels themselves are unaffected (Police Foundation, 1981; Clarke and Hough, 1984). At the same time, a number of developments have destroyed the primacy of foot patrol, and established crime prevention within the police service as a marginal specialism.

Unit beat policing

In August 1967 the Home Office issued a circular that advocated a new system of policing – known as 'unit beat policing' (UBP) – that reduced the number of officers on foot patrol, and put them into cars. This would have the advantage of allowing much wider geographical areas to be covered on a 24 hour basis and, together with personal radios, would enable officers to respond much more quickly to calls from the public. One of the unintended consequences of this reorganisation, it has been argued (Holdaway, 1984; Reiner, 1992), was to highlight the 'crime fighting' aspects of police work, and to devalue the 'service role' (Punch, 1979). Although UBP is now widely condemned for its supposed effects on police-public relations (Manwaring-White, 1983), it was to remedy just such difficulties (among other things) that the new system was introduced (Weatheritt, 1986).

According to its proponents, UBP would enable a better service to be offered to the public in all the major areas of police work: in the maintenance of public order, in the detection of crime, and in the prevention of crime. Reiner (1992) has suggested that partly as a consequence of UBP, patrol work became transformed into a 'fire brigade' service, and that prevention in this system came to mean 'pre-emption'. In particular, the new emphasis on the collection and collation of low-level information changed the character of surveillance undertaken by the police. UBP, however, quickly fell into disrepute, there being little evidence that the new system was having the hoped-for impact on police-public relations (indeed, successive studies have shown that strong public support for increased foot patrols remains (Smith & Gray, 1983; Kinsey, 1984; Hibberd, 1985). Almost at the same time as the move to UBP, specialist crime prevention departments developed within the police, and the Home Office set up its Standing Committee on Crime Prevention.

Specialist crime prevention departments
Specialist crime prevention departments began to grow from a very small number after the publication of the report of the Cornish Committee on the Prevention and Detection of Crime (Home Office, 1965). This recommended that there should be specialist police officers who would be experts in crime prevention technology; that an officer of at least the rank of inspector take the role of force crime prevention officer; and that the police should develop more professional publicity material on crime prevention.

Anticipating a potential problem with this approach, the committee urged that the creation of the specialism should not be allowed to diminish the responsibility for crime prevention accepted by police officers in general. In what has by now become a standard crime prevention argument, it emphasised the importance of building relationships with organisations outside the police; to this end, it recommended the setting up of 'crime prevention panels'.

Crime prevention panels

Such panels have no formal status and have generally been chaired by the police themselves (Home Office, 1971). Their purpose is to consider crime prevention proposals and to help in the process of publicising campaigns and initiatives aimed at improving security measures (usually physical ones). Because there was no requirement to set them up, and because they lacked formal status, crime prevention panels developed unevenly; following the lead taken by the nascent crime prevention departments within police forces (Home Office, 1971), they tended to focus fairly narrowly on physical security (Gladstone, 1980).

Crime prevention officers

In the main, crime prevention is a small-scale police specialism. Crime prevention officers (CPOs) usually represent less than 1 per cent of a force's establishment (Harvey *et al,* 1989) and rarely occupy ranks higher than chief inspector. Crime prevention officers are usually located within departments with 'community' in their title (community liaison, community involvement and so on) or within CID. Crime prevention work remains fairly marginal. It rarely permeates 'the force much beyond the designated officers, whatever the line of responsibility upwards' (Harvey *et al.,* 1989:88).

The scope of crime prevention work within police forces, like that of crime prevention panels, is relatively narrow. An extensive job description for CPOs was provided by an ACPO working party in 1979, listing 68 tasks. This included a wide variety of jobs ranging from disseminating advice about physical security both inside and outside the police service, giving crime prevention advice to designers and planners, inputs into probationer training, collection and analysis of information, supporting the activities of CPPs, and many others.

Weatheritt (1986) believed that the tasks actually undertaken by CPOs have, in practice, been much more limited than implied by this ambitious job description, and recent research tends to support that view. Harvey *et al.* (1989) found that although a broad range of officers within community liaison departments or their equivalents felt they were engaged in crime prevention work, there was a tendency for force CPOs to make a clear distinction between crime prevention work and 'community' work. Particular emphasis, for example, was placed on the need for technical or hardware expertise, and this 'bias' was reinforced by the training CPOs received at the Stafford Crime Prevention Centre.

In a similar vein, research in London (Johnston *et al.,* 1993), based on observation and worksheets, concluded that the majority of work undertaken by CPOs fell into the following ten categories: residential surveys, commercial/industrial surveys, alarm problems, firearms, displays, talks, designing out crime, initiatives, crime panels, and training. Yet the vast majority of CPOs' time was devoted to only two of these activities: surveys, and meetings about firearms and alarms. The bulk of the work was concerned with target hardening, surveillance, entry/exit screening, and access control – all standard techniques of 'situational prevention' (Clarke, 1992).

Thus, the philosophy underpinning the CPO's actual role is significantly narrower than that implied by the ACPO description. As Weatheritt put it:

> 'Community-based' approaches to crime prevention have not, on the whole, formed a major part of the tradition of specialist crime prevention. Little attention has been given to how best to build up and maintain the kind of contacts and channels of liaison and communication that 'community' approaches imply. Whatever the expressed importance of these wider aspects of their role, crime prevention officers have in practice become... primarily physical security experts. [1986:51]

Johnston *et al.* (1993:5) have argued, furthermore, that because much of the work is of a fairly narrow technical kind most police 'crime prevention activity (is) largely *reactive*, responding to the demands of the public to do surveys...or responding to the need of the service in general to try to reduce the time spent of false alarm calls'. The work of crime prevention design advisers was more proactive, but did not arise from local crime problems. They concluded that although the work could be justified as a direct response to public demand, the delivery of the service 'was not coordinated with the rest of the police service, nor was it necessarily planned to focus on the Division's main priorities for crime prevention'.

Where more socially-based or 'community' initiatives were undertaken, their objectives were generally unclear. Thus, Harvey *et al.* (1989:90) suggested:

> In the plethora of activities initiated and encouraged – soccer, netball, youth clubs, 'Cops, Kids and Carols' concerts, shooting [sic], and schools liaison – the common good seems to be the encouragement of friendly relationships between police and juveniles. Work described as crime prevention sometimes appears, in fact, to be principally public relations with no clearly articulated connection between a good press and crime preventive effects.

This was a theme running through many of the initiatives carried out in the study forces.

Community policing

As crime continued to rise, despite the increase in resources devoted to policing in the early 1980s, the police service increasingly emphasised that it could not be expected to carry responsibility for the prevention of crime unaided. Increasing emphasis came to placed upon the 'community' both in relation to policing generally and, more specifically, in relation to crime prevention (Willmott, 1987). A strong early impetus to these developments had been given by a Home Office circular (211/1978), which became known as the Ditchley circular. This recommended improved coordination between criminal justice agencies, together with community-based initiatives, in place of what was seen as a piecemeal approach to dealing with juveniles.

'Community policing' is most closely associated with John Alderson, at one time Chief Constable of Devon and Cornwall, who emphasised the importance of close relationships between police and public and, consequently, the broad service role of his constabulary (Alderson, 1979). The emphasis upon community and inter-agency cooperation broadened the scope of crime prevention from its previous preoccupation with technology, target hardening, and opportunity reduction, to the social conditions that provide the context of behaviour defined as criminal, and the organisations that are involved in regulating it. Such an approach has been widely referred to as 'social crime prevention' (Clarke, 1981) to distinguish it from 'situational crime prevention' (Clarke and Mayhew, 1980; Clarke, 1992); although this distinction is not always helpful (Bottoms, 1990), it nevertheless retains considerable currency within criminology. The changing emphasis within crime prevention was also reflected, for example, in the curriculum at the Home Office Training Centre at Stafford which, according to Laycock and Heal (1989:320), moved away from 'the previous locks and bars emphasis towards community involvement, crime pattern analysis and inter-agency work'. Although community-focused policing initiatives were many and varied during the 1980s, little rigorous evidence is available, and there is little to suggest that much success has been achieved. Thus, research on community constables (Brown and Iles, 1985), directed patrolling (Burrows and Lewis, 1988), focused patrolling (Chatterton and Rogers, 1989), neighbourhood policing (Irving *et al.*, 1989) and neighbourhood watch (Husain, 1988; Bennett, 1990; McConville and Shepherd, 1992) has illustrated the difficulties in planning, implementing and evaluating community-focused crime prevention measures. It has been argued that most of the problems have stemmed from programme failure (Hope, 1985) rather than fundamental flaws in the underlying philosophy.

Wider developments and the police role

Although crime prevention within the police service had initially been treated as a peripheral specialism of low status and interest when placed alongside crime fighting (Graef, 1989), it became increasingly emphasised during the 1980s and was given considerable publicity to the point that Reiner (1992:99) even felt able to assert that crime prevention departments had become 'the belles of the ball'. Although this is a considerable overstatement of the position within the police service, there had indeed been a number of significant developments in crime prevention more widely. Bottoms (1990) highlighted the setting up of the Crime Prevention Unit in the Home Office in 1983, the issuing of the 1984 interdepartmental circular on crime prevention (Home Office, 1984; followed by Scottish Office, 1984), the two seminars on crime prevention held at 10 Downing Street in 1986 – one chaired by the Prime Minister the other by the Home Secretary – the 'Five Towns Initiative' launched in 1986, followed by the Safer Cities Programme in 1988, and the launch of the charity *Crime Concern*. To this list can be added the reconstituting of the Home Office Standing Conference on Crime Prevention, the second Home Office circular which updated 8/84, and the formation of the ACPO sub-committee on crime prevention. Bottoms (1990:5) concluded that:

> By any standards, this is a formidable list of developments. The 1980s, we can safely assert, has put crime prevention firmly on the map: a conclusion which is true not only in Britain, but also, at a minimum, in France, in the Netherlands and in the Council of Europe.

However, the intended role of the police in the development of crime prevention remains obscure. In some contexts, central government argues that the prevention of crime should remain a central part of the policing function, but it has also supported other agencies that are active in the field, such as NACRO, has directly initiated its own programmes, such as Safer Cities, has created its own voluntary organisation in the field (Crime Concern), and has tried to ensure that local authorities continue to be involved (as evidenced by the two crime prevention circulars).

Again, the police themselves are quick to support the idea that this area of their work remains fundamental, yet the reality is different. CPOs and the departments within which they work remain marginal within most police forces, and crime prevention work remains a narrowly defined specialism.

Situational versus social crime prevention

The distinction between situational and social crime prevention is relevant to an analysis of the role of the police in this field. The idea of situational crime prevention has it origins partly in what was then the Home Office Research Unit (now Research and Planning Unit). Ron Clarke, its leading advocate within the Home Office in the early 1980s, has offered the following definition:

> Situational crime prevention... refers to a pre-emptive approach that relies, not on improving society or its institutions, but simply on reducing opportunities for crime... Situational prevention comprises opportunity-reducing measures that are, (1) directed at highly specific forms of crime (2) that involve the management, design or manipulation of the immediate environment in as specific and permanent way as possible (3) so as to increase the effort and risks of crime and reduce the rewards as perceived by a wide range of offenders (1992:4).

As Clarke himself has pointed out (1992), situational prevention owes a major theoretical debt both to Oscar Newman's theory of 'defensible space' (Newman, 1972) and to the notion of 'crime prevention through environmental design' (Jeffrey, 1971). It was Newman's view that a link could be demonstrated between high-rise public sector housing and increased crime rates. The design of the buildings was such that residents were discouraged from looking after and protecting them. He went on to specify aspects of design, such as unsupervised access points, that contribute to levels of crime. Opportunities for crime could be reduced by correcting such design faults. Newman's ideas have been influential in many countries, including the UK (see for example, Coleman, 1985). Situational prevention took from Newman the idea that the opportunities for crime arise from the structure of the environment and extended it to a wide variety of areas other than public housing.

In the passage quoted above, Clarke referred to 'improving society or its institutions'. In doing so, he was drawing a line between situational prevention and 'social' crime prevention measures. Critics of situational prevention tend to view it as a superficial response to what they regard as the more 'fundamental' causes of crime such as poverty, poor housing, unemployment and inadequate education. As Weatheritt has put it, 'On this view, it is not the physical environment which needs to be manipulated, but rather the social conditions and psychological dispositions that create offenders in the first place... What is needed, therefore, is programmes of action which will help change people's attitudes to offending, encourage respect for law and reduce the wish to commit crimes' (1986:57).

Situational theory explicitly states that crime arises from an interaction between dispositions, perceived opportunities, and perceived risks (Clarke, 1992) and therefore accepts the importance of dispositions. However, the essence of the theory is that, since crime is caused by a multitude of factors, prevention must concentrate on those factors that are easiest to manipulate, namely the concrete aspects of specific situations that influence crime opportunities. Clarke contrasted this modest and piecemeal project with the grander one of 'improving society and its institutions', which is sometimes called 'social crime prevention'. This is an altogether vaguer concept, which does not seem to lead to specific action programmes. It might be used to refer to any programme designed to deal with basic social problems, such as poverty, unemployment, sub-standard education, or family discord, that are thought to be among the causes of crime, but it is better to avoid that usage, because such programmes will never have crime prevention as their only or even their main objective.

More plausibly, the idea of social crime prevention can be linked with a 'social control' theory of crime. From that perspective, the starting point is the need to explain why most of the time most people do not commit crimes, not why some of the time some people do. Deviant behaviour is inhibited by informal social controls, and by the social bonds tied by reciprocal relationships. The apparatus of criminal justice only comes into play when these normal controls have broken down. Social crime prevention is a set of programmes for maintaining and reinforcing informal social controls and social bonds. Although this more limited interpretation of social crime prevention is perfectly coherent, specific and concrete programmes that act in the intended way are hard to find.

If social crime prevention is interpreted as reinforcing social controls and social bonds, then it means enabling social units to regulate themselves more effectively. That leads directly to the notion of 'community-based crime prevention' which has also been promoted in recent years (see Hope and Shaw, 1988). Community-based crime prevention programmes have tried to involve a range of agencies and to use both situational and social measures to promote crime prevention, fear reduction and community safety. This kind of philosophy was the starting point for the Safer Cities programme that the Home Office launched in the late 1980s.

Indeed, a number of attempts have been made by central government to stimulate this type of activity, notably the 1984 circular which emphasised the need for a partnership approach between the police and local government to ensure a comprehensive crime prevention strategy for a 'safer Britain'. In encouraging community-based crime prevention initiatives, the Government stressed the importance of broadening responsibility to the point where 'preventing crime is a task for the whole community'. What was known as 'the multi-agency approach' became the official doctrine underlying a wide range of new projects. These generally aimed to encompass both situational and social crime prevention measures.

Police crime prevention work, however, continues in the main to be dominated by situational measures. Nevertheless, the language of the community-based approach has permeated police discourse about crime prevention, which tends to stress the importance of community involvement and inter-agency cooperation. This is illustrated by the following extract from the submission by the Metropolitan Police Service (MPS) to the Sheehy Inquiry (MPS, 1992):

> The prevention of crime is one of the highest priorities of the MPS. For many years the emphasis has been on crime in its micro perspective, which has caused officers to concentrate on detection of offenders. This produces a more immediate measure of success. However, the approach to reduction, prevention and investigation has to be interactive.

> The Partnership Approach recognises that in order effectively to reduce crime and reverse crime trends it is necessary to view crime in its macro environment. This is a long term option attacking the socio-economic factors that perpetuate crime and targeting multi-agency resources at the heart of the problem.

References in this statement to 'the partnership approach', the 'macro environment', 'the socio-economic factors that perpetuate crime' and 'multi-agency resources' all revolve around the idea that the police are but one agency among many in the 'fight against crime'. This avowed approach to crime prevention evolved from the realisation first that the police working in isolation had only a limited impact on levels of crime (Burrows and Tarling, 1985), and that situational measures were themselves only of limited utility if not supplemented by other approaches to crime reduction (Matthews, 1990). However, much of the discussion about inter-agency cooperation to prevent crime has been conducted in a largely uncritical manner as in, for example, the much quoted circular 8/84 which claimed that 'crime prevention schemes *are more successful* where the police and local agencies work together in a coordinated way towards particular aims' (emphasis added). Although it is attractive to believe that this is the case, there are few rigorously evaluated examples to prove it.

Neighbourhood watch (NW), which is the best known and most widely adopted crime prevention programme in Britain, can be regarded as a form of social or community-based crime prevention. NW appeared first in Britain in the early 1980s, and was promoted force-wide by the Metropolitan Police in 1983. Sir Kenneth Newman sold the initiative as something that would involve community or neighbourhood self-help, with the support of the police. Neighbourhood groups would be formed to carry out informal surveillance, thereby deterring thieves, and to feed information back to the police. Subsequent evaluations have indicated that NW has little or no success in achieving its primary objective of reducing crime (Rosenbaum, 1988; Bennett, 1989), although it is argued that the fault may lie in the failure of both the police and the public to put the idea fully into practice. Nevertheless, considerable police resources have been and continue to be devoted to supporting NW.

CHANGE IN POLICY AND PRACTICE IN FOUR PROVINCIAL POLICE FORCES

Crime prevention and organisational structure

As reported above, recent research (eg Johnston *et al.*, 1993) has suggested that crime prevention remains fairly marginal within police forces. That was true of three of the four study forces. The organisational structures varied somewhat between the four forces, although in most cases the crime prevention department was located within a 'community affairs' or similar department. In force A, the structure and staffing of crime prevention came under review during the course of the fieldwork. Before this review, community relations activity was divided into two parts: the headquarters community relations branch, and the staff on the territorial divisions and sub-divisions. The community relations branch was part of the Traffic and Operational Support Department, which in turn was headed by a chief superintendent reporting to an ACC (support services). The HQ community relations branch itself was headed by a superintendent, and comprised his deputy (a chief inspector), a force CPO (an inspector), a research and support sergeant, a design advice sergeant, a civilian alarms administrator and a clerk typist. Each of the four territorial divisions had a community relations establishment of one inspector and one sergeant, together with a sergeant and two constables designated as CPOs. These officers were responsible to the divisional commander. Each sub-division had at least one Schools Liaison Officer (SLO), of whom there were 21 across 14 sub-divisions. The SLOs were responsible to the sub-divisional commander.

In force B crime prevention was a more important function accounting for a larger number of staff than in the other three forces. The main responsibility lay with the Community Crime Prevention Department (CCPD). This large department covered situational crime prevention, schools liaison, administration of the force's employment and youth training schemes, management of the force expedition centre, the firearms section, race relations, press and public relations, and contacts with the community such as the committee set up to develop victim reception suites. Senior officers thought it important that the CCPD came under the responsibility of an assistant chief constable (ACC) who was also responsible for CID. Thus, prevention and detection were, according to the head of the CCPD, given equal importance by the police organisation in the fight against crime.

The CCPD had its roots in a department put together in 1982 called 'Community Services'. This covered physical crime prevention and included schools liaison and the expedition centre, but according to the current force CPO, had not laid a great deal of stress on the social crime prevention side. The department evolved gradually into the current CCPD, and became an exact reflection of a model department laid down in an ACPO report. The department was large, with a total staff of about 150 of whom 85 were police officers. At HQ there were 16 officers, including the head of CCPD (a chief superintendent), and two deputies (superintendents, one a 'situational' CPO and the other a 'social' CPO). There were four chief inspectors, one responsible for race relations, one for youth and employment training schemes, and the other two having territorial responsibility for three divisions each. On each division there was an inspector and a sergeant with responsibility for crime prevention and a number of SLOs and CPOs, apparently working across sub-divisional boundaries.

Crime prevention in force C came under the HQ department called 'Force Services'. This department was part of the bigger Management Services Department which reported to one of the two ACCs. Force Services was headed by a chief superintendent and divided into three sections comprising community relations, prosecutions, and force solicitors. Crime prevention came under the community relations section which was headed by a superintendent. Below him there were two chief inspectors, one of whom was the force CPO while the other was in charge of the 'inter-agency branch' (which dealt with schools liaison and public relations). The HQ crime prevention section consisted of the chief inspector, a sergeant, a constable and some civilian support. Each of the force's 10 sub-divisions had a CPO who was based in the sub-divisional coordination unit. This unit was made up of the CPO, a juvenile liaison officer, an accident prevention officer, two collators and a civilian support worker operating the force incident recording system. In force D crime prevention was one of the responsibilities of the community affairs department at headquarters. At the time of the research, this department was headed by a chief superintendent, with a superintendent deputy, two inspectors (the force CPO and the force community relations officer), one sergeant (Architectural Liaison Officer), a constable (technical services), a civilian NW coordinator, and three civilian clerks. The force had four territorial divisions, and on each the community relations complement was one sergeant and six constables (two juvenile liaison officers, two schools liaison officers and two CPOs). This made a total of 34 police officers and four civilians working in community relations.

Crime prevention and organisational change

The thinking behind the organisation of crime prevention and community relations in force A was to devolve ownership and responsibility for preventive policing strategies to the local level. The study certainly found differences of approach in different localities. On one division there was a 12-month crime reduction experiment in which the responsibility for crime prevention was shifted to CID with one CPO on each of the four sub-divisions. Another division had two CPOs who adopted a traditional security-based approach to crime prevention. Another division adopted a broader community relations approach; projects were initiated in which, for example, schoolchildren produced small plays with a crime prevention theme, new property recording schemes were promoted, and this was coupled with an enthusiastic approach to obtaining sponsorship from outside the police service. The main organisational change in crime prevention following a force review in 1986 had been a partial devolution of responsibility to divisional level: at the time of the fieldwork on sub-divisions it was up to the divisional commanders how they organised crime prevention (for example, whether they put it under CID or uniform control). This led to some ambiguity about where the main line of responsibility for crime prevention lay. The role of the HQ department was to oversee the strategy of the force as a whole towards crime prevention, a strategy whose central part was the devolution of responsibility for local issues down to the local area. At the same time HQ was supposed to liaise with the Home Office, keep abreast of national developments and initiatives in other forces, monitor local initiatives within the force and disseminate good practice. Within this framework, different divisions appeared to have significant freedom to develop their own policies, and this was illustrated by the difference in approach on the two sub-divisions visited as part of the research.

There were further changes following an extensive review of crime prevention policy in 1990. The review was initiated in response to a number of factors, including dissatisfaction over the role of community relations and crime prevention within the force, and national developments, in particular the issue of the inter-departmental circular 44/90 which requested forces (and local authorities) to submit reports detailing current arrangements, or proposed arrangements, for inter-agency structures in crime prevention. The review body recommended that a community crime prevention branch should be created within CID; it would be headed by a superintendent, and would comprise a crime prevention unit, a community affairs unit, and a multi-agency unit. The multi-agency unit was to be headed by two chief inspectors, one for each of the administrative counties covered by the force. The activities of the multi-agency unit would be linked with a force-wide chief officers' inter-agency group, which would comprise senior representatives of police, education, health, probation, and highways from both administrative counties covered by the force. Deciding to go further than the review had recommended, the force command team created a community crime prevention department headed by a chief super-intendent (rather than a branch headed by a superintendent). Most other recommendations were accepted, and the sub-divisional CPOs became responsible to the HQ department.

Home Office guidance was a major influence on both waves of organisational change in force A. The first set of changes emerged from a Force Structure Review carried out in response to Home Office circular 114/83. The issue of circular 44/90 was an important impetus to the more recent review of the structure of crime prevention. However, individuals also had an influence. The force CPO had been considering the development of a new structure before the issue of 44/90. Personalities were also important at the local level. The experiment of putting crime prevention under CID in one division was closely related to the personal priorities of the divisional CID head.

Force B had also experimented with changing the organisational structure of crime prevention. As in some other forces, the overall aim appeared to be devolution of responsibility to sub-divisions and spreading ownership of crime prevention within the police organisation. In 1987, the superintendent in charge of crime prevention formulated a policy which gave some responsibility for crime prevention to the deputy divisional and deputy sub-divisional commanders. This was to try to create a local ownership of problems, and to move away from the notion of crime prevention as a headquarters specialism. There was a force-wide meeting of all these deputy commanders with the superintendent CPO to brief them on their responsibility for crime prevention. At the same time, all uniform shift officers and permanent beat officers (PBOs) on sub-division were given a crime prevention manual to enable them to give basic crime prevention advice (mainly on physical security) to the public. There was no requirement for the deputy divisional and sub-divisional commanders to do specific things in relation to their new responsibilities. The aim, it seems, was simply to raise the profile of 'crime prevention' in the territorial units of the organisation. Headquarters was supposed to retain a coordinating and disseminating function.

The effect of this organisational change was unclear. The CPO whose responsibilities included one of the sub-divisions we visited complained that he had too many bosses. Formally, he had responsibilities to HQ, to the division and to the sub-divisional management. The sub-divisional commanders reported little change in terms of local ownership of problems resulting from the organisational developments in the CCPD. The force had already set up a structure of communication with the chief executives of the six metropolitan district councils in the force area. This was simply submitted to the Home Office in response to 44/90.

There was little evidence of any recent major change in the organisation of crime prevention in force C. However, a report into the force structure carried out by management consultants in 1981 continued to exert a strong influence upon the organisational structure. This report had argued for devolution of responsibility to the lowest possible level, for reducing the number of divisions and for breaking the force up into 10 smaller sub-divisions. The report even laid down the exact geographical boundaries of the sub-divisions, which senior officers were (apparently) still loath to change. Nearly a decade later, there was still a strong leaning among senior managers in the force in favour of sub-divisional autonomy, and against the setting up of specialist units. This may explain why the CPOs were based on sub-division rather than division. Nevertheless, they had a close relationship with the HQ crime prevention department although they were supposed to report to the local commander. A former sub-divisional commander said that he saw little of crime prevention policy-making when he was on sub-division, and that policies simply 'appeared from on high'.

Until late 1988 the community affairs department in force D was headed by a superintendent. The chief constable wanted to introduce another chief superintendent post, and in a report to the police authority he asked that the head of community affairs be upgraded to a chief superintendent post, in order that the department would henceforth have an input into force corporate policy deliberations (the force policy group included officers of chief superintendent rank and above). The first chief superintendent was a young and innovative officer who was immediately tasked to carry out a review of the department. The review involved interviews with members of staff in the department, and visits to outside agencies and to other forces. It concluded that there was an ambiguity about the aims of the department because the staff, who were based at divisional level, reported both to headquarters and to the divisional management. Officers at sub-divisional level had little contact with community relations officers, and were unclear what the department was there for apart from public relations. This suggested one of two courses of action: either centralise the department completely and make all officers fully accountable to HQ; or decentralise to the sub-divisional level. The new head of department chose the second option saying: 'I wanted the sub-divisional commander to think about crime prevention when he thought about crime detection'. He thought it was a common assumption in the police service that crime could only be tackled by gaining evidence from people after they had been victimised, which meant assuming that there had to be an increase in the number of victims before the problem could be tackled by catching more offenders. He wanted to attack that assumption by re-emphasising the importance of crime prevention as a central force objective.

In 1989, the force set up what was widely referred to as an experiment, which involved the 'sub-divisionalisation' of community relations staff on one division. Two sub-divisions within this division were visited during the research. All officers interviewed spoke of the 'experiment' in a highly positive light, although there was no evidence of any systematic evaluation of its results. Sub-divisional commanders and CPOs were equally enthusiastic about the CPOs being based on sub-division. In both sub-divisions, the CPOs said that their workloads had gone up, because both the sub-divisional officers and the general public were more aware of the services which they could offer. By workload they meant requests to carry out security surveys, and advice on target-hardening measures. Although they argued that the whole nature of crime prevention was changing, there was little evidence of changes in the kind of work that the CPOs were doing, just the amount. There was no evidence of systematic analysis of local crime trends, although one CPO described this as 'the thing of the future'.

One consequence of the experiment was a further clouding of the role of the community affairs department at headquarters. The divisional community affairs sergeant was in theory the link between HQ and the sub-divisional officers, but in practice there was little contact. The HQ role was described by the sergeant and his officers as one of coordination and supervision, but little evidence was found of such a role being filled (partly because the experiment was set up on the assumption that crime prevention needed to be a local response to local problems).

It appears that the chief constable was the key influence on the decision to up-grade the community affairs department and create a chief superintendent post. The sub-divisionalisation experiment sprang directly from the departmental review which was set up by the first chief superintendent in charge of the department. He was a young and innovative officer with strong views about the direction that community affairs should take. Many of the changes in the organisation of community affairs can be attributed to him personally. The departmental review largely reflected his beliefs about the future role of community affairs. These contrasted strongly with the more conservative views expressed by his successor. The police authority in force D had little influence over these developments.

Neighbourhood watch

Force A faced the familiar problem that support for NW tended to stimulate further demands on police time and resources. Also, it was comparatively difficult to establish schemes in high-crime areas where they are most necessary. The force CPO expressed the need for more police resources and encouragement to be put into NW. It was decided to take on 12 part-time NW coordinators, funded by the Employment Training Scheme, who were to liaise with the public and help set up new schemes. However, the coordinators were not allocated from the centre. Instead, after discussions at force management level, it was decided to leave it to each sub-divisional commander to decide how NW was to be supported on that patch.

In one of the two sub-divisions examined, policy strongly encouraged NW. The NW coordinator was enthusiastic about the close working relationship she had with the CPOs. Also, a full-time coordinator has been appointed as a civilian member of the police staff, which was seen as a sign of higher than usual commitment to the NW principle. The NW coordinator evaluated activity by the total number of schemes and the perceived enthusiasm of participants. In the other sub-division, a part-time NW coordinator funded by Employment Training had been brought in (whereas previously there had been no coordinator at all). She feared that once the year's funding was exhausted there would be a return to the old situation. She evaluated NW in similar terms to the other coordinator. The CPOs in both sub-divisions were in favour of NW and wanted the police to encourage its development, although one was aware that research had found little effect of NW on crime levels. He thought the main role of NW was not crime reduction but raising public awareness of crime prevention and improving police-community relations. He was arguing strongly for the sub-division to fund a full-time NW coordinator.

The main policy initiative taken at HQ level was the decision to take on 12 coordinators funded by Employment Training. As stated above, it was an explicit decision by the force management team not to lay down policy in this area but to allow the sub-divisional commanders to decide their own priorities, although there was talk of the need to improve the servicing of schemes and to extend them to new areas. In one of the sub-divisions examined, a local decision was taken to employ a full-time coordinator using police funds.

The police authority played no active part in deciding policy, but were kept informed of developments by the chief constable's reports. The NW groups expected and demanded police support, but played no part in the development of policy about how that support would be provided and what form it would take. They adopted a responsive role and remained dependent on the police.

Force B gave the greatest degree of support to NW of all the four police forces studied. At the time of the research, there were about 2,600 schemes in the force area, and from the early 1980s the force had taken the initiative in setting up schemes. The force CPO's comments on how NW started gave an interesting insight into the way the idea took hold within the police organisation:

> We were aware that it was going great guns in the States, and then we heard that Cheshire police had started the first scheme in this country, and thought that we would try out a couple of pilot schemes here.. both in high crime areas. As always, pilot schemes were successful (or apparently successful!), so guidance was given to the rest of the force in establishing another set of schemes within the sub-divisions.

A review of NW was carried out when the idea became so popular it threatened to become a significant drain on police resources. This led to a set of detailed guidelines for all sub-divisional commanders on how to manage NW (an impressively produced, glossy-covered volume), which suggested that they prioritise high-crime areas and have a single monthly meeting with all coordinators. In 1991, Urban Programme funding enabled three NW development officers to be employed at HQ to oversee the force policy in this area. Each sub-division was given a civilian NW assistant to service the local schemes, and be a point of contact with the police organisation. Also, there was what the force CPO called 'an ongoing evaluation of NW' in which specimen schemes were selected each year, and the force research department carried out some survey work to assess the perceived benefits of NW and come up with suggested improvements.

The CPO in force C described the process by which they came to adopt NW as part of its crime prevention policy as 'policy-making by default'. The approach of the force followed directly from the views of the chief constable. Prior to 1986, the chief had been opposed to NW and the force did not set up any schemes. However, it was clear by 1986 that HMIC supported the concept as did public opinion in general. Persuaded by this, the chief set up a few pilot schemes in the force area, which were evaluated by the research department. Although this evaluation showed little effect on crime rates, the chief decided to go ahead with NW force-wide. In the view of the force CPO, the chief constable could not withdraw from NW at this stage because of the pressure of opinion from HMIC and Home Office in favour of it. In 1988 the chief issued an instruction to the force that they were not to initiate any more schemes, because those that were being set up by the public were already taking up a lot of police resources. The original idea had been that the NW schemes would be serviced by special constables, but not enough had been recruited. At the time of the research, there were 2,400 schemes in the force area. The force CPO explained that it was very difficult to service them with information about crime and incidents. Schemes received information at irregular intervals, and even then the information was often out of date. The NW schemes were very police-dependent. A permanent beat officer on one sub-division described how he would respond to requests to start NW schemes by circulating and collecting questionnaires; he would then arrange and address the initial meeting, and would try to provide each scheme on his beat with up-to-date information.

NW schemes came to force D fairly late in the day. The superintendent (community affairs) said that this was due to the resources that the force had needed to invest in policing the miners' strike in the county. The first scheme was set up in August 1985. The chief constable appeared to take a positive but cautious view of NW, and stressed in a report to the police authority that it could not in any way be seen as a substitute for the regular policing of an area. The same report explained that the force had taken on an MSC-funded civilian at HQ to administer NW schemes force-wide. At the time of the research the force area had about 400 schemes of differing sizes. It was quite difficult to identify a tangible force policy on NW. Senior officers talked in somewhat vague terms of the need to enhance community spirit and good neighbourliness. The overall view of NW was quite positive. The force actively encouraged schemes to start up, sending out an information pack and providing funds for signs and stickers if there was enough enthusiasm. The local CPO would attend and give a talk to members at the outset. At the same time, senior officers remained cautious about NW. A number of officers stressed that NW should not be police-led, and expressed concern that more and more police resources would be needed to keep it going. On visiting sub-divisions, the researcher observed both schemes that were highly dependent on the police, and schemes that functioned with almost no police contact.

There was no attempt to evaluate the effects of NW schemes. On this issue there was a vagueness from the top of the department to the bottom. The superintendent (community affairs) said that he had heard of Bennett's (1990) research, but that things like community spirit and neighbourliness could not be measured. The CPOs talked about the 'success' of NW in terms of the absolute number of schemes, but felt that effects on crime rates could not be measured. The CPO at one sub-division argued strongly that it was NW which, through displacement, had led to the increases in autocrime (due to reduction of opportunities for domestic burglary). However, he admitted that this was 'gut feeling' rather than a provable contention. The local coordinators appeared to evaluate schemes by the activity of members and the number of meetings held. Overall, all those interviewed saw NW as a good thing, but this was more a matter of faith than demonstration.

This was one area in which the force D police authority did appear to have exerted some influence. The minutes record that in 1984 two councillors visited the Kingsdown project in Bristol and reported back, recommending that the chief constable support the NW principle and introduce experimental arrangements. The chief constable of the time appeared to adopt a policy of cautious encouragement, which allowed police input to vary according to demand. However, this policy led to a degree of uncertainty: NW was regarded as a good thing but people within the force appeared unsure of exactly why. The local schemes were some-what isolated: there were no local sub-divisional scheme coordinators, so that the chances of coordination between different schemes were restricted.

Special projects

Design advisory services
All four of the study forces provided some kind of design advisory service with the objective of giving advice to local authorities, architects and building developers about crime prevention implications of design features. The design advisory service was described by one of force A's CPOs as 'the biggest change we've seen'. The force introduced the project in November 1987, and the service was staffed by HQ personnel. The local CPOs were also involved. They obtained lists of the local building developments in the area from local authority planning applications. These were sent to the Architect Liaison Officer (ALO) at HQ who coordinated the service and took personal responsibility for crime prevention advice to major building developments. The ALO decided which developments could benefit from a crime prevention input, contacted the architect and developer and offered police assistance and advice. This included advice about security hardware as well as the interpretation of crime trends, and

social and environmental factors that might influence crime at that location in the future.

Secured by Design was a local regional initiative with which the force A CPO had strong personal links (he was mentioned by name by the force D ALO as promoting the project nationally). According to the project information pack, the project was aimed at 'actively encouraging the adoption by housebuilders of important guidelines to upgrade the security against crime and fire safety of new houses'. If the developer designed the required amount of security measures into the proposed dwellings (after consultation with the police) then he could use the 'secured by design' police logo, which was intended to help sell the properties.

At the local level, CPOs had been working with the local authority for some time, according to the force CPO. The annual report outlined some examples of the CPOs working with the council housing department and technical services department to improve security in local authority housing. The report said that 'the council architect has put into practice the concept of designing out crime on all new building projects'. On one sub-division, after pressure from the police consultative committee, the local borough council had appointed a secure homes officer to the housing department. In another part of the force area, such developments were beginning to take place at the time of the research. The CPO outlined a project in which they targeted a high-crime industrial estate with the help of the design advisory service in order to make improvements. He also liaised with the local authority and the Electricity Board on a project to improve the street lighting in an area of high car crime. The local council were in the process of redesigning the town centre, and after consultations with the design advisory service a series of recommendations were submitted to the planning department. The CPO felt that the local authority could take more notice of crime prevention advice from the police, and hoped that the introduction of the circular 44/90 would encourage this.

Since 1987 force B had employed two ALOs at headquarters. The first post had been funded through the Urban Programme, although both posts were subsequently funded through the force budget. Both ALOs held architectural qualifications. They attended monthly planning surgeries of all the local authority planners in the force area, which examined planning applications and recommended alterations for reasons of crime prevention and security. A senior officer in the force stated that planners were usually 'quite happy' to comply with such recommendations, although there was evidence that this was not always the case. A researcher accompanied the head of the community crime prevention department (CCPD) on a visit to a recently-built retail site. The development had been built in such a way that it was extremely vulnerable to ram raiders. A few design alterations could have improved the security significantly. When asked what had happened to the ALO input in this case the head of department said he was not sure and would investigate the case.

The ALOs were working closely with the local development corporation, and had made a crime prevention input to its housing, commercial and leisure developments. The CCPD also had a continuing link with the Department of the Environment looking at DoE-funded estate action projects in the force area. The DoE agreed to make local authority consultation with the ALOs a condition of granting estate action funding, to ensure that measures of security are built in.

Unlike some of the other forces in the study, this force was not in favour of the *Secured by Design* project. The ACPO region was not in favour of implementing the project. The superintendent (force CPO) explained that the project applied mainly to the private housing sector, which was not the main problem area for the force. Even so, *Secured by Design* reached less than half of private house builders. The main problem anticipated was that the project would be highly resource-intensive for the police. The force decided not to commit resources to it until there was some kind of evaluation that revealed what resource input was needed and what the benefits would be. As in the other forces, discussions with the CPOs in the two sub-divisions showed that the ALO function was very much a headquarters activity, with little involvement from the sub-divisional level.

Force C had also considered the *Secured by Design* initiative but decided against supporting it for similar reasons. The force had a trained ALO who was a sergeant in the force services department. Two other officers (one of whom was a sub-divisional CPO) were booked to go on training courses at the Stafford crime prevention centre to become ALOs. When the force decided to employ an ALO the policy was that the service be police-driven (the officer would try to influence the planning decisions he thought to be most important) rather than spend time responding to requests for the service.

In force D, there was a single force ALO (a sergeant) at force headquarters. The divisional and sub-divisional CPOs had little to do with the provision of this service: it was almost totally managed and delivered from HQ. The ALO post had existed since 1982 although staff shortages during the miners' strike, and the ill-health of the previous post-holder meant that little was achieved until 1986. The ALO in post during the study explained that he had no specialist crime prevention experience before coming into post, which had been a significant disadvantage at the outset. A few referrals came from CPOs, but the bulk of the work was generated by the ALO himself sifting through planning applications to the various district councils and selecting cases where he felt he could have an effective input. Because he was the only ALO, the officer had to be very selective about the cases he took up. He pointed out the contrast with the county's large number of fire prevention officers. He had negotiated a crime prevention input into a course at the local University School of Architecture, and had established a liaison with the education authority on the matter of school security (he had persuaded the education authority to set aside a section of the budget specifically for the security of school buildings).

At the time of the research, force D had yet to become fully involved in the *Secured by Design* initiative. The force CPO had met his counterpart from another police force, who was promoting the scheme nationally. One of the ACPO regions had agreed to try to obtain sponsorship to start the scheme, and the chief of each force in the region had agreed to give £1,000 to start things off. Although the force CPO was very keen on the scheme, the ALO expressed reservations that as the only specialist member of staff, he would be totally over-run if the scheme started. He was concerned that he would have difficulty in checking that the required standards were being met, and claimed that he had heard from colleagues in the other regions that the scheme logo was being used for buildings that had not actually met the required criteria.

Burglar alarm policy

All four forces reported that over recent years, the amount of police time wasted in responding to false burglar alarm calls had increased. In response to this problem, the crime prevention sub-committee of the ACPO crime committee formulated a national policy to start from January 1990. The aim was to make commercial central alarm stations (which handled most alarm calls) bear a greater responsibility for validating alarm signals received before contacting the police for response. The policy laid down that following seven false alarms over a 12 month period from a single alarm source, the police would withdraw response for at least three months, or until the situation was rectified. The four police forces in the study had all adopted the ACPO policy.

'Social' crime prevention schemes

All of the forces were involved in schemes that could broadly be described as social crime prevention (see the earlier discussion of this rather vague term). Force A had sub-divisional SLOs, who set up a 'crime theatre' scheme by which school children were encouraged to develop short plays with a crime prevention theme. Force B ran training schemes and a programme of activity holidays for young people. Force C also ran an activity holidays programme and in addition maintained a coordinated schools liaison programme. Force D gave specific responsibilities to two CPOs on each sub-division, calling them the CPOs for 'physical' and 'social' crime prevention. The force ran a series of visits to schools.

Senior officers in the community crime prevention department (CCPD) in force B were very proud of the extensive use that the force made of employment and youth training schemes. The chief superintendent who was head of the department explained that although it was not unusual for police forces to employ trainees from government schemes, it was unusual for a police force to be the 'training managers' of their own schemes, as was the case in this area. It was certainly true that youth and employment trainees were involved in a wide variety of tasks in the force. The youth training scheme concentrated initially on office administrative skills, and in every police office with an administrative element there was at least one youth trainee. The trainees had four six-month training periods, at least one of which was in a specifically police environment. According to the chief superintendent, there was a high demand for these young people once they had finished the training, not just because of the skills they had picked up, but also because private companies knew that they had not been in trouble with the police, since that was one of the criteria of selection. According to the head of CCPD, over 1,000 young people had been put through the force's youth training scheme. The force took people on placements for up to 12 months, and 40 per cent of this time consisted of training tailored to individual needs. The researcher saw trainees working in front offices and counters, as crime pattern analysts, and as NW assistants, and giving administrative support to permanent beat officers.

This youth training scheme was clearly seen by senior officers in the CCPD as part of their social crime prevention work. On one level at least the results were impressive. The force was able to offer its permanent beat officers and NW coordinators far more support than in any of the other forces covered by the study. Also, the contribution to local employment prospects was impressive. However, the crime prevention aspect of these training schemes was less clear. For example, the head of CCPD seemed to think that the objectives of the scheme were to break the link between unemployment and crime, and to foster good relationships between young people and the police. But he also said that applicants were closely vetted, and those with criminal records or associates were screened out. This was a point explicitly recognised by a an inspector in the CCPD who said 'some argue that we only get the nice kids anyway, and we could do a lot more in the direction of targeting kids, and I think there is some truth in that'.

Like other forces, force B had a network of specialist schools liaison officers (SLOs). There were about 40 SLOs across the force. Officers in the CCPD explained that the schools programme had in the past been somewhat unstructured, and largely left to contacts between individual schools and individual SLOs about the level and nature of the input. At the time of the research the force was in the process of putting together a more coordinated programme, with a full-time 'schools adviser' examining what input the police could have in the curriculum of different year groups. In addition to the SLOs, the force had for many years run an expedition centre, with a police-funded civilian employed as the outward bound instructor. This was used to give children from the inner-city areas the opportunity to have an activity holiday in the country. The emphasis on this kind of 'social crime prevention' did not escape criticism from other sections of the force, particularly some of the CID officers who were interviewed. This was perhaps not surprising, as even those who believed most strongly that the police should do this kind of thing seemed rather vague about the crime prevention effects. One of the officers in the CCP department explained that it was not possible to justify such projects on the basis of hard data:

> We do work on the social side; our schools liaison teams and the expedition centre. We must put several hundred kids though there every year. A lot of operational police officers would question the value of it, but it's something you can't really evaluate. At the end of the day, do you want contact between police and young people, and if you do then that sort of thing is one of the best ways of doing it, allowing them to work together. We can't prove that it works, the only thing is the response from the kids themselves that go there – we have hundreds of letters of appreciation.

This seemed to sum up many officers' position on police involvement in such things. There was, it seemed, an acceptance on the part of some senior officers that there were strong arguments in favour of the proposition that such things *are not* a primary police task, and that perhaps the police should concentrate resources upon those functions that *are*. However, the force remained committed to such schemes, apparently because of a 'gut feeling' that they are self-evidently 'good' which overcame any more practical concerns about effective resource allocation.

Senior officers in force C were very proud of a project known as 'Operation Lifestyle'. This was a scheme intended to provide children of 11-15 with activities during the school holidays. The scheme started in 1989 and was initially sponsored by a local communications company, although a national petrol company provided sponsorship the following year. The scheme involved schoolchildren being encouraged to design and carry out projects in small teams during their summer holidays. The projects were supposed to benefit the local community or the environment. Each team was supervised by an adult, and at the end of the summer the teams submitted a short report of their activities as part of a competition. The best project would win a holiday in Canada. A promotional video was produced which was shown by neighbourhood beat officers in all the secondary schools in the force area. In its first year the scheme involved more than 9,000 children. Projects included helping the elderly and the disabled, cleaning and gardening, renovation of playgrounds, and recycling of paper and tins.

Privately, even the most enthusiastic supporters of police involvement in the scheme admitted that it could not be justified by reference to direct impact on juvenile crime. During the first year there was an 8 per cent drop in juvenile crime, but police officers volunteered that this was the result of a number of factors, including demographic changes. Despite this private reluctance to link the project with changes in the crime figures, the 1989 Annual Report implied that the scheme had reduced the numbers of juveniles reported to the police for criminal matters by 3 per cent during the summer holidays. The chief superintendent who headed the Force Services Department argued that the project should not be seen primarily as crime prevention at all. He viewed the project as a large and highly successful public relations exercise. Nevertheless, the force's commitment to the project was shown by the amount of police time devoted to it. Within the inter-agency unit, the inspector in charge of public relations, along with a sergeant and a constable were working full-time on the project. In addition, there was a lot of work for the sub-divisional neighbourhood beat officers, who made the visits to schools to set the projects up, and monitored the kinds of projects that were being implemented. The scheme was very popular with officers at the sub-divisional level, who again saw it as a way of fostering good contacts between the police service and young people.

At the time of the study, the responsibility for schools visits in force C lay with juvenile liaison officers (JLOs) and neighbourhood beat officers helping to set up Operation Lifestyle. The JLOs visited primary schools, although there did not appear to be a coordinated pattern of visits. The force was in the process of developing schools liaison work into a model by which there was a police input into a programme delivered by teachers. In 1989 the force set up a steering group chaired by one of the ACCs including a deputy director of education from the county council, a curriculum design expert, an inspector and a seconded deputy headteacher. The aim was to have a more coordinated approach overall, and to develop a more detailed input into the school curriculum on crime and order issues.

Crime pattern analysis

In 1985 force B made it policy that each sub-division should have a police officer dedicated to analysing the local crime patterns and presenting the information to management and operational officers. At the time of the research, some of these crime pattern analyst clerks used computers, but many just used a paper-based system. Both of the sub-divisions visited had crime pattern clerks in the latter category. Both produced a weekly bulletin of crime figures, picking out the main problem areas and trying to identify patterns. Crime and incident figures were extracted from the force computer and broken down, sometimes to the level of individual footbeats. This information was given to the sub-divisional management, CID and uniform shifts, and also to the NW assistants. Each analyst had a YTS trainee giving administrative support. The information given was from a fairly basic level of analysis, in fact more description than analysis. One of the officers in this role was used in his sub-division as a source of information on performance, and he showed what he called his 'arrest league table' which compared the numbers of arrests between shifts. This information was communicated to shift supervisors if the 'productivity' of their shift went down. Although this analysis was neither detailed nor elaborate, it was still a way of targeting particular problems. The officers said that when types of crime, time and geographical location patterns had been established, they could respond by targeting patrols and alerting NW coordinators. The crime pattern analyst post was due to be civilianised and merged with the criminal intelligence function.

Crime prevention panels (CPPs)

All the police forces in the study had set up crime prevention panels, most usually one per sub-division. The aim of CPPs was to extend participation in crime prevention projects. Most CPOs felt that the CPPs had some benefits, in particular in terms of helping the police to raise the public awareness of crime problems. But CPPs were not an important part of any force's approach to crime prevention. Most members were strongly supportive of the police, and enthusiastically promoted low-level publicity and property-marking schemes. However, these were nearly always initiated by the CPOs, upon whom all the CPPs were heavily dependent.

'Theme of the month'

This was an initiative which formed part of the superintendent's attempt to structure the approach to crime prevention across force D. In his view, different parts of the force were targeting different things and he wanted a more coordinated effort. The community affairs department (in effect, either the chief or his deputy) would decide on a theme for the month in question which would then be given to a particular division to promote for a month. This amounted to no more than a public information campaign, with displays, exhibitions and the use of the force mobile crime prevention caravan. The CPOs in both sub-divisions that were studied were somewhat dubious about the usefulness of theme of the month. They felt that the chosen themes bore little relation to their local problems.

In a similar fashion, force B regularly ran force-wide 'campaigns' which lasted for 6 months. These were basically public information campaigns on particular types of crime. They involved the production and distribution of leaflets and posters, and public conferences held at force HQ. Also, divisions and sub-divisions were encouraged to respond to the force campaign with specific initiatives. The setting up of an experimental domestic violence unit on one division was apparently part of that division's response to a force-wide campaign against violence.

'Light Against Crime'

This was mentioned by the force CPO (force D), although nobody else appeared to know much about it. The superintendent (community affairs) did not mention it, and when asked directly about it, the ALO said he had never heard of it. However, according to the CPO, the project involved a campaign launched by the community affairs department, the local Electricity Board, and a private company. According to the force annual report, the purpose was to encourage householders to reduce crime in the dark winter evenings by increasing the level of lighting around their properties. The police designed an information leaflet funded by the Electricity Board. There was no evidence of any attempt to evaluate the project.

Autocrime prevention

This was a central priority of force D. In fact, the Safer Cities coordinator felt that the police were over-focusing on 'taken without owner's consent' (TWOC) as an offence and exaggerating its significance as part of a political campaign to raise its profile. The CPO explained how he had tried to analyse the patterns of autocrime across the county, but had failed to come up with results which could relate the problem to a particular time or place. They developed a force-wide scheme which involved information leaflets, car stickers and property marking drives. A car company etched windows free of charge for one week, and a local car dealer helped to promote the project. The force CPO evaluated the scheme in terms of the number of leaflets distributed (apparently, about 100,000 people were covered in a 6 month period).

Coalition against crime

Another project mentioned by force B was similar to a programme singled out as an example of good practice in a Home Office circular. The 'Coalition Against Crime' was a team of seconded business people whose task was to look at ways of promoting crime prevention. Like Crime Concern, the coalition was a registered charity. The coalition was answerable to a management board serviced by an executive team to which the force seconded a police officer. Member companies and local councils provided representatives to set up and manage crime prevention initiatives. The coalition was responsible for distributing a set of posters featuring a character called 'Barney the Bloodhound' who urged the public to 'take a bite out of crime'.

Multi-agency work

One of the elements common to all four forces' presentation of their crime prevention policy was an emphasis on the 'multi-agency approach' – although the strength of the emphasis varied between the forces. Multi-agency work was widely viewed as being either the most or one of the most significant developments in the field in recent years. For example, within force A, it became clear from early discussions at HQ that the policy of crime prevention was regarded as undergoing significant change. Several officers referred to the 'old school' of crime prevention, which basically involved traditional specialisms of advice about security and target-hardening measures – 'bolts, bars and burglar alarms'. This was contrasted with the 'new school' which was based on a much broader concept of crime prevention, involving special targeted projects, crime pattern analysis, and an emphasis on joint working with other agencies. Some of the most enthusiastic proponents of this new kind of approach were not trained specifically in crime prevention. The chief superintendent in charge of traffic and operational support at HQ (which covered crime prevention) thought the role of the crime prevention branch was uncertain and tended to be misunderstood in the force. He thought this was partly because there was no crime prevention strategy, and because many police officers saw crime prevention as something narrow and technical, and did not believe it deserved its own resources and structure. In many ways, he felt, it was not regarded as 'proper' policing which was widely seen as being about detections and arrests.

The 'multi-agency approach' was a term used frequently by officers in crime prevention. The force CPO (force A) repeatedly used it to describe the policy the force was trying to develop: he stressed that the police are part of a wider forum and not necessarily the leading agency in the fight against crime. At the higher levels, this kind of approach was illustrated by the inclusion of the police on the County Council Risk Management Group, which consisted of the chief officers of finance, audit, insurance, education, fire and police. One of the things the group discussed was the design of school buildings. The group was set up at the request of the police after they had had a number of dealings over the previous two years with individual county council departments on crime prevention matters. The force CPO argued that the police simply did not have the resources available to become actively involved with every crime prevention plan, but could help to pilot promising schemes and disseminate information about good practice to raise awareness, with the aim of setting a self-sustaining model in process.

One of the main claims of force B to 'leading the field' in crime prevention was based on its self-proclaimed commitment to the 'multi-agency approach' in crime prevention. The chief constable emphasised that multi-agency work in the area predated Home Office circulars such as 8/1984. The force CPO (a superintendent) said that 'the main commitment since 1982 has been the inter-agency aspect of crime prevention and the police role within that'. A complicating factor was that the force covered six different local authority areas, which caused problems of coordination. For example, when the force asked local authorities for advice on policing racial attacks, the six chief executives came back with six different sets of proposals. The force certainly did appear to be operating within a number of 'multi-agency' structures, although despite the chief constable's claim, most of those appeared after 1984 (they may or may not have been initiated in response to the circular).

During interviews with senior officers in force C, there was a ready acceptance that the police were not necessarily the leading agency in crime prevention and the need for cooperation between a number of different agencies was an often-mentioned topic. The ACC who was ultimately responsible for crime prevention felt that the police were falling between two stools. One option was for the police to make crime prevention a much more important part of what they do and use this as a way of getting more resources from the government. The other option was to concentrate their existing resources on their core functions, and leave crime prevention to some other organisation. The ACC leaned towards the latter option, but displayed a similar reluctance to officers in other forces to rid the police of non-confrontational 'service' aspects of the job that are so often a part of crime prevention initiatives. The overall approach of the force reflected this ambivalence.

The term 'multi-agency approach' was extremely popular with officers of all ranks in force D, although there did appear to be some ambiguity about what such an approach actually involved. Many of the police officers interviewed as part of the study claimed to be enthusiastic advocates of the multi-agency approach which, in line with officers in the other three forces, they seemed to equate with any work involving liaison with agencies other than the police. At HQ, the perception of senior officers was that the police had fully embraced the principle behind circular 8/84, but it was the local authorities who had failed to do likewise. This was a consistently-expressed view; from the chief superintendent (who said that the various different tiers of local government cannot even work together let alone with the police); his superintendent (who said that whereas the police were compelled to respond to the Home Office circular, local authorities and businesses took it only as advisory); to the ALO (who said that local authority departments were not easy to work with). The Safer Cities coordinator later commented that the police failed to appreciate or understand decision-making processes in other less hierarchical organisations. The superintendent (community affairs) strongly supported the view that the police should be the lead agency in crime prevention, saying: 'The police should still be the lead agency, holding the reins and promoting enthusiasm'. However, at the sub-divisional level officers were less clear about who should lead. One CPO said that which was the lead agency should depend on 'the nature of the problem and the circumstances', a view supported by his sergeant who explained that 'a real multi-agency approach would have a number of agencies and different ones taking the leading role depending on the situation'.

Safer Cities

Force B, C and D areas all included Safer Cities projects. The schemes were set up with Home Office funding with a remit to tackle crime, the fear of crime, and community safety in general. They represented three of the 16 projects set up across Britain. Each scheme had broadly the same structure including a steering group intended to produce and coordinate a local action plan, about the same number of staff and the same core objectives.

Force B: The Safer Cities coordinator was a seconded police inspector. The project was well supported by the police authority who were represented on the steering group by one of their members. (By contrast, in force D area, the chair of the police authority had complained that the money spent on Safer Cities should have been given to the police authority to spend on crime prevention.) Apparently, there was only one other Safer Cities project with a police coordinator (the decision as to who coordinated was taken by the Home Office). The steering committee consisted of 14 people: local councillors (including the leader of the local borough council), one police authority member, the chief executive, a senior probation officer, representatives from victim support, Council for Voluntary Service (CVS) and council officers. All initiatives funded by the project had to undergo an evaluation for the Home Office, although the coordinator was rather vague about the nature of such evaluations.

The project had given rise to various initiatives, including the following.

- *Estate-based schemes.* Safer Cities worked with the local authority to address the problems on a high-crime estate in the area. A Housing Association was set up which refurbished some properties, removed graffiti and litter, and provided funds to a group of residents who wanted to set up a community centre. The main input into this kind of scheme was not money, but time and coordination.

- *Soccer in the community.* The project arranged special soccer coaching sessions with players from the local league football club for children in three particular deprived areas. These operated during the summer holidays, two or three hours a day. The schemes were very popular, and again were not very costly. The total cost to Safer Cities was about £3000, and over 600 boys participated.

- *Car park schemes.* This was a larger project which involved total funds of £200,000 between Safer Cities and the borough council. The result was improved lighting, target hardening, security patrols, repainting, closed circuit television.

- *Industrial schemes.* One of these involved setting up a Port Users Security Group in one of the cities in the area. After a questionnaire survey, the project helped the group to improve lighting and physical security measures, and advised security officers on systems and methods. Reported crime was reduced by 50 per cent in the first few months.

- *Offenders job-club.* This was led by the probation service, and involved an accommodation support project for homeless young people, a diversion scheme for young autocrime offenders in which they built their own buggies and drove them.

The coordinator explained that the Safer Cities project was trying to prioritise initiatives that had a good chance of continuing after the Home

Office funding ceased. That meant setting up mechanisms, transferring the ownership of initiatives, or demonstrating that something worked in the hope that another agency would take it on after the Safer Cities funding had ended. In spite of these intentions, no detailed consideration had been given to setting up permanent mechanisms of this kind. The coordinator said that the project was seen as the central body to advise, facilitate and coordinate crime prevention initiatives, but seemed unclear about what would happen after the project finished:

> The project is widely seen as a benefit to the town, a positive crime prevention input. Most people would say that our work has been of positive benefit and would hope that things would carry on. That is not only political leaders but grass roots as well; at the end of the day the project is an asset. I think that we are leaning towards more provision of central government funding for crime prevention

This contrasts markedly with other areas, particularly force D, where the coordinator saw the primary aim of Safer Cities as using the temporary funding from central government to set up permanent local structures and mechanisms to support crime prevention activity after the funding had ceased.

Force C: The Safer Cities project grew from one of the Home Office 'Five Towns Initiatives'. A number of police sources felt that the police authority had been less than encouraging about Safer Cities (along with Crime Concern), and claimed that when representatives from these projects came for an initial visit they were not even met by people from the county council. It was left to the police to look after the visitors. There was some feeling that this was because the chair of the police authority had political objections to crime prevention initiatives being run by central government rather than the local authority, and that was supported by an interview with the chair. His request to be included on the Safer Cities steering committee had been turned down by the Home Office, for reasons that were not made explicit. The leader of the City Council was included. When asked why the chair of the police authority had not been allowed to join the committee, the Safer Cities coordinator said it was because the size of the group had to be kept to a minimum, and because 'the chair of the police authority has no direct link with what the police do: he might be in favour of something but they might not do it'.

At the time of the research, the Safer Cities project had been running for just over a year. The project had started with a detailed crime profile of the city based on information provided by the police. Crime data by police beats along with some census data had been supplied, but analysis had been held up because the project did not have the necessary computer software.

The coordinator emphasised the problem that no agency provides detailed information about crime in a satisfactory way. The police would perhaps be in the best position to do it, or alternatively local government could take on the task, adding in relevant information about housing, education and other services. Using Safer Cities funding, a number of projects went ahead in the first year. These included improved lighting in the bus station (the main Saturday evening trouble spot), a target-hardening and property-marking scheme in a particular area of the city, and a project against obscene telephone calls (with the aid of a local telephone company).

Force D: The visit to the Safer Cities scheme in force D area did uncover evidence of some attempts to set up genuine inter-agency work. Two points in particular stand out. First, the work of the Safer Cities scheme appeared much more suited than many of the police-led projects to the term 'multi-agency'. Second, very little of what was going on in the Safer Cities scheme was revealed in discussions with police officers: this showed that they were either unaware of the developments or felt that they were too unimportant to mention.

In force D area, the Safer Cities project was established in April 1989, its steering group comprising the chief executive of the city council, the senior community relations officer, the chief probation officer, the chief constable (who in practice sent his head of community affairs), the director of the local Chamber of Commerce, the deputy director of Planning and Transportation, the secretary of the DTI City Action Team, and the director of the local CVS.

The project started with a crime profile of the city, and a survey of public experience of and attitudes to crime. Given that the Home Office funding was time-limited, the broad aim was to develop a corporate planning mechanism for dealing with crime and the fear of crime that would be locally owned and driven once the core funding ceased. This was intended to be primarily located in the local authorities. The first aim was to put a 'value-for-money' tag on crime prevention through a crime audit which showed the costs of crime to the city council. This was intended to provide a financial incentive towards development of the hoped-for mechanisms. The scheme targeted in particular three areas of the city: personal safety on a problem estate, a burglary reduction project on a council estate, and a target-hardening programme in another area. Additionally, at the time of the research there were two issue-based pieces of work under way. One was a racial harassment project and the other was a project dealing with women's safety.

There was police involvement in many aspects of the Safer Cities work. For example, the burglary project was coordinated by a seconded police inspector, a sub-divisional CPO carried out security surveys and provided advice for the target hardening programme, and the police were represented on the working groups set up to examine racial harassment and women's safety. Significantly, none of this was mentioned by the head of community affairs. The only mention he made of Safer Cities was in connection with its funding of a crime prevention shop in the city centre precinct. This was a development 'dear to the heart' of the chief superintendent (according to the Safer Cities coordinator), although it did not to be appear highly significant compared to the other projects. The chief superintendent did not appear to be very enthusiastic about Safer Cities, and he made critical references to the first chair of the steering group. The attitude of the head of community affairs may have had real effects on police cooperation with Safer Cities. The coordinator said that he was a very different kind of police officer from his predecessor, adding:

> The climate has definitely changed since X came along; he wants a higher profile for the police and for community affairs. He is not intuitively in favour of multi-agency crime prevention that is led by other agencies, and he has fairly deep-seated feelings about some of the other agencies that he might be working with. But he cannot entirely set the police policy.

This clearly implies that the coordinator saw successful cooperation with the police as more likely to happen despite the head of community affairs rather than because of him. Other officers in the department had a more positive view of Safer Cities, for example the ALO said of the project: 'It's a very useful vehicle, and has opened a lot of previously closed and almost locked doors in the relatively short time it's been in existence'.

So despite the attitude of senior officers, officers lower down the police hierarchy were participating in Safer Cities projects with more enthusiasm. The coordinator made some very interesting observations about the relationship between police attitudes to inter-agency work and the nature of the police organisation and decision-making structures. Within the police the emphasis is upon quick delivery; it is a task-oriented organisation which demands quick and tangible results. Many other organisations however, do not hold to the same time-scales, and the process of information-sharing and decision-making can take considerably longer.

Overall, the Safer Cities project in force D area seemed to have set up some genuine inter-agency work in crime prevention. That was certainly the view of the coordinator:

> It is simply the case that prior to April 1989 there was no history of inter-agency cooperation on crime prevention. There may have been

links with the police working with single agencies, for example the education authorities, but not any genuine multi-agency projects.

Other multi-agency projects

Since 1988 force B had in each division what were known as 'multi-agency crime prevention initiatives' (MACPIs). The roots of this development lay in the force's leading role in one of the Home Office Five Towns Initiatives. In this force area, that project involved police officers working to steering panels of voluntary bodies. It was widely considered to be a success, and in 1987 the chief recommended to the police authority that there should be a similar structure in every local authority area in the force. The police approached the local authorities who were in favour of this, and the MACPIs came into being. The basic structure of each MACPI was the same, with the police providing a coordinator (usually an inspector), working to a steering panel with representatives from the relevant agencies, and administrative staff (often employment or youth trainees on the force scheme). The local authority provided accommodation, as well as some finance and administrative support.

The MACPIs tended not to focus on a whole local authority area but worked instead on a particular high-crime area of a division, an estate or a few police beats. The MACPIs all had similar terms of reference, a similar staffing structure with coordinator and steering panel, and a similar programme of work. All of the schemes carried out crime profiles of their respective areas, including business and residential surveys. All had the same computing facilities and research packages (developed by the force research department). The steering panel of one MACPI was quite a high-powered body with either the director or deputy director from all the main local authority departments, including education, social services, public highways, public works and planning. In addition, there was representation from the local Chamber of Commerce, church groups, and probation service. As the project developed, representatives from the transport executive, local councillors, residents' associations, and other voluntary bodies became involved.

The MACPI coordinator gave the following account of how the priorities for the project were initially defined:

> Initially, so I could give them something to work on I approached the three commanders for the sub-divisions covered by my area and asked each for one or two suggested target areas with reasons why. They each produced suggestions so I put together mini crime profiles on each of the areas and ended up with six of these – really to give the committee members some basic information on why the police thought those areas were suitable for action. It fell upon the panel members to go back to

their own organisation and discuss these suggestions and come back with preferred ones or even other ones. In [one town] there was a fairly unanimous decision to go into the area which was eventually chosen. I think all of the organisations that were involved had problems in that area. It didn't work out quite as easily for all the initiatives.

It is worth noting that the coordinator clearly felt that the local police managers were the first people to approach when trying to formulate goals for a crime prevention project, although the other involved organisations had the opportunity to raise different priorities. In the event, it seems there was little conflict over the aims.

There was still a strong tendency to see multi-agency structures like the MACPIs as a way of educating agencies outside the police in the true nature of the problems of crime. The coordinator said that they had produced an in-depth crime profile that broke down the local crime statistics for the previous year:

I already knew a lot about the area having been a working policeman there. Putting it down on paper brought it home, but for the others [non-police] involved, we needed to get back to basics and show them what we were talking about, what these offences meant, how many, where, who was committing them.

The coordinator was vague about what the MACPI actually did to address the problems highlighted by the various surveys they had carried out in the early part of the project. He explained that the steering committee tried to coordinate action where more than one agency was already working in a particular area. In response to the problem of residential burglary, the housing department resolved to grant resources to replacing all the back doors of council accommodation in the area with more secure ones. This led to other departments introducing target-hardening measures. The coordinator appeared to evaluate the project in terms of the effects on reported crime in the surveys. For example he said there was a clear effect on the figures for residential burglary. When asked about the lasting effects of the MACPI, the coordinator was unsure that effects like lower rates of burglary would continue. The MACPI was a permanent structure, but moved on to concentrate on other areas and problems within the division. What it had achieved was a much better network of communications within the division between the various agencies involved in crime prevention.

The coordinator was asked directly about his experience of working with other organisations, and his reply supported some of the observations made the Safer Cities coordinator in area D (see above) about the different organisational culture of the police force.

> Initially I did [find it difficult working with people from very different kinds of organisation], but I did find some like minds. Working in the police you get used to asking someone to do something and getting a response within a deadline. A lot of the other organisations were not used to working to such tight deadlines, there wasn't the same sense of urgency.

A more unusual development in force B was the long-standing inter-agency structure on a particular problem estate which included a working group with representatives from management level in the police, other local authority services, and community groups. Below this there was a 'task group' consisting of front-line workers from the different agencies. This was an example of a 'priority area team' and was based in one of the sub-divisions visited in the study.

Finally, in force C area a working party on inner-city disorder was set up in 1988 following a conference at the local University on crime prevention attended by the force CPO and a sub-divisional superintendent. The commander of the sub-division covering the central city area had favoured a combination of short-term high-profile policing of the city centre area, with a more strategic inter-agency approach. The working group was chaired by a city councillor, and included representatives of the main brewers, licensees, taxi and bus companies, environmental health department, and fast food shops. This had come up with a number of actions. These included reducing the number of times that half-price drinks were offered by pubs in the early evenings, detailed instructions to door staff, and afternoon closure of public houses on some days before Christmas (when in the previous year trouble had been at its highest).

This working party also became the centre of a controversy between the police authority and chief constable over closed circuit television (CCTV). The police favoured installing CCTV in the city centre, but were keen that this should not to be seen as a police initiative. The working party discussed the matter, decided in favour, and applied for funding from the Safer Cities project. Meanwhile, the police authority complained to the chief that the matter had not been discussed with them, and called for a report. A number of police authority members had strong reservations about the civil liberties implications of CCTV. At the time of the study, the matter had not been resolved, but it is an interesting example of how different levels in the system can conflict. The police authority was aggrieved because they had not been consulted about CCTV. However, the chief constable clearly did not feel it was a matter for the police authority, partly because he did not consult about things in general. However, CCTV was supported by representatives of the city council (also Labour-led) and it was a city councillor who chaired the working group. The issue can thus also be seen as partly about conflict between the city and county council, which according to the police authority chair, transcended party loyalties.

Evidence of a shift towards multi-agency working

In forces B, C, and D there was some police involvement in activities initiated by the Safer Cities Projects, and within force B there was also police involvement in multi-agency crime prevention initiatives. However, the level of police resources devoted to these activities was not substantial, and the police had not fully accepted the principle that they should share responsibility equally with several other agencies. The shift towards multi-agency working in forces B, C, and D was therefore partial and limited.

In force A area there was no Safer Cities project, and even less evidence of a shift towards multi-agency working. The CPOs in one of the sub-divisions appeared dubious about what they called the 'new school' of thought in crime prevention, and preferred to concentrate on the traditional approach. While they did not express hostility to the concept of inter-agency working, the examples they gave were simply of contacts with agencies outside the police. For example, they were enthusiastic about the design advisory service, but in reality this only involved giving advice to the borough council. Although the CPO on another sub-division claimed to be a supporter of a new kind of crime prevention, once again he perceived multi-agency work as any liaison with outside bodies and assumed that the other agencies should take the lead from the police. The CPO complained that the local authority did not take on board his recommendations, and was not sufficiently open to police advice. The 1983 Annual Report had stated that 'locks, bolts, bars and intruder alarms continue to form the basis and main area of the department's work'. Although there was disagreement about which should be the lead agency, all officers appeared to be united in the view that crime prevention was substantially shifting away from this narrow definition. There were a number of special projects that involved working with agencies and bodies outside the police, but these were isolated and on a small scale. At the sub-divisional level, the officers talked enthusiastically about how the devolution of crime prevention responsibility had dramatically shifted the kind of crime prevention work that they did. In practice, however, the main change appeared to be an increase in quantity of the same target-hardening work they had been doing before.

Thus, where there had been a limited shift towards multi-agency work, in forces B, C, and D, the impetus had come largely from outside the police service, principally from the Safer Cities projects. In force A, where there

87

was no Safer Cities Project, even this limited shift seemed not to have occurred.

Reasons for the lack of fundamental change in police crime prevention policy

The previous sections have shown that there was evidence of a considerable number of crime prevention initiatives of one sort or another in the four study forces, and of some increase in the level of crime prevention activity by the forces over the 1980s. For example, all of the forces had specialist crime prevention officers and central departments; in one the central crime prevention department was larger and better funded than in the others, and had grown over the 1980s. NW schemes had rapidly proliferated during the 1980s, and had attracted considerable policing resources. All four forces had introduced new policies for dealing with burglar alarms following recommendations made by ACPO in 1989. A wide variety of special projects with crime prevention objectives were introduced or supported by the police over the 1980s, including design services, training schemes and organised activities for young people, crime pattern analysis on a limited scale, and participation in specific crime prevention initiatives. The police in three of the areas had been involved in a number of local initiatives launched within the framework of the Safer Cities Programme; in one area they had been involved in multi-agency crime prevention initiatives within each of the constituent local authority areas; in another they had taken the leading role in setting up a working party on inner-city disorder, which had come up with various actions.

In spite of these developments, there was evidence of a wider failure by the police to make substantive changes towards introducing effective crime prevention policies. Except in force B, crime prevention departments remained small and had not grown. Any police contribution to community-based crime prevention schemes was minor. Although there was a huge growth in NW schemes, they were inadequately supported by the police, and were probably largely ineffective. There was generally a lack of resources and expertise within the study forces to support proactive crime prevention; for example, the impact of architectural liaison officers, with their limited knowledge base and small numbers, must have been minimal. Social crime prevention initiatives initiated by the police had tenuous links with concrete crime prevention objectives. There was a general failure of the forces to develop crime pattern analysis or to take an analytical approach to crime prevention strategy. There was little evidence of concrete policy initiatives embodying a major transformation away from narrow target-hardening initiatives and towards the multi-agency approach.

Finally, none of the crime prevention activity by the study forces was adequately evaluated, and there was little evidence that it was effective.

It is important to consider why some limited changes in crime prevention policy occurred, and why more fundamental changes did not.

One over-riding feature is that with the partial exception of force B, the forces did not have an overall crime prevention strategy. In fact, they did not have a policy at all, taking that to mean a tangible set of proposals or objectives, and methods for achieving them. The way the force CPO in area A put it was 'there are no tablets of stone'. Partly influenced by Home Office circulars, senior officers at HQ in force A had some ideas about crime prevention policy, but the new organisational structure placed the responsibility with divisional commanders. The department could not force policy onto the divisions. For example, the force CPO stated explicitly that the police should not always be the lead agency in crime prevention, and yet at the local level the police did lead the initiatives in which they were involved.

It is possible that the police find it hard to combine a strategic approach to crime prevention policy with the requirement that local initiatives should be a response to local problems, and should be mounted in partnership with other agencies. Certainly the best example of a policy formulated at the centre and implemented locally was the ACPO policy on burglar alarms. In this instance, the problems caused by false alarm calls were similar everywhere, and the police were able to impose their new policy rather than work with other agencies to develop it. This was also interesting as an example of a national policy formulated by ACPO (with the active encouragement of the Home Office) and then implemented with rare exceptions by all police forces.

However, there is no reason in principle why local initiatives should not take place within the framework of a central strategy. Yet police discussion of crime prevention is almost never strategic: it is dominated by the fortunes of particular schemes that become fashionable and talked about for a time, then later fall out of favour. In this process, the Home Office seems to act as a central clearing house. The idea for a particular initiative originates in one force, becomes known by the Home Office, in rare cases is evaluated by the Home Office Crime Prevention Unit, is publicised in a circular, is taken up by other forces, proves disappointing or too demanding of police resources, and falls out of favour. For example, circular 44/90 described a number of case studies of good practice, two of which originated in force A.

At first sight, force B may seem to be an exception. The force perceived itself as leading the field in terms of police involvement in crime prevention, and certainly, compared with the other three, force B showed a greater commitment in terms of staffing and resources, a wider and more long-standing development of multi-agency structures, and a stronger public commitment to the concept of crime prevention. Yet on closer examination, most of the activities of force B in this field lacked substance in that they were not directed towards achieving concrete and clearly defined crime prevention results.

The large and relatively well-staffed Community Crime Prevention Department was a powerful player in the internal politics of the police organisation. A representative from the force's research department (Inspection and Development) mentioned that the CCPD was of such high status in the force that it did not need to use the research department to back up its claims for resources. The importance of the department was a fact noted and not always welcomed by other sections of the police force. Informal conversations with CID officers on sub-division gave rise to a number of critical comments such as the following one by a Detective Inspector: 'Have you come across "Barney the Bloodhound" yet!?... This force has quite a healthy crime prevention department, well resourced. But we've still got a 10 per cent rise in this sub-division, it's hard to see what good they're doing.' Then, in response to the question 'Does the fact that the CCP department and CID answer to the same ACC make any difference substantively' the DI said:

> You tell me. I see the CID and uniform as totally different, they have different rules of engagement. I suppose I'm a dyed in the wool detective. You will find officers on sub-division who during the course of their work feel they need to get in touch with CCP. They will find 17 pages of little venues that guys have dived into away from operational policing, some of it is good and necessary. We must educate the public to take greater care; they seem to think there are thousands of us here. But I saw one thing in particular which annoyed me. Before Christmas there was a crime prevention shopping trip to [a city in a neighbouring county] organised by the CCPD. The idea was to sell tickets on a bus to a new shopping centre in ---. On the way down, officers from the CCPD would give crime prevention advice and show videos. I don't think they found enough to fill the bus... To hire a bus to --- to tell people about crime prevention is obscene to me, when I'm struggling to resource my detectives to make inroads into crime. The best crime prevention for me is when they're in... jail... I don't see much of the CPO, he goes off to factories and does things with Safer Cities. They've got a healthy budget, but what the hell they do I don't know!

There was also criticism from other departments of the way that CCPD was seen to 'hijack' responsibility for certain initiatives even when they were not the obvious choice for such a function, the case in point being that of the experimental domestic violence unit.

Discussions with the main research department in force B gave some interesting insights into the process of policy formulation within the police organisation. The head of the department was quite frank in admitting that the force had a 'progressive' image and a chief constable with a high public profile. The problem with this combination was that the force, along with other police forces in the country, was sometimes almost desperate to be recognised as progressive. This led to hasty public statements from the chief constable which were reported widely by the press, and then led to a force working party being set up to investigate the implications of what had been claimed. This, according to the officer, was the wrong way around. He saw the main impetus for many innovations in the police organisation, as the desire to be noticed, on the part of both individual officers eager for promotion, and entire forces eager to impress the Home Office. This often led to policy initiatives being introduced over-hastily, without proper planning, and resources being committed without the aid of an objective and detailed evaluation. Thus, the fact that Home Office circulars had made the issue of domestic violence 'sexy' meant that it was very difficult to evaluate critically the effects of a specialist unit. The tendency was to see it as self-evidently beneficial, and worthy of resources. The same problem applied to the introduction of administrative support units and many crime prevention initiatives.

Much of this criticism seems to be justified. Compared with the other forces visited, force B appeared to be more committed to evaluating initiatives and gathering hard information about projects, yet there was still a tenuous connection between the results of such evaluations and decisions on policy. Thus, officers in CCPD said that the domestic violence unit had been a success, and they knew it would be adopted as force policy, even before the official evaluation had been completed. The various initiatives in social crime prevention were not really evaluated at all. Senior officers in CCPD were slightly uncomfortable about this, and were aware of the criticisms, but still supported the force involvement in such projects. The way that the force CPO rationalised the contradiction in this position was to argue that the crime prevention part of policing is one of the most important service aspects of policing; to remove it to other agencies would leave the police with just a repressive function, which would substantially reduce the co-operation received from the public in carrying out law enforcement tasks.

In contrast to senior officers elsewhere, for example in force D, those in force B did not believe that the police should always take the lead in crime prevention. Both the chief superintendent who headed the CCPD and other officers of the department independently agreed with the proposal that the crime prevention structure should be based on local government, and none suggested that the police should always take the lead because of their knowledge of crime and criminals. However, in practice there were few crime prevention initiatives in which force B had participated on equal terms with other agencies.

It was because of the views of the then chief constable that crime prevention was given a higher priority in force B than elsewhere. In fact, the appearance of a progressive crime prevention policy in force B had been an important influence on national policy. It was partly because of this relationship that national policy, like force B policy, lacked substance. Despite a considerable level of activity in force B, and a number of initiatives that were noticed both locally and nationally, there was little or no evidence of concrete results. Specific initiatives were not evaluated, and at an aggregate level the force experienced higher than average increases in recorded crime levels over the 1980s.

The lack of a crime prevention strategy was particularly clear in force C. The police, as was admitted explicitly by one senior officer, were sitting on the fence. On the one hand, they saw themselves as primarily a law-enforcement agency, and perhaps not well-suited to running a programme like 'Operation Lifestyle'. They recognised that other agencies might be able to run such projects better and more cheaply, and that they divert resources from the core police functions. On the other hand, officers felt the need to emphasise the service aspect which is so often a big part of these schemes. They felt that such projects improve relationships between the police and the public at large, thus creating the conditions for more successful exercise of the law enforcement function.

Although there was talk of the move to the multi-agency approach in force C, actual developments of this kind were particularly limited. This seemed to stem from a somewhat strained relationship between the police and the county council. The chair of the police authority had strong reservations about the development of crime prevention projects such as Safer Cities and Crime Concern in so far as they took crime prevention out of the hands of the county council. The conflict between the city council and the county council tended to inhibit the development of multi-agency work, as in the case of the closed circuit television proposal.

Discussions with senior police officers in the force gave rise to some interesting comments about the development of a crime prevention structure. Although it was accepted, as in other forces, that the most appropriate agency for coordinating crime prevention would probably be local government, there were more reservations about this in force C. The chief superintendent in charge of the force services department (which covered crime prevention) had an interesting angle on the police service's reaction to the AMA's proposals for development of the crime prevention structure:

> A lot of aggro came from the police service. The AMA had got quite a detailed plan on which they would take responsibility for crime prevention, and generally that was rebuffed by the police service. They felt that the budget for it should be centrally funded, but it was highly likely that the budget would come from the police budget which understandably the police service would be against. Also, if it was put out to them, it would no doubt assign it to the chief executive, but that would really mean the chairman of the police committee to do the organisation and direction, and they thought in terms of using police officers to do that... The partnership approach is a response to pressure from the police

On this account, the police service as a whole had resisted the proposal that responsibility for crime prevention should be given to local authorities because this would mean losing resources to local authorities and ceding operational control over some aspects of policing.

During the 1980s there were a number of positive developments in crime prevention taken by the force D. The community affairs department was upgraded by placing a chief superintendent as its head, which was intended to give the department more credibility both outside and within the organisation. It also meant that department now had a representative on the force policy-making team. The first appointment to the post was a young officer with interesting views about the role of the police in the community and crime prevention. He was also willing to experiment and innovate. He completed a wide-ranging review of the community affairs department, and set in motion the project of devolving responsibility for crime prevention to the level of the sub-division.

The force cautiously encouraged NW schemes, had followed the ACPO burglar alarm policy, and had established a design advisory service. It is likely that the idea for the design advisory service came to force D from another force (possibly force A), perhaps through the central clearing house of the Home Office. (*Secured By Design* was mentioned in the 1990 crime prevention circular.)

But there were a number of factors that may have reduced the positive benefits from crime prevention initiatives. As the force review pointed out, although appointing a chief superintendent as head of department was an important signal, it was not enough on its own to bring about lasting change. The force's lack of strategy was shown by the replacement of the first head of community affairs by a more traditional successor, who had entirely different attitudes and perspectives. The new chief superintendent and his deputy believed that the police must always be the leading light in crime prevention. They were suspicious of the ability or willingness of local authorities to work with the police, believed in the over-riding importance of autocrime, and tended to see the multi-agency approach as mere cooperation or liaison with one or two outside agencies. These views were influential, although they were not replicated throughout the organisation.

Although responsibility for crime prevention was thought to have been successfully devolved to the sub-divisions, there was little evidence that local crime prevention strategies were being developed. Policy-making on crime prevention was fairly centralised. This applied to NW (which reflected the chief constable's views), the devolution of the crime prevention function (initiated by the department head), and centrally-administered policies like the design advisory service and the burglar alarm policy (which had little to do with the sub-divisions). However, in other senses, policy was diffuse and ambiguous. The sub-divisionalisation experiment had further clouded the role of HQ, and the Safer Cities project was beginning to introduce projects explicitly shared amongst a variety of agencies. In many ways, policy in this area had only just begun to develop, and a number of officers talked of crime pattern analysis and targeted projects (which are basic to crime prevention) as future projects. In the words of the Safer Cities coordinator the police had some way to go, and at the time were 'just scratching the surface'. He added that 'it's amazing how much information they have which they have simply not got a clue how to use'. The Safer Cities project tended to produce a shift in crime prevention policy away from a narrow security-based and police-led approach, and towards a more general inter-agency effort. Although the police claimed that they were the only agency to respond positively to Home Office circular 8/84, there was little evidence to support this. In general, police officers tended to view multi-agency work as anything involving contact with an outside agency, and the chief superintendent's view that the police should take the lead in crime prevention was reflected in the views of a number of his staff. However, the officers who were involved in the Safer Cities projects appeared to be enthusiastic and committed. The move to the approach embodied in the Safer Cities project was not, of course, initiated by the police, nor by the police authority, which had little input into any shift in the approach to crime prevention.

Taking an overview of all these influences across the four forces, it seems that the impetus for positive developments in police crime prevention policy often came from outside the police service: in particular, from the Home Office directly, or from the Safer Cities projects established by the Home Office. Where ideas came from other police forces, it was often through the Home Office acting as a clearing house. The development of crime prevention in force B arose from the enthusiasm of the then chief constable, but lacked substance.

The failure to change crime prevention policy in a more fundamental way seems to be tied up with a lack of strategy. The police service was not sure whether this was a function that it should seriously take on. It did not know how to combine a strategy on crime prevention with encouragement for local initiatives launched in partnership with other agencies. It was not under strong pressure to make a fundamental shift (unlike in the case of the response to crimes against women and children). Finally, the police service was unlikely to formulate a viable strategy amid the wider confusion of government policy in the field of crime prevention.

POLICY-MAKING AT THE NATIONAL LEVEL

The lack of a crime prevention strategy at the force level was matched by vagueness and deliberate ambivalence within central government. The department concerned with crime prevention policy within the police service was the Home Office, although the Department of the Environment had also been responsible for launching a substantial crime prevention initiative (the Priority Estates Programme). Of course, a comprehensive approach to crime prevention would require the active participation of all departments, since all government-funded activities have implications for crime and its prevention. However, at the present early stage in the development of crime prevention policy, substantive developments are likely to come from the lead department.

Interviews with a number of senior Home Office officials gave a clear picture of the stages of policy development during the 1980s. The paramount influence was the view of the department rather than that of politicians, and senior officials had the decisive say in forming the departmental view. One senior official thought that the key event was the arrival of a new Permanent Secretary in 1979, and not the coming to power of the Conservative government in the same year. Officials did consider the advent of the new Conservative administration to be an important development, although a strong commitment to change in the field of crime prevention was not part of their initial agenda. Rather, a new administration was likely to be looking for ideas and initiatives which it could pick up and develop. At least initially, it seemed that pressures from elected politicians contributed only indirectly to the development of crime prevention policy.

The then Deputy Under Secretary for the Criminal Department described the influences over development of crime prevention policy as follows:

> One was the arrival of the Conservative administration. More important was the arrival of [the new] Permanent Secretary at that stage. The original emphasis on crime prevention was very much [his] own initiative... Originally this was [the] Permanent Secretary looking for and finding a new theme to develop in the Office irrespective of the political administration. It wasn't until quite a bit later on that the political administration seized on it as an attractive political programme.

This account was confirmed by other senior Home Office officials. According to the then Head of the Research and Planning Unit, discussion within the Unit of the need for a policy on crime prevention had started in the 1970s. During the 1980s the focus of attention moved from a narrow emphasis on situational measures toward broader social or community-based initiatives. John Patten, a junior Minister at the time, had been on an official visit to France and Germany to look at social crime prevention measures and decarceration initiatives. He had been impressed by some of the things he witnessed and a subsequent Green Paper, it was suggested, included some ideas imported from these visits.

Clearly John Patten, the elected Minister, was of key importance in this development. However, in the opinion of senior civil servants he was firmly nudged in the direction in which the officials wished him to go. The policy-making model in operation in this case, according to several senior officials, was one in which policy is largely framed by experts and then 'sold' to ministers.

While ministers took a secondary role in the initial development of crime prevention policy, later stages saw a greater assertion of the political agenda. According to Home Office officials, William Whitelaw did not see a major role for crime prevention, and was only marginally involved in the development of policy, although unlikely to interfere with it. (For a discussion of the politics of crime prevention at this time, see Heal, 1991.) Since Whitelaw's successor, Leon Brittan, was less sceptical about crime prevention, senior officials then took the opportunity to suggest several initiatives. In 1983, the Crime Prevention Unit was set up within the Police Department of the Home Office, which apparently signalled that the police were to have an important role in crime prevention. At about the same time, the Five Towns Project was started. This was an initiative directly managed by the Home Office that aimed to establish multi-agency crime prevention programmes. At about the same time, NW was developing within local police forces; officials and ministers in the Home Office were, in the Deputy Secretary's words, 'pleased to seize on it' as another new idea.

Two years after the issue of the inter-departmental circular 8/84, crime prevention began to receive support from the highest political level. In 1986 the Prime Minister chaired a special seminar on the subject at 10 Downing Street, attended by the Home Secretary and other ministers. This seminar placed a particularly strong emphasis on the need for the business community to support the development of crime prevention measures, and it led directly to the creation of the Ministerial Group on Crime Prevention.

Following the 1987 election, the new Home Secretary, Douglas Hurd, decided to make crime prevention a major plank of policy. The Conservatives had made a manifesto promise in the 1987 election that they would put more resources into crime prevention. John Patten, was put in charge of developing a 'total response' to crime, and the Ministerial Group on Crime Prevention (consisting of 13 ministers) attempted to coordinate crime prevention initiatives between government departments.

The role of circulars
There have been two major circulars on crime prevention. The first was issued in 1984 (8/84) and the second in 1990 (44/90). The 1984 circular had a long history. According to one senior Home Office researcher there was 'at least ten years of discussion' leading up to the publication of circular 8/84. It arose from a developing tradition of research and analysis within HORU about the causes of crime and the feasibility of different kinds of crime reduction policy. Ron Clarke, then Head of the Research Unit, played the central role in the development of this new thinking. Along with a number of American writers such as James Q Wilson, Clarke was critical of theories that concentrated on explaining why some individuals are more disposed towards crime than others. He shifted attention to those factors that increase or reduce the chances that someone will commit a crime in a given situation. He argued that there was more scope for public policy to change criminal opportunities and risks than to influence criminal dispositions. The circular reflected this theoretical position stating that:

> whilst there is a need to address the social factors associated with criminal behaviour, and policies are continually being devised to tackle this aspect of the problem, these are essentially long-term measures. For the short-term, the best way forward is to reduce through management, design or changes in the environment, the opportunities that exist for crime to occur.

The circular then outlined (in very general terms) the argument that the police alone could not be expected to deal with crime. It stated that inter-agency cooperation between the police and other local agencies was essential to successful development of local crime prevention initiatives, and suggested that individuals at chief officer or director level be identified to ensure satisfactory liaison between Departments.

The process of consultation before the issue of the circular is somewhat unclear. AMA representatives said that their association had been sent the circular in draft and had responded formally by setting out their 'policy stall'. However, their representatives explained that the matter of crime prevention was not only one for the AMA police committee, but also for individual local authorities. The AMA was not asked to coordinate the views of member authorities and reply to the Home Office on their behalf; rather, the draft circular was sent directly to individual authorities.

Whereas the circular 8/84 was a brief outline of the need for agencies to work together in developing crime prevention initiatives, the following crime prevention circular 44/90 was a more detailed statement of the same principles. This time, it was decided (by Home Office officials) to make specific examples of good practice a central feature of the circular, with common themes between them outlined in the text. In February 1990 a draft circular was sent to about 30 organisations including the police staff associations, the local authority associations, the Association of Chief Officers of Probation, the Fire Unions, NACRO and Crime Concern. These organisations had six weeks in which to make comments on the draft. An official from the Home Office Crime Prevention Unit (who drafted the circular) said that the comments that came back did not lead to major changes in the final document: 'We gave them all six weeks to comment. Their views were largely complementary and complimentary... Detail and margins apart, they were happy with the document that was emerging.' The official responsible for drafting the circular strongly denied that the consultation process had led to major changes of substance in the circular. He did say, however, that the local authorities strongly supported the notion that they should play a central role in developing crime prevention. However, this was not perceived as diminishing the role of the police.

This leads to an important crux in the development of national crime prevention policy. Interviews within the Home Office revealed an ambiguity as to which agency should take the lead in crime prevention. Officials were not prepared to be drawn into saying whether responsibility for coordinating crime prevention should lie with the police, with local authorities, or with some other agencies, perhaps voluntary organisations. This ambivalence comes through clearly in both the circulars 8/84 and 44/90. Many Home Office officials argued that this was a deliberate and thought-through policy. This is illustrated by the answer given by one official from the Home Office crime prevention unit who responded to the suggestion that failure to put one organisation in the driving seat was simply a way of avoiding the issue by saying:

> No, it isn't, no. No, I'd reject that. We could find ourselves in the position of broker between two sectors that are jockeying for position. That's not our role. Our role is to foster and develop it first in the police, secondly with the local council... It's equality. All the evidence points towards a joint effort being the most effective. Now we're not going to spoil that by suggesting the police should always be in the lead... So it's not avoiding the issue at all.

This interpretation of the Home Office approach was supported by interviews with officials from F3 division (covering police operations and crime prevention). A senior member of that division said:

> In practice we couldn't possibly have given the Safer Cities money to the police because we would have seriously endangered our relationship with local authorities who expect to have some involvement in this area. If we gave the money instead to local authorities, that would endanger our relationship with the police. The policy is to keep all the players in play. It's a balancing act. The Home Office can't decide how it will develop, which agency will play the greatest role. We can only start things off, and act in a Machiavellian way if necessary to keep them going, to keep everyone involved, then wait and see how they develop. We can't directly control it.

However, the Deputy Secretary in the Home Office at the time explicitly contradicted the views of other, less senior, officials, when he said 'there is this gap in the structure of who is actually in charge locally, which we have never actually settled. That's the fundamental weakness of the whole crime prevention programme'.

Special projects

Home Office circulars expounded the general principle of 'multi-agency' crime prevention without making clear which agency should be in the driving seat. Another central part of national crime prevention policy during the 1980s was the setting up of centrally-funded local initiatives such as the Five Towns, Safer Cities and Priority Estates projects. The first two of these were funded by the Home Office, and the last was funded by the Department of the Environment.

The Five Towns project was set up by the Home Office Crime Prevention Unit in early 1986. It established local crime prevention projects in five towns, each to last 18 months in the first instance. The areas chosen were intended to represent a wide geographical spread and a range of social conditions. The Home Office funded a project coordinator in each of the towns to oversee inter-agency structures with representation from public services and the local authorities. The approach first established by the Five Towns project was extended in the Safer Cities project, which started in 1988 as part of the government's Action for Cities project. However, the Safer Cities programme was carried out on a much broader scale, involving 9 local authority areas in its first year, and with the ultimate aim of including 20 local projects. It was intended to provide a more coherent approach than the five towns project, focusing on the delivery of public services generally and the wider structure of society in a medium- to large-sized local authority area. The local authority had a more central role than in the five towns initiative. Home Office funding for Safer Cities was more substantial, covering the cost of a coordinator and two other staff, accommodation, running costs and grant funds to support local initiatives.

The Priority Estates Project (PEP) is an example at the national level of the ambivalence about who is ultimately responsible for crime prevention. As outlined above, it was an initiative funded by the Department of Environment (it funded the priority area team examined during the research in force B). Although crime and justice are not primary concerns of the Department of the Environment, the DoE interest in crime prevention sprang indirectly from its concern with the effect of vandalism, incivility and crime on the local environment. Both central and local government expressed concern over 'the declining popularity of many housing estates' (quoted in Rock, 1988) and in 1979 the Priority Estates Project (PEP) was launched. Its primary aim was to improve housing management and reduce the number of vacant properties in the most run-down housing estates. Thus, although they were run by different government departments, and departments with significantly different priorities, PEP and the Safer Cities programme overlapped to a considerable extent. Of course, they did not directly compete on the same housing estates.

Another important initiative was Crime Concern. According to the Deputy Under Secretary in the Home Office, this was an initiative driven by senior politicians independently of the officials who had taken the lead in other areas of crime prevention policy. Proposals for a national crime prevention body were included in the manifesto for the 1987 election, as outlined by this official:

> The Conservative Party had worked up its proposal for a national crime prevention body which featured in the manifesto. That was generated on the political network, and the Home Office didn't have a great deal to do with it, and I'm not sure we entirely understood what was in politician's minds in putting it in the manifesto, but eventually it was given effect as Crime Concern, after quite a lot of discussion... about what form this national body might take.

Crime Concern is a curious hybrid, in that it sprang from a pledge in a Conservative Party manifesto, it was established by the incoming Conservative government, it was funded initially by the Home Office, but it is a voluntary organisation. Its initial task was to attempt to improve the quality of life by stimulating crime prevention. The plan in the beginning was to build on what was already in existence: NW, crime prevention panels, and crime reduction programmes like Safer Cities. Crime Concern received three years' 'pump-priming' money from the Home Office, but quickly attempted to engage the cooperation of the private sector in developing good practice models and communication networks. Thus, for example, a consultancy service providing crime audits for businesses was set up early on and this has been followed by a number of initiatives aimed at raising financial support from the private sector. However, Crime Concern did not become financially self-sufficient within the target period of three years, and Home Office funding was extended for a further period.

The Crime Concern model built on earlier experience with the National Association for the Care and Resettlement of Offenders (NACRO). This was a genuinely voluntary organisation, in that it was originally established without government support. By the early 1980s its interests were broadening to include crime prevention on unpopular council housing estates. Its Safe Neighbourhoods Unit launched a number of pioneering schemes, increasingly with support from the Home Office and the Department of the Environment.

Other national influences

One method by which the local authority associations can attempt to exert influence over developments at national level is to set up working parties examining particular areas of policy, and disseminate their findings. Following this strategy, the AMA set up a major working party in 1988 tasked with examining the local authority role in crime prevention. The report suggested a three-tier structure for crime prevention based on central government, county councils, and district councils. County and district councillors working together would draw up a corporate plan setting out both general strategy and specific policies. The report recommended that crime prevention be resourced on the basis of a specific grant from central government. A representative of the AMA explained that central government was the main target of reports of this kind: as he put it, 'the heavyweight stuff is directed at central government more than anyone'. It seems, however, that central government was not moved by these representations. The government made no proposals to give local authorities either statutory responsibility for crime prevention, or funding to cover it.

By contrast, ACPO had an important influence nationally. A working party of ACPO's crime committee formulated national guidelines in 1989, and its report set up the model of a community crime prevention department which was later followed by forces A and B. The chief constable of force B was clearly a strong influence upon this working party, and both the CPO from force B and the recommendations of the ACPO report appeared to have had a strong influence on developments in force A. In the report of the review of crime prevention which preceded the creation of a new CCP department, there were numerous references to the ACPO recommendations.

As set out in an earlier section, a senior officer in force C believed that opposition from ACPO had been crucial in dissuading the government from adopting the AMA's proposals to give the central responsibility for crime prevention to local authorities. Because ACPO declined to participate in this research, this theory could not be tested further, but it seems highly plausible.

The other key national organisation in the development of crime prevention policy was NACRO. It established a Crime Prevention Unit in 1979 and the Safe Neighbourhoods Unit in 1980. NACRO used crime prevention a means of reorienting the emphasis in debates about crime and the treatment of offenders away from concern with punishment, deterrent sentences, police strength and police equipment. This found favour with officials in the Home Office and in October 1982 what one senior civil servant described as 'the really quite critical seminar' [to the development of thinking on crime prevention] was held at Bramshill, attended by police, central and local government and Vivien Stern, Director of NACRO. From this point onwards NACRO became increasingly involved in a variety of crime prevention initiatives, particularly on 'problem estates'. The first schemes NACRO had been involved in had been in the late 1970s in Widnes (Osborn, 1982); by the time that 8/84 was issued in the mid-1980s NACRO had worked on almost twenty estates in London alone (Rock, 1988). By the late 1980s, NACRO was a source of significant practical knowledge about crime prevention, was one of the organisations consulted about the draft of circular 44/90 and eventually was the source of several of the recruits to the new quango, Crime Concern.

Effect of national policy on police forces
The preceding sections have shown that the idea of crime prevention as a new field of policy arose among central government officials as the result

of a train of thought which started from the failure of traditional responses to crime. By 1986 it had been taken up enthusiastically by the most senior figures in the Conservative administration. Yet within two or three years, the new policy had begun to run into the sand when no agency had been appointed to run it, and the only budgets assigned to it were for centrally administered initiatives like Safer Cities.

In particular, the police had not been assigned any specific responsibility in the field of crime prevention. Messages from the Home Office about the police role were contradictory: for example, whereas the crime prevention unit was established within the Home Office's police department, the Five Towns and later the Safer Cities initiative promoted multi-agency work in which the police had an uncertain function; the same applied to Crime Concern. Central government policy was equally unclear about the balance that should be struck between target hardening or physical crime prevention and more broadly based programmes intended to build up the capacity of communities to control and resist crime. Which agencies should be responsible for which types of crime prevention activity remained equally unclear.

This confusion or indecision in central government policy was probably among the reasons why police forces generally failed to develop convincing crime reduction programmes, as set out in an earlier section.

THE INFLUENCE OF POLICE AUTHORITIES

There was little evidence of active input into the process of decision-making about crime prevention from any of the four police authorities covered by this study. The police authority in force A was party to quite a high level of information about policing from the chief constable. However, little input was made into the development of crime prevention policy. The chair of the authority suggested that their main role in the development of crime prevention was to appoint the chief constable and then give him support. There was little evidence from the minutes of any attempt by the authority to influence crime prevention policy in a substantive way.

Force B had perhaps the most active of the police authorities studied. The minutes of authority meetings showed that the chief constable was often asked to provide fairly detailed information about what the force was doing in terms of crime prevention, and also the overall strategy and philosophy underlying it. The police authority had set up a specific crime prevention sub-committee, though the chair of this sub-committee did not confirm the impression given by the minutes of active member input into the development of policy. In fact, he appeared to have little time for the concept of crime prevention, and made it clear that he favoured a stronger policy of enforcement. Despite the more detailed interventions of this particular police authority, there was no evidence of the authority developing its own ideas on crime prevention and pushing them. The overall impression was still one of the chief constable driving policy, with the authority perhaps taking a greater interest in what was happening than was the case in other forces.

Policy in force C was influenced little by the activities of the police committee. This was despite what were perhaps more strident efforts on the part of the chair to have some real input into policing in the area. The chair clearly felt that it was the local authority that should have responsibility for crime prevention and that the police should take its lead from them. The chief constable, however, jealously (and successfully) guarded his independence. For example, he refused for several years to support NW despite vocal representations from some members of the police authority (and from others).

In force D, leading police authority members' enthusiasm about the commitment of their force to crime prevention was not matched by their level of knowledge about what was actually going on. Again, their main contribution was to choose the chief constable and give him support. However, in contrast to force C, police authority members had taken the initiative in the matter of introducing NW.

DEMOCRATIC INFLUENCES AND CRIME PREVENTION

Equity

In one important sense an increasing emphasis on crime prevention as a policing task is associated with increased equity in the provision of services. Much of policing – that, at least, which is focused on the tasks of crime control and order-maintenance – is unequally focused on working class or relatively disadvantaged sections of society. These communities are characterised by high crime rates (although there is, of course, more than an element of self-fulfilling prophecy in concentrating policing in 'high-crime' areas) and therefore suffer disproportionately from rising crime. A general policing strategy which includes a vastly increased commitment to the prevention of crime in those areas which are most badly hit would, if it were at all successful, have the effect of reducing the disparity between the levels of victimisation in different communities. Undoubtedly, a large proportion of crime prevention activities – especially of the design or target-hardening variety – have been concentrated in such communities. The major exception to this is probably NW.

Of course, crime prevention would only help to achieve the democratic ideal of equity *if successful*. Although many crime prevention projects have been evaluated in one way or another, there remains little firm evidence that many of them have had much impact on crime rates. One of the central problems in attempting to measure such effects is the problem of 'displacement'. It is suggested, particularly in relation to 'situational' initiatives, that if opportunities for a particular kind of crime are effectively blocked in one area, then similar offences will be committed elsewhere, or at some other point in time, or in another way, or else offences of a different type will be committed instead. Although displacement would weaken crime reduction effects, it could help to achieve a redistribution of crime victimisation in accordance with the principle of equity. Even if a given initiative cannot reduce the total amount of crime, it may displace crime from one neighbourhood to another – from a neighbourhood with very high crime rates to one with lower rates – and evening out the crime rates in this way would be equitable.

Barr and Pease (1990) have described a policy similar to this as 'crime deflection', and Pease (1994:677) has argued that 'deflection may be a success. Displacement is never referred to as a success. Crime deflection is benign when the deflected crime causes less harm or misery than the original crime.' Although straightforward deflection would not necessarily result in less harm or misery being caused, it might have the effect of equalising some of the impact.

It should be noted that crimes prevented are not necessarily displaced. Furthermore, Clarke (1992) has argued that there is a complementary phenomenon of 'diffusion' whereby crime prevention directed at a particular kind of crime or at a particular area also tends to prevent crimes of a different type or in adjoining areas. However, to the extent that displacement occurs, it may be used to help achieve the democratic objective of equity.

Delivery of service

Although crime prevention has been an explicit function of policing ever since the development of the modern service, it is only within the last 20 or so years that resources have been devoted to specialist crime prevention initiatives as opposed to relying on the supposed preventive element in such activities as patrol. Even so, crime prevention activities continue to account for only a very small proportion of overall policing budgets. Pease (1994: 684) has observed that 'those forces with the highest rates of recorded crime tend to be those with the lowest proportion of the force's strength devoted to crime prevention. It is almost as though crime prevention is a luxury to which forces may devote resources when there are no more pressing demands on their time.'

Despite the problems associated with measuring the success or otherwise of crime prevention initiatives, and the questionable methods used to evaluate some crime prevention activities, nevertheless this area of policing has been regularly scrutinised by researchers. There is now a minor industry of academics and others engaged in the search for successful crime preventive techniques and there have, on occasion, been some successes (see reviews in Clarke, 1992; Pease, 1994). Probably the majority of crime prevention initiatives remain unproven in terms of their success in preventing, reducing or deflecting crime. However, the continued search for innovation together with a trend towards rigorous evaluation is likely to lead to a more effectively delivered service in the longer term.

Responsiveness

Although there is a strong body of public opinion that seeks significant reductions in levels of crime, it is not clear that there is any direct link between public opinion and the developing interest in crime prevention among professionals inside and outside the police. From the evidence presented above, it seems that crime prevention policy has largely been the product of a specific political and administrative élite (this idea is developed further below in relation to *participation*). Where crime prevention policy has perhaps been most responsive has been in relation to those areas of policing considered in the following chapter: sexual assault, domestic violence and child abuse. In each of these areas – though to differing degrees – an increasingly vocal public (or sections of the public) have made policy change within the police almost inevitable. This was much less true of the crime prevention initiatives discussed in this chapter.

None of the four police authorities covered by this study had any significant influence on the development of crime prevention policy. Even where the police authority's influence was highest (in force B), it expressed itself by requests for detailed information from the chief, and not by actively initiating policy developments. In the other three areas, the influence of the police authorities was markedly less. Thus, developments in crime prevention cannot be portrayed as in any way a response to local representative bodies.

Distribution of power

This is an especially interesting element in relation to crime prevention. The Home Office has been extremely reluctant to place the main responsibility for crime prevention policy in the hands of one agency. This may have happened because a bid by the local authorities to take on the main responsibility was blocked by ACPO, although it is represented by many Home Office officials as a deliberate policy of keeping all the players on board (in practice, more or less the same thing). Another factor was that whereas the obvious candidate for lead agency status was the local authorities, giving them more statutory powers would have been in conflict with the Conservative administration's approach to local government.

The Crime Prevention Unit, the division within which much policy in this area was formulated, was itself part of the Home Office Police Department. It is hardly surprising, therefore, that much of the responsibility for crime prevention has continued to lie with the police. Although in recent years there has been an increasing emphasis on inter-agency and multi-agency cooperation, this has not resulted in anything approaching pluralism in this area. The creation of Crime Concern has not changed the balance of power in a significant way, since this apparently voluntary body remains heavily dependent on the Home Office.

Information
In spite of the trend towards evaluation mentioned above under *service delivery*, and despite the rapid development of crime prevention over recent years, there remains a striking lack of hard evidence about the effectiveness of different kinds of approach. Few of the initiatives within the police forces visited during this study were evaluated in the strict sense. For example, officers in all forces tended to evaluate NW in terms of number of schemes or number of households covered, rather than in terms of real effects on crime. On the other hand, it is possible that NW could provide a structure through which more complete and more pertinent information than is usually available could be delivered to the public. Although this happens only occasionally at the moment, there is no reason in principle why NW should not become an important forum for police-public communication. As in other areas of criminal justice policy, a wide body of research on crime prevention has provided a range of information about the causes of crime and effectiveness of police methods in dealing with crime. However, much of this information is created by the 'experts', and is in the main only accessible to them. Public opinion, therefore, is informed only indirectly by such research.

Redress
If the policy is not working, can the wider public bring the decision-makers to account and bring about a reversal in policy? Where geographical communities or communities of interest have resolved that they are being insufficiently protected by the police from increasing crime and incivility, and where this has resulted in an increased emphasis on a policy of crime

prevention, then some *redress* has been made. This is perhaps true in some senses of NW. As fear of crime has apparently increased so have demands for increased surveillance. Because police resources were insufficient to provide the degree of surveillance required, a police-facilitated self-help programme (NW) developed. What is more, it continued to develop in the face of police and central government scepticism about its value. This is a point at which *redress* and *participation* overlap: it is difficult to disentangle what is the development of new policy as a consequence of public participation, and what is the overturning or redirecting of previous policy as a result of public dissatisfaction.

Participation

The wider public participated in the development of crime prevention only in a very indirect way. The adoption of the notion of crime prevention became politically attractive to the Conservative Government during the mid-1980s. Crucial in this regard was the fact that despite increasing expenditure on the police and criminal justice in general, rates of recorded crime and survey-based rates of victimisation continued to rise. Law and order increasingly became a hot political issue. The pressure on the government to take some initiative was enhanced by the Labour Party's reconciliation with the police service and its attacks on the Conservatives' reputation as the self-styled party of law and order.

Thus in a broad sense, 'public opinion' was a crucial factor in giving impetus to the adoption of a new policy initiative. The specific focus, however, was provided by 'experts' within the Home Office who had been developing a policy on crime prevention for some time. Public opinion, together with the arrival of a new Permanent Secretary looking for new avenues to explore, provided the political conditions conducive to 'selling' such a policy to political masters. Moreover, these political masters were also 'new', were themselves looking to make a mark, and were more open to the general philosophy which underpinned crime prevention than their predecessors. In this sense then, the public participation in the broad policy was minimal and indirect, essentially restricted to electing the party whose ministers eventually chose, or were persuaded, to go down the crime prevention route.

But when considering individual elements of crime prevention policy it is possible to discern a greater degree of direct public participation. Thus, although both CPPs and police consultative committees appeared to be largely ineffective public forums, the case of NW, which formed the centre-piece of the crime prevention policies of many police forces during the mid-1980s, provides something of a contrast. It does appear that the

NW initiative was demand-driven, rather than something developed by Home Office officials or government ministers. They were quick to pick up on and support the concept but, initially at least, NW appears to have been largely a grassroots development. The support given to NW both by the Home Office and by nearly all police forces seems to have been related to the perception that this was something which was popular with the public. It presented an opportunity to involve people in crime control initiatives rather than have them rely on the police or other agencies. In that it stressed individual private initiatives rather than state agencies, NW was in tune with prevailing Conservative philosophy. However, interviews with senior Home Office officials, and the experience within the individual police forces suggested that they had increasing reservations about the practical benefits of NW. Within the Home Office there was a sense at the time that the NW experiment was impossible to stop once it was under way. Besides, the perception was that it had police as well as public support.

The train of thought within police forces was similar. There were doubts not only about the efficacy of NW but also about the costs involved. However, there seemed to be significant public support for the initiative and, furthermore, the Home Office still supported it. The rapid growth of NW threatened to become a significant drain on expensive police resources, and research about the effectiveness of NW remained at best equivocal.

Hence, both the Home Office and individual police forces found themselves in the position of responding to public demand by putting resources into NW when they were far from sure that it actually worked. This raises an important question about participation in the democratic system: what balance is to be struck between public opinion, professional opinion and 'expert' opinion? The 'expert' opinion of Home Office and other researchers was crucial in laying the theoretical foundations for the crime prevention policy that was later formulated. There was perceived to be public pressure for 'something to be done' but, perhaps with the partial exception of NW, public opinion did not have a specific focus. The prime movers behind the development of policy were members of an intellectual and administrative élite.

3 New Policing Responses to Crimes Against Women and Children

The last 20 years have seen a marked increase in awareness of issues surrounding the role and status of women in society. Whilst a major focus has been on sexual discrimination and disadvantage in the labour market, there is also a substantial body of research on the women's experiences of the criminal justice system (see *inter alia*, Gelsthorpe and Morris, 1990). An important part of this has concerned way that the criminal justice system deals with crimes of sexual violence against women. The same period has also witnessed increasing recognition of the vulnerability of children to criminal victimisation (Morgan and Zedner, 1991). During the 1980s, there were a series of public scandals involving incidents of child sexual abuse. One of these (in Cleveland) led to a major public inquiry and an official report which provided a number of recommendations for procedures to be adopted by the agencies involved in such cases (Butler-Sloss, 1989). Partly due to increased public awareness of these sorts of crimes, there has been pressure on the police in recent years to change the way they approach crimes against women and children. The general aim has been to encourage more sympathetic and respectful treatment of the victims of crimes of sexual violence. This has occurred against the background of a renewed interest in victims in studies of the criminal justice system (see *inter alia* Maguire and Corbett, 1987; Mawby and Gill, 1987; Shapland *et al.*, 1985).

Rape and domestic violence

There has, therefore, been increasing attention paid in recent years to the difficulties faced by women victims of sexual assault or domestic violence in reporting incidents to the police, and in the process of complaints through the criminal justice system (Dobash and Dobash, 1970). This increasing scrutiny, and the changes this eventually brought about, have their roots in the re-emergence of the feminist movement in the 1970s (Coote and Campbell, 1987). It has been argued that the agents of the criminal justice system tend to treat women complainants in a way that amounts to 'secondary victimisation', especially in the case of sexual assault. There is evidence from the late 1970s (see for example Berger 1977, Katz and Mazur 1979) and early 1980s (Chambers and Millar, 1983) that women who reported sexual assault to the police often had their character and morality questioned in such a way as to imply some responsibility for their victimisation. Public attention was focused sharply on such issues in early 1982, when a judge imposed a fine on a man convicted of rape on the grounds that the victim was guilty of what he called 'contributory negligence'. This was followed shortly after by a BBC television 'fly-on-the-wall' documentary about Thames Valley Police, one episode of which concerned the interview of a woman who was reporting that she had been raped. So intimidating was the investigating officers' approach that a considerable public furore followed the broadcast. Much concern was voiced about the lack of sensitivity and sympathy being given to the victim's rights and feelings. As Adler (1987) put it some time later: 'All but the most transparently flawless victim was liable to be bullied by interrogators and prosecutors, exposing her to a form of secondary victimisation'. Feminists argued that sexual and domestic assault, and the failure of the criminal justice system to deal effectively with such phenomena, were a reflection of the subjugation of women's rights to male supremacy in society as a whole (Rape Research and Counselling Project, 1981).

Policing policy in this area appears to have lagged behind other developments – at least within that part of the voluntary sector in which the Women's Movement was particularly influential. A campaigning body, Women Against Rape (WAR) was established in 1976, roughly coinciding with the importation into the UK from the United States of Rape Crisis Centres. Reinforcing the point about the unattractiveness of the criminal justice system as an option for women who had been assaulted, the first of these Centres took over 600 referrals in its first two years of operation of which under a third involved incidents that had been reported to the police. Following Roger Graef's 1982 television documentary, and research conducted by the Scottish Office which found that lack of sympathy and tact by CID officers and uniformed policewomen appeared to be quite widespread (Chambers and Millar, 1983), the Home Office issued a circular to chief constables (25/1983) which contained advice on how investigations should be conducted, on the timing and conduct of medical examinations, the number of officers involved in an investigation and, where possible, the importance of having female officers centrally involved.

The following year a governmental advisory group, the Women's National Commission (WNC), set up a working party to examine the issue of violence against women. Smith (1989) suggests that the major concern of the WNC 'was to try to effect certain practical changes – for example, to help ensure that female victims receive the legal, medical, social and psychological help which they need and that their role as court witnesses be made as tolerable as possible. But it was also concerned to offer practical advice to the police and to court personnel on their procedures and to bring home to them that these procedures could be contributing to a lack of effectiveness' (Smith, 1989:6). The WNC focused upon improved training as one of the key areas in which effective change could be implemented, with a view to developing a small number of highly trained specialist officers. The working party also reflected on broader criminal justice issues. Its report, *Violence Against Women*, criticised the police for 'reluctance to interfere in domestic disputes, and in particular, for their reluctance to arrest and prosecute the perpetrators of the violence' (Women's National Commission, 1985). Further guidelines were issued in October 1986 by the Home Office via circular 69/1986 which dealt with victims of both rape and domestic violence. This made a number of suggestions, including that police forces should consider setting up special victim examination suites, more advice and information for rape victims, follow-up visits, and enhanced training for officers who deal with rape victims.

Many accounts of the development of domestic violence as a social problem show the phenomenon as rooted in the traditional unequal power relationship between men and women. English Common Law clearly outlined the rights that a man had over his wife; including the complete control over her property and of her daily affairs. This notion that a woman could be a man's property was fundamental to the idea that a husband had the right to administer physical 'punishment' to his wife. Similar arguments have been made as regards the police approach to domestic violence as have been made for sexual assault. That the police do not treat the victims of domestic assault with the required degree of sympathy, that they do not take a sufficiently serious view of the offence of domestic violence (indeed, may not really regard it as a criminal offence at all), and that they may often regard the victim as in some way responsible for what has happened to her. These are all themes which have arisen from a body of research into the policing of domestic violence from both the USA and the UK. One of the earlier pieces of research regarding the police approach to domestic violence was the 'Minneapolis experiment' in the USA (Sherman and Berk, 1983). This project attempted to randomly allocate domestic incidents to one of three alternative police responses; arresting the man, sending the man away for a period of hours, or giving advice and counselling. The conclusion of the experiment was an apparent clear-cut 'success' for the arrest option, as over a six-month period, repeat calls fell much more when this option was used. The authors of the study favoured a policy of a presumption of arrest – that police officers should make an arrest unless there are clear stated reasons for doing otherwise. This led to a number of police departments in the USA adopting more active arrest policies with regard to domestic disputes. However, subsequent research has cast some doubts on the approach which was suggested by the Minneapolis project. Sherman himself has argued more recently that in some cases the effect of arrest may be to exacerbate the violence experienced by women rather than reduce it (Sherman *et al.*, 1992). Research in the UK context has also provided support for a more active arrest policy in the police response to domestic violence (See for example, Edwards, 1989). Others have questioned the concentration on possible police interventions and argued that the most effective response will be a coordinated effort amongst a number of concerned agencies (Levens and Dutton, 1980). There continues to be disagreement over the most appropriate role for the police in this area, and although it has been argued that inadequate police responses result in only a very low proportion of incidents of sexual assault and domestic violence being reported to the police, it is neither completely clear how a higher reporting rate might be encouraged, nor is it self-evidently the case that this would necessarily be a good thing.

There have been a number of practical developments in each of these areas. The Women's Movement has been instrumental in setting up rape crisis centres and women's refuges in many towns and cities in the UK. The first refuge was set up in 1971 (Pizzey, 1974) and there were over 150 by 1978 (Binney *et al.*, 1981). It was, however, the Parliamentary Select Committee on Violence in Marriage that heralded the beginnings of change in public policy and the Committee's Report, according to Dobash and Dobash (1992), signalled government support for refuges. The Working Party's survey of police forces found that domestic violence was not perceived by them as an area where their procedures fell down or where new measures were necessary or important. However, 'despite criticism of law enforcement stressed by activists and some fairly pressing questioning of the police by MPs when taking oral evidence, this concern virtually disappeared in the text of the Report and from the recommendations. Instead all that was recommended was that the police keep statistics and that chief constables review their policies' (Dobash and Dobash, 1992:125). The ineffectiveness of the criminal justice system – and especially the police – was one of the major focuses of the women's movement in this area. The central and most often voiced criticism of the police was that they remained reluctant to intervene in domestic incidents, and that this reluctance was underpinned on the one hand by the perception that the threat to officer's personal safety was high (Parnas, 1972) and on the other the widespread belief that such work was not 'real' police work (Pahl, 1982). Police officers have suggested that this is largely due to their frustration at victims' unwillingness to fully cooperate when the police try to take firm action.

Pressure for change remained high and, as far as the police were concerned, it was the Metropolitan Police that led the way. During 1985, they set up a working party to look into the problems of policing domestic violence. Reporting in 1986 it recommended a more active arrest and prosecution policy, better collection of statistics on the nature and extent of domestic violence, and the introduction of improved training for the police officers who deal with such incidents. It was particularly critical of existing training which, it said, 'perpetuate[d] current terminology ('domestic dispute') which helps to trivialise marital violence rather than treating it as an allegation of crime'. A Force Order encouraging arrest was issued in 1987, and the Metropolitan Police quickly set up a number of specialist domestic violence units, being followed in later years by a small number of provincial forces (West Yorkshire and the Welsh forces being prominent). The Home Office issued further guidance to police forces about domestic violence in 1990 (circular 60/90), and senior ministers made a number of public statements drawing attention to the seriousness of the problem and the need for action to address it.[1]

Child abuse
This issue of child abuse, in particular child sexual abuse, is one in which the criminal justice agencies have been required to review policies and practices over recent years. In terms of policing policy, it is often placed with responses to rape and domestic violence, because all involve the need for a more sympathetic and tactful approach to the victim. In addition, where the police have set up specialist teams to deal with child abuse, they often have the investigation of rape and domestic violence within their terms of reference as well. However, the development of the police role in dealing with child abuse has been quite distinct from developments concerning sexual and physical violence against adult women, and these in turn have been almost completely separated from any broader consideration of victimisation. Rape and sexual assault, domestic violence and child abuse have remained unconnected to other areas of criminal victimisation, allowing the general subject of victimisation to remain largely unpoliticised and the dominant image of the crime victim to remain androgynous or sexually neutral.[2]

Early work on child abuse focused its attention upon physical assaults or neglect of children. In 1962, C. Henry Kempe, a US-based paediatrician and his associates coined the term 'battered child syndrome'. This described the process leading to physical assaults by parents on their young children. Kempe went on to argue both that the abuse was more common than was generally recognised and that professionals had been turning a blind eye to the phenomenon. His view was that child abuse stemmed from emotional or psychological problems with the parent(s) and the response should involve therapy for the parent(s) combined with temporary protection for the child. This model of child abuse was extremely influential in the USA during the 1960s and 1970s and, largely thanks to the efforts of Kempe and his colleagues to publicise the subject, it became a major social issue there. Developments in the UK were strongly influenced by those in the USA. During the 1960s, the two main groupings involved in dealing with child abuse were the NSPCC and GPs. During the late 1960s and early 1970s, the NSPCC published a large number of studies on the subject of child abuse (For an overview see Parton, 1985).

However, as well as the actions of bodies working in the area of child abuse, it is the repercussions of specific highly-publicised incidents of abuse which have done as much as anything to raise the profile of the issue in Britain. A key example, and the first major case, is that of Maria Colwell in 1973. Maria was seven years old when she was killed by her stepfather. She had previously been removed from home by social services for fostering but had later been returned and had been both beaten and starved before eventually being murdered. It was this case, and the ensuing public outcry, which led to the acceptance of the term 'child abuse' and to the establishment of a new system of child protection in the UK – involving area child protection committees, inter-agency case conferences, the development of specific training and so forth. The legal framework for the treatment of children who had been abused was set out in two Acts of Parliament – the Children and Young Persons Acts of 1933 and 1969.

Certainly it was not until the early 1980s that the idea of *sexual* abuse of children, as opposed to physical abuse, gained any sort of real recognition. The pressure on the police around this time to introduce more sympathetic means of dealing with adult victims of sexual violence was quickly extended to children. Once again the Metropolitan Police were at the forefront, and in 1984 established a pilot project in the Borough of Bexleyheath where training of officers was undertaken jointly with that of social workers and, subsequently, investigations of allegations of abuse were also handled jointly (Metropolitan Police and London Borough of Bexley, 1987; and for a critique see Kelly and Regan, 1990). Following the end of the pilot project the general approach was endorsed and efforts were made to introduce it universally. Home Office Circular 52/1988, for example, encouraged joint investigations by the police and social services. Two other crucial developments in 1986 and 1987, however, did more to frame the issue of child abuse in the UK at this time than perhaps any others. The first of these was the setting up of 'Childline' in 1986. The television programme *That's Life* late on in the year had embarked upon a special investigation of child abuse. The response was huge and it prompted the programme's host, Esther Rantzen, to launch a telephone helpline for any child wanting to report abuse or seek help. Tens of thousands of calls were made on the first day of Childline, and although the service was not without its critics,[3] the publicity that surrounded its operation did as much as anything to draw public attention to the issue of sexual abuse of children.

It was, however, the 'Cleveland affair' in the summer of 1987 which brought the issue of sexual abuse to the forefront of public debate. The scandal involved two local paediatricians who had over a period of months been instrumental in bringing over 100 children into care on place of safety orders. On the basis of a particular physical test – the anal dilatation test which later came under question – the doctors argued that many of the children had been anally abused. Before long stories of large numbers of children being taken into care in Cleveland began to surface in the national press, and parents in the area began to mobilise. The parents of the children gained the support of the MP for Cleveland, Stuart Bell, who raised the matter in Parliament and campaigned vigorously on their behalf (Bell, 1988; Campbell, 1988). The eventual outcome was the establishment of another public inquiry.

The Inquiry chaired by Judge Elizabeth Butler-Sloss was surrounded by massive media and public attention. The report (Butler-Sloss, 1988) made a number of detailed recommendations for the agencies involved in dealing with child abuse. These included procedures for joint investigation of child abuse cases by police officers and social workers, joint training of police and social workers, new interview techniques, and a network of communication between all the involved agencies. In contrast with the above cases of physical abuse, the main criticism of social workers in the Cleveland case was that they had been over-zealous in their desire to take action to protect children. Crucially, the Report recommended that it was the interests of the child that should form the primary focus of any policies established to deal with the problem. Indeed, it is this general philosophy that found expression in the 1989 Children Act.

This has been far from the end of the story. From 1990 onwards stories of 'ritual abuse' have appeared in the media and a number of social services departments have become involved in dealing with cases in which highly ritualised and organised abuse of children has been alleged – the most notorious of which were those in Nottingham (where police and social services disagreed publicly over an investigation of alleged 'satanic' abuse); in the Orkneys (where police and social workers had to return a number of children they had taken into care because there appeared to be little evidence of child abuse); and the more recent investigation of a large number of allegations involving children's homes in North Wales and Leicester.

POLICY CHANGE IN FOUR PROVINCIAL FORCES

The central aim of the research was to establish how far change had taken place in relation to the policing of sexual assault, domestic violence and child abuse, and following that to analyse how and why these changes had come about. Thus, whilst a good deal of the research effort was focused on force-wide policy making, visits to the two local sub-divisions were undertaken in order to collect evidence on the substance of policy change, and the difficulties of implementation.

Whilst it is the case that every police officer has a responsibility for the prevention and detection of crime, all police forces have a specialist criminal investigation department (CID) whose main function is crime detection. In the four forces in this study the (CID) command structure was capped by an assistant chief constable. In each force, interviews were carried out with the detective chief superintendent (head of CID), and in some cases other representatives of the headquarters CID involved in policy-making at force level. From these interviews as full a picture as possible was built up of the force policy in relation to the investigation of sexual assault and child abuse, and the handling of domestic violence. Within the local sub-division, interviews were conducted with the head of the local CID (generally a DI), together with interviews with detective constables about the procedures involved in dealing with cases of alleged rape, and with officers – in specialist units or otherwise – who were tasked with the investigation of child sexual abuse.

In the four forces studied, the policies adopted in relation to the policing of sexual assault, domestic violence and child abuse contained a number of common features. Consequently, for the purposes of this chapter, the findings of the research in relation to each of these three areas are summarised together. The major developments in policy and practice are summarised under the following six headings: the setting up of specialist teams; the creation of new facilities; improved training for police officers;

detailed written force guidelines; new inter-agency structures; and other developments.

Specialist teams

All four of the forces included in the study had set up specialist teams. The primary concern of the majority of the teams was child abuse, though in three forces the units were also involved – in some way – in dealing with cases of rape and sexual assault. Generally speaking, domestic violence generally came fairly low down on the agenda in such units. The teams varied not only in terms of their coverage, but also in structure and terms of reference.

Two forces had developed specialist teams on a divisional basis. In the first of these, force A, the specialist teams which were set up from 1987 onwards, were called 'special enquiry units' (SEUs), and consisted of 4 to 6 officers (mainly women). Officers worked in plain clothes but did not belong to CID (although their line management was through DIs). The vast majority of their work involved the investigation of child abuse (physical and sexual), although they also had a responsibility for missing children, and some juvenile crime. The units were also used as a resource to provide a female officer to take an initial statement from a woman alleging rape, should there not be a sub-divisional WDC on duty. The sergeant in charge of one of the SEUs indicated that her unit had a responsibility for monitoring incidents of domestic violence as well. The officers in the units were carefully selected, having several years' experience before applying to join the unit, and thereafter undergoing specialist training in the investigation of child abuse.

The second force with specialist teams on a divisional basis called these 'child protection teams'. Force B's teams were introduced in 1986, and the two that we visited during the research each had four officers, over half of whom were female (WPCs). Each team also included a male detective constable. The main work of the teams involved the investigation of child sexual abuse by family members or someone else with custody or care of the child. As in force A, the units were also occasionally used to provide support in cases of sexual assault, as they were known to specialise in 'sensitive' interview techniques. Once again, officers had to meet strict selection and training requirements. The teams had no role in dealing with incidents of domestic violence, but at the time of the research the force was considering the introduction of divisional domestic violence units. This followed one division which had set up one such unit two years previously (consisting of 2 WPCs). The unit provided a back-up to the uniform relief officers who initially dealt with domestic incidents. Victims were informed of the existence of the unit; follow up letters were sent to addresses of repeat calls with a returnable slip asking the informant to tick one of two boxes; 'I would like to discuss this matter further' or 'The matter has now been resolved'. The unit also carried out an analysis of the pattern of domestic incidents on the division. There was a flagging system, so that the controller could inform an officer attending an incident of any details from previous call-outs. The unit's officers accompanied a victim to court if she so wished, and also liaised closely with other involved agencies including the local Women's Aid, social services and the women's refuge.

The third force (force C) was particularly interesting because the over-riding management philosophy over recent years had been against the setting up of specialist units. Following a report by management consultants into the force structure some years previously, the emphasis had been upon decentralisation and sub-divisional autonomy. As far as crimes of sexual assault and violence against women and children were concerned, this resulted in a policy of introducing a number of 'victim liaison officers' (VLOs) on each sub-division. These were nearly all female police officers, who had undergone a two-week course in dealing with victims of such crimes. The officers were operational, and worked in various departments, but were available to be called out if required to carry out a rape interview, or deal with a child victim.They also provided the liaison with other agencies (notably social services) in child abuse investigations. However, senior officers on one division decided that a specialist unit would improve the police response to cases of child abuse, and eventually a force working party recommended the introduction of such units across the force area (whilst retaining a number of trained VLOs as a back-up resource).

The fourth police force (force D) had also set up a specialist unit called the 'family support unit' (FSU). According to the unit's terms of reference, it was set up in 1988 'primarily to provide operational support to sub-divisions and specialist departments in respect of investigations concerning violent or sexual crime against women, and child abuse'. The unit consisted of four WPCs, and two male DCs, and a full-time sergeant (female). As with specialist units in other forces there were particular requirements for experienced officers (at least five years service), and specialist training (see below). Although the terms of reference gave the unit responsibility for dealing with rape, domestic violence and child abuse, in practice the unit dealt mostly with physical child abuse. In theory, sub-divisions could turn to the unit if they were unable to find a trained female police officer to take the statement from the victim in a rape case, but this happened only infrequently. The FSU did not play a major role in the force's approach to domestic violence. This point was explicitly made in interview by the officers of the FSU, as well as by a Women's Aid representative and the county council women's officer. A leaflet had been produced which was designed to inform victims of domestic violence of the existence of the FSU, and although the force sent these leaflets to addresses to which police had been called to a domestic incident it did not elicit much response. One problem experienced by the FSU was that when there was a major inquiry, the detectives from the unit would sometimes be removed due to staff shortages elsewhere. This resulted in something of a credibility problem for the unit with some sub-divisional DI. There appeared to be differing views about what the unit was capable of dealing with, with some DIs only prepared to refer relatively minor cases of non-accidental injury of children, whilst others would use the unit's services for serious cases of child sexual abuse. The FSU was a single centralised unit, and was available to support all territorial divisions in the force bar one (a large rural division). The force was planning to double the size of the unit and extend its 'catchment area' to the whole force.

The creation of new facilities

Following the lead taken by the Metropolitan Police and others, a number of forces examined the facilities they had for victims of sexual assault. In particular, victim examination suites have been established which provide more comfortable surroundings than would normally be available in a police station in which the victim can make a statement and be examined by a doctor. Of the four forces visited during the course of the research, two had set up special facilities of some kind. Force B was in the process of setting up two large victim reception suites within its force area at the time of the research. These were influenced very much by the St Marys Centre in Greater Manchester, which is a hospital-based reception centre incorporating interview, medical examination, showering and counselling facilities. After a comprehensive force review into the investigation of rape and serious sexual offences, it was decided to develop two victim reception centres, one in each of the main cities in the force area. These were to be funded partly by the police authority, but with additional funding from the Urban Programme and local authorities. Even though it appears that the police were key movers in the decision to develop these special facilities, the officers with whom we spoke were keen not to portray the centres as police-run. They said that the facilities would also be open to women who did not want to involve the police. So whilst it would be force policy to refer most women reporting that they were victims of rape within the last 28 days to be examined and interviewed at the centre, other women could approach the centre directly without prompting police inquiries. Force D established a rape victim examination suite in 1986, and issued a written force order that it was to be used for all examinations for sexual assaults which took place in the main conurbation within the force area.

By contrast to these two areas, force A had considered the feasibility of setting up a 'rape suite' but had decided against it after fairly lengthy consideration. The force had responded to the Home Office circular 25/83 by setting up a working party chaired by an assistant chief constable. This was tasked to examine training, investigation techniques, examination facilities and other implications of the circular. Following the report of the Women's National Commission (1985), the working party looked at the possibility of creating a victim reception suite in the force area. The working party found against providing facilities at one central location. Police surgeons in the county had expressed reservations about such an idea, as many would have to travel long distances meaning delay in obtaining forensic evidence and adding to the distress of those awaiting examination. However, it remained force policy that no victim underwent a medical examination at a police station; examination taking place at doctors' private surgeries, health centres or hospitals situated at strategic points throughout the force area. A similar policy existed in the other police force without special rape suites (force C), victims underwent medical examination away from police stations, usually at doctors' surgeries but sometimes at hospitals.

Improved training for police officers

All four police forces which participated in the study had made efforts over recent years to improve the training of officers dealing with rape and child sexual abuse investigations. Once again, however, domestic violence was less often the focus of any of the new initiatives or developments.

Following the report of the Women's National Commission in 1985, force A set up a working party to examine its procedures for investigating sexual assault. As a result of this review all male and female uniformed police constables and sergeants received basic training in dealing with sexual offences. Emphasis on rape trauma syndrome (RTS) and care for the victim was a central feature of this training. Detective training on both initial and development courses was revised to include sessions on sexual assault and on child abuse. In addition, women police officers received additional specialist training in dealing with sexual offences. In 1987, the force set up joint training for social workers and police officers. This was a seven day course taken by groups of 12 (six police officers and six social workers). The courses included sessions identifying personal attitudes towards sex, insights into the guilt feelings of the victim, and specialist interview techniques. The training was set up on the personal initiative of a sergeant who had a interest in this area of police work, and who drew on her own experience of working with children, as well as investigating the approach adopted in some other police forces.

Reflecting the special role played by female police officers in the investigation of sexual offences, there were three specialist courses open only to female officers in force B. These were all of one week duration, and were at the initial (12 months service), intermediate (3 years experience) and advanced (5 or more years experience) levels. A common theme of all these courses was the provision of information on RTS and the need for sympathetic treatment of the victim. At the time of the study, all police officers in this force received a basic legal training in the recognition of various sexual offences, but as a working party review of the force's approach to this area stated, 'much of the training in sexual offences is denied to the non-detective male officer unless he reaches a very senior rank'. This problem was partially addressed in 1989 when a one-week course on sexual offences and child abuse was introduced into the stage two phase of probationary training, and this too stressed the need for sympathetic treatment of the victim, and an awareness of RTS. Male detective sergeants in this force became eligible to attend the advanced courses offered to female officers. Thus, the main change was that increasing numbers of male officers were being trained in dealing with serious sexual offences. Officers from the training department particularly stressed the importance of including detective sergeants on the sexual offences course, since in practice it is they who took charge of rape investigations. According to the training department officers the role of the trained police women in rape investigations was not properly appreciated by the detective sergeants until they themselves underwent the training. At the time of the study, a quarter of all the detective sergeants in the force had been on this training course.

This force also reported significant developments in the training of police officers for dealing with the investigation of child abuse. The major change here was the introduction of joint training courses for police and staff from other agencies involved in dealing with child abuse. All officers in the specialist child protection units had done a 5 day child protection course which also involved health visitors, social workers, and education staff and was basically aimed at introducing the procedures to be followed. Since 1987, there had been joint training of police officers and social workers in interview techniques. Once again, there did not appear to be any new initiatives in this force for training police officers to deal more effectively with domestic violence. In one of the sub-divisions the police and representatives from a local women's refuge were involved in discussions about arranging an informal training input for probationers about domestic violence, but at the time of the fieldwork this was still to be confirmed.

As outlined above, rather than setting up specialist teams, force C had designated victim liaison officers who had received specialist training in dealing with victims of sexual assault and child abuse. About 100 officers in the force (nearly all women) had done the week long VLO course, which involved lectures and role playing, an input from other agencies such as Rape Crisis, Victim Support, and Women's Aid. There was a further two-day course on techniques for interviewing children, and the use of telephone games and anatomically-correct dolls. In addition, there was a joint investigation course which lasted one week, given to groups made up of equal numbers of social workers and police officers.

During the 1980s, force D made efforts to extend its training on sexual offences. All female officers were required by force policy to attend a specialist course soon after completing initial training. This five day course included information on victim awareness, interview techniques, understanding domestic violence, and involved inputs from other agencies such as the NSPCC and social services. The force introduced a special course in 1987 aimed at training those female police officers who would not have qualified for the above training due to their probationary period being over before its inception. There was not a comparable commitment to that of force A to extending this kind of training to male police officers.

The force had made significant changes to the methods (and the extent) of training for police officers who deal with child sexual abuse. Each of the officers of the family support unit had to attend a four week training course, one week of which was spent on secondment to a social services office. The course was designed by the force training officer in consultation with senior CID officers and the social services' training department. Following the inception of the specialist unit, the force began a series of two-day courses designed for CID officers who deal with child sexual abuse investigations. Officers from the family support unit also had an input to this course which was run jointly with social services, and occurred every six weeks. It usually involved seven social workers and seven police officers. In response to the necessity introduced by the Children Act 1989 (which came into force in 1991) that only designated officers may deal with child abuse, the force was planning to further expand its training programme.

Only in force D was there any new training initiative specifically in relation to domestic violence – and even in this case it was confined to probationers. A year before the study, the force introduced a change whereby all recruits were to be given a half-day session on domestic violence led by a volunteer from Women's Aid. Positive though such a development was, in interview one volunteer expressed frustration both at the limited time that was given to the subject, and at some of the attitudes that she encountered from some recruits. However, she was also involved in a sub-divisional experiment whereby uniformed officers were required to report back to the sub-divisional DI after having attended a domestic incident, and justify the course of action (or non-action) that they followed. The experiment involved visits to the local women's refuge for all uniform reliefs and discussions with the volunteers there, as well as informal discussions led by the Women's Aid worker whom we met. She said that she was encouraged to see officers who she had spoken to at training school challenging the attitudes of some of their older colleagues.

Detailed written force guidelines

Most police forces have a set of 'standing orders' which lay down broad force policy, legal requirements and procedural guidance. These form the basis for written force policy. It is common practice in police forces to issue guidance and information across the force in the form of written weekly orders.[4] Changes in policy resulting in revisions to force standing orders are communicated through these weekly orders. The legislative and administrative demands on the police service have risen dramatically over recent years. This has resulted in the growth of standing orders, as more and more revisions and additions are made. A number of officers across all the forces visited as part of the research called into question the effectiveness of standing orders in terms of changing policy. They had a symbolic value, but their sheer size and detail undermined their usefulness as a practical guide to action, or as an effective way of communicating change. Nevertheless, written orders do provide information about the broad approach of a police force to a particular areas of policing policy.

As a result of increasing emphasis on the specific handling of serious sexual assault cases forces had a number of set procedures written into force policy concerning the treatment of victims. All four forces had guidelines which referred to rape and sexual assault, and two forces had specific instructions regarding the handling of domestic violence.

The working party established by the chief constable in force A endorsed a set of six guidelines in relation to the treatment of victims of rape, and a meeting of the police authority in November 1986 was informed that these now formed part of the force's policy. The guidelines, which were not dissimilar to those introduced in other forces, read as follows:

(a) All victims will be interviewed by an experienced woman police officer;

(b) wherever possible the interview will be at a location other than a police station;

(c) medical examinations will always be carried out at a location other than a police station;

(d) all victims will be given the option of an examination by a woman police surgeon

(e) an experienced detective officer, working under the supervision of a detective inspector, will conduct the investigation;

(f) all victims of sexual offences, subject to the availability of suitably trained members, will be referred to the victim support scheme.

Standing orders in force B contained detailed procedures for investigating and handling rape and serious sexual offences. These were much more detailed than the above guidelines, but contained most of the same elements. This element of the standing orders opened and ended with an explicit reference to the treatment of the victim. For example, the introduction states: 'the offence of rape particularly, is surrounded by strong feelings, and insensitive interviewing of a victim, already humiliated and degraded, may cause further trauma. Whilst it is accepted that some allegations of rape are false, any investigation must commence on the premise that the complainant is a genuine victim' (original emphasis). The standing orders then stated that a policewoman trained in understanding of rape trauma syndrome should be involved in the investigation from the earliest possible stage, that an adult female victim must be given the option of being examined by a woman doctor, that the medical examination should take place in a designated hospital, health centre or surgery, that the interview should be in a location other than a police station if possible, that victims receive full information, and that efforts are made to continue to support the victim if possible by the officer who took the main statement.

There was also reference in the force standing orders of force B to the police role in domestic violence. The guidelines cautiously raised the issue of arresting the offender, although in a very general way: 'In minor cases, reconciliation may be the best course of action, but where incidents are of a more serious nature the arrest of the offender may be more appropriate'.

Force C had a standing order on rape and sexual offences. This went into some considerable detail about the force policy, stating explicitly that it was based upon Home Office circulars 25/83 and 69/86. As in other forces, the standing order laid down that an experienced woman police officer would take the victim statement, that the medical examination should take place away from the police station, and stated that a VLO should be appointed in every case. The working party into rape, domestic violence and child abuse reported that in previous years force standing orders had been revised to note the shift in the police approach to domestic violence, away from mediation and towards intervention and victim support. However, the report also raised doubts about the lack of structures within the force for the monitoring of the extent of such changes on the ground.

Force D had a system of written weekly orders which were used to promulgate policy changes from headquarters. There were two written orders of relevance. First, although there was no written force policy specifically on the treatment of rape victims, there was one weekly order concerning the employment of a female police surgeon. This said that the female surgeon should be used for examinations of victims of sexual assault from the main conurbation as long as a number of criteria were satisfied. These included having a request from a victim to be examined by a female police surgeon, followed by agreement from the supervisory officer that her specialism is required and that this is supported by another police surgeon. In contrast to the views expressed in other forces the order added that 'it is important to note that [seeing a female surgeon] should not be the practice... merely because the prisoner or victim is a female.' Finally, the order also informed officers of the availability of a victim examination suite which should be used for the examination of all victims of sexual assault from within the main conurbation area.

A second force order received a lot of attention in the force area, as it represented a commitment from the chief constable to deal effectively with domestic violence. The weekly order was signed by the chief constable, and stated that 'assaults in the home are just as serious as assaults in other places' and police officers must 'where necessary intervene in a positive manner for the immediate benefit of the victim'. Attached to this weekly order was a copy of the revised force standing orders (dated March 1988). These stated that 'domestic violence is a crime which occurs on a significant and disturbing scale', and laid down the following procedures for a police officer attending the scene of a domestic incident:

'...a) remain calm, be patient, tactful and courteous;
b) display a positive, helpful and impartial attitude;
c) stop the verbal dispute and listen to both sides of the story;
d) appear sensitive to the problems;
e) indicate a willingness to help;
f) advise against extremes of behaviour;
g) obtain full information but avoid the impression of prying;
h) take positive action in the detection of any offences under the criminal law.....'

The standing orders went on to instruct officers to make a full recording of the particulars of incidents that are not the subject of a crime complaint. Details must be shown of what action was taken. In the case of an assault or wounding, if it was of 'a serious nature' then the perpetrator was to be arrested. Officers were instructed to inform the victim where appropriate of the available services of other agencies like Rape Crisis, women's refuges, Victim Support, Citizens Advice Bureaux and local law centres (details available from the control room). The standing orders went on to give details of powers of arrest under the Police and Criminal Evidence Act (1984) and of the Domestic Violence and Matrimonial Proceedings Act (1976).

New inter-agency structures

The most significant changes in terms of inter-agency working were the structures and procedures set up to deal with child abuse. As outlined above, all four police forces set up joint training for police officers and social workers involved in dealing with child abuse. Police and social services were also involved in multi-agency structures at various levels, in all force areas. Those forces that set up specialist units tended to use those units as a main point of contact with other agencies involved in these areas.

The main forum for developing and reviewing policies for child protection was the Area Child Protection Committee (ACPC). In each of our force areas there was an ACPC for each local authority area, on which the police sat along with representatives from social services, community health workers, schools, and medical practitioners. They developed management policies and strategies over and above the co-operation at the individual case level (where police forces were also represented). Again in each of the four areas, forces participating in these inter-agency structures had set up joint training and investigation with social services. It should be noted that the mere existence of such structures does not prevent difficulties threatening the ability of different agencies of working effectively together. In force D, for example, an extensive outline was provided of the inter-agency structures for dealing with child abuse, and a description of the joint training and investigations with social services. However, during the course of the study, a major public disagreement occurred between the police force and a group of social workers. It was generally agreed that these developments caused substantial harm to the ability of police and social services in this area to work effectively together.

Police involvement in inter-agency structures was mainly confined to the area of child abuse. However, force D was represented by its chief constable on an inter-agency panel on domestic violence which was set up by the county council in 1987. This later was to hold a major conference about domestic violence, and the chief constable's directive and the change to force standing orders was one of the responses to this. The inter-agency contact was limited in this case to very senior levels, and it was suggested by several critical respondents that what was needed for effective responses to domestic violence were new approaches at the sharp end of organisations. This is considered in more detail when the implementation of policy at the sub-divisional level is examined below.

Other developments

Three other major developments were noted among the four forces, some of which were referred to in the written force procedures outlined above. Thus, for example, one change from the previous practice in relation to the treatment of rape victims is the increasing tendency for victims to be offered the services of a female police surgeon for the medical examination. In force A, as was set out in the guidelines, it was force policy to actively give all victims of sexual assault the option of being examined by a female doctor. Force B had for a number of years run what it called its 'women doctors scheme'. This was introduced in 1983 because all of the police surgeons at the time were male. The scheme sought the agreement of women doctors in the force area to participate in police training on the implications of examinations, forensic evidence, statement writing and court appearances. These doctors were listed on a rota as available for call-out in the event of the need for an examination of a victim of sexual assault. After that time, the number of doctors on the scheme remained between 30 and 40, and the group became more autonomous, organising its own training sessions and meeting groups to discuss cases, findings and court appearances. The group retained close contact with the police force, and met quarterly with representatives of the community crime prevention department.

Force C had recognised the role of female doctors in the medical examination of victims, and had appointed four female doctors as deputy police surgeons. A weekly order in force D announced in 1986 the appointment of a female police surgeon. However, this was not such a major development as it was, for example, in force B, as the order made it clear that it was up to the woman victim to specifically request a female doctor, and in addition, the new police surgeon was only to be used in cases from part of the force area.

The second more general area of development is in relation to the support of victims. The basic aim of many of the changes in police policy and practice in relation to rape, domestic violence and child abuse is to treat the victims of such crimes with more understanding and respect. The four forces had all, in varying degrees, introduced specific ways of giving continual support to the victim, even though these were not always an explicit part of written force policy. For example, at least one officer in each of the forces suggested in interview that it was the practice for a police officer to attend court with the victim, and in some cases take the victim to the court room before the hearing to explain carefully what she may expect. On occasion, this might be the police officer who took the initial statement, and thereafter maintained contact with the victim throughout the case. In addition, in at least one force victims were referred to Rape Crisis Centres if they so wished. In three of the forces, the police initiated training courses for selected volunteers from victim support schemes to act as rape counsellors if required.

Finally, all four police forces had increased the proportion of their total establishment made up by female officers over recent years. This reflected a national trend in which the proportion of female officers in the police has risen from 9 to 11.5 per cent in the last 5 years. The proportion of total officers who are female in forces A to D were 9.5, 9.2, 7.7 and 9 per cent respectively. In force A the highest ranking women officers were two chief inspectors, forces B and C each had a female superintendent, and force D's highest ranking female officer was an inspector. Force C's relatively low proportion of female officers was noted in the 1991 HMIC report, which strongly urged the force to take special steps to recruit more women. All the forces reported an increase of female detectives, although the figures for this are not available.

IMPLEMENTATION OF NEW POLICIES

For a number of reasons it is difficult to change the ways in which police officers carry out their tasks. One of the most important is the nature of the job itself; much police-work is carried out by individual officers away from direct supervision (Muir, 1977). This limits the degree to which the pattern of policing is determined by sets of laws, rules and procedures (Smith, 1986). Furthermore, critics have argued that policy statements at the top of an organisation are largely meaningless if further action is not taken to ensure that these are translated into real change at the bottom (Johnston, 1987).

As was stated above, we did not have the available time and resources to carry out detailed evaluation of implementation of policy changes within forces. There is a wide body of research which describes such evaluations, for example of new police approaches to domestic violence (Smith, 1989). Thorough evaluations of this kind require a good deal of time to be spent at the local level, including detailed observations of police approaches and carrying out in-depth interviews with officers and victims. However, although this study is primarily about the process of police policy-making, it is clearly relevant to assess how decisions taken at the top level translate into practice. It was also important to examine the extent to which policy initiatives could develop at the local level. To this end fieldwork was undertaken at two sub-divisions in each force, and interviews with civilians and police officers of all ranks, as well as representatives of some local organisations were conducted. This gave insight into the intra-force process of policy-making, and allowed some assessment of the degree to which real change had actually occurred.

Rape and sexual assault

At the sub-divisional level semi-structured interviews were carried out with an experienced detective (usually a detective inspector). From these interviews it was possible to assess their knowledge of, and attitudes towards official force policy, as well as their views on the extent to which practice had changed and why change occurred. Whenever possible, interviews were also undertaken with people outside the police who might offer an informed view on the implementation of policy in the sub-divisions.

In terms of the investigation of rape, in all four forces (to differing degrees) there was evidence of new approaches at the policy level. In one force, however, what change there had been was presented as a process of reinforcement or consolidation rather than significant movement. Unlike the three other forces which were generally very open about the limitations of past approaches, the detective inspectors (DIs) interviewed in force A emphasised that in their experience, victims of sexual assault were by and large treated with tact and sympathy by the police. The introduction of a written force policy, they argued, simply codified what was generally happening on the ground in any case, perhaps making some minor improvements. Thus one DI referring to the 1982 BBC documentary on Thames Valley Police which had shown two police officers insensitively questioning a woman who was reporting rape said:

> That was nothing like the way that we treated the victims of rape. It spurred our senior officers to discuss and tell us how we should treat rape in the future. But what they dictated was no different to what we were doing anyway. This view was reinforced by a DI from the second sub-division:

> The Thames Valley programme highlighted certain aspects of rape investigation and other external organisations put pressure on the police to make sure a woman did the interviewing. But we did try to do this

> before. I can remember investigating rapes 10 or 12 years ago, and I have always got a policewoman to do the initial interview

The detective chief inspector (DCI), in assessing the extent of policy change on the ground, concluded that it had 'formalised rather than changed significantly. You don't need to be ordered that a rape victim would rather give her statement to a woman. Seemingly some police in the country did need to be told. So it became formal policy even though that's what we always did anyway'.

On the whole, when questioned officers recounted the main elements of force policy that had been outlined at the top of the organisation; all officers said that an experienced police woman carries out the interview, that the medical examination takes place by a female doctor away from the police station. The use of trained victim support counsellors was also mentioned, as was the continued contact with the victim maintained by a policewoman. Interestingly, even though the force had decided against providing its own victim examination suites, both sub-divisional DIs said that victims are taken to a 'rape suite' in the locality. It transpired that these were facilities provided by the local social services. Although all officers agreed that the force had formalised or tightened up policy in this area during the 1980s, they had no particular recollection of how this was communicated within the organisation. This was partly related to the fact that they did not perceive there to have been a significant change in practice. For example, when one DI was asked whether the policy had been communicated in written guidelines, he said that officers did not refer to written policy to find out what to do:

> A lot of the way policemen behave is shaped by the way they are taught on the job. By word of mouth and following the example of older and more experienced officers. So when a rape case comes in, a given officer will not say to himself, 'Rule 47 in standing orders states that a woman officer shall carry out the interview' after consulting the rule-book. The officer simply *knows* that this is the way that things are done and acts accordingly

It was pointed out to him that policing styles would never change if this was the case, passed down from older to younger officers. He argued that the styles of policing develop gradually, rather than change suddenly in response to a new policy from headquarters. The other DI referred to written guidelines that were based on Home Office circulars being distributed throughout the force, but could not be more specific.

Although it appeared that some improvements in the way that the police deal with rape victims had been made, doubts were raised about the extent to which this new enlightened approach had extended. When past criticism of police treatment of rape victims was raised with a rape counsellor in the force area, she replied 'It still goes on I'm afraid'. However, she would not elaborate further on this and accepted that in her experience generally, the police approach to rape victims was highly satisfactory. More serious criticism of the police approach came in a meeting of the local police consultative committee in one of the force sub-divisions. A local councillor raised the subject of 'no-criming' of rapes allegations, and implied that unsympathetic treatment by male police officers was leading rape victims to retract their complaints. A local Women's Aid worker made more sweeping accusations against the local police, attacking the 'macho' image of CID and stating she knew of examples of rape victims who had been interviewed by a male officer, against force policy though this was firmly denied by the local DCI.

Of the four forces, force B appeared to be perhaps the most progressive in its approach to this area of police work. Even though its current procedures were more detailed and extensive than those of the other forces, at the time of the research the force had just completed a major review of possible improvements to the investigation of serious sexual assault. This had supported the introduction of victim reception suites, and various improvements to existing force policy (for example, introducing set procedures concerning the taking of intimate photographs for evidence). Officers also gave a strong impression that this policy had effectively been passed down to sub-divisional level.

Compared to force A, the sub-divisional DIs in forces B and C appeared to be less defensive about accepting that substantial improvements had been made on previous police practice. One, for example, commented that in the past rape victims had been required to meet certain 'arbitrary criteria' before they were taken seriously by the police, and on the whole victims were not given proper sympathetic treatment. Both DIs recalled past ways of dealing with rape that would not be accepted now. Similarly, one VLO from force C said that there was a 'completely different approach now'. A second commented that 'our initial response to a rape allegation has changed. You used to feel you had to prove it was a lie. Now our attitude has changed totally', and another that 'It wouldn't be thought wrong before that a man would speak to the woman initially. If there were no policewomen on duty then a man would talk to her... the location (of the interview) was never considered. The location of the medical was never considered, it would be wherever and whenever. There was no back-up, you would interview the female and never see her again'.

Officers from forces B and C gave a clear account of the main points of the force policy on treatment of victims of sexual assault. Written directives were the main method used to communicate these policy changes. One officer suggested that Force Weekly Orders had announced amendments to Force Standing Orders on the investigation of rape, backed up by verbal briefings by supervisors, the other that a copy of the Home Office circular was sent to sub-divisional CID, and DIs and detective sergeants briefed DCs on the new procedures. In the same vein, it was striking the degree to which senior CID officers in Force D were prepared to be critical of past police approaches to the investigation of sexual assault. They were unequivocal that attitudes and procedures in the past were unsatisfactory, but that great efforts had been made to change.

However, in contrast to the other three forces, in force D there appeared to be mixed findings about the degree to which the policy changes outlined above had been translated to the sub-divisional level. One of the sub-divisional DIs had started in his new post the day that he was interviewed, so could not explain the police approach to rape on that sub-division. However, he was still questioned about his experience of force policy. His answers were somewhat vague. Thus, whereas force policy was that a female police officer carries out the interview with the complainant, he said 'we like to have a policewoman present', and made other very general references to treating the victim with more sympathy. He said that the police were now more aware of the work of 'other agencies' but when asked to do so could not specify any particular examples. When asked what had influenced changes in policing policy regarding the investigation of rape, he said 'after Cleveland the public have become much more aware of how we deal with rapes and that', even though Cleveland concerned child sexual abuse. The DI could not remember how changes in policy had been communicated, but thought there had been 'various written directives'. He was unaware of Victim Support having a role in rape counselling. It appeared that this particular detective was not well-versed in the new force policy. However, and by contrast, an experienced detective constable on the same sub-division displayed a detailed knowledge of the procedures as outlined at HQ, and remembered the communication of the policy through written weekly orders backed up by verbal briefings from supervisory officers.

Domestic violence

As was outlined in the previous section, force policy changes in relation to police responses to domestic violence were minor, particularly when compared with the other two areas covered in this chapter.[5] Nevertheless, there was evidence of policy change at the sub-divisional level. Although there was no written force policy specifically concerned with domestic violence in force A, in one sub-division the police-community consultative committee had initiated some changes. This involved the development of a referral card carried by uniformed officers, containing the telephone numbers of the Local Housing Advice Centre (where Women's Aid were situated), and also gave clear guidelines to police officers. Representatives from the committee stated that whilst they knew that not all officers carried the card in practice, many did, and that there had been a clear change in attitudes on the part of senior officers in recent years.

Force B's standing orders contained a somewhat short and general reference to domestic violence at the time of the research. On one division, there was a new approach to domestic violence as part of a divisional initiative. A specialist domestic violence unit had been set up, a written divisional order had been circulated outlining how officers should deal with domestic incidents. Supervising officers were told to brief individual shifts on the new approach. The division also had a domestic violence unit of two WPCs. In addition, domestic incidents were recorded separately from other incidents of violence. None of the officers interviewed on the two sub-divisions (which were not a part of this division) could remember any specific guidance in recent years, written or verbal, from senior officers as to how domestic incidents should be dealt with. The officers mentioned how their worksheets were examined by their supervisors as one indicator of their 'productivity'. However, most domestic incidents were not recorded on the worksheets. In one of the sub-divisions the coordinator of a women's refuge was interviewed. She was working with senior officers in the sub-division to try to bring about a new approach to domestic violence. She argued that while more senior officers had been convinced of the need for a new approach, this had not significantly filtered down to the officers at the 'sharp-end'. This meant, in her view, that the police response to domestic violence in that sub-division remained unsatisfactory.

On one sub-division in force C the superintendent said that domestic violence was investigated more thoroughly now as a result of changes in force policy. However, it was unclear exactly what these particular changes were, other than revisions of force standing orders. By contrast, as outlined above, there were a number of significant changes in policy in force D, including the changing of standing orders, and a well-publicised statement by the chief constable to the effect that domestic violence would be taken seriously by the police. This involved circulating details of women's refuges throughout the force, issuing a written order about the police role in domestic disputes, and establishing of a family support unit (although the unit's role regarding domestic violence was unclear).

In the two sub-divisions informal interviews were undertaken with three uniformed officers with wide experience in dealing with domestic disputes. One officer was clearly in tune with the new force policy; whereas two were somewhat more dubious about the policy change, and were unaware of where to refer victims for further help. Both said that on the ground the new policy had not really changed things, and that policy statements at the top of the organisation often amounted to public relations exercises. Both stressed that they took domestic violence seriously, and the sergeant said explicitly that 'each domestic is a potential murder'. They simply felt that the new policy did not make what they were supposed to do any clearer. This view received some support from a local Women's Aid worker who although aware of more positive attitudes among officers was critical of the lack of back-up in some parts of the force where policy change at the top meant very little on the ground.

In another sub-division in the force area, the local police had started an initiative aimed at ensuring that the spirit of the chief constable's guidelines on domestic violence was kept in their sub-division. The sub-divisional head of CID (a female DI) oversaw the project. She had examined control room messages and written records, and concluded that the new guidelines were not being followed on the sub-division. She introduced a new domestic violence register which would record the history of incidents so that an officer attending a repeat call could be fully briefed by the control room. Additionally, she briefed all the inspectors on the sub-division and urged them to encourage officers to take more positive action in cases of domestic violence. For a period she monitored records of domestic incidents, and the officer who handled it would be de-briefed, during which he was asked to justify his action or lack thereof. Finally, there was a sub-divisional written order issued by the commander which emphasised that the police could take action independently of whether or not they have a complainant's statement. A representative of Women's Aid reported a strong improvement in the police approach to domestic assault on this sub-division.

Child abuse

The police response to the investigation of child abuse has clearly changed substantially over recent years. All four forces had set up specialist units, undertook joint investigations with social workers, sent police officers on joint training courses with social workers, and participated in multi-agency structures. At the time of the fieldwork the forces were working to implement the requirement in the Children Act 1989 that the police must have 'designated officers' (who fulfil certain experience and training requirements) to deal with child abuse investigations.

In force A, the role of the sub-division in the investigation of child abuse was limited due to the existence of SEUs. The specialist units dealt with all cases of physical and sexual abuse, and usually received referrals direct from other agencies (most commonly social services or the NSPCC). As the specialist units worked office hours, sub-divisional officers would occasionally play a role in the initial stages of a child abuse investigation, but the SEU would then take it on. However, the specialist units were usually ultimately responsible to a DI who oversaw investigations, and occasionally attended case conferences. The female sergeant in charge of one of these units did state that the nature of their work tended to set them apart from the rest of the police organisation, and was not regarded by more traditional 'macho' officers as real police work.

Force B had the longest-established specialist child abuse units of all the forces. The officers of the unit gave clear indications that their approach was markedly different from other types of police work. The specialist 'child protection units' were completely autonomous, and received most referrals direct from the other involved agencies. This was substantiated by the research on the two sub-divisions, which it was clear would only play a limited role in the initial phase of a child abuse enquiry should it be reported when the specialist unit was not on duty. Both sergeants from the units made the point that they were insulated from, and perhaps not understood by, other parts of the police service due to the nature of the work. One said that officers of the unit tended to look to people in the other agencies dealing with child abuse for support, rather than to other police officers. The other sergeant said that they were known as the 'Marks and Spencer' squad by certain officers who did not understand the type of work they did.

Force C eventually decided to set up specialist units, but had used specially trained victim liaison officers for some years. The VLOs interviewed during the course of the study had clearly built up a great deal of expertise in the area, a result both of specialist training and from experience. They formed the links with social services and other agencies in the cases of joint investigation, and reported little difficulty with this arrangement. However, in this force, the sub-division did take a more active role in the investigation of child abuse, as it came under the responsibility of the sub-divisional DI. The DI would appoint a VLO from the sub-division, if there was one available. A force review outlined a number of problems with this approach and recommended the setting up of specialist units. The main problem was that over half the designated VLOs were members of uniform shifts, and therefore even though the sub-divisions tried to allocate them evenly it was often a matter of luck whether or not a VLO was available when a case came in. Furthermore, the other duties of the VLOs often intruded upon the work of maintaining ongoing contact with victims and other involved agencies, so that the continuity vital to such cases was lost. One VLO said that they were set apart from other parts of the service, and older male officers often did not understand the complexities of their work, thinking that it was simply a matter of being 'good with kids'. There seemed to be strong support amongst VLOs and senior CID officers within the force for the setting up of specialist units to deal with child abuse.

Force D had, as stated above, a single central family support unit whose main area of work was dealing with child abuse. Unlike the specialist units in forces A and B, the FSU was there to support the sub-divisions, who still retained primary responsibility for the handling of child abuse cases. It remained up to the discretion of the sub-divisional DI which cases were referred. The DIs at the two sub-divisions that we visited said that they referred about one third of the cases that came in. The officers of the unit said that this proportion varied according to the individual DI on a sub-division. Some had a great deal of confidence in the unit and were prepared to refer quite complex cases of child sexual abuse for the unit to investigate. Others did not believe that the unit had the necessary CID expertise, and would only refer relatively minor physical abuse cases. The lack of CID expertise was cited explicitly by both the DI and an experienced DC on one of the sub-divisions, as a reason for not referring more work to the unit. The DC said that the unit consisted of uniform WPCs who were not able to investigate serious crime. This DC explained that he had not had any specialist training in joint investigation techniques or in the investigation of child abuse. However, he said that he carried out child abuse investigations despite this; he knew of no force rule that said an officer must have had specialist training to handle this sort of offence. He was asked whether there has to be a designated officer to investigate child abuse, and replied that if he was the only detective available when a case came in, then he would be the designated officer, regardless of training. On the other sub-division, the DI said also that there was a policy of handing child abuse cases to experienced DCs, but cited the sheer volume of work that the unit had to deal with rather than the lack of investigative expertise. Either way, it appeared that in force D the sub-divisional CID still played the major role in the investigation of child abuse, whether or not the officers concerned had received the specialist training in the area.

INFLUENCES OVER POLICY CHANGE

As the general discussion in the earlier part of this chapter will have made clear, there are a large number of individuals and agencies that may potentially have an influence on the development of policing policy in relation to sexual assault, domestic violence and child abuse. This section examines in more detail the relative influence of all the key 'players' in these areas. It is based on data gathered from interviews with representatives from the major bodies and an analysis of the articulated policy-preferences of the key groups in the policy debate.

The Home Office

An interesting picture emerged of how issues relating to the policing of rape, domestic violence and child abuse came to be raised in the Home Office during the 1980s. The development of the Home Office circular 69/86 on rape appears (primarily) to have been a reaction in the first instance to the Women's National Commission report. The principal in charge of F2 division had been unaware that the Commission were addressing this subject until a draft of the report arrived on his desk in 1986. However, there had been pressures on the Home Office to give advice to forces on the way they deal with sexual assault, stemming from a rising concern in general about the way that victims were dealt with, but in particular following the Thames Valley Police documentary in 1982.

The problem in F2 division was a lack of expertise on the subject: a circular was issued but it did not amount to much in terms of specific advice – it was more of a general exhortation to be more sympathetic. However, the WNC report was a catalyst for a more detailed and comprehensive circular which was issued in 1986. The recommendations appeared to senior officials in the Home Office to be 'inherently sensible'. The head of the division was at this time also in contact with a senior officer in the Metropolitan Police who was often used as a source of advice or statistics to respond to parliamentary questions and other queries. The same officer had been in charge of the force's policy on sexual offences, and had heavily influenced the WNC report. Much that was recommended by the WNC was already in place in the Metropolitan Police area. This made the report's recommendations even more attractive to senior Home Office officials; if they were largely in place in one police force then it was felt that they could be considered to be both practical and workable.

The normal procedure within the Home Office with reports such as that produced by the WNC is for it to be circulated between the relevant divisions, and then a view formed once all of the replies have been received, collated and weighed. This is potentially an extremely time-consuming exercise. On this occasion, however, the official concerned decided to formulate a set of recommendations arising from the report and circulate them for comment. The strategy worked, and a Home Office 'view' on the subject was formed relatively quickly. The next stage was to produce a draft circular for ACPO. According to this official, in order to have most effect, the circular needed to be brief, clear and practical: to lay down as precisely as possible what the officer put in charge of the force response to the circular needed to do.

According to Home Office sources, ACPO generally operates an internal consultation process not unlike that in the Home Office to deal with responses to draft circulars and reports. On this occasion, however, the main person ACPO were likely to consult was, again, the same officer who had advised both the Home Office and the WNC in the first place. In view of this, and as many of the recommendations were already in place in London, ACPO raised no objections in principle to the draft circular, and it was published largely unchanged. As was the usual procedure, HMIC followed up the circular advice in its annual inspections of police forces. The Home Office officials felt that although they could not in theory require police forces to respond, in practice most of them would respond. However, the speed with which they did so would vary between forces. As one senior official commented:

> There's nothing to stop them, when an Inspector (HMIC) comes along and says 'how many examination suites have you got', saying 'well, none – we don't hold with that nonsense. We're not going to do it'. But in fact it generally doesn't work like that. Once you've got to the point by which it's enshrined in a Home Office circular which has been approved by ACPO, they all grumble, but they will go along with it... and the issue generally tends to be the pace with which they implement it.

The background to the development of the child abuse circular within the Home Office was somewhat different. In this case the Home Office were more proactive in developing the circular. In the words of one senior official: 'we were ahead of the game for a change'. F2 division had become more active in developing advice for police forces with the response to violence against women, and were looking for the next area to develop. The same senior official who had taken charge of the response to the WNC report discovered (largely by chance) that the Metropolitan Police and the London Borough of Bexley had initiated an experiment of joint working in dealing with child abuse investigation. He took a close personal interest in developments and also found out about pioneering work in some provincial forces. It was decided (it seems by this senior Home Office official and his colleagues) that there was a great deal of potential for the Home Office to act as a catalyst in the promotion of good practice in this area. Because the key to the Bexley experiment in this area was multi-disciplinary work, in particular the important role played by social services departments, it was decided to set up a multi-disciplinary working party. As the official described it himself:

> We couldn't sit around with a few officers and dream up a circular, which is very often what happens in the Police Department... in this case we had to carry social workers and... the DHSS because dealing with child abuse was clearly a multidisciplinary responsibility and the heart of it was police/social services co-operation.

The official drafted a circular, drawing heavily on the experience of the Metropolitan Police, and this was discussed by the working party. The draft was also circulated to the police staff associations. Whilst this was in progress, the Cleveland controversy broke. This was a key factor in promoting acceptance of the circular by the police themselves. The public outcry following Cleveland put many police forces in a difficult position in that they were suddenly, and without warning, receiving a great number of questions about what they were doing in the area of child abuse. They therefore welcomed the fact that the Home Office were already developing advice for them. In the words of one senior Home Office official, 'the police were screaming for it'. Another official described the situation after Cleveland as one in which 'instead of seeing (the circular) as another burden being imposed on them by wet liberals at the Home Office, suddenly they were surrounded by a terrible crisis – had no idea how to respond... and so saw it as a lifeboat'.

The Home Office also produced a circular advising police forces on the ways to approach cases of domestic violence in 1990 (circular 60/1990). The background developments to this circular were again heavily influenced by the personal priorities of senior officials. The same senior official who dealt with the circulars on rape and on child abuse explained to us that the political pressures had not been as great in the case of domestic violence. However, he was aware of pressure group criticisms of the police response to these incidents and had seen reports in the press. He saw domestic violence as the next area to look at giving advice to the police. Again, contacts with senior Metropolitan Police officers with a particular interest in the subject were important, and these officers communicated the developments that the Metropolitan Police had made in response to domestic violence.

As with the first circular on rape in the early 1980s, the Home Office found themselves with the problem of feeling that guidance needed to be given to forces but not having the information available on which to base this. They therefore commissioned a literature review on domestic violence from their Research and Planning Unit which was later published (Smith, 1989b). This enabled officials to draft circular advice. According to the key official involved in this drafting process, more resistance to advice on domestic violence was expected than had been the case for rape or for child abuse. This was partly because there was a lot more division both politically and within the police force about the subject. For example, we were told of a Home Secretary who was strongly opposed to the Home Office intervening in this area, whilst one of his junior ministers was extremely keen that something should be done. Similarly, there were senior members of ACPO on both sides of the argument. The circular was drafted and sent to the ACPO crime committee for comment, and they commissioned a chief constable with a particular interest in domestic violence to work with the Home Office to produce a redraft. The revised circular (which came out as 60/90)was heavily influenced by the US and Canadian research of the mid-1980s which encouraged a greater use of arrest in domestic violence cases, though in the circular this was drafted to read that chief officers should 'ensure that in all cases their officers are aware of their *powers of arrest* in dealing with cases'. In addition, there was encouragement that the police should develop links with other agencies with an interest in the problem, in particular women's refuges.

The Metropolitan Police
The Metropolitan Police certainly see themselves as the most progressive force in Britain. In terms of the response to rape, domestic violence and child abuse they did appear to play an important role in developing good practice. They are the largest force in the UK, cover much the largest population, have the largest expenditure per head of population, and have the Home Secretary as their police authority. This means that they are in a unique position to influence the Home Office and through this the 41 provincial forces in England and Wales.

They appear to have been one of the forces at the forefront of developing improved policing responses to crimes against women and children, thereby influencing Home Office circulars and consequently practice in other forces. A primary instrument by which the Metropolitan Police addressed new responses to sexual crimes and domestic violence during the 1980s was the working party. There was a working party on each of the three areas of rape, domestic violence and child abuse. The rape working party was the first of these, set up in February 1984 and chaired by a female commander. It was run in an *'ad hoc'* way (according to a senior officer who sat upon the working party) but, because it had quite senior representatives from different sections of the police organisation, it became an extremely effective mechanism for bringing about policy change. It even resulted in the commissioning of one officer to undertake research in the United States on initiatives there. Not least because of the 'forceful personality' of the female officer chairing the working party, a number of changes in the Met's policy were effected, including a force rule that rapes would in future be handled by DIs or above, a new improved training package which trained the DIs alongside WPCs and WDCs, and the introduction of 'rape suites' in the force area.

Not long after the rape working party had been set up, the then Commissioner (Sir Kenneth Newman) – who was particularly interested in developments in Canada in police responses to domestic violence – ordered that a working party be set up to look into improving the police response in the Metropolitan Police district. It reported in 1986 amidst widespread publicity. A senior officer who was involved with this explained that although there were a number of recommendations about improving training and the setting up of specialist domestic violence units, no extra resources were set aside to support new developments, and this proved to be a major hindrance to their implementation. However, a new force order on the recording of domestic violence incidents was issued in 1987, and a number of Metropolitan Police divisions set up domestic violence units, a move which also received considerable media attention. The senior officers involved with the domestic violence working party had a number of meetings within the Home Office to discuss the draft Home Office circular, and as has already been suggested, it seems that civil service deliberations were influenced as a result.

In the area of child abuse, the Metropolitan Police were (it seems) the initial impetus to the development of Home Office circular 52/1988. The Metropolitan Police set up a child abuse working party in January 1985, which oversaw the Bexley social services experiment outlined in the introduction. The report of this was published in 1987. The work of the working party came to the notice of a senior Home Office official who had been instrumental in developing the Home Office circulars on rape and domestic violence. He took a close interest in what was being developed and officials began to develop a draft circular on child abuse. This meant that the work on this was quite far advanced by the time that the Cleveland controversy broke.

The Police Federation
Much of the Police Federation's activity in this general area followed the report of the Women's National Commission: 'Violence Against Women'.

The Police Federation has a committee structure within which the most important committee in terms of policy-making is the Joint Central Committee (JCC). A representative of the Police Federation explained how the JCC took the decisions to encourage new police initiatives in this area. The Federation supported the development of improved training packages for investigating serious sexual offences, and also strongly supported the setting up of specialist units in this regard. The policies were worked out at the Police Federation conference and subsequently in committee. The Promotion and Training Sub-Committee was responsible for the proposal that a national training package in relation to sexual offences should be developed, a proposal that was then taken up by the Police Training Council. Additionally, the views of the Federation were expressed in letters to the Home Office (setting out the case for specialist units to deal with serious sexual offences and requesting information about the follow-up within police forces to the Home Office circular 69/86), and to the Law Commission (expressing sympathy, but ultimately disagreeing, with the WNC proposal that rape within marriage should be made a crime under all circumstances).

Local authorities
The major national associations of local authorities are the Association of County Councils (ACC) and the Association of Metropolitan Authorities (AMA). Representatives of both these bodies were interviewed, and they made it clear that policing responses to rape, domestic violence and child abuse were not really within their remit. They allowed that, if concerns were expressed by member authorities about the way that police forces were dealing with such crimes, then there could be a role for the national associations to raise the matter, but did not feel that this had been a major influence on the developments within police forces. The local authority associations did, however, take an interest in the area of policy from the point of view of resources. In public relations terms this had put them in a tricky position as they would be appearing to drag their feet over making widely-approved improvements in policing. But they felt that it was important to recognise the fact that changing policy was not simply a matter of the Home Office laying down progressive circulars, and things following from there; extra resources had to be found to pay for improvements (or resources diverted from other areas of policing). This was a particular problem in the light of the capping restrictions on local authority powers to raise revenue. This fear is summed up in the following quote from a senior official in the ACC, given in response to a question about the Association's views on policing rape, domestic violence and child abuse:

That's operational. Police authorities can and do call for a report from the chief constable and the outcome may be to ask for something to be done. There is no way that a trade association can take effective action about rape, domestic violence and child abuse. What we can do is hoist storm cones when the Home Office get all enthusiastic. If the Home Office say after consulting ACPO that police are to be allowed to go into peoples' houses and start taking real action then the ACC must say, this is an additional duty which means additional resources. When central government starts saying things like that it must recognise that there are resource implications. But we've now come out publicly against the devoting of more resources to child abuse particularly, even when there is universal condemnation of the crime. The ACC has this PR problem about the things that it has to say about applying resources. If you put more resources into something then you either have to raise more money which you can't because of poll tax capping, or transfer resources from other areas. But that's what local accountability and democracy are all about.

So the actual influence on the changing policy at ACC level was cautionary if anything, due to the resource implications. There was some evidence of AMA involvement in encouraging the development of rape suites in force B. Police authority members asked the chief constable to consider the implications of the St Mary's Centre in the Greater Manchester area. Apparently, police authority members from force B heard about the St Mary's Centre in an AMA presentation given by members of the Greater Manchester Police Authority. At the level of the individual local authority, we found little evidence of police authority involvement in the changing response to rape, domestic violence or child abuse, although there had been a number of significant developments in all four force areas. The police authorities were, on the whole, kept informed of developments within their forces, but the general rule appeared to be that the police took action and then informed the authority about what was being done. The impetus for change seemed to come mainly from the police themselves, and the Home Office.

Pressure groups and representative groups

Changes in policing policy towards rape, domestic violence and child abuse have largely been considered together here, in the main because of the broad areas of similarity in the methods and structures adopted by the police to deal with such crimes. However, this is not meant to imply that there are not important differences between these kinds of crime, both in the approaches to dealing with them, and in terms of the influences leading to change. One important difference which distinguished policy change in the sphere of rape and domestic violence from child abuse, was the relatively important role played by pressure groups representing women's rights in campaigning for change. Informal interviews with representatives from several organisations, both national and local, who had an interest in bringing about changes in the way that the police deal with rape and domestic violence. These included several women's groups. The interviews sought to obtain the stated policy preferences of the different groups concerned, and also to find out the ways in which the groups represented these views in the policy-making process. These could then be compared with the actual outcomes in terms of the changes in policy and practice that we found in the police forces studied.

The Women's National Commission (WNC)

The WNC was established in 1969, replacing the Women's Consultative Council set up in 1963. It comprises representatives of national organisations with a large and active membership of women, including the women's sections of the major political parties, of the trade unions and of the churches, professional and business women's organisations and other organisations broadly representative of women generally. There are currently 50 constituent organisations each appointing one representative. There are two vice-chairpersons, one appointed by the government and one elected by the Commission.

WNCs 1986 report, entitled 'Violence Against Women', was, as has already been alluded to, very influential in raising the profile of domestic violence and sexual assault on women. It had a strong influence on the subsequent Home Office circular 69/86, and also had a significant impact on the Police Federation. During the early 1980s, the issue of violence against women was increasingly raised in meetings of the Commission. One representative of a Scottish trade union raised a number of concerns. In July 1983 the meeting of the Commission was addressed by Lady Ralphs (who was chair of the Magistrates' Association) and chief superintendent Sheila Ward (from the Community Relations Branch of the Metropolitan Police). The subject of the address was women and violence, and the following discussion resulted in the WNC setting up a working party to look at violence against women. The working party was addressed by a number of speakers during late 1983 and 1984, including representatives from the Metropolitan Police and also representatives of rape crisis and other victims organisations.

The principal starting point of the report is described by Smith (1988: 6) as 'the need to try to bring about changes in the way both rape and domestic violence are perceived'. In particular 'they saw a need to take these crimes out of the context of private relationships and into the same arena as any other type of criminal behaviour'. The WNC collected information from forces on their policies and practices in relation to both rape and domestic violence. In relation to domestic violence, over half of police forces in England and Wales either made no comment on their current policies or indicated that they were satisfied with their current practices. A number of *ad hoc* developments in forces were described and one force – the West Midlands – singled out for good practice. The information collected about practices in relation to rape was slightly more encouraging, and suggested that there was a willingness to change. The report was drafted in the summer of 1985, and was circulated to all relevant government departments. It recommended improved training for police officers, and improved liaison and consultation with voluntary bodies and support groups. In relation to domestic violence it concluded rather pessimistically saying that it was 'not frequently perceived as an area in which police procedures "fall down", or where new measures are feasible or important'.

Other women's organisations

There are a number of key agencies helping women who have been physically and emotionally abused. Women's Aid groups provide emergency accommodation (through a network of refuges), advice, information and support. The groups are locally-based and autonomous, but in the mid-1970s national coordinating bodies were set up, including the Women's Aid Federation in England (WAFE). These national bodies lobby and campaign on the law regarding the abuse of women, and also provide training resources and information for local women's refuges. *Women Against Rape* were founded in 1977 and campaign at a number of levels to influence the law and policy concerning rape and other violence against women. *Rights of Women* is another feminist pressure group campaigning on women's issues generally but in particular on rape and domestic violence. Although these are different groups with different histories and purposes, there were number of areas of common ground between them in terms of interest in policing policy.

The representatives from the above groups shared the view that inadequacies in policing responses to rape and domestic violence were often due to the attitudes of police officers, and the culture of what is a male-dominated organisation. The Women Against Rape representative argued that officers had an automatic tendency to disbelieve the victim or to blame her for what happened. They added that women from ethnic minorities have the added difficulty of having to cope with racist attitudes on the part of some police officers. Rights of Women said there was a general hostility to women on the part of the police, who generally failed to understand the concerns behind rape and domestic violence. The Women's Aid representatives described the police approach to domestic violence in the past to have been 'very, very bad'. The criticisms were that the police had strong stereotypes of battered wives, their attitudes and behaviour constituted secondary victimisation of abused women, and they lacked basic knowledge and understanding about the underlying issues. This led to a total lack of effective action in many cases of domestic violence.

Women Against Rape produced a report during the early 1980s called *Ask Any Woman* which listed detailed requirements for police procedures in dealing with rape (Hall, 1985). The recommendations included general requests that incidents of rape and sexual assault should be given higher priority by the police. The report also stated that women must be certain of a sympathetic response regardless of who they are. It made special reference to the fact that rape allegations made by prostitutes tend not to be taken seriously by the police and demanded that this be changed. Women reporting rape must be allowed to make their report in the presence of a friend or counsellor if they wish. Female doctors must be available to carry out the medical examination, and these doctors must have special training in dealing with rape victims. No woman should be pressured to undergo a medical examination if she does not want to. Finally, the report argued that the police should give progress reports on what they are doing to improve policy and practice in this area. The representative from Rights of Women did not give a detailed outline of what the organisation wanted from policing policy, but in general wanted improvements in police attitudes to women, increased numbers of female police officers, and in cases of domestic violence for the police to 'do what the woman wants'. Women's Aid representatives laid down a number of requirements for the police response to domestic violence. These included clear guidelines as to the police role, an increased use of arrest and prosecution to indicate that domestic violence is unacceptable to society, the police to put the safety of the victim first, and a policy of referral to other agencies in appropriate cases. There was broad support for the setting up of domestic violence units, and support for increased training for officers in this area.

All of the organisations visited said that they attempted to gain publicity through the media in order to influence policy. Women Against Rape had produced a number of papers, one of which was on the issue of rape within marriage and was presented to the Law Commission, and also the publication about women's experience of rape which received considerable media attention (Hall, 1985). All of the groups were also active in lobbying members of parliament and local government. There was little evidence of formal contacts with the police. Women's Aid said that they had too few staff to be proactive in influencing policy, and that most of the contacts with police were informal and local. The representative from Rights of Women said that the organisation had objections to formal contacts with the police, but liaised with some individual officers on an informal basis. Women Against Rape had experienced direct contacts with the police, it appears to complain about the way particular cases had been dealt with. The strong impression was still one of rather hostile relationships between the police and campaigning women's groups.

At the local level, there was more evidence of contact between police and women's groups, although on quite a modest basis. The strongest formal contacts were in force B, where representatives from local Women's Aid refuges and Rape Crisis volunteers were part of a forum which met periodically with representatives from the community crime prevention department to discuss developments in force policy in general and the development of victim reception centres in particular. In force A, one sub-division had a consultative committee which was a sub-committee of the local borough council. This included representatives from the local Women's Aid group and Rape Crisis. The meeting of the committee that attended by a PSI researcher focused upon police treatment of rape victims, and the local police were vigorously questioned on this matter. In addition, it was the initiative of this committee to develop the referral card for officers dealing with incidents of domestic violence. Informal contacts between police and representatives of women's groups varied between forces and between sub-divisions. In one force (force D), there was provision for a Women's Aid representative to contribute a half day training for probationers about dealing with domestic violence. As has been outlined already, the same woman was involved in what she regarded as a more successful experiment on one sub-division, in which local officers met her to discuss possible responses to domestic violence. In force B, there was informal contact on one sub-division between the coordinator of the local women's refuge, and the local sub-divisional commander, to discuss particular cases. These local contacts were therefore largely informal and *ad hoc,* and often dependent on local personalities.

Victim Support
The first victim support scheme started as an experiment in Bristol in 1974 (Holtom and Raynor, 1988). A BBC TV programme about the scheme lead to considerable publicity which eventually resulted in the establishment of a number of other similar schemes in other parts of the country. In 1979,

schemes came together to form a national organisation, called the National Association of Victim Support Schemes (subsequently Victim Support). The Home Office made a small amount of money available to support the activities of the national organisation, but local schemes had to find their own finance either from local authorities or charities. In 1987, the government announced that it was to fund the main coordinators in every local victim support scheme, and in subsequent years the funding has grown from £2 million in 1987 to £6 million in 1991-2.[6] There are currently over 400 local schemes. Interviews were conducted with the director of the national association, and a number of local coordinators in the police sub-divisions that were visited within the four forces studied. From this some idea was gained of the views of the organisation. It should be stressed that this is a very different kind of organisation from the women's groups described above. They are fundamentally campaigning organisations – whereas Victim Support largely avoids major campaigns – although Women's Aid is more concerned with giving practical help to abused women. All of the women's groups are independent of government, whereas Victim Support is funded by the Home Office. Victim Support has tended to be more closely connected with the police, and less critical of them. Victim Support deals with people who have been referred by the police, and thus has few dealings with people who have had very bad experiences with them.

Victim Support representatives (national and local) tend to be supportive of the police and were cautious about laying down policy preferences in detail. In terms of the investigation of rape, the organisation had initially felt that its volunteers were not qualified to play a part in helping the victim, but after a working party report in 1988, it was decided that there was a role for the organisation. A training package for volunteers was developed, and was being put into action in the four study forces.

With regard to the police response to domestic violence, Victim Support published a report in 1992 of a national inter-agency working party, which made a number of recommendations for all agencies involved in dealing with the problem including the police (Victim Support, 1992). This welcomed the recommendations of the Home Office circular 60/1990, but outlined some areas for improvement. For example, it recommended the introduction of central classification systems which distinguish domestic violence from other violent incidents. It also recommended that at the scene of an incident, the primary concern should be with the safety (immediate and future) of the woman, and that she should be given information about other agencies who may be able to offer help. Another recommendation was that there be regular monitoring of arrest rates for domestic violence across the country. The report also welcomed the establishment of domestic violence units, but recommended that they should be separate from units dealing with child abuse.

At the national level, Victim Support is present on a number of forums for discussing policy. The organisation is represented on the Home Office victim steering committee. Its central council includes a representative from ACPO, and they have worked out a national policy on referral from the police. At the local level, Victim Support schemes usually have a steering group upon which there is formal police representation, usually the local community affairs officer. It is usual to find victim support represented upon the local police-community consultative committees. Informally, there are regular contacts between Victim Support volunteers and police officers dealing with individual cases. Although the organisation is not primarily a campaigning one, the outputs of working parties (such as that concerning domestic violence) are disseminated to receive wide publicity. At the local level, Victim Support counsellors were directly involved in a part of police policy towards victims of sexual assault. In all four police forces studied, the police had initiated specialist training for selected Victim Support volunteers in counselling victims of sexual assault. Thus, there were a number of contacts with the police at the local level in which Victim Support representatives could put forward their views and ideas.

Members of Parliament
Interviews were undertaken with two opposition spokespersons – the late Jo Richardson (then spokesperson on women) and Joan Lestor (then opposition spokesperson on children), and there was also some contact with the secretariat of the Ministerial Group on Women's Issues. This was set up in May 1986 as a response to the UN 'Decade for Women'. Its aim is to coordinate policies between different government departments with an interest in women's issues. It meets every three months to consider papers submitted by officials and issues press releases after each meeting. It was chaired for a while by John Patten, and then Angela Rumbold (neither of whom was available for interview). The issues that it had addressed included childcare, domestic violence and public appointments. In 1989, the group met to discuss the publication of Lorna Smith's Home Office literature review on domestic violence. A press release dated 21.7.89 outlined how the group had 'set in hand' further work on use of the criminal and civil law and the response to domestic violence by the criminal justice agencies, an examination of the way in which social service and health service departments could give more effective help to victims, and examination of guidance and materials currently available to schools in this

area. There is little detail of substantive practical work though, aside from general awareness-raising activity.

Jo Richardson, unsurprisingly, was quite critical of the group. She argued that the group had been partly set up as a response to Labour's proposed Ministry for Women, and was largely a public relations exercise. The group needed to find itself an agenda without committing significant resources, and so focused first on child care (making general statements that it was a good thing) and then on domestic violence. However, Jo Richardson did welcome the Home Office circulars on the subject. She also said that the group had commissioned some research on the issue of rape in marriage. Jo Richardson herself tried to raise awareness of the issues surrounding domestic violence, through asking a number of parliamentary questions during the late 1970s to determine the effects of the 1978 Matrimonial Proceedings and Domestic Violence Act which introduced the possibility of women obtaining injunctions to keep violent partners away from them. Jo Richardson wanted to find out whether judges were attaching powers of arrest as often as they should be, and what kind of regional variations there were in the application of the act. In 1989 she organised a seminar at the House of Commons involving representatives from the police, social services, women's groups, and the Association of London Authorities.

POLICY-MAKING AT THE NATIONAL LEVEL
As should be clear from the preceding section, the process of policy-making differed somewhat between the three separate areas of policy under consideration in this chapter. However, crucial to all three areas were the issuing of the Home Office circulars on rape and sexual assault, child abuse and domestic violence.

There were interesting comparisons between the way that the circulars came about. In the case of the rape circulars, it was in direct response to the WNC report. The Home Office was acting in a reactive way (which it was suggested was the usual mode of approach). The case of the child abuse circular was different in that the Home Office was proactive; hearing about good practice in one force the particular senior official involved in drafting the rape circular decided that the next step was to look at the way the police dealt with child abuse. Domestic violence followed on from this. One theme which was quite striking was the importance of the personal priorities of senior officials in the development of all this. Peter Hennessy (1989:343) has drawn attention to the importance of officials in developing policy generally:

> The truly skilled seekers after influence know that it can often be more
> productive to approach the man (sic) who drafted the departmental letter
> (the civil servant) rather than the man (sic) who signed it (the minister).

So there appeared to be little direct political influence from ministerial level. Senior Home Office officials did refer to an exception to this rule in the case of domestic violence. Apparently, one Home Secretary was opposed to the Home Office intervening in the way that police forces deal with domestic violence, whereas a junior minister was strongly in favour. The impression was that senior officials needed to bide their time for the political conditions to allow the development of a domestic violence circular.

The next point which stands out is the process of consultation. The importance of ACPO and the experience of the Metropolitan Police in the formulation of national guidelines was crucial. In many ways, ACPO was the 'joint author' of the circular on rape and that on child abuse. Once again the case of domestic violence was somewhat different in that there was more division within the police service about whether the Home Office should give advice in this area, and if so, what kind of advice it should give. The Home Office clearly placed ACPO as top of the list of organisations to consult, because they were responsible for delivering the response. However, as far as the second rape circular went, there was arguably less need to consult more widely than this. The draft circular was a direct response to the recommendations of the WNC report which the official responsible for the drafting viewed as inherently sensible. The WNC had included many of the interested groups to the debate.

Other national influences
Pressure groups such as women's organisations and victim support were not, it seems, consulted directly by the Home Office with regard to the details of the circular. But it could be argued that the main strength of their impact lay in the wider effects of raising awareness of problems with the current policing response through lobbying politicians and the media. The BBC Television documentary on Thames Valley police had a major impact on the public debate, and arguably led to the first circular. One senior Home Office official working in this area at the time commented that in his opinion there had been 'a long-standing concern about police treatment of rape victims going back to the television programme... I think that programme won the argument'. One national broadsheet crime correspondent confirmed this view of Graef's documentary saying: 'The single most important thing was the Thames Valley documentary'.

Pressure groups continued to press for change, and as noted earlier, Women Against Rape's publication about rape victims received wide attention. WAR also produced papers for the Law Commission. The resources of Women's Aid are primarily geared to the provision of direct help for assaulted women, and thus they were limited in their ability to campaign for change. Whilst such groups may have had relatively little impact individually, collectively they provided the basis on which national governmental and local policing policy developments could be formed. The changes in policing policy that were described above were located within a context in which increasing attention was paid to the impact of criminal victimisation on women and the role and effectiveness of the criminal justice responses to such victimisation. This increased scrutiny, it is suggested, had its roots in the re-emergence of the feminist movement in the 1970s. It is worth at this stage unpicking this observation, thus outlining more concretely the context in which the changes described took place.

It has become commonplace to observe that the role of women in British society has changed significantly since the second World War. Most often this is linked to changed or changing employment opportunities and practices. Thus, for example, although there was a slight drop in the rate of female employment after the War, by the early 1950s this position was reversed and numbers began to rise quite sharply despite a concerted ideological campaign to return women to their 'natural place' (Weeks, 1981). A booming economy and full employment, based largely on domestic consumption, increased the pressure on women to 'return to work', and by the late 1950s 40% of married women were working.

Despite such changes, employment continued to be one of the key areas of discrimination throughout the 1950s and 1960s (Department of Employment, 1974). Women were expected to be both 'wives-and-mothers – spending home-makers – *and* (part-time) working women' (Hall, 1980). There existed a highly complex maternal and domestic ideal which confined women, ideologically, to the *private* and the *personal*. Whilst relatively few advances in either the economic or political spheres occurred during the 1960s there was, however, a reorientation of traditional classifications with a declining emphasis on the domestic, and an increasing emphasis on the 'feminine' and the sexual (Newburn, 1991). Despite the relative lack of economic and political progress during this period as far as women were concerned, there was significant change in women's 'consciousness of discrimination' (Carter, 1988), a consciousness stimulated and supported by the feminist movement.

Women's protection and safety quickly formed one of the cornerstones of the emerging feminist movement, and the areas of rape, sexual assault and domestic violence were quickly politicised though, importantly, these 'issues transcended the cultural trendiness associated with the late 1960s, affected women of all social classes and ages, and were issues on which new women's groups could link up with the established and more conventional women's organisations, enlisting the sympathy of men' (Carter, 1988:69). By the mid-to-late 1970s, demonstrations by women's groups against attacks on women and portrayals of sexual violence in film and on television began to take place, and this trend was consolidated during the period in which the hunt for the 'Yorkshire Ripper' was taking place in the early 1980s.

One of the most crucial challenges that was undertaken by the women's movement was that to traditional models of the boundaries of the 'public' and the 'private', and this challenge was of particular relevance to the issue of policing. The ideology of domesticity, so prominent in the 1950s and well into the 1960s, presented 'the home' as a place of security and safety for women (Stanko, 1988), and also as an essentially private sphere largely outside the purview of the police. Prior to the campaigning undertaken by the women's movement, violence occurring in this sphere, in the main, remained largely invisible and was frequently described by police officers as either simply 'domestic' and by implication 'private', or alternatively as 'not real police work' (Hanmer *et al.,* 1989). To the extent that such campaigns have been successful, they have been successful in relocating certain forms of violence and aggression within the public sphere. A significant element, then, in unpicking the history of policing policy in relation particularly to domestic violence and child abuse, but also more generally to rape and sexual assault, concerns the progressive incorporation of these areas within the 'public', with consequent increasing pressure on the police to recognise the pervasiveness of male violence and intervene in ways which ensure women's and children's safety.

Although the priorities and decisions of senior officials in the Home Office were important in shaping policy nationally, the activities of politicians were also important, with the formation of the Ministerial Group on Women. A chair of this group, John Patten, became a strong supporter of raising the issue of domestic violence and the need for a changed police response whilst he was a junior minister at the Home Office. The Opposition was also active, through its spokesperson on women.

In the case of changing policy towards child abuse, possibly the key development was the major scandal in Cleveland, although as suggested above, the Home Office had already started to develop guidelines in this area of policy. The Home Office used the Metropolitan Police/Bexley experiment as the basis for its recommendations, thus acting – as it did more frequently in relation to crime prevention policy – as a kind of clearing house for what were perceived to be best practices. However, the external development of Cleveland meant that the Home Office circular was received with very little comment at all, in fact it was positively welcomed by the police. In the words of the senior official involved in the drafting of this circular, the Cleveland controversy 'generated the public concern which created the political will to change'.

LOCAL FORCE LEVEL

Whilst many of the key parties to the policy-making process were active at national level, there were also those who operated at the level of the local force. All police forces made some changes in policy in relation to rape and child abuse. At the time of the study, there was less activity in the area of domestic violence. However, within this there was significant difference of approach between the four forces studied, as was outlined above. For example, force B appeared to be ahead of the other forces in terms of the investigation of child abuse and the response to rape, and seemed to have begun this process independently of Home Office pressure. In fact, force B was mentioned as one of the forces whose practices informed the Home Office circular on child abuse. Although all forces moved towards the setting up of specialist units, there were substantial differences in the organisation, structure and role of these units between the forces. Whilst the Home Office circulars on rape were clearly an important impetus within the forces, there were different levels of response. For example, whilst two forces set up rape suites, two others decided that this would not be an appropriate course of action in their forces. There were more similarities in the policy changes regarding child abuse than was the case for rape and domestic violence. Perhaps this was because of the high degree of public pressure on the police following the Cleveland incidents leading to conformity. As Home Office officials made clear, there was more division within the police service as to the appropriate response to domestic violence. There is a further important point to be reiterated at this stage. Baldly put, it is that policy changes should not be conflated with changes in practice. It is clearly the case that policy statements at the top of an organisation do not necessarily reflect what is happening on the ground. This, women's groups were quick to point out, appeared to be especially so in relation to the policing of rape and domestic violence. As one spokesperson for Women's Aid talking about policy and practice said in interview, 'everything's phrased to look right on and trendy basically, but when it comes down to street level the policies are only as good as the people that are going to implement them'. The view generally from representatives from women's groups was that although some progress had undoubtedly been made, there remained a very long way to go. It is important, therefore, that discussion of changes in policy here should not necessarily be taken as proof of changes in practice.

Furthermore, changes in policy should not be assumed to have been successful in achieving the aims set out for them. One of the influences for change within forces was the fact, explained in some detail by one chief superintendent, that 'everyone wants to have a winner'. What he suggested was that there exists within forces an internal pressure to be seen to be doing something new and innovative, especially when looking for promotion. This, he argued, led to the establishment of initiatives that were never properly thought through or evaluated. Thus, in relation to domestic violence units in his force he said:

> There we have it again. It's a sexy issue with the Home Office, the Met have got a unit up and running... [the Commander] wanted to be noticed – what better than to pilot this scheme as part of the response to the force concentration on violent crime that year... [He] was promoted so it worked!.. It's not meant to sound derogatory, that's just the way the system works.

The influence of police authorities
Another player at the local force level was of course, the local police authority. Whilst the interviews with the AMA and ACC made it clear that the actual police response to such crimes was considered an operational matter, there were important resource implications for local forces in, for example, the setting up of special rape suites or examination facilities. The analysis of the police authority role within development of policy in these areas did find, overall, that at the local level it was the police themselves who took the initiative. But this is not to say that all the police authorities made no contribution.

Force A had perhaps the most compliant and supportive police authority of all the four studied. However, in terms of the quantity and quality of information it received from its chief constable, it was relatively well-served, even though it appeared from the minutes of meetings that this information was rarely requested. There were a number of reports to the police authority dating from the publication of the WNC report, and explaining that the force had set up a working party to review practice in dealing with the victims of serious sexual assault. The working group considered the feasibility of introducing special victim reception suites, eventually deciding against these for practical and resource reasons, laid down in the report to the police authority. All recommendations were accepted by the police authority. The only evidence of matters pertaining to rape being raised at police authority level was in response to a member from one of the constituent county councils on the authority, who mentioned that his council had recently passed a motion expressing concern about the level of reported rapes, and requesting the police to review their practices to make sure that victims were being treated in a satisfactory manner. Although there were significant developments in the way that child abuse was investigated within this force, there is little evidence that the police authority played an active role in this. Again, it appeared to be largely a police-driven initiative.

Force B appeared to be the most progressive force regarding new policing responses to each of rape, domestic violence and child abuse, and analysis of the police authority minutes revealed a good deal of information coming from the chief constable about developments within the force. There had been a number of important developments in this force area regarding child protection (indeed, the research within the Home Office suggested that they had influenced national policy in this respect), and more recently on domestic violence. There had been a comprehensive review of policy on dealing with sexual offences, and the force was developing two victim reception centres. The police authority in this force area appeared to be kept relatively-well informed by its chief constable, and members played an important part in the more recent developments of victim reception suites. It was police authority members who, through contact with members of the Greater Manchester Police Authority, became aware of the development of the St Mary's Centre. The police authority minutes recorded that the chief constable was asked to report back on current arrangements for dealing with victims of sexual assault, and on the implications of the St Mary's Centre. So the police authority did appear to have an important role in change in this policy area.

Force C had also introduced policy changes into the areas of rape, domestic violence and child abuse. The role of the local authority in bringing these about was rather limited. The general rule in this area was that the police authority was informed of changes after the event, and was not always fully-informed (in the view of the chair). The chair explained that the police authority tended to use its power under the 1964 Act to call for reports from the chief constable on particular areas of policing, because that was the only way of obtaining information about what was going on. However, in the area of crimes against women and children, the police authority may have had some initiating role in that the chair directly raised the issue of domestic violence with the chief constable. The chief constable's response was to propose specialist units with a remit to deal with the investigation of rape and child abuse, as well as to follow up domestic violence incidents. However, this may well have been on the chief's agenda already, given the apparent impotence of the police authority in most other areas of policy.

In force D, there was little evidence from the minutes of meetings or interviews with members, that the police authority had played a major role in developing policy in any of these three areas. There was no evidence of the reporting of developments back to the authority to the extent that was occurring in forces A and B. In fact, leading members of the police authority seemed unclear about exactly what the developments were within the force. Again, the authority appeared to broadly support all measures taken, although having said that it is difficult to find any area in which the chief constable did not receive broad support. However, while the police authority may not appear to have had a major input into any of these policy areas, in the area of domestic violence at least, the county council played an important role. The general purposes committee of the county council, along with the council women's officer, organised a conference in 1987 on the response to domestic violence. The conference received a great deal of local media coverage, and included senior representatives from a range of agencies dealing with domestic violence, including the chief constable of the police force. As a direct result of this conference, the chief issued a force order laying down guidelines for his officers, and stressing the need to treat incidents of domestic violence as serious crimes, 'potential murders' in his words. Whilst there remains debate about the degree to which these guidelines have been followed, it does provide some evidence of the local authority having some influence over change.

DEMOCRATIC INFLUENCES AND RESPONSES TO CRIMES AGAINST WOMEN AND CHILDREN

Equity

As was suggested in the introduction to this book, although many of the commentators on issues of policing policy and police accountability use the notion of democracy as the basis for many of their arguments about current practices and future prospects in this area, few of them ever make explicit what it is that they take to constitute democracy. The major exception to this is the work of Jefferson and Grimshaw (1984) in which a model of democracy is advanced at the centre of which is a commitment to equality. Thus, they suggest (1984: 155) that 'the fundamental basis of democratic political authority is the notion of equal rights'. They argue that the inputs of policing should be adjusted so that the outputs are more equal, for under the current structure, policing impinges more heavily on certain groups. Working class people, ethnic minorities and women do not receive an equal amount of policing protection and/or are subject to an unequal amount of police coercion. They also suggest that the police should prioritise offences which bear hardest on those least able to defend themselves. Indeed, they specifically argue that more resources should be put into offences such as rape because of the social impact of the offence upon women.

As outlined in Chapter 1, influencing policing policy is about affecting the decisions about priorities and methods. The police have finite resources; the setting up of a domestic violence unit (or any specialist unit) may have an impact on the organisation's ability to respond to other calls on its services. The emphasis over recent years has been on encouraging the police to place greater priority on areas like child abuse and sexual violence. To the extent, therefore, that policing (accepting again that practice has not always kept pace with policy) has changed in a direction which emphasises sympathetic treatment of victims of rape and sexual assault, of domestic violence and of child abuse, and which increases the emphasis on the arrest of spouse abusers, a degree of inequity has been overcome. In this manner an element of democratic influence has been exercised. Though the law may still in Jefferson and Grimshaw's terms be being applied unequally, the changes outlined above may nevertheless represent an equalisation of the odds. Under current conditions, the odds remain stacked against the abused woman or child who needs the protection of the legal system, though the current trends appear to be towards redressing the balance. Such trends are, however, not primarily the product of the influence of outside groups, but rather are part of and reflect a wider cultural shift in which the needs and concerns of women and children have, albeit slowly, moved progressively centre-stage.

Delivery of service

A key 'democratic' role of policing is to provide a service which protects basic freedoms in order that individuals may develop their lives. For sexually and physically abused women and children, inadequate responses on the part of the police (and the criminal justice system as a whole) have substantially affected these basic freedoms. This element therefore concentrates on the degree to which the changes in policy brought about in policing have addressed this problem, rather than how the changes came about. The main argument for facilitating the input of a variety of individuals and groups involved with this area of policy is to bring about the most effective response possible.

Doubts still remain about the effectiveness of response across all three areas of policy. For example, it is worth noting the problems with child abuse investigations in one of the force areas, and the continued concerns of women's groups in others about the degree to which police responses to rape and domestic assault have actually changed on the ground. In terms of rape and child abuse, there does appear to be strong evidence that these crimes are dealt with in a completely different way than was the case 10 or so years ago. There are clearly still problems, but the available evidence presented above provides little support for the 'no real change' argument. In relation to domestic violence the findings are less clear. Changes of policy and practice in police forces were much more limited and patchy. The changes that did occur were mostly local initiatives. Some were regarded as successful in terms on the effect of policing outputs, for example the sub-divisional initiative in force D. In others, for example the domestic violence unit in force B, the overall benefits of the initiative were as yet unproven and, indeed, it was quite forcefully suggested by one senior officer that little attention was actually ever paid to the process of evaluation. Local women's groups remained sceptical about the extent to which useful change had been managed. However, it was not within the remit of the study to carry out in-depth evaluation of policy-implementation at the local level, so the data do not provide the basis on which the effect of policy change on actual policing outputs might be assessed. Overall though, it would be difficult to argue against the proposition that developments of policing policy in these areas, particularly regarding the investigation of rape and child abuse, constitute a significant improvement in delivery of service.

Responsiveness
This refers to the idea that policing policy should, in some way, be responsive to public demand. Whilst any significant degree of *responsiveness* was difficult to detect in relation to the development of crime prevention policy, this is not the case in relation to crimes against women and children. Indeed, it is hard to imagine that policing policy would have changed in these areas either in the ways or to the extent that it did, were it not for (organised) public opinion. Thus, for example, the very issue of violence against women only properly entered the political arena because of the power of the Women's Movement. The WNC, the refuge movement, and organisations such as Rape Crisis were powerful advocates on behalf of victimised women. In relation to the treatment of rape victims, the public outcry that followed the broadcast of the 'Thames Valley' documentary ensured that the subject was placed firmly on the agenda.

It is perhaps in relation to child abuse that the impact of 'public' opinion is to be seen most clearly. The evolving scandal in Cleveland gave rise to such strength of public feeling that it was, in the opinion of many of those interviewed as part of this study, inevitable that some form of change would occur. As one official said in relation to the Home Office circular which followed Cleveland, rather than seeing it as some form of imposition the police 'saw it as a lifeboat'. There was little evidence, however, that policing policy had been particularly influenced by or had developed in response to anything said or done by local police authorities, or local consultative committees. In many cases this appeared to be the result of a lack of imagination and desire on the part of the members of these bodies rather than resistance by the local constabulary.

Distribution of power

The Home Office and ACPO were probably the key players in bringing about specific changes in a number of these areas. But the complexity of the process and the interaction of a number of different players did show some dispersal of power over the decision-making process. More general background influences included those of the media and public concern. The actions of pressure groups impinged upon this, and more directly onto the policy-makers through the report of the WNC. Whilst the contacts between women's groups and the local police organisations were rather limited, there were still some examples of input into policing policy. For this to happen of course, the police themselves needed to be open to such input. The breadth of consultation prior to the issue of Home Office circulars was less than was the case for civilianisation (see Chapter 4). However, the local authority associations clearly saw these kinds of areas as 'operational', and only within their remit in so far as they had resource implications for police authorities. This is in part no doubt the explanation for the Home Office concentrating its focus for consultation in these areas upon the police staff associations, most notably ACPO.

The effect of women's groups and some pressure groups is far from easy to describe. Thus, although it is clear that the women's movement generally had a profound impact on the social and cultural landscape within which the policy changes described here took place, individual women's groups still largely feel excluded from the process of decision-making and remain highly critical of policing responses to sexual assault and domestic violence. However, the fact is that a number of important changes did take place, and it appears that some of these changes coincide with the policy-preferences and priorities of these groups. Their contribution, individually, to the process of change was indirect, largely via *ad hoc* local contacts or inputs to bodies like the WNC. The development of policy in this area does confirm the overall impression of a system of decision-making heavily tilted towards the centre. The centre in this case is the Home

Office jointly with ACPO. At least in relation to rape and domestic violence the two organisations framed policy jointly. Once broad policy had been agreed at the national level, individual constabularies made plans to act on the recommendations relatively quickly. The policy-making model, therefore, whilst containing elements of pluralism – the Home Office responding to cultural and social pressures from a variety of groups – nevertheless remains dominated by the centre. It is important, however, not to over-simplify the complexity of the process. Thus, the balance of influences differs in each of the three areas considered here. With regard to child abuse, the Home Office, for example, took a largely proactive and steering role, whereas in relation to rape and sexual assault it was much more reactive and responsive. By contrast with both these examples, its profile remained relatively low-key in relation domestic violence, reflecting a far more resistant stance on behalf of the police, together with less insistent public pressure for change.

Information

Nationally, the quantity and quality of information about policing has increased a great deal in the last decade or so. HMIC publishes reports which include information about what forces are doing about these areas of policy, and this can be effective in encouraging change.[7] It remains limited, however, and despite occasional examples to the contrary such reports remain generally uncontested. Locally, the amount of information available about policing these kinds of crime varied between forces. Force C had by some way the least 'informed' police authority (in terms of the amount of information released by the chief constable), but in some ways the most informed in terms of acting to a clear political agenda. The next 'worst off' in terms of information was force D, whose leading members appeared unclear about the exact nature of what the force was doing in relation to rape, domestic violence and child abuse, and whose minutes recorded no discussion of these issues during the five years prior to the study. Forces A and B received a great deal of information from their respective chief constables generally, and on the areas focused upon by this chapter in particular. The difference was that while the police authority in force B specifically requested much of this information, that in force A received it almost against its will. In force A, the police and public safety committee received a good deal of information from the local police upon which it based an effective input into the formation of local policing policy, particularly in the example of domestic violence.

Redress

The notion of redress here is particularly relevant to individual incidents. To what extent is it possible to change or to reverse police policy and practice in the aftermath of incidents in which police action has been considered to be inadequate or ineffective? Could complaints about the general approach in past instances lead to changes in force policy? Furthermore, on those occasions when force policy did change, what steps were taken by the organisation to ensure that this translated to effective action on the ground?

First of all, it is important to recognise that prior to the period covered by this study, the police appear to have been particularly resistant to major changes in policy and practice in these three areas. In other words, the possibility of redress was very limited. The situation was changed by a number of major public controversies. In the area of child abuse, a number of cases in which children died as a result of abuse and where social services departments were deemed to have failed in their duty to protect the child from harm established the issue in the public mind. Following this, the problems highlighted by the Cleveland affair had significant repercussions for child protection policies in social services departments and police forces nationally. The Home Office responded quickly with a new circular and the Department of Health with the Children Act 1989. The Act represents a significant shift in the powers given to local authorities, and a significant increase in the expectations of the services local authorities and police forces should deliver to children and their families. It encourages new practices and attitudes in relation to parents, children and other family members, treating them not as passive recipients of services, but as partners who themselves have both powers and responsibilities. As was described above, at this time the police were especially nervous about the issues surrounding child protection and were particularly open to policy revision and change.

In a somewhat similar way changes in policing policy in relation to the investigation of rape and the treatment of rape victims was, in part, brought about by public pressure for redress. In particular, the public outcry that followed from the example of extremely aggressive interviewing by a Thames Valley officer of a woman who had been raped, was a key influence in having policy changed there and elsewhere. Changes in the policing of domestic violence still appear to be less extensive, but as public attention is focused on this, the chance of redress increases. First there needs to be an official acceptance that there is a problem with the traditional way of doing things. How this might be brought about it difficult to speculate on, but perhaps increased public knowledge and scrutiny of domestic violence cases involving police officers might be one avenue. In addition, there needs to be official support for a change in policy and finally there has to be effective follow-up of the change so that real changes occur at ground level. It is arguable that in terms of child abuse and sexual assault, there was evidence of change from all three levels. However, women's groups (and others), whilst welcoming changes in official policy and the recognition from senior officers that the previous approach was wrong, still felt that there had yet to be significant change at the most important level, that of the individual officer dealing with the problem.

Participation

The nature of the participation of the wider public in the changes in policy regarding rape, domestic violence and child abuse was varied, often indirect, but frequently influential. The role of the media in bringing the issue of the treatment of rape victims to the awareness of the wider public was central, and as was suggested at several points above, the women's movement in general provided the cultural climate within which it became increasingly difficult for officials in government and the police not to respond. However, at both national and local levels, this public awareness produced the pressure for something to be done, rather than led to specific changes in policy. Once again, it was frequently the personal priorities of senior Home Office officials who took it upon themselves to respond to perceived public concerns. Arguably, from time to time there is a good deal of publicity (through the media or otherwise) about some other areas of public policy to which officials choose *not* to respond. So there needed to be an added element, which was that the Home Office officials' personal priorities supported changes. The role of elected people in changes appears to have been fairly minimal. Although there was general political support for improvements in the way that the police deal with these sorts of crimes, the main initiatives came from the Home Office and the police themselves. This was certainly true in relation to rape and to the very limited policy changes attempted in relation to domestic violence, but was perhaps less true in connection with child abuse. As one Home Office official put it: 'With child abuse I think the Home Office played a major part in getting the policy established...whereas with rape I think we tagged along'.

At the local level, although there was more involvement of police authorities than some sources would suggest, it would be stretching things to say that they actively initiated policy in these areas. Their involvement usually stemmed from either their own response to, or their police force's response to Home Office circulars. In relation to domestic violence, policy change – let alone change in practice – had (by the time of the study) been slow and limited. The groundswell of opinion which underpinned change in the other two areas studied in this chapter failed to impact on policing in the same manner in connection with domestic assault. Through a variety of means, however, both sexual assault and child abuse found themselves fairly high on the agenda for change, conspicuous enough for the Home Office to feel compelled to examine current practice and to recommend new practices. Police forces also felt the need to examine their practice independently of central government scrutiny, or be aware of the necessity to respond to Home Office guidance. It is probably fair to conclude that although widespread social pressure for change existed and was (in varying degrees) successful, there was no clear mechanism of participation in bringing change about, and the main role was left for the 'experts'.

Notes

1.	See for example John Patten quoted in the *Daily Telegraph* 23.3.90

2.	For a similar argument in relation to policies adopted by the National Association of Victim Support Schemes see Rock, P. *Helping Victims of Crime* Oxford: Oxford University Press, 1990

3.	See *Community Care* December 1987.

4.	Since the research was carried out, a number of forces have sought to reform the somewhat cumbersome and over-detailed nature of standing orders. For example, one of the forces in the study is presently computerising the system, and dividing them up into legal information, broad force policy, and procedural guidance. Weekly force orders will then simply go out on the database.

5.	The position may well have changed since the fieldwork was carried out. For example, since this time force C has started a multi-agency initiative about domestic violence with input from the local university.

6.	For a full history see Rock, P. (1990) *Helping Victims of Crime* Oxford: Oxford University Press.

7.	Note for example the recent criticism of Merseyside police by HMI Geoffrey Dear for its apparent failure to respond to the domestic violence circular.

4 Civilians in the Police Service

By 1993, about 38,000 civilians were employed by the 41 provincial police forces in England and Wales. This constituted 28 per cent of the total staffing level of almost 136,000 people.[1] The expansion in employment of civilian staff in the police service has received increasing attention during the last 10 years or so. Supported by Home Office circulars, the policy of 'civilianisation' has formed an important part of the drive to improve the efficiency and effectiveness of police forces.

Although civilianisation was an important development in policing policy during the 1980s, the policy has a much longer history. The employment of civilians within police organisations dates back to the earliest days of the police service, when forces employed some civilians in ancillary and clerical posts. Recent developments have included not only the increase in absolute numbers of civilian staff, but also changes in the kinds of tasks they are employed to do. Thus, civilians are increasingly found in higher grade positions within the police organisation, and carry out tasks which were traditionally the preserve of sworn police officers. Although, the transfer of tasks from police to civilians is clearly a crucial element of civilianisation, it should be borne in mind that an expansion of civilian staff also results from increased demands on police resources. Additionally, developments in new technologies and policing methods create new functions within the police organisation. Such developments may result in increased numbers of civilians in important positions in the organisation without these positions ever having been filled by police officers. In the broader sense then, civilianisation means more than the simple transfer of police tasks to civilian staff, but more generally the increasing importance of the civilian element within the organisation.

There are also wider political and organisational implications stemming from the fact that as a consequence of civilianisation, a substantial proportion of the police service is staffed by a group with different employers, different terms and conditions, and a different occupational culture, from police officer colleagues. In exploring the policy of civilianisation, this chapter uses the definitions adopted by the Home Office in its Memorandum of Evidence presented to the House of Commons Expenditure Committee in 1977:

> 'civilian' covers anybody employed for police purposes who is not a police officer or a special constable... 'civilianisation' embodies the deployment of civilians in any capacity whether or not the work was once performed by a police officer.

Civilianisation, policing and democracy

Civilianisation was selected as an area of study first because it fulfilled the criterion that it was a policy area in which there had been substantial change over recent years. A detailed examination of the process which led to change addresses the central objective of the research. In addition, civilianisation highlights two central issues about the nature and organisation of the police. First, the employment of civilians in what were previously police posts raises the question of what the core functions of the police are; that is, what are the tasks that can only be performed by police officers? In so far as civilianisation was part of a wider government drive towards achieving better value for money in the public sector, it raises the question whether the police function is unique and distinct from that of other public services. Second, civilianisation raises questions about control of the police organisation. The increasing proportion of police staff who are directly employed by local authorities may be thought to weaken the chief constable's control of the force. At present, civilians working in the police service (outside London) are employed by the county council or police authority. Consequently, the terms and conditions of a significant group of employees within the organisation are outside the direct control of the chief constable. While many commentators say this has little practical significance,[2] it does raise the possibility of increasing influence by local authorities over policing policy. Police civilians have the right to join a trade union and take industrial action and, as is sometimes rather melodramatically argued, through this they may have the power to decide whether the police service continues to function. In both of these ways civilianisation may perhaps act as a constraint on the 'operational control' of the chief constable.

Civilianisation is also interlinked with the level of central government control over policing. As was pointed out by senior representatives of at least one force, civilianisation provides a potential source of growth in expenditure on policing outside the direct control of the Home Office. As subsequent sections establish, the only direct controls that the Home Office exerts over the expenditure of provincial police forces are over police officer establishment and capital spending. Civilian employment is not

167

something the Home Office can control directly. Analysis of some of the implications of civilianisation gives special insights into the ambiguities and complexities of the tripartite system of control for provincial police forces.

HISTORICAL DEVELOPMENT OF CIVILIANISATION
The Metropolitan Police Act 1829 recognised that the Commissioner could employ civilian clerks, which he did from the early days of the force. Furthermore, there was a 'civilian' influence in quite senior positions within the police. Loveday (1993) noted that before the 1950s there were a number of Metropolitan Police Commissioners appointed from outside the police service (Loveday, 1993). He added that most senior positions in provincial forces were given to 'civilians' – often ex-military personnel – during this period. However, lower down the police organisation it seems that the majority of civilian staff in the provincial forces were confined to clerical or ancillary posts, and it was the post-1945 period which saw the main expansion of civilian employment in the police service (see Table 1).

Table 1 shows the total numbers of civilian and police staff employed in provincial forces in England and Wales since 1955. A 1977 House of Commons expenditure committee report estimated that the number of civilians employed by provincial forces in 1945 was about 1,000 (House of Commons Expenditure Committee, 1977). Although the figures may not be directly comparable, this still suggests a rapid expansion of civilian employment after 1945, which continued up until 1975. The second half of the 1970s saw a sharp drop in police civilian employment, before the period of the 1980s, when the total number of civilians (and eventually the civilian proportion of total staff) began to expand again, this process continuing into the 1990s.

Similarly, official interest in the policy appeared well before the 1980s. An analysis of official documents and reports gives a more detailed picture of the background to the trends outlined in Table 1. One early pronouncement on civilianisation can be found in the Oaksey Committee (Oaksey, 1949) report on police pay, pensions and other aspects of police service conditions. This report recommended that 'police establishments in general should be thoroughly overhauled with a view to releasing policemen for police duty wherever possible by the employment of civilians'.[3]

The significant growth in the number of civilians employed by the police service post-1945 was noted by the Select Committee on Estimates Report of 1957-58. The Report suggested that this was partly due to the growing realisation that some tasks may be more economically performed

Table 1   Civilians and police officers employed by provincial forces in England and Wales since 1955

	1955	1960	1965	1970	1975	1980	1985	1990	1993
Civilians	7,345	9,935	13,943	21,758	26,344	26,007	27,935	34,361	38,174
Police Officers	49,211	54,616	62,243	69,927	79,752	89,316	91,173	95,883	97,473
Police staff	56,556	64,551	76,186	91,685	106,096	115,323	119,108	130,244	135,647
Civilians as % of total staff	13.0	15.4	18.3	23.7	24.8	22.6	23.5	26.4	28.1

Source: CIPFA Police Statistics

by civilians than police officers, but mainly due to the difficulty in filling police posts in the face of increasing demands on the service (House of Commons, 1957-8).

In its Interim Report of November 1960, the Royal Commission on the Police (Royal Commission on the Police, 1960) noted that progress had been made with civilianisation, but qualified this with the view that the potential number of civilian posts was limited by the need to keep a reserve of trained manpower and a number of sedentary posts for sick or injured police officers. Although the Final Report of May 1962 (Royal Commission on the Police, 1962) did not mention civilianisation, the 1964 Police Act which followed, recognised that police authorities and county councils have the legal power to employ civilians to work for the police organisation. Section 10 (1) of the Act states that police authorities or county councils may employ civilians for police purposes.

In 1965 the then Home Secretary, Roy Jenkins, set up a working party of the newly-formed Police Advisory Board (PAB) to look into the staffing shortages being experienced by the police service. Its 1967 report, *Police Manpower, Equipment and Efficiency* was the first official document to examine in some detail the issue of police civilians. It stated that there was significant room for an increased use of civilians in most police forces, and suggested a number of functions which might be carried out by civilians rather than by police officers. These suggestions were perhaps modest in relation to the functions which were later deemed suitable for civilianisation. They included school crossing patrols, duties under the Diseases of Animals Act, domestic duties, supervision and maintenance of buildings and garages, purchasing of police uniforms and stores, and physical training instruction. The report went on to list a number of slightly-more contentious areas where further progress could be made, including clerical work in connection with CID, scenes of crime, fingerprinting and photography. The report did not seek to constrain civilian employment to relatively lowly levels within the police organisation, arguing that although the tendency in the past had been to allocate the more responsible positions to police officers, the committee felt 'that civilians can develop the necessary skill and experience to carry out duties at the higher and more responsible levels, with advice as necessary from serving police officers'(Home Office, 1967). The report recognised the need for an improved career structure for police civilians and argued that this could be best provided by integration with the wider local government career structure.

The Estimates Committee examined civilian police staff in its first report for 1966-67 and noted that civilianisation had continued to progress with the encouragement of Her Majesty's Inspectorate of Constabulary (HMIC). The Committee felt, however, that in some areas civilianisation could not be taken much further. The Home Office continued to adopt the general view that police officers should not be regularly employed on tasks which did not require police powers, training or experience. But by the mid-1970s it appeared that the Home Office felt that the scope for further civilianisation was rapidly disappearing. In a series of guidelines on civilianisation prepared for the Police Advisory Board in 1975 the Home Office stated that '...most forces have now passed the point at which further substantial savings by the employment of civilian staff can be attained'. The guidelines were fairly cautious and stated that posts should be civilianised only given the availability of suitable staff and taking into account the threat of industrial action. The Home Office even began to suggest a reversal of the policy in official circulars to police forces. Home Office circulars 138/75 and 191/76 called for reductions in civilian staffing, and numbers of police civilians in provincial forces fell during the late 1970s.

A 1977 report of the Expenditure Committee (House of Commons Expenditure Committee, 1977) revealed that the Home Office was at that time giving priority to police officer recruitment. In the light of public expenditure cuts, the Home Office had suggested to police authorities that economies should be made in capital spending, goods and services, and civilian staff. The Home Office stated that restrictions in the recruitment of civilian staff were a temporary measure due to the climate of economic stringency.

During the 1980s, there were major developments in the policy of civilianisation. The Conservatives came to power in 1979 and immediately implemented the recommendation of the Edmund Davies Committee that police pay be linked to average earnings. As private sector earnings expanded over the decade, so did police pay so that by 1991 a constable was earning 41 per cent more in real terms than he or she did in 1979. Edmund-Davies, and subsequent police pay awards during the 1980s made police officers a relatively expensive commodity, and according to Loveday (1993) made further civilianisation inevitable, given the context of a government committed to a drastic reduction in public expenditure. Loveday suggested two further factors which provided an impetus to civilianisation from the 1970s onwards. First, increased levels of training and improved service conditions meant that a larger proportion of police officers' time was spent away from 'operational duties'. Second, the increased demands of paperwork and the growth of specialist units also meant that increases in police officer numbers were not reflected in the numbers available for 'operational duties'.

The rapid escalation in police expenditure resulted in the Home Office coming under increasing pressure from the Treasury to impose limits, and in 1983 it issued the circular 114, *Manpower, Effectiveness and Efficiency in the Police Service*. This signalled the extension to the police service of the government's 'Financial Management Initiative' (FMI), which sought to improve the effectiveness and efficiency of government departments by applying private sector management methods and imposing market disciplines upon them. The circular explicitly reversed the policy of the late 1970s, stating that 'the levels of civilians recommended in previous Home Office circulars are no longer relevant and should be disregarded'. In addition, it stated that the Home Secretary would not normally approve applications for police officer establishment increases in forces where police officers were filling posts 'which could properly and more economically be filled by civilians'. Civilianisation was now a necessary condition to the granting of increases to authorised establishment. A National Audit Office report found that this principle was applied in practice, and quoted the example of the West Midlands Police which was refused an establishment increase and subsequently launched an extensive civilianisation programme (National Audit Office, 1991).

The pressure for increased civilianisation was supported by independent bodies like the Audit Commission which from 1982 onwards conducted a major inspection of all aspects of the police service with a view to increasing financial efficiency. A 1983 report by the Department of Environment's Audit Inspectorate found that the average cost of employment of a civilian was about half that of a comparable officer (Department of the Environment, 1983). In 1988 an Audit Commission report commended the increased use made of civilian staff by police forces over the previous decade, and suggested further developments, in particular the setting up of civilian-staffed 'administrative support units' (ASUs) (Audit Commission, 1988a).

Home Office circular 105/88 addressed civilianisation as part of a more general staffing strategy. It required forces to inform the Home Office (through HMIC) of their medium and long-term plans for staffing. It recommended that forces review their staffing levels and deployment, and provided a checklist of tasks deemed suitable for civilianisation. It also drew attention to the need for grading structures, career development and personnel management. The circular explicitly recommended that forces develop ASUs as laid down in the Audit Commission's report. In effect, the Home Office was recognising the existence of a substantial civilian workforce within the police service which had its own identity and needs.

The end of the decade saw a slowing down of the civilianisation programme. In 1988, the Audit Commission argued that disincentives to civilianisation were caused by anomalies in the system for financing the police (Audit Commission, 1988b). Whereas the Home Office police-specific grant was paid on all police-related local authority expenditure, since 1987 the police element of the Department of the Environment Revenue Support Grant (RSG) was related only to police officer establishments. Thus, although the Home Office was encouraging the increased use of civilians, there was a financial incentive for forces to concentrate on increasing police establishments. The issue of community charge capping provided a more serious threat to the continued policy of civilianisation. In order to remain within the Department of Environment's capping criteria, a number of forces had to cut civilian strengths and some even reduced their actual police officer strengths. The policy of civilianisation cannot, therefore, be seen in isolation from the wider questions of the determination of police staffing levels, and the complex system for financing the police service. It is important to view civilianisation within the context of these wider constraints.

Central controls and the determination of police staffing levels
The Home Office has a central role to play in the determination of police officer staffing levels. Policing is a labour intensive activity, and labour costs take up by far the largest part of police expenditure. By the end of the 1980s, staffing costs were estimated to take up about 85 per cent of total police expenditure (National Audit Office, 1991). The rapid escalation in expenditure on the police service led directly to increasing concern with value for money and provided a major impetus for the policy of civilianisation. As the figures in Table 1 show, there was a steady increase in police staff over the 1980s; over the decade police officer numbers grew

by about 9 per cent. The main part of the increase in police expenditure was salary costs.

One of the main central controls over provincial police forces is the police staffing controls of the Home Office. Police authorities submit bids annually to the Home Office for increases in police officer establishment, bids which can be accepted or rejected wholly or in part. It is important to note that there is no provision for the Home Secretary to *reduce* authorised establishment of a police force. The Home Secretary has no statutory responsibility for approving the number of civilian staff, although some have detected efforts from the Home Office to increase its influence here. This was a particular concern of representatives of the Association of County Councils interviewed during the study. Police pay and conditions are negotiated in the Police Negotiating Board by representatives of police authorities, the police staff associations and the Home Office. Agreed terms are subject to the final approval of the Home Secretary. The terms and conditions of civilian staff in the police service are negotiated nationally in the local authority pay structure. The National Joint Council (NJC) for Administrative, Technical, Professional and Clerical Staff is the forum in which representatives of the trade unions and local authorities come together to negotiate terms and conditions.

When the Home Office is assessing police officer staffing bids, it takes a number of factors into account. These factors were laid out in circular 114/83 and signalled a slowing down in the rate of growth of police expenditure. The factors included the effectiveness with which existing resources were being used, whether or not a specific case had been made for the increase in posts, and whether the police authority had agreed to fund its share of additional posts. The circular 105/88 further systematised the staffing mechanism by requiring forces to inform the Home Office (via HMIC) of medium and long-term staffing plans. It reinforced the conditions for establishment increases, and recommended that forces review staffing levels and the scope for further civilianisation. If forces were to bid for additional police officers, then the precise duties and locations for additional staff had to be specified.

HMIC play a central role in advising Home Office decisions over staffing bids. HMIC gather information from each force and compare it with other forces of a similar size and character. There have been moves during recent years to standardise the kinds of information and analysis available to HMIC, as well as ways of measuring the demands upon and the performance of police forces (Weatheritt, 1993). A police staffing formula was introduced in 1989 and was used to support HMIC judgement on the relative needs of forces. This formula takes account of the size of population of a force area, the number of traffic accidents, reported crimes, and measures of social deprivation. It is important to note, however, that the formula does not totally determine the Home Office decision on police establishment bids. The aim is to identify relative over- or under-provision, which is one of the factors used by the Home Office in assessing bids.

As was outlined above, after a rapid escalation in policing expenditure during the early 1980s, the Home Office attempted to exert control over this growth through exerting control over increases in police staffing levels. However, it should again be emphasised that these controls are limited to police *officer* establishment. The number of *civilian* staff employed by a police force is entirely a matter for the police authority. If a police authority decides to fund a certain number of posts then that is the number there will be, and the Home Office must pay 51 per cent police grant to support that. In this sense, civilianisation provides an important source of potential growth in police expenditure outside the direct control of the Home Office. This is especially the case as civilianisation, under the current structure, means absolute growth in expenditure. The Home Office cannot reduce police establishments, so the number of police officer posts does not decline with the increase in civilian ones.

The system for financing the police fully reflects the ambiguities and tensions of a part-local and part-national police service. The Home Secretary pays 51 per cent specific grant on all police expenditure, and local authorities meet the remaining 49 per cent. However, this 49 per cent is not all raised by local taxation. Central government provides support to local authorities through the Department of the Environment. This is given in the form of Revenue Support Grant (RSG). The government calculates and allocates a 'standard spending assessment' (SSA) for each authority. This SSA is based on a set of indicators which are supposed to reflect the spending needs of an authority. The SSAs are calculated annually using principles which reflect the demographic, social and physical characteristics of each area. The only element relating to the police force is the authorised establishment of police officers, which leads to the anomalies outlined earlier. Taken together with the 51 per cent of Home Office grant, the RSG means that over 70 per cent of spending on policing in provincial police forces comes from central government grants.

CIVILIANISATION IN FOUR PROVINCIAL FORCES

Civilians as proportions of total staff

Table 1 presented total figures for police officers and civilians for the 41 English and Welsh provincial police forces. Table 2 shows the breakdown

Table 2 **Civilians as a percentage of total staff in four provincial police forces 1975-93**

	1975	1980	1985	1990	1993
Force A	24.4	23.1	23.3	25.8	27.6
Force B	23.2	22.5	25.3	27.1	27.6
Force C	24.9	23.3	23.8	28.8	27.1
Force D	24.3	22.0	23.6	23.5	25.5
England & Wales*	24.8	22.6	23.5	26.4	28.1

* outside London

Source: CIPFA Police Statistics

for the four forces included in the study, and compares the proportion of civilians of total staffing with the average for England and Wales.

The table shows how the development of civilianisation has varied in extent and timing between forces. In all four forces studied, the proportion of civilians fell during the late 1970s, the sharpest drop occurring in force D. Again for all four forces, the early 1980s saw an increase in the proportion of forces made up by civilians (the biggest increase being in force B). During the latter half of the 1980s, there were substantial increases in the proportion of civilians in force C, a slight increase in forces A and B, and little change in force D. During the early 1990s, forces A and D showed the largest increase in proportions of civilian staff. Force B continued to increase gradually, whereas force C showed a decrease. This general trend is based on the overall proportion of civilians within the force. However, as outlined above, the implications of civilianisation go further than the absolute numbers or proportions of civilians within the police service. Of crucial importance also are the tasks which these civilians undertake. The broad totals give a general overview of how civilianisation developed across the four forces. Information about the kinds of posts which were involved can be gathered from HMIC figures on the proportion of 'key posts' which have been civilianised in each force.

Key posts
As mentioned above, Home Office circular 105/88 included a check-list of functions which it deemed suitable for civilianisation. This was

Table 3   Percentage of key posts civilianised (1987-90)

Force	1987	1988	1989	1990
Force A	67.7	69.7	69.6	75.3
Force B	64.9	66.3	65.9	67.0
Force C	66.2	69.5	71.1	74.1
Force D	64.1	73.6	69.2	73.3
England & Wales*	64.7	67.7	69.2	72.1

*   outside London

Source: HMIC Matrix of Indicators

incorporated into the annual inspection process so that HMIC could monitor the progress of civilianisation in police forces. Since 1987, HMIC have collected statistics on the proportion of key posts which have been civilianised. The key posts include about 60 different types of policing function into which at least some police forces have introduced civilianisation. Table 3 outlines the progress of the four police forces covered by the study.

All four of the chosen forces made progress in the late 1980s towards civilianising key posts. All of the forces with the exception of force D were above the average for England and Wales, force A being the furthest advanced. By 1990, all forces had civilianised more key posts, but force B had civilianised at the slowest rate and was actually below the England and Wales average. The HMIC figures break down for each force the relevant percentage of posts in the function which are taken up by civilians. Whilst 60 posts is too many to analyse in detail here, Table 4 compares the four forces in terms of the civilianisation of 10 key functions.

This table begins to show how the analysis of totals (whether it be total number of civilians, total civilian percentage of all staff, or total percentage of key posts civilianised) hides the different approaches taken by forces. The similarities between the four forces is clear. All had comparable levels of civilianisation in the CID administration, traffic administration, control room, and research and planning functions. However, individual forces tended to stand out when the other functions are analysed. For example, all forces except force D kept the scenes of crime department about half civilianised, whereas force D had civilianised virtually all of the department. Taking enquiry or station officers, all forces bar force B had almost completely civilianised this function. Force B however had

Table 4   Percentage of key posts civilianised in given functions (1990)

	A	B	C	D
SOCOs*	50	50	51	92
CID administration	97	100	100	100
Traffic administration	100	100	100	87
Station officers	100	28	100	97
Gaolers	100	18	100	100
Control room	51	53	47	53
Driving school	50	50	33	33
Personnel	20	86	85	84
Research & planning	20	27	30	33
Computing	45	80	100	82

*   scenes of crime officers

civilianised only 28 per cent of these posts. This force took a similarly cautious line on civilian gaolers. Whereas force A took a quite radical approach towards civilianisation of the above functions, this did not extend to support functions such as personnel, research and computing. The force preferred to retain an extremely high police presence (relative to other forces) in the personnel and computing departments, and also a relatively high proportion of police officers working in research and planning. A closer analysis of key posts shows that it is difficult to generalise about a force's overall approach to civilianisation. The general picture is one of a uniformity of approach in certain functions, but very different approaches in others. The strong implication is that there is considerable further scope for civilianisation in the key posts as defined by HMIC. Additionally, the definition of 'key posts' may change, which makes it difficult to make comparisons over time.

Officers released to operational duties
A commonly-stated objective for civilianisation is that it should release police officers from administrative and other tasks not requiring police powers or training. Table 5 shows the number of police officer posts released each year since 1985 for the four police forces covered by the study.

These figures support the claims made by both forces B and D that they started releasing officers through civilianisation early. In force A, the bulk

Table 5 **Officers redeployed to operational duties because of civilianisation 1985-90**

	1985	1986	1987	1988	1989	1990
A:	0	35	0	0	6	3
B:	22	19	2	3	11	21
C:	6	1	32	23	0	0
D:	40	4	17	13	0	3

Source: Home Office Statistics quoted in Parrett (1992)

of civilianisation which released police officers took place in 1986, and although its civilian staffing levels increased substantially since that point, it appears that little of this resulted in police officers being released for operational duty. The figures also support force C's claim that the main drive to releasing officers through civilianisation occurred during 1987 and 1988.

The intra-force development of civilianisation
Overall figures may well hide a great deal about general attitudes and approaches to civilianisation. For example, a force may invest resources in relatively senior civilian posts within the organisation. This could reflect a strong commitment to role of civilians in the police service not reflected in simple comparisons of absolute numbers or proportions of civilians. This section draws upon data from interviews with senior police officers and civilian staff within the four forces and focuses on the details of their approaches to civilianisation.

The rationale for civilianisation
One theme which was addressed by the interviews was the perceptions of senior officers and civilians of the rationale behind civilianisation. All four forces gave broad support to the policy, as is clear from the figures above. All four forces appeared to see the policy first in terms of cost savings, but later claimed to be developing broader concerns about organisational effectiveness. All were suffering recruitment and retention problems among civilian staff which seemed to be strongly related to the predominance of low grades among such posts. This reinforces the view that the initial rationale behind civilianisation was financial economy. Despite this, the primary aim in civilianising still appeared to be to justify bids for increases in police officer establishment. No forces actually

replaced police officer posts with civilian posts, so civilianisation always meant real growth.

Mechanism of implementation

All forces appeared to have made efforts to approach the policy of civilianisation in an integrated and systematic way, but the method by which civilianisation was implemented differed between forces. Some forces appeared to operate a bidding system in which divisions and departments applied to headquarters for more staff and resources, and headquarters personnel and finance departments assessed these requests and took staffing decisions. This was the case in two forces – A and D. Clearly, this left some control with the divisions and sub-divisions, in that local commanders were encouraged to identify posts for civilianisation. However, when a post was civilianised, the freed-up operational time did not always go to the division or department which suggested the post, which was something of a disincentive for police managers. In both forces attempts had been made to rationalise the process, with an annual bidding cycle (rather than bids for more staff coming in *ad hoc* during the whole year) and close cooperation between personnel departments and finance and administration divisions in reviewing staffing.

The other two forces had different ways of implementing civilianisation. In force C, this was done through force staff reviews, carried out at irregular intervals by a combination of senior police officers and representatives of the county council management services unit. The late 1980s saw a change in the approach adopted by force B towards civilianisation. Senior officers explained that the civilianisation programme up until the mid-1980s had not been a systematic process, but had been approached in a rather piecemeal way. There were no force reviews of civil staff, and the effects of civilianisation were not monitored. In 1988 the force took the decision that the process of preparing the staffing bids should be formalised rather than the rushed 'knee-jerk' reaction that had been the case before. The result was that a computerised establishment system was developed, one for the regular force and one for civilian staff. Each force post was defined and recorded in the system, and updated weekly. This made it a fairly simple and immediate job to find out the exact distribution of the force's civilian and police staff at any one time. The system incorporated a staffing formula in which the independent variables were recorded crime, population and recorded incidents. This was used to determine the staffing needs of the territorial sub-divisions. Posts that were suitable for civilianisation arose from this constant 'trawling' process. Civilianisation thus became part of a wider ongoing staff review. This left little role for the local policing units in identifying posts for civilianisation or in more general staffing issues. The police inspector in charge of developing this system compared it very favourably to the bidding system which he described as 'decibel planning'.

The impetus to civilianisation

Out of the four forces, two claimed to have started the substantive drive to civilianising posts prior to the issue of Home Office circulars. For example, force B claimed to have civilianised over 100 posts prior to 1982, and in force D, the chief constable sent a memo to the police authority claiming that 'a tremendous amount of civilianisation' had occurred in the force prior to 1980. In terms of both numbers and proportions of civilians within the organisation as a whole, this is broadly supported by the figures in Table 2 (however, in terms of the kinds of posts civilianised, the figures in Table 3 suggest that by the late 1980s neither force had civilianised as extensively as the other two in terms of HMIC key posts). Prior to 1980, forces B and D had the highest proportions of civilian staff of all the forces in the study. Force D also claimed to have been the first force to use civilian scenes of crime officers (SOCOs), and pioneered the use of civilian gaolers. The source of D's early support for the policy of civilianisation appears to be the personal influence of the long-serving senior force administrative officer, who was a civilian but in a position previously filled by an assistant chief constable. He was highly respected by the senior police officers in the force, and exerted a strong personal influence over the way that policy developed.

Interviews and documents from force C suggest that the main drive to civilianisation came much later, during 1987/88 (supported by the figures in Tables 2 and 3 above). Representatives of the force said that the Home Office circular 114/83 was a key incentive to this stage of civilianisation. In force A, the impetus to civilianisation during the 1980s followed publication of the circular 114/83, which led directly to a force structure review. The findings of this review identified a number of posts for civilianisation. Following the publication of the later circular 105/88, the force introduced a regular process by which all heads of departments and territorial sub-divisions were asked to identify suitable posts for civilianisation. Table 3 shows that force A made particular progress in civilianising key posts during the late 1980s. However, the chief constable expressed strong reservations about extending civilianisation too far in certain areas recommended by HMIC. Circular 105/88 had a central effect on the mechanism of civilianisation used in force B. The new force staffing review system was developed as a direct response to the circular. The evidence set out above comparing levels of civilianisation of key posts shows how forces differed in the degree to which posts listed in the circular should be civilianised.

This shows that although Home Office circulars may have provided an important impetus to civilianisation in general, there was still room for different approaches as regards the details of policy. This is summed up by a statement from the civilian personnel officer of force A who reflected his chief constable's concern to keep police officers in some functions which other forces had totally civilianised:

> We take a more cautious view than the Home Office. They take the view that if one force civilianises a top post, and another a deputy, why shouldn't a force civilianise both? We must not blindly follow the lead that other forces have given... we're looking at *our* needs.

A similar argument was made by a senior officer in force B who said that 'we still do resist the Home Office and HMIs, what they define as key posts we won't necessarily accept are civilianisable'.

The anomalies of the grant system

The Audit Commission (1988) argued that the grant system for financing the police contained anomalies which meant there was a financial penalty for civilianisation. Funding for policing comes from both central and local government. The Home Office provides specific grants which amount to 51 per cent of all police expenditure. Revenue Support Grant (RSG) to local authorities provides a further substantial amount, leaving only about 30 per cent for local authorities to raise from the non-domestic rate and council tax. Since 1987/88, the policing element of the RSG (in England) has been related to police officer numbers rather than to indicators of need (crime levels, population density, and so on). Thus, forces which prioritised police officer establishment increases would be rewarded with a greater RSG. The extent to which this 'perverse incentive' was actually effective is not clear. Table 1 showed that civilians as a proportion of total police staff declined slightly in force D and slowed its rate of growth in force B during the latter half of the 1980s following the introduction of the 'disincentive'. However, during the year of our research, force D did not bid for any increase in police establishment and concentrated on increasing its civilian staff, which suggests that the disincentive to civilianisation was not strong. In the other two forces, civilians as a proportion of total staff grew significantly during the second half of the 1980s. However, the disincentive effect of the grant system was acknowledged as a real constraint on civilianisation by senior staff in two forces: 'The other thing which works against civilianisation is that your Standard Spending Assessment is based on your establishment,

181

ignoring civilians. So you're penalised for civilianisation' (chief finance officer, force B)

In force C, the finance officer also outlined the disincentive effects of the grant system, but added that the greatest obstacle to continued civilianisation was seen as the general financial position of the relevant county council. Although the chief finance officers of forces B and C explicitly referred to the disincentive effect of the SSA, more general central government controls were seen as a greater threat to civilianisation:

> You must bear in mind that the Metropolitan forces were rate-capped for three years after the abolition of the Metropolitan Counties, which artificially kept our growth down. But when that came off in 1989/90 the members had more freedom to put more money into repairing buildings, and quite drastically increase the civilianisation programme (finance officer, force B).

At the time of the research, the Metropolitan forces were all facing charge capping, and it was this (in combination with the anomalies within the method of calculating the RSG) which was threatening the continuation of the programme of civilianisation.[4]

Proposals set out in the current Police and Magistrates' Courts Bill would reform the system of financing the police and remove this disincentive effect. The major change would be that the Home Secretary would no longer control the number of police officers in each force, something which would in future be decided by the chief constable and police authority. This would give them greater freedom of choice over how to divide expenditure on police officers, civilian staff, vehicles, plant, equipment and computers.

Personnel management

Home Office circular 105/88 encouraged forces to 'foster the career development of civilian staff and other aspects of their personnel management'. The research found that all four forces had a personnel department for civilian staff headed by a civilian. All these departments had developed during the 1980s. One force (force A) had just appointed a full-time training officer to develop training for civilian staff. All forces had a senior civilian in charge of administration and finance, although the influence of this position varied between forces. In only one force was there a civilian who was a member of the command team. This was the long-serving and highly-respected person in force D who was equivalent to an ACC. In his capacity as force administrative officer he was a member of the force policy team. None of the other forces had a civilian post at ACC level. When the idea of creating a similar post in force A had been raised the chief constable opposed the idea because it would reduce 'operational flexibility' and would reduce opportunities for career development for police officers. This force also insisted that the position of force computer officer remain a police post, despite opposition from the civilian personnel department. However, after the research had been completed in force A, the chief superintendent (administration) post was civilianised creating the most senior civilian post in the force. Force B had a senior civilian as force finance and administration officer, but he was not a member of the chief constable's command team. In fact, this officer made clear his frustration at being excluded from the command team on the grounds of his being a civilian:

> Senior officers – the chief, deputy and ACCs meet fairly regularly. There is no written agenda that senior (civilian) officers like me get to see. We don't know which items they will discuss. We are never asked to attend, and the only way we find out about decisions on policy is if the ACC tells us.

Whilst all forces underlined the need to develop career structures for civilian staff, it appeared that progress towards this was slow. Only two forces had taken active steps towards the development of a career structure for its civilian staff. In one of the forces the personnel officer said that it was difficult to create a career structure for police civilians in isolation from the wider local authority structure, and saw integration into this as the likely development. On the other hand, the chief constable of force A supported the development of a national organisation for police civilians (outside local government), with training and promotion opportunities to be developed within this structure.

The threat of industrial action

Police officers do not have the right to take strike action or join a trade union. This was identified by the Sheehy Inquiry as one of the distinguishing characteristics of the police compared with other public services. One argument which has been used to oppose civilianisation is that civilians retain the right to take industrial action. The argument is that further civilianisation may place a key emergency service at the mercy of union action. Senior officers in two out of the four police forces (force A and B) did not appear to see this as a real threat, and pointed to the example of the national NALGO action in 1989. This had little substantive effect upon the running of their forces. One force however (force C) reported that the dispute had real effects on the operational running of the force, with civilian SOCOs and communications staff coming out on strike in answer to the union call. In this force a number of senior police officers stated that the threat of industrial action was a barrier to further civilianisation within the force. Although the force administration officer in force D reported that industrial action had exerted a negligible effect on the force, he saw the issue one which would constrain further civilianisation. He said that the threat of strike action was 'the one main barrier to further civilianisation'.

Home Office circular 105/88 recommended that chief constables develop contingency plans to keep key areas running in the event of industrial action. Two of the key areas most often mentioned in this context are SOCOs and control/communications room staff. In the case of the latter, all four forces retained a 50:50 split between police and civilian staff. The same was true for most forces in relation to the SOCO function, except for force D which had an almost totally civilianised SOCO department. Representatives of NALGO highlighted the findings of the Operational Policing Review to support their claim that the threat of strike action had been exaggerated. This found only a small number of chief constables who had considered the danger serious enough to actually make contingency plans, as recommended in the circular.

Administrative Support Units (ASUs)
The Audit Commission (1988) and Home Office circular 105/88 both suggested that one particularly effective form of civilianisation was the development of ASUs. These are centralised units, specialised in dealing with administrative tasks such as file preparation and other paperwork. Two forces had developed specific forms of ASU. In one force (force A), the ASUs were introduced following a pilot scheme in 1986. At the time of the research there were separate crime process units (mainly dealing with CID support) and uniform process units (dealing with non-crime matters such as minor traffic items, document checking, and accident witness statements). In the other force with ASUs (force B), the development of such units was seen as quite distinct from the force policy of civilianisation. However, it was recognised that ASUs would potentially provide an opportunity for further civilianisation in the future. The main rationale was to develop specialised units to improve the quality and the speed with which files were prepared for the Crown Prosecution Service (CPS). They also provided a central point of contact for the local CPS should a particular case need to be discussed, or general prosecution policy changed. So although ASUs may often be discussed in the context of civilianisation, in this force (force B) these units were almost entirely staffed by police officers. In both forces with ASUs, local representatives of the CPS were strongly supportive of their development, and reported an improvement in the

quality of process files, and in communications. However, the CPS appears to have had no direct influence on the decision to implement ASUs, or in way that they were organised.

In force D the file processing system for the whole force was centralised. The force had spent some years moving away from divisional administrative file process support, and developing a large 'administration of justice' department in the force headquarters. Following the research in force D, it emerged that the force had decided to review policy in this area with a view to devolving the function to divisional or sub-divisional level. In the other force, force C, there was pressure for ASUs which had so far been resisted by a senior management who were not disposed towards specialist units of any kind. On one sub-division, there was an experiment in centralising support for CID officers with the creation of the post of CID office manager.

Officers in all forces were aware that the notion of ASUs was popular with the Home Office and HMIC. In fact, in force B, a senior officer expressed frustration with the process by which the force had adopted the concept, without (in his view) the necessary planning and research. This contention was supported by the fact that the force first invested a good deal of time and effort on setting up sub-divisional ASUs (concentrating on court files process), but then switched to the development of larger multi-purpose units at the divisional level.

Employing authority and control of civilians

The current Police and Magistrates' Courts Bill includes a provision that all civilians working in the police service should become employees of the police authority. In two forces covered in this study, it was already the case that the employer of police civilians was the police authority (in the metropolitan and combined police authorities). In the two single county police forces the employer of civilian staff was the county council. In three of the forces, both senior officers and civilians argued that because the chief constable, under the Police Act 1964, directs and controls his force (including the civilian component), the question of which is the official employing authority was not significant. However, in force C, senior officers stressed that a lack of management control resulted from the employment of a larger group of people whose terms and conditions are not directly managed by the police. An ACC further suggested that there was a danger that employees of the county council may be used by the police authority to exert a 'political' influence over policing policy. There was no evidence of this happening, but such views perhaps reflected the difficult relationship between senior police officers and the police authority in the area.

The findings provide evidence that being the employing authority for police civilians may provide an important source of influence for the local authority or police authority. There was evidence of a number of conflicts over the appropriate grading of civilian posts, not just between police authority and chief constable, but within forces (between chief constable and his own civilian personnel officers). The influence of the police authority in this regard is illustrated by the following quote from the personnel officer in force B:

> We analyse and produce our report which obviously recommends a salary grade. But we've not only got to convince the police authority, but also the personnel adviser to the police authority that the grade is correct... We are employed by the ------- police authority, we being civilians, not the operational side. So our paymaster and our bosses are the elected members on the police authority. But for practical purposes we are employed by the ------- Police which is of course headed by the chief constable. So to some extent we've got two bosses... it's a different matter for police officers; they are employed by the chief constable and the ------- police authority has got little control over operational matters on the police side. But on grading structures and so on, of civilians, they can and sometimes do oppose what the chief constable himself would think... Not everything goes to the police authority, but everything with financial implications must go to the police authority to get their support. No matter what the view of the chief constable is, if they don't agree with those policies then they are not adopted. He can shout until he is blue in the face, but they are not adopted.

The personnel officer went on to recount how the appointment of the force's chief finance officer became a matter of conflict between the police authority and chief constable. The chief constable wanted the post to have a high grade, a grade which the advisers to the police authority considered too high. The chief threatened to put a superintendent into the post if he was not allowed to recruit a civilian at that grade, and the police authority backed down. Although the police authority lost out on this occasion, a number of sources claimed that police authority influence had kept the grades of civilians in the force very low until relatively recently (illustrating that it viewed civilianisation primarily in terms of cost savings rather than the need to match skills to jobs or continuity in certain posts).

A similar example of conflict over grading, although with a different outcome, came from force C. This also concerned the grading of the chief finance officer. On this occasion, the police authority wanted the post to be given a higher grade and the chief opposed this. The view of the police authority prevailed:

I don't know whether you know that there was a dispute over my post.
The chief wasn't happy with the post being paid at the grade it was.
Members insisted that it was. (Director of Finance and Administration)

The study uncovered no evidence of any overt conflict between police authorities and chief constables over the grading of civilians in forces A or D. However, it remained clear that the local authority influence was important. For example, in force A, one of the county councils covered by the force was carrying out a job evaluation exercise on the civilian staff side, for the police authority. In force D, the civilian personnel officer felt that the emphasis on equal opportunities in civilian employment was a direct result of county council policies. He felt that more resources were put into equal opportunities because of county council pressure than would otherwise have been the case. The force administrative officer explained how the staffing part of the budget plans were negotiated with the police authority over a period of time. He added that 'the county council could object to certain points or reappraise their resource proposals for the later years; so there must be a healthy dialogue with the people who provide the resources'.

There was an interesting example of conflict between senior officers and senior civilian staff within one force over the grading of civilians. The personnel officer explained that he was having an ongoing argument with a chief superintendent head of department over the grading of a civilian post within that department. The attitude of this police officer was causing him considerable annoyance, and said he was tired of senior police officers interfering in things they knew 'f--- all about!'. He later went on to describe how some police officers put recommendations directly to the command block to avoid the influence of the civilian personnel department. As the decision was often taken before he could do anything about it, this strategy appeared to work.

The consequence of this discussion is to undermine the simplistic assumption that for all practical purposes civilian staff are under the control of the chief constable. Furthermore, it would also be inaccurate to think of the management of such staff as a means by which local authorities effect 'political' control over policing policy. Although civilian employment was not used as a way of extending local authority influence over policing policy generally, there were still important aspects of civilian employment which lay outside the control of the chief constable.

INFLUENCES OVER POLICY CHANGE
As outlined in an earlier section, the policy of civilianisation in the police service has a long history. It is also a complex history and, as a senior police

officer from one of the forces covered by the study said, investigating from where policy initiatives come is like 'tracing the sources of the Nile'. He meant that the development of policy is determined by variety of influences, some of them consciously exerted by key actors in the policy-making process, and others the product of wider developments outside the control of such actors. It is often difficult to establish how and why some changes in policy came about.

However, the previous sections suggest that a number of influences were important in the development of civilianisation policy. For example, the approach adopted by the Home Office has clearly been crucial. This was particularly the case during the 1980s, when Home Office circulars began directly to address civilianisation. This was, of course, part of a wider government approach to encourage 'value-for-money' measures in the police service, and in public services as a whole. The discussion also shows that individual police forces, and to differing extents their police authorities, also had an input into the development of the policy. This remains, however, a rather broad picture of the process by which policy change occurred.

A comparison of stated policy preferences with actual outcomes (in terms of what happened within the police forces) would broadly support the notion of Home Office primacy within the policy-making process. The Home Office wanted forces to pursue the policy of civilianisation, and to differing degrees the forces studied complied with its wishes. But a number of different parties influenced, or tried to influence, the way that the policy developed. These included the relevant Home Office divisions and HMIC, the local authority associations, the Audit Commission and National Audit Office, the police staff associations and main trade union (then) representing police civilian staff, the National and Local Government Officers union (NALGO).

The information about the inputs to the policy process comes from two main sources. First, from a number of semi-structured interviews carried out within the organisations listed above (with the exceptions of ACPO, HMIC and the National Audit Office). Second, analysis of a number of documentary sources, including parliamentary reports, academic papers, articles, reports of studies carried out by some of the above organisations, police authority minutes and reports, and the internal files of the local authority associations.

The Home Office
It is perhaps unsurprising that the Home Office played a crucial role in the promotion of civilianisation as a policy. Of course, the Home Office has over the years adopted a fairly consistent position of upholding the general

principle that police officers should not be employed on work which does not require their skills or training. However, prior to the 1980s this took the form of general statements of support for the principle rather than active encouragement of forces to civilianise. It was during the 1980s that the Home Office began to take specific action to encourage police forces to pursue the policy.

The Home Office is not of course a monolithic organisation, but is made up of a number of different divisions and departments. The relevant divisions to the development of civilianisation policy were F1 division (which deals with police staffing and the provincial forces), F9 division (dealing with the Metropolitan Police, but with a special interest in value for money in the police service as a whole), and the Police Requirements Support Unit (PRSU).[5] It appears that F1 division took the lead in developing the Home Office circulars that promoted civilianisation (as both were signed by the then head of F1 division). F9 division liaised closely with F1 about developing value for money initiatives generally, of which civilianisation, and more particularly, the introduction of ASUs were considered an important part. PRSU was particularly concerned with the development of ASUs. It participated in an influential experimental ASU in the West Midlands police force, and also produced a wide range of practical suggestions to help forces reduce the administrative burden on operational officers.

As outlined earlier, circular 114/83 extended the government's financial management initiative to the police service. Although it covered much wider ground than civilianisation, it nevertheless signalled an important shift in emphasis in policy on civilianisation. The circular stated that 'the levels of civilians recommended in previous Home Office circulars are no longer relevant and should be disregarded'. Of course, the Home Office had given broad support to the notion of civilianisation since 1945. What was new about the approach encapsulated in 114/83 was that civilians were no longer seen as shoring up the gaps in the police service caused by failure to recruit enough police officers. Rather, 'civilians were now perceived as an economic means of satisfying ever escalating demands for police services' (Parrett, 1992:88).

As was the case in the other policy areas studied, Home Office circulars concerning civilianisation did not simply appear as edicts from central government. There was, behind the scenes, a process of consultation for both 114/83 and the later 105/88, with interested parties to the debate. Circular 114/83 arose from a narrower process of consultation than did the later civilianisation circular. The shape of the circular was determined in the Tripartite Forum, which includes representatives of the Home Office,

ACPO, and the local authority associations. The later circular, 105/88, appeared after consultation through the Police Advisory Board(PAB),[6] which also includes the Superintendents' Association and the Police Federation. The senior official in F1 interviewed could not remember exactly why the process of consultation had been different for the two circulars. In retrospect, he felt it was probably a mistake not to have included all the police staff associations in discussions about the earlier circular. However, he noted that their inclusion in the consultation process for the later circular had done little to make them happy with the outcome on that occasion.

There was more detailed information available concerning the appearance of the later civilianisation circular. This appears to have been initiated by Home Office officials wishing to systematise and build upon the approach laid down by 114/83; this was certainly the impression given by the senior F1 official. There appears to have been a two-part process through which the Home Office consulted about the contents of the circular. First, officials in F1 division (in consultation with F9), put together a draft circular, together with the checklist of key posts. This was then sent out to the member organisations on the PAB with formal requests for written comments. The draft was also the subject of discussions within the PAB standing committee meetings. There appear to have been a number of objections to the first draft, not least from the local authority associations (see below), and the Home Office withdrew it, and began the process again with a new draft which had been altered to meet some of these objections.

Although the Home Office circulars clearly played a pivotal role in developing the policy of civilianisation during the 1980s, it is important to remember that this was part of a wider shift in government policy. The FMI was a general attempt to improve efficiency and effectiveness in the public services and government departments, and the development of civilianisation (along with performance indicators, a strengthened inspection process, standardisation of information, etc.) must be seen as part of this drive. It is interesting, in that context, that the most powerful of government departments, the Treasury, also played a role. In his evidence to the Public Accounts Committee (1 May 1991), Sir Clive Whitmore (Permanent Under-Secretary at the Home Office) made this clear when referring to a joint Home Office/Treasury study on police staffing:

> ...the provenance of this study was – going back a bit – an initiative that I took in 1988 shortly after coming to the Home Office when I discovered, rather to my surprise, that police manpower planning did not extend much beyond the current year... It seemed to me we wanted to move to at least a three year rolling programme which matched the public expenditure survey. The Treasury, when we put this to them, while

> feeling that in principle this was a sensible way of proceeding, were not
> prepared to give it the go-ahead because, understandably, they felt that
> we had not yet got in place measures for assessing the use which the
> police were making of their resources in which they could have
> confidence. It was that which led to this particular study which we and
> the Treasury did jointly... (House of Commons Committee of Public
> Accounts, 1991)

Two interesting points arise from this statement. First, how important
the official's own views and priorities were in developing policy. Second,
civilianisation was just one part of a broader concern with efficiency and
effectiveness within public services which in turn sprang from the high
priority given to the control of public expenditure. Clearly, the Treasury
was both a crucial influence on this broader policy, and also made particular
inputs into its application to the police service.

The influence exerted by the Home Office, whilst strong, was indirect.
Officials in both F1 and F9 divisions repeatedly emphasised the limits to
Home Office powers regarding the process of civilianisation. The only
direct controls available to the Home Office under the current arrangements
are over police establishment increases, and capital spending. As outlined
above, it was by relating police officer establishment bids to civilianisation
that the Home Office attempted to persuade forces to civilianise posts.

Her Majesty's Inspectorate of Constabulary (HMIC)

Her Majesty's Inspectorate of Constabulary played a crucial role in keeping
up the pressure on forces to civilianise. In particular, they have kept
statistics comparing the rate at which similar police forces have civilianised
'key posts', and were able to ask questions of forces which resisted Home
Office guidance. The ultimate sanction available to HMIC is to fail to certify
a force efficient for the purposes of receiving police grant. Although this
has for many years been regarded as something of an empty threat, this
changed in 1992 when HMIC refused to certify the Derbyshire police force
efficient for police grant purposes.

There is no documentary evidence about how HMIC contributed to
change during the 1980s, but a number of senior officers in the forces
covered by the study, talked about 'pressure' from HMIC to civilianise
particular posts. Senior officers in forces A and B made it clear that they
had not always yielded to HMIC pressure to civilianise particular posts.
Earlier analysis showed how these two forces retained high proportions of
police officers in some functions where other forces had civilianised much
more extensively. Since 1990, the annual inspection reports of HMIC have
been published, and these contain some information about how HMIC have
tried to keep up the pressure to civilianise. The 1991 reports contain a

number of references to civilianisation, although mostly these are framed in very general terms. For example, in the report on force A HMIC commended the force on the progress made but recommended that the force prioritise civilianisation in posts which will release operational time. It noted that a 'nil cost' civilianisation was recommended by the HMI to the chief and police authority (which means that extra police are not recruited). The report on force B noted that the percentage of key posts civilianised in the force was below the national average and noted that there was room for expansion of the programme in the communications, scientific support and general office duties. In force C, the HMIC report commended the progress that had been made so far and urged the reinstatement of the civilianisation programme (which had been suspended due to budgetary restrictions on the council). Force D was praised for its decision not to apply for an increase in police establishment that year and to concentrate on civilianisation. Although these were rather general comments, taken along with the comments of senior police officers and civilians within the forces visited, they show how HMIC was able to keep up the pressure to civilianise posts.

The local authority associations

Both the Association of County Councils (ACC) and the Association of Metropolitan Authorities (AMA) take a close interest in policing matters. As outlined above, representatives from these bodies sit on the Tripartite Forum out of which came circular 114/83, and are consulted on other draft circulars in which the Home Office judges they have an interest. Both the ACC and the AMA have a police committee, which consists of members from police authorities in England and Wales, and has advisers from all local authority disciplines. The committees liaise with other ACC/AMA committees, and report quarterly to the full association.

Both associations have generally supported the policy of civilianisation, and it appears that they had an important influence upon the way that the policy developed during the 1980s. Representatives of both the AMA and the ACC felt that they had exerted a strong influence over the development of circular 114/83. A senior representative of the AMA said that the Association had had 'a great deal of influence over that circular'. He added that whilst the Home Office do not always send the AMA draft circulars for formal comment, it was only very occasionally that they were not consulted when they felt they should have been. AMA officials did not feel that the amount of consultation by the Home Office had declined over the 1980s, and quoted an example of a more recent draft circular on football charges, saying 'the football charges draft circular was fairly precise and specific and we didn't like it, so a year later it hasn't come out yet – so we do have some influence!'.

The internal files of the ACC suggested that both the local authority associations had managed to influence the development of the civilianisation policy. Files from 1975 onwards were examined, and they contained a number of references to consultation by the Home Office prior to the issue of circulars. For example, in March 1979 the ACC received a draft circular on police expenditure from the Home Office with a request for detailed comments. An internal ACC memo of the same time records how the ACC and AMA made clear their displeasure at the way that the Home Office tried to prescribe levels of civilians before 1977. This, according to the memo, was taken on board by the Home Office, which produced a revised circular.

In December 1987 the ACC received the draft circular on civilians in the police service (which became 105/88), sent by F1 division to a number of organisations for comments. Drafts were also sent to representatives of the AMA, ACPO, Police Federation, Superintendents Association, NALGO, and the Department of Environment. The ACC circulated this draft amongst its member police authorities and also invited comments from chief constables. A number of replies were on file, from chief constables and county councils. In general, chief constables tended to support the draft, but most of the county councils that replied expressed reservations. In February 1988 the ACC wrote to the Home Office expressing concern about a number of points in the draft circular and requesting that the issue be deferred until Home Office representatives had met with ACC advisers. The Home Office agreed to this and met with the advisers to discuss the reservations about the draft. The outcome was that the draft was withdrawn completely, and the Home Office agreed to submit a new draft in due course.

In the summer of 1988, the local authority associations held a joint seminar to discuss the issue of civilianisation in the police service. When the circular 105/88 came out in its final form, an internal ACC memo recorded that the final document was 'much more acceptable', partly as a result of the deliberations of the seminar. This suggests that the Home Office was willing to consult over circulars and respond to suggestions. Interestingly, the personal perceptions of some senior representatives of the ACC did not conform with the general impression given by the files. One official referred to a drastic reduction in both the quantity and quality of Home Office consultation during recent years, and referred to the Home Office as the most 'militantly centralist' of all government departments. Fears were raised that the Home Office was planning to involve itself more closely in matters concerning police civilians, including the monitoring of sickness rates and matters of training and qualifications.

The Association of Chief Police Officers (ACPO)

ACPO represents all police officers in England and Wales above the rank of chief superintendent. ACPO have published a number of reports into civilianisation, and there are a number of references to the position which they have adopted in the ACC internal files which were referred to above. In recent years ACPO has played an increasingly important role in the formulation of national policing policy generally. The secretariat, funded from the common police services budget, has been strengthened, and there is a policy analysis unit and a public relations officer. The chief constable of one of the forces covered in the study (force A) was a past president of ACPO. He said in interview that he had tried to strengthen the policy-making power of the organisation by introducing the doctrine of cabinet responsibility. This meant that if an individual chief officer wished to dissent from official ACPO policy they would have a duty to come before council and explain their reasons. He saw advantages in local control, but stressed the need for ACPO to produce coherent national policy.

ACPO's position on civilianisation has changed over the years. Before the 1980s there is evidence that chief constables took a cautious view of the employment of civilians in their forces. The ACC files revealed correspondence from September 1976 in which the chief of a county force expressed concern that 'key personnel' in the service were outside the direct authority of the chief constable. The letter called for more integration of the civilian element into the police service, with career development independent of local authority structures. This caution was mirrored in 1977 by an ACPO report on trade union recognition, which expressed concern about departments becoming operationally dependent on civilians, given the danger of industrial action. Minutes of the PAB meeting of October 1978 recorded that ACPO had presented a report on civilians in the police service, which had argued for the development of a national police civilian service, outside the control of local authorities. The minutes noted that 'in general, it was agreed that there was scope only for piecemeal and not substantial civilianisation in the future'.

However, during the 1980s ACPO effectively abandoned its opposition to the policy of civilianisation. An ACPO report in 1988 recognised the importance of the civilian element in the police service, and noted that chief officers had striven to follow Home Office guidance on this matter. The report noted the conflicting pressures coming from central government on the policy, with Home Office and HMIC pressure upon chiefs to press on with civilianisation, but restrictions on local authority spending, and disincentives inherent in the RSG, working against civilianisation.

As noted above, ACPO was represented on the Tripartite Forum which was responsible for the development of circular 114/83. The senior representative of F1 division explained that this was such a far-reaching circular, that the main discussions over it took place in the 'essentially management forum of the tripartite working party'. ACPO was, of course, also represented on the PAB which formed the forum of consultation for circular 105/88. There was no direct evidence available about the kinds of pressures which ACPO brought to bear on the shape of either of the civilianisation circulars. However, it would be very surprising if this was insignificant. However, looking at the outcomes of policy, it does seem that ACPO gave ground on a number of issues. For example, it has consistently expressed cautionary views on the issue of control, and trade union recognition, and pressed for a national police civilian service. These are all referred to, but only in a very general way, by the circular 105/88, which merely said that chief officers and police authorities should give these matters attention.

The Police Federation

The Police Federation is the staff association which represents police officers below the rank of superintendent. Not surprisingly, the Federation has generally opposed the development of civilianisation in the police service. Although the Federation claims that its attitude to civilianisation has changed over time, it has consistently expressed cautious views on the subject, arguing at several stages during the development of the policy that it should go no further. For example, in July 1981 the Federation submitted a paper to the PAB which expressed concern at the growth in the civilian element in the police service, given the climate of industrial militancy at the time. The paper stressed that no civilian should be employed on duties including supervision of police officers. The paper recommended no further growth in civilian employment, and also a gradual reversal of the policy so that some duties such as SOCOs would revert to being filled only by police officers. The fact that this was just before the Home Office issued the circulars 114/83 and 105/88 underlines the extent to which the Federation lost the battle. Their position is, of course, hardly surprising. It is the job of the Federation to represent and promote the interests of police officers, and civilianisation was perceived as a real threat to these interests. Whittaker (1982) argued that the opposition to civilianisation was due to the fact that civilians could undercut police officers in many functions. Civilianisation provides a potentially far cheaper way of executing some tasks within the police organisation. It also limits the career structure of police officers and reduces the number of sedentary posts for sick or injured officers. The Federation maintains that its position is based on the need to protect the quality of service as well as the interests of officers. It argues that civilianisation can undermine 'operational effectiveness'; for example, a control room operator with police experience will be able to make a more effective assessment than a civilian of the appropriate response to a reported incident. The Federation fears that police forces are in danger of becoming a 'rump service'. This means that the only police posts left would be those involving confrontation with the public, with major implications for the legitimacy of the police service as a whole.

A representative of the Audit Commission felt strongly that Police Federation opposition to civilianisation had been exacerbated by the terms of the debate over the policy. It had been presented purely as a method of cost-cutting rather than a method of improving organisational effectiveness and reducing administrative burdens on operational officers. It is interesting that the Police Federation was *not* one of the parties consulted prior to the issue of the circular 114/83, although this circular had considerable implications for the work of those officers it represented. This point was stressed by a senior representative of the Federation who was understandably concerned by this aspect: 'It was a very wide-ranging circular and we were not consulted about any of it. We immediately wrote to the Home Office to complain, especially after we had bitten the bullet and accepted that in the 1980s some civilianisation would be necessary'.

As mentioned above, a senior Home Office official admitted, with hindsight, the failure to consult the Police Federation had been a mistake. The later circular 105/88 was developed through consultation with the wider range of bodies on the PAB, including the Police Federation. However, as the official himself noted, this did not make it more popular with the Federation. The Federation representative accepted that there was more opportunity for them to comment in that they received a draft of the circular and a request for their views. They submitted a number of objections, mainly to particular posts which were recommended for civilianisation. However, these representations had little effect, and none of these recommendations were followed when the circular was finalised. In fact, the Police Federation's representative said that the final version, from the Federation's viewpoint, was even worse than the draft. He was extremely doubtful about the worth of the consultation exercise:

> In relation to 105/88 we made a number of what we thought were valid points which seem almost to have been brushed aside. You begin to wonder whether the consultation has any value, or whether it is a

cosmetic exercise in that they have to ask but don't have to take on board any of the points made. One would expect at least some of the points you make would be taken on board.

Despite the fact that the Police Federation's natural opponents in the debate over civilianisation were the civilian trade unions, it seemed that NALGO and the Federation maintained cordial relations. The two organisations had a number of formal and informal contacts, and relationships were described by a senior NALGO official as 'cordial and extremely frank'. Of course, the two shared some common interests. For example, representatives of both organisations expressed strong opposition to perceived government plans to privatise certain policing functions altogether. In the long run, NALGO's success in promoting improved wages and conditions for its police members strengthens the Federation argument that civilianisation does not lead to major cost savings. There has even been a suggestion from within the Federation that the civilian element of the police service could be incorporated into its ranks. Although senior Federation representatives remained opposed to this, they recognised the implications such a move would have for the overall influence of their organisation. In the words of the Police Federation deputy secretary at the time of the research; 'it could make the Police Federation a very powerful body; it currently represents about 125,000 police officers, add civilians establishments to that and you would have a staff association that would rival NALGO and the TGWU'.

The National and Local Government Officers' union (NALGO)

Before its merger with health unions to form UNISON in 1993, NALGO was the union with the highest membership amongst police civilians, and by 1991 had an estimated 25,000 members in British police forces. In general terms, NALGO's position was one of support for civilianisation for two main reasons. First, that it provided for a more effective use of staffing resources in the police service. Second, in the sense of its own organisational interests, the policy clearly expanded the potential membership base and influence of NALGO. The internal structures for dealing with police-related issues were as follows. Under the national and local government committee which covered all local government matters, there was a national police advisory panel which advised on service conditions for police civilians. There were fourteen district police panels (with one representative from each police branch in the district) who nominated representatives to this panel. Police NALGO branches fell into two categories; 'proper' police branches that consisted only of police civilian members, and branches that formed part of a wider local government branch. The latter generally occurred where there was a single county police authority, although NALGO was encouraging the trend toward more separate police branches. Representatives outlined the need to deal with police civilian matters separately from those concerning other local government employees.

An important part of NALGO's influence over policy concerning police civilians was through its negotiating position on pay and conditions. The pay and conditions of civilian employees in the police service are negotiated nationally in the National Joint Council (NJC) for Administrative, Technical, Professional and Clerical Staff. The local authority associations form the employers side of this body. During the 1980s, NALGO pressured for matters concerning police civilian employees to be seen as distinct from those of the wider local authority workforce. This was strongly opposed by the employers' side. An ACC memo of June 1980 expressed strong opposition to a NALGO suggestion that white collar staff employed by police authorities should have a separate negotiating body outside the NJC. This subject occasionally surfaced in subsequent years, with a strong memo from the NJC in 1987 to the PAB stressing that matters of police civilian pay and gradings are matters for the NJC and individual authorities only.

In 1987, the NJC decided to set up a special advisory sub-committee dealing with the special interests of police civilians. This was supported strongly by NALGO. The local authority associations appeared to have mixed views on this development. They remained fearful of any link between civilian and police pay, because of the huge cost implications for them as employers. The AMA made this explicit with a letter to the NJC in 1987 expressing concern that the specialist sub-committee should not become a negotiating forum, and should not develop links with the PNB. However, minutes of an NJC meeting in 1988 explained that an important part of the employers' acceptance of a specialist sub-committee was to enable more effective resistance to Home Office interference in matters concerning police civilians:

> The employers' decision was taken against a background of concern that increasing Home Office interest in civilianisation would lead to central government and sectional police service influences growing over issues affecting numbers, gradings and conditions of police civilians, to the detriment of the role of police authorities and of the national council.

As well as influencing policy through its role in collective bargaining, NALGO was one of the bodies consulted by the Home Office about draft circulars. Interviews with senior representatives of NALGO gave little support to the contention that Home Office consultation has been declining in quantity and quality over recent years. On the contrary, representatives felt that the Home Office was increasingly likely to consult with them. With 114/83 NALGO had to 'chase' the Home Office in order to make an input, and representatives reported a tendency to ignore the existence of civilian trade unionism in the police service. However, a national NALGO official said that this position had changed and that their comments were now 'genuinely invited'. As well as members of the PAB, NALGO were formally consulted about the circular 105/88.

The Audit Commission and National Audit Office

The Audit Commission was established by the Local Government Finance Act of 1982. Its purpose is to be an independent body appointing auditors to all local authorities in England and Wales, and to undertake and promote value-for-money (VFM) work amongst its clients. About 70 per cent of local authority audits are done by the District Audit Service (the public sector audit wing coming under the Audit Commission), the rest is done by private firms who are hired by the Audit Commission. The work on promoting VFM in provincial police forces began in about 1986. Audit guides for use in forces appeared in 1988, and a series of published 'police papers' began at about the same time, many of them receiving significant media attention. The general theme of its work is that of applying principles of business management to police forces, and disseminating good practice. The research papers started off by examining support services, and then gravitated to more sensitive areas, for example operational command structures. At the time of the research, the group at the Audit Commission working on policing issues was quite small, with one person seconded from the Treasury working on police issues full-time. The team varied depending on the current subject of research; at the time of the study there were two others. Over the previous year, the group had employed the services of a retired Home Office official, and a former chief constable, and had commissioned work by private firms on a fixed-fee basis.

The Audit Commission played an important role in stimulating the development of ASUs. Its 1988 paper *Administrative Support for Operational Police Officers* appears to have been very influential, both within local forces and nationally. Senior officials in F9 division argued that this report led directly to the specific recommendation of ASUs in the circular 105/88. The District Audit Service can also follow up on themes from police papers at the local force level. An HMIC report on force A notes how the district auditor carried out a thematic audit of the force, with special attention paid to civilianisation and ASUs.

A representative of the Audit Commission's police group explained that the Commission had developed important contacts with ACPO and the

HMIC. ACPO set up a special committee, initially chaired by James Anderton (then chief constable of Greater Manchester), to liaise with the Audit Commission. The Commission also gave twice-yearly seminars to chief officers on their particular subjects of study. A particularly close working relationship had developed with chief officers of HMIC, who were consulted by the Commission before it decided on new areas of study. HMIC also made extensive comments on draft reports by the Audit Commission prior to publication. The representative of the Commission stressed that they were not 'led by the nose' by HMIC. It was the 'quality of advice' which characterised the relationship, and the Audit Commission remained 'an independent body'. The Commission also had a number of informal contacts with the Home Office, in particular with F9 division.

The Audit Commission has been critical of the role played by local authorities in policing; in a paper on performance measurement it argued that police authorities should take a more active role in developing policy. According to the representative of the Audit Commission, a lack of relevant expertise appeared to hamper the local authorities' inputs. He accepted that the Audit Commission had exerted a considerable impact on Home Office thinking, but underlined that this was not because of the statutory position: 'The Home Office isn't obliged to take us seriously but it does because we produce things which get written about and talked about and which we think are right'.

The subject of value for money in provincial police forces has, in recent years, also come under the scrutiny of the National Audit Office (NAO). The NAO (headed by the Comptroller and Auditor General) is an independent agency that certifies the accounts of all government departments and a range of other public sector bodies. It has statutory authority to report to Parliament on the economy, efficiency and effectiveness with which departments and other bodies use their resources. The NAO takes an interest in provincial police forces in so far as it must audit the accounts of Home Office grants paid to these forces. It has no power to examine the books and records of local police forces or police authorities. In 1991 the NAO published a report into the value for money measures in provincial police forces (National Audit Office, 1991).

The House of Commons Public Accounts Committee

In 1991, this powerful Select Committee of the House of Commons examined value for money in provincial police forces, and considered in particular the report of the NAO mentioned above. The Permanent Under-Secretary at the Home Office, along with the Chief HMI, Sir John Woodcock, were questioned very thoroughly by MPs about the role of the

Home Office in promoting value for money in provincial police forces. The Committee criticised the inability of the Home Office under the present structure to exert direct control over the progress of civilianisation. At the same time there was the feeling that attempts should have been made to overcome these structural constraints.

A number of MPs on the committee, most notably Labour members, strongly criticised the Home Office for its tardiness in trying to exert more central controls over provincial forces. The main thrust of the argument was that provincial police forces absorbed a large amount of public expenditure, £3 billion in 1989-90. The fact that so much of this came from central government meant that it would have been an abdication of the Home Office's public responsibility *not* to seek to ensure that this public money was spent in the most effective way possible. Alan Williams MP made very strong criticisms of the lack of central control over spending in provincial police forces, describing it as 'one of the most appalling shambles I have heard in my time on this committee'. Tim Smith MP closely questioned the Permanent Under Secretary about the tripartite system:

> What is so special about this tripartite system? Now nearly 90 per cent of local government spending across the board is financed either by the business ratepayer or by the central taxpayer and yet we allow local authorities considerable independence in the way in which they manage their resources. (House of Commons, 1991:18)

Alan Williams strongly criticised the Permanent Under-Secretary on the HMIC findings about relative over- and under-provision of staffing in provincial police forces (and the lack of Home Office action to rectify the situation). Sir Clive Whitmore had to remind him that police officers and civilians were not employed by the Home Office, and that under the current legislative arrangements the Home Office did not have the power to transfer resources from one force to another.

So the pressures upon the Home Office to increase its influence over provincial forces did not simply come from within government, as a response to Treasury pressures. The all-party House of Commons Public Accounts Committee made very strong criticisms of the Home Office's lack of control, and certain members strongly implied that it was failing in its duty, given the amount of centrally-raised taxation revenue that was used to fund provincial forces.

POLICY-MAKING AT THE NATIONAL LEVEL

A number of themes arise from the preceding section examining the main influences over the policy of civilianisation. First, it was the national level which was the crucial forum for the development of the policy. There was relatively little impetus from individual local forces or levels below this, in terms of initiating the policy. This was summarised by the representative of the Police Federation who said: 'the main discussions of the policy emanating from the Home Office take place at PAB level... if we lose the battle within the PAB or its standing committee there is little that can be achieved locally'. A second important theme was the central importance, within this national level, of the publication of Home Office circulars 114/83 and 105/88, which were the main factors in initiating the policy. The first circular laid down the principle of civilianisation, and the second systematised the approach with more detailed advice. Information about exactly why the Home Office came to adopt the approach embodied in the circulars was hard to locate. A senior official from F1 explained that the subjects for circulars arise in a variety of ways:

> It's not really possible to generalise about how a topic assumes such importance that central guidance seems to be called for. Perhaps new legislation or regulations may require extra guidance. The police service or the local authority associations may be particularly concerned by a particular issue and say that it would be helpful to have central guidance on this, that or the other. The HMIC, as they proceed on their programmes may pick up on areas where forces are acting differently, and it would be helpful to have guidance on best practice. It could happen in any one of a number of ways.

What the official did not mention, however, was the pressure from within government, which led to extension of the FMI to the police service. This pressure, it seems, came largely from Treasury officials, concerned at the rapid expansion of expenditure on the police at a time when control of public spending was the central plank of government policy.

It is also interesting that the senior official did not mention the Home Secretary in his discussion of sources for the subjects of circulars. This underlines another important feature of the national level policy-making process; the central role played by officials in deciding upon and formulating policy. Of course, the importance of controlling public expenditure, and the FMI, were initiated by elected ministers. But the particular application of the policy to the police service, and the timing, seem to have been related more to the agendas of senior civil servants than members of the Government.

A good deal of attention has been focused upon the centralisation of power in the process of police policy-making. However, an important feature of the findings about civilianisation concerned the incomplete nature of the controls at the disposal of the Home Office. Thus, paradoxically, the findings show the power of Home Office advice in stimulating forces to civilianise, but also relative weaknesses in controlling the implementation of the process. So although the dominance of the Home Office in policy-making has been frequently criticised, it is clear that the Home Office could not issue instructions to forces; though influential the circulars are only advisory. This was a point openly accepted by senior Home Office officials:

> The advice is probably pretty general, but that's because they are essentially local issues which vary from force to force and need to be worked out separately. (Senior official - F1 division)

> The Home Office has no direct control over civilianisation. The only direct controls we have are over police manpower and capital spending... it is up to a police force to decide how many civilians it employs. It only needs the police authority's readiness to foot the bill. (Senior official - F9 division)

Thus, the influence of the Home Office was exerted indirectly, through controls over police officer establishments, and backed-up by HMIC in its annual inspections. The uneven development of civilianisation between the four forces covered in this study is testimony to the indirect nature of Home Office controls. This was a point which was repeatedly used by members of the House of Commons Public Accounts Committee to criticise senior Home Office officials. However, as officials explained, the statutory limitations on the Home Office under the 1964 Police Act largely prevented a more effective control of the growth of staff in provincial forces.

An important feature of the background to the Home Office circulars was the importance of the consultation process prior to publication. Details about this process were uncovered for the two circulars 114/83 and 105/88. A senior F1 division official gave a brief description of the criteria applied when deciding which bodies should be consulted:

> Once it becomes clear that one must take action, then the first step is to ask who the other interested organisations are. Usually ACPO have to be brought in because they are responsible for actually making it happen. The police authorities, represented by the AMA and ACC, ought to be involved if expenditure is involved because they would provide 49 per cent. If it had a direct impact on the actual work of police officers then there would be a case for involving the Police Federation and Superintendents Association.

Even though some sources were sceptical about the degree to which the Home Office was prepared to take advice on board, there was some strong evidence that the Home Office did in fact respond to criticism. For example, it withdrew its first draft of 105/88 following criticisms from the local authority associations.

A further interesting point about policy-making at the national level was that a number of different coalitions came together over different aspects of civilianisation policy. Although the parties to the debate had broad positions supporting or opposing civilianisation, there were differences over particular issues. This resulted in several shifting coalitions and different strategies adopted by different groups to put a strong case in the PAB. One example was contained in an internal Police Federation paper from 1989, which gave insights into the Federation's strategy to effect the development of civilianisation at PAB level. This paper recognised the need for civilian support in the police service, but stated that the policy was now being taken too far. It identified the two parties most strongly pushing for more civilianisation; what it called a 'strange coalition' of central government and the trade unions. The paper outlined the basis on which these could be challenged; central government by calling into question the evidence in support of the cost-effectiveness of civilianisation, and the trade unions by highlighting the danger of industrial action.

Another 'strange coalition' arose from the positions adopted by NALGO and ACPO on civilian career structures. During the 1980s, ACPO argued at the PAB in favour of a national police civilian service. NALGO argued that police civilians were a distinctive group, and sought to set up structures to deal with their issues separately from those of other local government employees. This, of course, is in opposition to the local authority associations who wish to develop career structures within the wider local government context. The ACC's strategy at the PAB to oppose a separate police civilian service was to stress the implications of giving power to the unions on a national basis. It appears that this was sufficient to convince the Home Office. An ACC memo from 1980 recorded strong opposition to a NALGO suggestion that white collar staff employed by police authorities should have a separate negotiating body. The ACC wanted them to remain within the National Joint Council (NJC) for Administrative, Professional, Technical and Clerical staff.

ACPO and the Police Federation have united in using the fear of industrial action as a cautionary pressure against civilianisation. In 1981, the Police Federation submitted a paper to the PAB highlighting public sector union militancy and the likely effects of strike action in the police service. This has also been a concern of ACPO over the years.

Not surprisingly, there were a series of formal and informal contacts between the various parties to the policy-making process which facilitated information exchange and discussion. For example, NALGO reported meetings with representatives of HMIC, and an annual meeting with senior representatives of HMIC. There were also on-going contacts with the local authority associations at all levels. NALGO representatives explained they had a 'steady liaison' with the Police Federation. By the end of the 1980s, NALGO officials also had contacts with ACPO level officers through inputs into Bramshill and Hendon training courses for senior officers. The Audit Commission referred to the informal contacts with the Home Office and the close relationship with HMIC, as well as their desire for a more fruitful input from the local authority associations.

The developments at national level show the limitations of concentrating too much on overt conflict. The main party to explicitly oppose the policy was the Police Federation. There was little evidence of overt challenges from ACPO, although arguably they had far more influence over the development of policy. Although the Home Office did have a central role in developing policy, as the above has shown, there was a process of consultation prior to any circular. This suggests that the Home Office comes to adopt an approach after taking the positions (or expected positions) of other groups into account. Thus, the Home Office, although powerful, perceives that it has to consult with various bodies when building new policing policies. It is even possible to argue that the Home Office and ACPO may be joint authors of some circulars. Commenting on the relationship between the Home Office and ACPO, for example, Rock (1990:15) has argued that:

> ...the Home Secretary would be wary about issuing a circular or initiating a policy which would meet with strong resistance in public. Overt conflict is rare. In this sense, chief constables comply with advice which they are not reluctant to accept. They work within a negotiated order that anticipates most of their responses. Instead of being subject to peremptory, public and unexpected commands, the politics of their relations revolves around nuanced and solicitous gestures. The role of the Home Secretary and his officials... remains akin to that of a constitutional monarch, not that of a director.

LOCAL FORCE LEVEL

Most of the bodies operating to influence development of policy at the national level also had, to different degrees, links with the local force level. ACPO is of course made up of chief officers from the local police forces, and the views of individual chief constables would clearly be crucial to the development of civilianisation in each force. For the local authority associations, police staff associations, and NALGO there were a number of links with the local force level. The Edmund-Davies Committee (1978) recommended the establishment of formal consultative mechanisms via the staff associations within police forces. All the forces in the study had a joint consultative committee (JCC) including representatives of the Police

Federation, Superintendents' Association, NALGO and other civilian trade unions. There was little evidence of JCCs having a strong influence on the development of civilianisation. From discussions with senior officers, the JCC appeared to be a forum for informal discussions and information exchange rather than for negotiation over the details of policy. The nature of the police organisation has not encouraged the development of local bargaining between management and workforce. Local input from NALGO has also probably been limited, constrained by the lack of a uniform local framework for its organisation. Some police forces had their own police branches of NALGO, whereas civilians in other forces were subsumed in the wider local government union branch. The civilian personnel officer in force A supported this interpretation when he reported that, in terms of local policy, 'NALGO and the Police Federation had virtually no input into civilianisation'.

Findings about policy-making at force level also confirm the view put by the representative of the Police Federation, that the PAB, and therefore the national level, was the most important in developing policy. The room for negotiation at the local level was limited, according to this view, to the 'small level of discretion' left to chief constables in the area of sedentary posts. The best that could be hoped for was to try to soften the approach of the local chief constable on this matter. In so far as chief constables broadly followed Home Office advice to civilianise this was true. Nevertheless, the case studies of the individual forces showed that within the framework of broad support for the policy, there was considerable room for differences of approach.

Thus, for example, the actual mechanism of civilianisation differed between the force that used staff reviews, those which operated a staff bidding system (in which sub-divisions and departments needed to identify posts for civilianisation), and the force that operated a centralised establishment system with little role for the departments and sub-divisions. An earlier section has shown that the four forces civilianised at different overall rates, and that although there were similarities between the kinds of posts civilianised, forces retained an individual approach in some kinds of job. For example, force B retained a high proportion of police officers in front offices and custody suites, and force A had comparatively few civilians working in personnel and computing departments. In all the forces visited there were regular meetings between the command team and the staff associations, but these were not seen as having a major impact upon force policy. It is highly likely that the personal views of the chief constable were an important determinant of differences. For example, the chief constable of force A stated his belief in the importance of retaining a proper career structure for police officers with a variety of senior positions to be kept open for them. Perhaps this explained the high police presence in computing, personnel and research. This was not a position completely supported by the chief constable's own personnel department. The civilian personnel officer put a strong argument in favour of employing a qualified civilian to head the computing department, but concluded 'the force says it must be a policeman!'. A senior civilian employee in force C reported that the chief constable took the view that civilians should not be employed in jobs which involved supervision of a police officer.

The influence of police authorities

The police committees of the local authority associations are made up of members of local police authorities. Thus, a potentially important channel of influence for elected members was through the activities of the national associations described above. The other was, of course, activity on a local level. Civilianisation provided an area of potential influence for the police authorities over the police service.

In forces A and D, interviews with leading members of the local police authorities suggested a broad consensus in favour of civilianisation, though often based on different interests and rationales. There was little evidence that police authorities saw civilianisation as a potential for expanding their influence over the framing of policing policy. No police authority made a systematic effort to exert control over civilian staff and, it seemed that the authority accepted that civilians were part of a police service over which the chief constable had ultimate authority. Yet, as shown earlier, police authorities on occasion exerted a significant influence on decisions about grading and salaries.

The police authority of force B appeared to take a more active interest in civilianisation policy than their counterparts in other forces. The minutes recorded that the authority requested a report from the chief constable into progress with civilianisation, and plans for future development (which the chief duly provided). The final decision on grading matters in this force was the responsibility of a personnel sub-committee of the police authority, not the chief constable. Although the force personnel officer worked to gain acceptance for the chief's proposals, and these proposals were only occasionally rejected, this process of negotiation still had to take place. The example of the conflict over the chief finance officer's grade was referred to earlier. Additionally, the personnel sub-committee itself reviewed the Home Office circular 105/88 and considered the implications for the force. The police authority minutes note how the chief agreed to ask the personnel sub-committee's permission before a person in receipt of an occupational pension (ie. ex police officer) was recruited to a civilian post. According to the minutes, the chief fulfilled this promise. This close interest in civilianisation appeared to be particularly related to the authority's desire to make cost savings. A number of police officers in force B felt that this was a somewhat over-simplified approach to the policy. They said that the predominance of low grades amongst the civilian employees was a result of a deliberate police authority policy. The conflict over the grading of the force finance officer had arisen because the chief wanted to appoint someone at a higher grade than members thought was necessary.

Force C had the only police authority which had overtly difficult relationships with its chief constable. The chief tended not only to take action without the agreement of members, but provided minimal information about developments in the force. However, the issue of civilian staff in the police provided a rare example of police authority predominance over the views of the chief. This involved another example of conflict over grading, with the chief wanting a lower grade for a senior civilian post, and the police authority insisting the employment be made at a higher grade.

There is no evidence that police authorities initiated the policy of civilianisation, or indeed were instrumental in determining the different approaches between forces. However, it would not be accurate to portray them as passive 'rubber stamping' bodies to the policy of civilianisation. This finding is supported by an ACPO survey of 1988 which found that 48 per cent of local authorities *prevented* their police forces from employing people in receipt of an occupational pension in civilian posts. Although this is not evidence of police authorities making a comprehensive input into the policy of civilianisation, it does show that where police authorities had statutory powers, the view of the chief constable did not inevitably prevail. The Home Office was clearly the central influence determining the development of civilianisation policy, but that influence was more indirect, and the process of change more complex, than might at first appear from observation of the outcomes.

DEMOCRATIC INFLUENCES AND CIVILIANISATION

Equity

In contrast to the other specific policy areas included in the study, the 'equity' aspect of democracy appears to have little application to policy change in relation to civilianisation. The policy of civilianisation had more of a direct impact within the police service, and its implications were not a central feature of the public debate about policing. Thus, only in terms of internal organisational issues can the notion of equity or fairness be applied, for example regarding the lower status of civilians generally. A number of studies have shown that in terms of pay and conditions, and status within the police organisation, civilians have traditionally occupied a disadvantaged position within the police organisation. Although respective positions of civilians and police staff were not a key focus of this study, the research did reveal evidence of such inequalities, where for example, senior civilian staff were excluded from decision-making forums. Similarly, little evidence was found of proper career structures for civilian employees. Recent work by Loveday (1993) and Highmore (1993) has shown that these kinds of problems are still experienced within police forces generally.

Delivery of service

This aspect is the main focus of the policy of civilianisation. Although there is disagreement about the effects of the policy, in general terms it seems difficult to deny that civilianisation has increased the policing services available to the public. Operational time has been freed up by employing civilians on jobs that would otherwise have occupied police officers, and administrative structures have been rationalised. Additionally, in both forces with ASUs, the CPS reported a marked increase in the quality of police files that were sent to them.

However, in more specific ways, evidence about the effectiveness of civilianisation remains equivocal. Parret (1992) identifies three main objectives of the policy. These are the release of officers for operational duties, a more cost-effective provision of police services, and an improved delivery of police services (through civilian specialisms and continuity in post). The first of these appears to have been central to the initial developments of civilianisation in the UK, although arguably the next two objectives became more important as time went on.

In terms of release of police officers to operational duties, there are various estimates of the exact effects of civilianisation. For example, the Home Office circular 105/88 states that in the three year period from 1985 2,035 police officers were released through the employment of 3,040 civilian staff in the police service. The Operational Policing Review carried out in 1990 estimated that 4,303 officers were redeployed as a result of civilianisation between 1983 and 1989. However, Parret (1992) notes a perception at lower levels within the police service that the number of operational officers has not increased to the degree implied by such figures. These sorts of doubts were also expressed by officers working in sub-divisions of the forces covered by this study. A common question asked by such officers was, where had these 'released' officers gone to?

The actual effects of civilianisation on operational deployment are extremely difficult to measure. In the first instance, the definition of operational is unclear and may change. Secondly, there are civilians who are employed in new functions which were never carried out by police officers. Third, civilianisation may release pockets of police time, rather than release whole officer posts to other duties. However, during the latter half of the 1980s, the National Audit Office found no increase in the proportion of police officers available for operational patrol, despite civilianisation. As noted above, although forces could provide figures for numbers of officers released by civilianisation, few forces analysed where these released officers went. There was certainly a kind of 'leakage' in operation whereby operational officers are drawn upon for other requirements. There are a number of new functions within the police organisation – including career development and equal opportunities – which have sucked in some police officers. The administrative burden on police officers has increased due to PACE and increased levels of reported crime. Additionally, specialist departments have reduced operational patrol strength. Loveday (1991:12) used this finding to argue that civilianisation did not in fact lead to more effective delivery of service. He stated that in view of the static proportion of police officers available for patrol, civilianisation had 'only served to increase the overall cost of the police organisation'. Loveday's conclusion is, however, based on the assumption that the context of policing has remained unchanged during this period. The constraints upon operational patrol availability outlined above would have occurred whether or not forces had been civilianising. Thus, if civilianisation had not been introduced, it can be argued that operational availability *would* have significantly dropped.

The second of Parret's (1992) criteria concerned the cost-effectiveness of service delivery. There is no doubt that, due to civilianisation, the police service has been able to employ a much larger number of staff at a given cost. There have been a number of estimates of the direct cost savings of civilianisation, a Department of Environment Audit Inspectorate study in 1983 estimated that the average employment cost of a civilian was about half that of a police officer in a 'comparable' function. The National Audit Office (1991), on the assumption that each released officer would have otherwise been recruited, estimated a notional saving of £51 million from civilianisation in the period 1985-89. However, it should again be emphasised that in practice, civilianisation meant real growth. No forces actually reduced numbers of police officer posts with the expansion of civilian employment. Arguably, chief constables' main priority was still to expand police officer establishments, and civilianisation was simply a means of doing this.

In terms of improved delivery of policing services, the effects of civilianisation are hard to distinguish from wider factors. It would be hard to deny that the employment of specialists in functions such as computing, personnel and research benefits the police organisation. As noted above, the extent of the release of police officers to operational duties has been limited by the growth of other demands on the police organisation. The result has been that actual operational patrol time has not been significantly improved. Research evidence as to the influence of civilianisation upon public perceptions of policing style and customer satisfaction is limited. Shapland *et al.,* (1990) found that a majority of the public had no objection to being dealt with at the police station by a civilian for routine matters, but for crime matters the majority preferred to see a police officer. However, Parret (1992) notes that research into the civilianisation of the public enquiry role in the Metropolitan Police suggested that most customers did not even know that they had been dealt with by a civilian rather than a police officer. So the evidence on the effect of civilianising certain posts upon public satisfaction is inconclusive. However, there is also little evidence to support the contention that policing services have been reduced in effectiveness due to the lack of 'police experience' of staff such as control room operators. More research is required to provide evidence about the effects of civilianisation upon the delivery of policing services.

Responsiveness

Civilianisation was only in a limited way a response to local elected bodies. As the above sections showed, members on police authorities broadly supported the development of civilianisation, viewing it in narrow cost-saving terms rather than stressing the wider organisational implications. Elected members on police authorities did exert an influence, perhaps a rather negative one, in keeping grades low and in decisions on whether to employ ex-police officers. The interventions of local authorities could not really be represented as a coherent programme of developing civilianisation. Furthermore, the real impetus to civilianisation came from central and not local government. The policy was strongly encouraged by the Home Office, the central part of which was the extension of the Financial Management Initiative to the police service. Even though this was an area in which the police authorities had real financial responsibilities, the main drive towards change came from the centre. This was only in an indirect way a response to 'public' pressure. One of the above-stated objectives of civilianisation, the release of police officers to operational duty, can in part be presented as a response to the perceived public desire for 'more bobbies on the beat'. This certainly was a central consideration in the minds of police authority members when asked about civilianisation. However, the more detailed implications did not attract much attention in terms of public debate, and were more an internal matter for the police organisation. Civilianisation appears to have been a response more to shifts in the wider political and economic context than particular changes in public opinion or the activities of representative bodies. It was one of a series of 'value for money' initiatives developed by officials in the context of the Government's commitment to control the growth of public expenditure.

Distribution of power

The previous section described how a number of organisations came together in the system and made policy through a process of negotiation and bargaining. It is clear that power was not distributed evenly between the different actors within the decision-making process. The balance was clearly tilted towards the Home Office with regard to the other parties, and the chief constables with regard to the police authorities. However, it is important not to over-state the notion of Home Office dominance in such a way as to simplify the view of the policy-making process. In the first case, the influence of the Home Office in the case of civilianisation may seem greater than is the case in reality. This is because of the general agreement of most of the other key players (the Police Federation being the significant exception) with the broad thrust of the policy. The power of the Home Office was also partly counter-balanced by that of other parties to the process, whose influence varied with changes in the constraints of the system. These constraints included wider developments, such as the changes in police pay, and the reduction of industrial conflict which occurred during the mid-1980s (each of which strengthened the hand of the supporters of civilianisation).

Previous sections outlined the process of consultation which occurred prior to the issue of Home Office circulars. Although the Police Federation representative implied that this consultation was worthless, that the Home Office had already made its mind up on a course of action, there was evidence that the Home Office was prepared to respond to the comments of the local authority associations. There was a process of accommodation and negotiation which is not always recognised in examinations of the increase in Home Office influence. At the local level, there was also evidence of some checks and balances. Chief constables could not simply do as they wished in terms of civilianisation. Civilianisation required police authority funding, and there was evidence that police authorities had the power explicitly to go against the chief constable's wishes on certain matters. However, this rarely took the form of a positive and coherent input into the development of policy.

It is also important to note that the main players within the policy-making system should not be assumed to be monolithic bodies. Within organisations there are different interests and views which must work themselves out into an organisational 'view' on preferred policy outcomes. This is as true of the Home Office as it is of ACPO, the Police Federation or the local authority associations. There was a also process of negotiation prior to the final decisions within forces, with the civilian personnel departments, and then between these departments and the police authorities. With regard to civilianisation, although policy change did not conform to a pluralist model, power did appear to be more dispersed than centralisation theorists would allow.

An interesting theme which arises from the above discussion concerns the conflicting pressures which were brought to bear on the Home Office. On the one hand, there was criticism, in particular from the ACC, that the Home Office was exerting an increasing influence over civilianisation (and other policy areas) that were the proper domain of the local authorities. On the other hand, MPs on the select committee appeared to be arguing that there was too much pluralism under the present structure. With spending on provincial police forces running into billions of pounds, they expressed shock that it had taken so long for the Home Office to start developing more central controls. One of the main points made by the senior Home Office official was that strict controls were simply not possible under the current tripartite arrangements. It would require legislative changes for the Home Office directly to control the number of civilians employed for police purposes, or transfer resources between forces. MPs made the point that 70 per cent or more of policing expenditure is financed by central government. At least two MPs suggested that the Home Office had not exerted enough central influence to ensure that these resources were well-directed. This argument appeared to be that there was too much dispersal of power within the decision-making process to have optimum effectiveness in terms of service delivery.

Information
Policy development regarding civilianisation is a good example of an area in which both the quantity and quality of available information has increased over recent years. The Audit Commission and HMIC have developed a range of indicators with the aim of producing reliable measures of police performance. An off-shoot of this, along with the other VFM work being carried out, is that there is now a much more information available

about the organisation and outputs of policing. The central part civilianisation played in the VFM drive in the police service has meant that there are relatively good sources of information available about the implications of the policy. However, what is still lacking is reliable information about the actual effects of the policy. As outlined earlier, although there is a good deal of information available about the numbers of civilians employed and in what kinds of jobs, there is still little information about what the operational time released by their employment has been used for. The National Audit Office report referred to earlier found that irrespective of the number of posts civilianised, the number of police officers available for operational patrol during the late 1980s remained constant at 55 per cent. Parrett (1992) noted that police forces rarely monitor or evaluate the release of officers by civilianisation. His survey found that few forces carry out a pre or post-civilianisation review of posts to be civilianised, and rely on the general HMIC data to monitor developments. The Audit Commission has argued for a more proactive role for police authorities, not just in terms of the framing of policing policy, but also in informing the public about the options available so that the public is more able to have a real input into policy. A representative of the Commission argued that Police Federation opposition to civilianisation was significantly related to the way that the policy had been presented. The debate was framed in restrictive terms of narrow cost cutting and putting more 'bobbies on the beat'. This was in spite of the fact that research suggests little effect of visible patrol on actual crime rates.

> Instead of taking public opinion at face value, there is a job to be done in informing public opinion... It's all very well saying that you want more bobbies on the beat, but also you want to dial 999 and have a very quick response... so we've got the business of trade-offs and optimisation to do. You need to be getting public opinion in terms of priorities for action in a resource-constrained system whereas what you've got at the moment is 'we want more of everything and all out of the same pot', which cannot be done.

Redress
The policy of civilianisation has been reversed in the past, not as a direct decision about civilianisation itself, but rather as a result of the wider financial climate. It is unsurprising then that this change in direction of policy cannot be represented as a response to specific pressure from groups opposed to its implications. The only party in the debate which consistently argued against continuing the policy, and even occasionally for reversing it, was the Police Federation. As the previous section showed, on this subject at least, the arguments of the Federation became increasingly

marginalised. There are few who would now argue for a reversal of civilianisation.

Participation

The element of participation by the general public in the development of civilianisation was extremely indirect. Only in so far as the Home Office was responding to an elected government who had campaigned on a platform of reducing growth in public expenditure and introducing VFM measures in public service provision, did the wider public 'participate' in the development of policy. The other forum for the input of elected members was the police authorities. As noted above, they did not really initiate the policy change and contributed to the development of policy in a somewhat piecemeal way. Local consultative committees and other 'participatory' bodies had no real input into civilianisation. So this is as far as participation went: the participation in the process of choosing a national government who developed civilianisation as part of a broader policy, and in the process of electing local councillors who made some contributions to the development of the policy. Indeed, it would be unrealistic to expect a more direct participation than this. As with many details of public policy, it would be a fruitless task to look for a general public 'view' on civilianisation. This probably went as far as the general desire to see 'more bobbies on the beat' and no further. The local participatory mechanisms (such as consultative committees) and even police authorities themselves are simply not capable of framing and initiating detailed policy changes like civilianisation. Public participation in the development of the policy was participation in the sense of the democratic élitist model. The public took part in the process of electing people who took broad policy decisions and employed a series of experts, who themselves developed the details of policy.

This once again brings into question the idealism of placing participation as a central concern of democratic process. The participation of the wider public in policy change was not only limited, there was even some suggestion that it was somewhat negative in its effects. The Audit Commission representative argued above that the tone of the public debate over civilianisation had strongly contributed to opposition from some police officers. A precondition to more effective participation in the framing of policy was the provision of more information about the implications of the different options. This would require greater efforts, not least from police authorities, to inform the people they are supposed to represent about the available choices and their implications.

Notes

1. The figures are taken from the Chartered Institute of Public Finance and Accountancy (CIPFA) Police Statistics. The figure for civilians includes traffic wardens, and the figure for police officers is actual force strength rather than authorised establishment. The figures exclude London.

2. During interview, representatives of the local authority associations, the Home Office, NALGO, and the police service implied that the question of who actually employs police civilians is of little practical importance.

3. It is interesting to note that this encapsulates the principle of civilianisation later laid down in the Home Office circular 114/83.

4. The Department of Environment drew up charge capping criteria which meant that the force could either set up its planned budget and risk capping, or make cuts and halt its civilianisation programme. In early 1991 representatives of the Metropolitan Police Authorities jointly lobbied the Home Secretary, and a joint statement from the chief constables warned to the damaging loss of both police and civilian jobs if budgets were capped.

5. PRSU is dominated by seconded police officers, and has as one of its main functions to carry out research, keep up to date with current research in the police service, and to keep police forces updated with news of relevant research. One of PRSU's central functions is to maintain an information desk which keeps a centralised record of current research, and acts as a clearing house and a central reference point for individual forces who wish to develop research themselves.

6. The PAB includes representatives of the police staff associations, and the local authority associations. The full board meets twice a year with the Home Secretary in the chair. There is a PAB standing committee which meets quarterly. The purpose of the PAB is to advise the Home Secretary on general questions concerning the police service, but which are not matters for formal bargaining.

5 The Influence of Local Representatives

A central theme of the debate about accountability of the police service in Britain has concerned the role of local representatives in the making of policing policy. Various proposals for reform were suggested during the 1980s. These included proposals to increase the legal powers of police authorities; in particular to enable them to give the chief constables directions in policy matters. More radical commentators suggested that such reforms would not go far enough, and argued that new participative mechanisms of decision-making should be created below the level of the police authority. From the opposite end of the political spectrum, there were proposals to introduce market-style reforms to improve cost-effectiveness in service delivery. These reforms would circumscribe the policy making role of local representatives, and focus on effective service delivery rather than the process of decision making. All these varied proposals are based on different perceptions of what input local representatives can and should have into the development of local policing policies.

Before theorising about what level and nature of input of local representatives into policing policy can or should be, it is necessary to analyse what this input actually *is*. This chapter examines the role and impact in practice of local representatives on the development of policing policy in the four police forces studied.

Structures of accountability – a brief history

The origins of the 'modern' police begin with the establishment of a constabulary for the Metropolis via Peel's Metropolitan Police Act 1829. The Act established a new 'police office' at Westminster, and two justices, responsible to the Home Secretary, were to be responsible for control over the new force. Peel's Act made the Home Secretary responsible for approving the size of the force and gave him the power to command the two justices (later Commissioners) to execute specific duties. The power of the Home Secretary over the police generally, and not just the Metropolitan Police, has come in for increasing criticism. However, Lustgarten (1986) highlighted that in 1829 the electorate consisted of only a tiny fraction of the male population and that monolithic party government underpinned by the whip system did not exist. Given these conditions, he argued, the arrangements for the governance of the capital's police were 'designed to ensure the maximum accountability that the political system was capable of constructing at the time'.

The broad parameters of the system of accountability for the Metropolitan Police have remained largely unchanged since its inception; the establishment of elected local representative government for London in 1888 did not prise control away from the Home Office. Although the Metropolitan Police were the first of the forces to be established, the arrangements for its governance were not copied when other forces were set up and, indeed, the mechanisms of accountability for provincial forces continue to be organised on a different basis. With the growth of provincial police forces there developed two systems of local accountability. The Municipal Corporations Act 1835 established watch committees which possessed the power to appoint officers and establish regulations for the running of the town forces. Following this the County Police Act 1839 gave justices of the peace the power to appoint a chief officer of police who held statutory office and could only be dismissed at Quarter or General Sessions. The standing of the county force chief constable was much greater than that of the borough chief; at the same time the county forces were much more closely tied to the Home Office. The 1839 Act stated that all county forces were subject to rules concerning 'government, pay, clothing and accoutrements of constables' to be promulgated by the Home Secretary (Lustgarten, 1986:42).

The establishment of police forces did not become compulsory until the County and Borough Police Act 1856 which reinforced the power of the watch committee and of the justices. The Act did, however, introduce the first provision for central inspection of police forces, empowering the Crown to appoint three inspectors of constabulary to assess the efficiency of all forces. The power of the centre was at this point, and for some years to come, 'limited in both character and amount' (Critchley, 1978), but tended to grow thereafter. The Local Government Act 1888 established the administrative pattern for policing for almost all of the next century. It established county councils and, under their aegis, standing joint committees consisting of two thirds elected councillors and one third local magistrates to be the police authority for county forces, an arrangement which was applied to all police authorities by the Police Act 1964. Indeed, it was the proposal to change this basic arrangement that is one source of much of the discontent expressed in 1993-4 about the Government's plans for the police.

There were a number of well-publicised disputes between chief constables and watch committees around the turn of century, each of which revolved around, though none resolved, the question of whether a chief was entitled to act independently in enforcing the law. At the turn of the century practices varied greatly from force to force with some chief constables being largely subservient to their watch committee and others acting quite independently on occasion (Brogden, 1982; Spencer, 1985).

The First World War, and the police strikes that almost immediately followed its conclusion, were the source of the next important set of structural changes to policing and its governance. The Home Office had begun via Her Majesty's Inspectorate of Constabulary (HMIC) to oversee the activities of all police forces, and growing central control and supervision was made possible through the Police (Expenses) Act 1874, which increased the Exchequer grant to local police forces from one quarter to cover one half of police expenditure.[1] During the War, the government began to assume the role of a coordinating body, setting up committees and issuing circulars and instructions under the emergency regulations (Critchley, 1978), thus forging the first links between senior officers and the Home Office.

The police strikes of 1918 and 1919 led to the formation of the Desborough Committee whose recommendations were embodied in the Police Act 1919. This gave the Home Office increased powers over the regulation of pay, conditions and discipline in all police forces, and also set up an advisory body before which such regulations were to be laid (Critchley, 1978; Jefferson and Grimshaw, 1984). At the same time, a police department was set up in the Home Office which, similarly, had responsibility for provincial police forces as well as the Metropolitan Police.

From this point onwards, the history of police accountability is one dominated by increasing central control, generally at the expense of local police authorities (Jefferson and Grimshaw, 1984; Lustgarten, 1986). Lustgarten in fact suggested that from the 1920s two trends were visible. The first was increasing Home Office influence through legislation and through less formal means and, the second, was increasing freedom of action on the part of chief constables, eventually enshrined in the 'principle of constabulary independence'. In both cases, local police authorities were the 'losers'. The next major piece of legislation was the Police Act 1946 which gave the Home Secretary power to compulsorily amalgamate police forces with populations below 100,000.

By the mid 1950s there was increasing concern about the effectiveness of the police, and towards the end of the decade a number of well-publicised disputes between police authorities and their chief constables threw the issue of the accountability of the police into sharp relief. In 1958, for example, the Nottingham watch committee requested that the chief constable report on an investigation he had instituted in connection with corruption charges involving members of the city council. The chief constable refused and the watch committee used their power to suspend him. The Home Secretary ruled that such an action interfered with the chief constable's duty to enforce the criminal law free from political control and reinstated him. In 1959 the House of Commons debated a motion[2] censuring the Home Secretary for making £300 of public money available to settle an action brought against a Metropolitan Police constable as the result of an alleged assault. These, and a number of other *causes célèbres* put the issue of accountability high on the agenda – though the focus was on individual officers rather than on force policies – and led to the establishment of a Royal Commission on the Police.

The Royal Commission, set up in 1960, was given the central task of reviewing:

> the constitutional position of the police throughout Great Britain, the arrangements for their control and administration, the principles that should govern remuneration of police officers and, in particular, to consider:
>
> (1) the constitution and functions of local police authorities;
> (2) the status and accountability of members of police forces, including chief officers of police;
> (3) the relationship of the police with the public and the means of ensuring that complaints against police are effectively dealt with.
>
> (Royal Commission on the Police, 1962)

The Royal Commission began from the position that 'the problem of controlling the police can... be restated as the problem of controlling chief constables' – a statement which has been much contested since. It went on to note that chief constables were accountable to no-one, nor subject to anyone's orders for the way in which they settle general policies in relation to law enforcement and that, therefore, with regard to establishing more effective supervision, 'the problem [was] to move towards this objective without compromising the chief constable's impartiality in enforcing the law in particular cases' (para.92)

The Police Act 1964
This Act replaced the old system of watch committees and joint standing committees with a single system of police authorities. The watch committees had been composed entirely of councillors, whilst half of the

members of the joint standing committees were magistrates. The new authorities were to consist of two thirds councillors and one third magistrates and, outside London, these authorities took two basic forms – though a third emerged during the 1980s with the abolition of the metropolitan authorities. The most common type at present is the police authority which covers one county. This is a committee of the county council, usually referred to as the police committee, and is like other council committees except that none of its decisions, other than financial ones, can be overruled by the full council. The second type is the combined police authority which exists where police forces serve more than one county. They consist of councillors and magistrates from each county, and are wholly independent of each and all of the constituent councils.

All police authorities are under a duty to secure the maintenance of an 'adequate and efficient' force for their area, though these terms are undefined. In the event the Police Act 1964 empowered police authorities to:

- appoint a chief constable, his deputy and assistants, subject to the approval of the Home Secretary;

- determine the overall establishment, and number of each rank, of the force;

- provide vehicles, clothing and equipment;

- determine the overall budget of the force, subject however to the requirement that costs incurred under authority of central government regulations, or any statute, must be met.

- require its chief constable to submit a report in writing on matters connected with the policing of the area.

Consequently, the only statutory duty owed by the chief constable to his police authority is the submission of an annual report, though the authority may 'require' that he also provide a written report on any matter related to policing of the area. This is, then, a form of what Marshall (1978) termed 'explanatory' accountability, wherein the police are required after the event to explain the policies they have followed or actions they have taken. Though potentially powerful, this provision in the 1964 Act provides little actual leverage, for a chief constable may refuse to make such a report if he believes it would contain information 'which in the public interest ought not to be disclosed, or is not needed for the discharge of the functions of the police authority'. Furthermore, police authorities have no powers to instruct chief constables to change any policies set out in the reports provided them. The 'unsatisfactory, indeed somewhat ludicrous result' according to Lustgarten (1986) is 'that police authorities are dependent on their chief constable for information, making their ability to offer effective criticism subject to the co-operation of its primary target. And the position of the Home Secretary as ultimate arbiter quietly emphasises the power of central government in policing matters.'

A recurring theme within the work of Lustgarten and others (notably Reiner) during the 1980s and early 1990s was the centralisation of policy-making power in policing. Reiner (1985; 1991) lucidly documents the increase in influence of central institutions at the expense of local accountability. His argument is that by the end of the 1980s, the most important decisions about policing were taken by central bodies, in particular the Home Office. This left a kind of sham accountability at the local level. In a later study Reiner (1992) showed that chief constables often did take the views of their police authorities into account when framing policy. However, he argued that this was more a matter of the chiefs' 'wise statecraft' than an illustration of meaningful influence on the part of the police authority. He argued that *when push comes to shove* (in cases of real conflict between a chief and his police authority), the view of the chief would always prevail.

It is certainly true that one of the major changes made by the 1964 Act was the enshrining in statute of the principle that supreme responsibility for local policing lay with chief constables, each force thenceforward being 'under the direction and control' of its chief officer. In order to do this he was empowered by the Act to appoint, promote and discipline all officers up to the rank of chief superintendent. The Act also required chief constables to investigate complaints against the police and to submit all complaints that reveal that a criminal offence has been committed to the Director of Public Prosecutions.

The third pillar of what has since become known as the 'tripartite structure' is the Home Secretary. Many of the powers conferred on the police authority are only exercisable with the approval of the Home Secretary. Thus, although the chief, deputy and assistant chief constables are appointed by the police authority, these appointments must not only be approved by the Home Secretary, but they are subject to regulations promulgated by him. In addition, the Home Secretary can require a police authority to retire its chief constable 'in the interests of efficiency', though this provision has never been formally invoked.

This is the basic structure that, until 1994, underpinned the process by which the police in England and Wales were held to account for their general policies. That having been said, some amendments and additions to the system have been made since the 1964 Act and these are worth outlining at this stage before moving on to consider how the system of accountability worked in practice.

Joint Boards
The early 1980s were a time in which policing in general and the tripartite structure in particular came under increased scrutiny (Reiner, 1993a). In the local government elections in 1981 radical Labour councils were returned in all the metropolitan areas, and the police authorities in these areas gradually began to attempt to exercise some of their powers. There were a number of major clashes between authorities and chief constables and such conflict contributed to the overall disenchantment with which the Government viewed these particular councils. The Local Government Act 1985 abolished these authorities, and replaced them with joint boards which, it has been argued, proved more accommodating to police influence than their predecessors (Loveday, 1987; Reiner, 1993a). Joint Boards are made up of nominees of constituent district councils and, as far as it is practicable, the membership reflects the local party political balance. In general this meant a move away from Labour domination or control in the metropolitan areas (Loveday, 1991) and, additionally, resulted in an increased profile for the magistrate members of police authorities.

Police Community Consultative Groups
At approximately the same time that such changes were being proposed and later implemented, the urban riots in Brixton and a number of other inner-city areas, and the consequent inquiry by Lord Scarman, were also focusing attention on questions of local consultation and local accountability. Lord Scarman's chief recommendation on accountability was that local community consultative committees should be set up. In Scarman's view, there had been insufficient formal liaison between the black community and the police in and around Brixton, and the absence of such communication was both a symptom and a cause of the 'withdrawal of consent' that underpinned the policing problems in the area (Morgan, 1992). He concluded that 'a police force which does not consult locally will fail to be efficient'.

Scarman dashed the hopes of many critics of the existing arrangements by endorsing the 'tripartite' structure. He did, however, suggest that police authorities could act more effectively and vigorously if there were better arrangements for local consultation in areas considerably smaller than those covered by whole forces. He favoured the introduction of a statutory duty to make such arrangements 'at police divisional or sub-divisional levels'.

This, as Morgan (1992) concludes, 'was the participative mechanism on which he pinned his faith that policing would in future be more congruent with the wishes of people locally.'

Scarman's recommendation that local consultative committees should be established was quickly followed by a Home Office circular (54/1982) supporting such arrangements and, as an illustration of the influence of Home Office circulars in the area of policing generally,[3] a large number of police authorities, in the main supported by their chief constables, established such committees in their regions. Statutory provision for the making of arrangements 'in each police area for obtaining the views of the people in that area about matters concerning the policing of the area and for obtaining their cooperation with the police in preventing crime in the area' were introduced under s.106 of the Police and Criminal Evidence Act 1984 (PACE).

The 1993 White Paper on reform of the police service and the subsequent Police and Magistrates' Courts Bill had major implications for the role of local representatives in shaping policing policy. The Bill proposed to limit the size of all police authorities to 16 members, of whom three would be magistrates, eight would be elected local councillors, and five would be people appointed by the Home Secretary. The Home Secretary would appoint the chair from the total membership, so that police authorities would no longer be chaired by, or have a majority of, elected members. In addition to this, the Bill proposed that police authorities should have responsibility for drawing up an annual plan of objectives for policing the area. This would have to take into account national objectives laid down by the Home Secretary. The Bill also proposed the introduction of fixed-term contracts for senior police officers. These proposals were strongly criticised by representatives of the AMA and ACC, and opposition spokespersons, as an attack on local democracy. The police service also united in condemnation of the proposals. It was feared that chief constables on fixed contracts would be far more responsive to centrally-determined performance objectives than to local pressures. In any case, under the proposed structure it was argued that the Home Secretary would have unprecendented influence over the working of local police authorities.

Following extensive criticism in the Second Reading debate in the House of Lords in January 1994, the Home Secretary abandoned the proposal that he have power to appoint authority chairs, and that all authorities be limited to 16 members. He also presented a complicated procedure of appointment of the non-elected members of the new police authorities, in an attempt to allay the fears about increasing central influence.

The Bill's supporters argued that rather than weaken police authorities, the proposals would increase their ability to hold chief constables to account, and to develop workable policing plans for local areas. The Home Secretary argued that the non-elected appointees would provide a new source of expertise for police authorities. Additionally, the Bill proposed a new system for financing the police which, it was argued, would give greater freedom to local forces in financial matters. The proposal was that the Home Office should no longer decide how many police officers a force should have. Each authority would receive a cash-limited amount of police grant, and also receive money from council tax, RSG and non-domestic rates. The chief constable and his police authority would decide how to allocate their budgets between police and civilian staff, vehicles, equipment and so on. So there would be greater local freedom in deciding how to spend the money, but greater central control over total spending.

A common argument against the Bill's proposals was that reducing the number of locally-elected representatives and introducing non-elected appointees would undermine local democracy. The strong implication was that local police authorities were already fully capable of making an active contribution to the framing of policy in their areas. An ACC/AMA survey in 1994 found that police authority members already had 'a wide range of outside interests'. This included 62 per cent of elected members who were school governors, and 38 per cent with outside business interests. The survey also found a high proportion of elected members on police authorities had connections with other local services, through membership of the relevant committees.

LOCAL REPRESENTATION IN THE FOUR STUDY AREAS

Force A
The police authority for force A was an example of what is known as a combined police authority, since force A covered two administrative counties. The numbers of representatives from each council are prescribed by the terms of the amalgation order creating the force. Such authorities are wholly independent of the constituent councils upon which they levy a rate and, as such, are potentially less accountable than single county police authorities. Single county police authorities include representatives who are also members of other committees, and are thus aware of other demands being made on the local budget from which the police budget is drawn. Making choices among priorities in this manner is not something which need affect combined authorities. Lustgarten (1986) observed that combined authorities are most common in rural areas with Conservative majorities, and force A was no exception. At the time of the research the

political distribution of the councillors on the police authority was 13 Conservative, four Social and Liberal Democrat (SLD)(as they then were called), and three Labour.

Force A was the only force in the study which did not set up a new force-wide structure of consultative committees following Lord Scarman's recommendations. The police authority had two general sub-committees of which the more powerful was the finance and general purposes committee (FGPC). The members of this committee did not support the proposal to set up an authority-wide system of consultative committees. The chief constable's report of 1983 stated that local consultative initiatives were already reasonably established in the region before Scarman, though these arrangements were reviewed in 1984. A report by the chief in 1985 noted that new formalised links between elected members and local crime prevention panels (CPPs) were widely viewed as a constructive development. According to the report, CPPs had been expanded so as to become more representative of the community.

In addition, the chief constable reported on the arrangements in one of the two larger towns of the region for the establishment of a police and public safety sub-committee. He invited the police authority to recognise this forum as a suitable vehicle for consultation between the police and the community in one of these towns, and to regard it as appropriate for the purposes of section 106 of PACE. The police authority were initially rather reluctant, arguing that existing arrangements for consultation were sufficient. In the event police support for the sub-committee meant that the police authority were forced to recognise it. Indeed, official reluctance extended even further. The Conservative councillors from the borough council refused to take up their allocated places on the sub-committee because they felt that it would become a forum dominated by left-wingers wishing to use it to criticise the police. According to senior police officers in the region, the Conservatives had hoped that the police would have nothing to do with the sub-committee once they had pulled out, but this did not materialise. Police views of the sub-committee and its day-to-day workings are described in greater detail later in the chapter.

In the region's other main town, the local consultation arrangements were two-fold. First there was a twice yearly meeting with the chief executive and the leader of the borough council. Second, there was the CPP which the local sub-divisional commander described as 'of very doubtful advantage compared to the amount of police time expended', and which the chair of the panel admitted had a role that was confined to minor crime prevention issues. So, in contrast with other forces in the study, the Scarman proposals and section 106 of PACE had little substantive effect in the region as a whole. The 1985 chief constable's report stated 'it should be said that some councils have expressed reservations that such formal relationships are necessary in view of their already close informal relationships with the police'. The town where a local initiative produced a consultative forum which was unique to the county was perhaps the exception to the general pattern and, as will be described in greater detail below, that this was a forum which had a significant impact on the shaping of local policing policy.

The 1991 HMIC report on force A stated that the current consultation arrangements were not satisfactory, recommending that the police authority should review their arrangements. In particular, it was suggested that arrangements should be made consistent between the two administrative counties, that steps be taken to improve the public access to, and expand membership of consultative groups, and that the police authority should develop closer links with such groups. The work of the police and public safety sub-committee was strongly commended by HMIC.

In terms of force-wide mechanisms of consultation, force A was less advanced than the other forces in the study. However, in terms of particular initiatives, it was relatively progressive. One of these initiatives was the police and public safety sub-committee. Another initiative was taken by the force in 1989 when it commissioned a major survey of public opinion regarding policing. The survey was designed and analysed by university academics, and carried out by an independent company. Over 600 people from four areas were surveyed, half selected randomly from the electoral register, and the other half selected from people who had contacted the police in the preceding 12 months either regarding public order, theft from motor vehicles, burglary, or because they had been required to produce driving documents at the police station. There was a very strong commitment to the survey on the part of senior officers in the force. This was shown by the fact that after the survey, the chief and his deputy personally addressed meetings on divisions attended by all staff, and invited the force as a whole to respond to the survey results. More than 300 proposals for improving the quality of service were received.

An important debate arose during the course of the research concerning the structure of the police authority. There appeared to be significant feeling that the current structure was inefficient. It meant that there were a large number of meetings to attend every year, when sub-committee and full police authority meetings were added together. Additionally, much of the paperwork discussed at sub-committee level was duplicated at full authority level. Another criticism, from a minority of members, was that the committee structure tended to hide issues, so that important matters were never properly and fully discussed by the police authority. Two alternative proposals for change were suggested. First, abolishing the sub-committees altogether, and having six meetings of the full police authority each year. Additionally, there would be a series of seminars for members only (not the public or press) presented by senior police officers, to facilitate the sharing of information and opinions. This was the proposal favoured by the chief constable and the chair of the police authority. The alternative structure was a refined committee structure, including a smaller 'outputs' committee, with some responsibility for the monitoring of policing policy. This was supported by opposition members, but also by two prominent Conservatives, who had recently joined the police authority.

Force B

The police authority for force B was a joint board consisting of members nominated by constituent metropolitan district councils and magistrates from the different areas. Like other metropolitan police authorities, it had a 'lead authority', providing legal, financial and administrative support to the force organisation. At the time of the research the police authority had 28 members, 19 of whom were elected councillors nominated by their party groups – the Labour Party forming the ruling group: of the elected members, 16 were Labour, compared to two Conservative and just one SLD. The principal officer to the police authority described it as a 'non-political' police authority which had over the years consciously worked for cross-party consensus on policing matters. He gave three reasons for this. First, that the region had a long history of Labour-controlled local government, and that the Labour tradition had been a moderate one. Second, because Labour had always had a strong majority it had never really been necessary for it to be confrontational in its approach. Third, the chief constable of the time had been in post a long time and had developed strong working relationships with local politicians.

The full police authority met every month, and there were a number of sub-committees (notably more than in other authorities) which also met monthly. These were finance, personnel, complaints, 114/83, crime prevention, as well as some *ad hoc* committees which met as and when it was felt necessary. The local consultation arrangements were a network of 23 'police-community forums' set up in sub-divisions following section 106 of PACE. Each of these was chaired by a member of the police authority. These reported to a sub-committee of the police authority, the 'Scarman Report Members Panel' which met quarterly. This sub-committee processed the minutes of the forum meetings and could pass on any suggestions to the full police authority. Force B also had a network of CPPs (one per sub-division), and a growing number of NW schemes. The force gave substantially more support to the NW concept than other forces in the study.

Force C

The force C authority was a single county police authority and functioned as a committee of the county council. The police committee (as it was known) was dominated by Labour, who held 11 of the 21 seats, with three Conservatives and seven magistrates. The committee met monthly, and had a committee structure which included three sub-committees: finance and general purposes, community development, and a community liaison support group. Prior to each meeting of the police committee there was an 'agenda meeting' attended by the chair, vice-chair, shadow chair, chief constable, an assistant chief constable, the clerk and the secretary to the police committee. The chief constable exerted a strong influence over the subjects which finally appeared on the agenda. While the authority chair stated that the police authority was dominated by moderate Labour members, it appeared that the police authority here had a more terse relationship with the chief constable than was the case in the other force areas. The chair of the police committee was a young councillor who wanted the authority to be more active in the framing of local policing policy. He tried to pursue this end following his succession to the chair of the police committee in 1989. However, the chief constable took a more traditional view of the role of the police authority, and regularly stressed his operational independence when the committee attempted to involve itself in policy development.

On each of the 16 sub-divisions, a community liaison committee had been set up following the PACE Act in the mid-1980s. Apparently, the meetings of these committees were not made public until 1990. The chair of the police authority initiated the setting up of a police committee support group, which was intended as a support framework to the development of community links. The meetings of the police liaison committees were opened up to the public, and the support group was to provide secretarial support to these meetings (for example in the preparation of agendas and the writing up and circulation of minutes). In addition to the police community liaison committees there was a network of crime prevention panels (whose role seemed to be somewhat confused with the former). There was also a network of NW schemes, under an association partly funded by the police committee.

Force D

Like force C, this had a single county police authority and as such was a committee of the county council. At the time of the research it had 27 members, of whom 18 were elected councillors and the remaining one third local magistrates. The chair reported that the Local Government and Housing Act 1988 had had a substantial impact on the distribution of seats within the police authority. Prior to the Act the ruling Labour Group commanded 15 seats on the police authority, three were held by Conservatives. The Act stated that seats should reflect the distribution of power on the council as a whole. Consequently, at the time of the research, only ten of the seats were held by Labour, seven by Conservatives and one by the SLD. According to the principal officer to the police authority, one potential consequence of this was that the balance of power on the authority shifted away from Labour and towards the magistrate members. However, he then stressed that the magistrate members had in the past tended to take a fairly neutral line on police matters, and both the principal officer and the chair appeared keen to promote an image of bipartisan consensus. Their view was that confrontation with the chief constable tended to occur in authorities dominated by the 'hard left', and that policing should not be seen as a party political matter. The principal officer's view of the consensual nature of the authority was illustrated by his remark that 'we're not very political in ------shire'.

In addition to the police authority, there existed a number of other avenues through which local representatives could make their views about policing known. The county took a number of steps in response to the Scarman Report. The police authority devised a network of Police Liaison/ Advisory Committees (PLACs) in 1983 before PACE made local consultative committees statutory. At the time of the research there were 15 such committees, though the force was divided into only 12 sub-divisions. The reason for this apparent anomaly was that the force structure was re-organised in 1984, but the existing committee structure was left unchanged as it was felt that the new sub-divisions were too large in some cases for effective consultation to take place. In January 1982 a working party was set up to consider the recommendations about local consultation, and in the following month a letter was received from the Home Secretary explaining the nature of the proposed consultation arrangements. In particular, the Home Secretary's letter outlined the advisory as opposed to executive powers of the proposed committees, and police authority followed this line in drawing up its own plans. Organising the committees on the basis of the existing police sub-divisional structure, the police authority decided that each committee should be chaired by one of its own elected members. It decided that the core membership of the committee should, in addition to the chair, include one district councillor per district in the sub-division, one representative from each of the local parish councils, and one representative from the local trades council. In addition, the county council was to fund one full-time post to act as secretary to all the PLACs.

THE INFLUENCE OF LOCAL REPRESENTATIVES IN POLICY-MAKING

Chapter 1 outlined how the law can only set broad limits to possible patterns of policing. The factors which do determine policy within those broader limits can be termed policing policy. This section examines in detail the ways in which local representatives influenced the patterns of policing in the three chosen policy areas. The material is based on four main sources of data. First, was an analyis of the minutes of police authority meetings for a period of about 5 years prior to the research (where possible, minutes from further back in time were examined). It was also possible to examine the papers and reports provided for the meetings of the authorities. Second, it was possible to attend a police authority meeting in three of the four forces studied and observe the authority in operation. Third, a number of semi-structured interviews were carried out with principal officers to the authorities, chairs, opposition spokespersons and some other leading members. Finally, visits were made to two sub-divisions in each of the four forces and, where possible, interviews were conducted with representatives of other forms of local organisation such as CPPs and NW schemes.

Force A

Analysis of the minutes of (and reports to) meetings of the police authority in force A, gave rise to noticably more documentation than in some of the other forces. The agendas for meetings tended to be long, and the reports from the chief constable were lengthy and detailed. This was partly because each of the sub-committees also presented full reports of their meetings to meetings of the full police authority, which tended to increase the bulk of papers.

The first mention of crime prevention in the minutes was found in the chief constable's quarterly report of June 1982. This gave details of the force's 'Let's protect [the county]' campaign, which involved the distribution of 36,000 copies of a letter about crime prevention written by the chief constable to elderly people. The report asked for the police authority's support for the campaign, which was duly given. The following year, a report of the FGPC expressed concern at the amount of wasted police time spent responding to false burglar alarm calls. The report stated that the chief constable would withdraw response from the worst offenders for three months whilst they examined their systems. The chief constable's report to a meeting of the sub-committee in 1983 informed them of 'Crime Alert' schemes in the county. In 1986, a chief constable's report announced a review of NW in the force with a view to finding ways of keeping up the momentum of the NW movement. In December 1987, the chief constable's quarterly report gave details of the introduction of a design advisory service (following discussions with the county secretaries and departmental directors). Finally, in February 1990, the chief constable's quarterly report stated that the force was now following the national burglar alarm policy developed by ACPO.

The first reference to the investigation of rape was in April 1986, when a comprehensive report from the chief constable explained developments in the force policy regarding rape victims. The report outlined how in response to the Home Office circular 25/83 a force working group was set up which examined training, investigation techniques, and examination facilities. The 1985 report *Violence Against Women* led to a renewed interest in the force which specifically examined the feasibility of developing a rape suite. It was later decided that a rape suite in the area would not be feasible, although other recommendations were put into effect. The reasons were laid down in a report to the sub-committee in September 1986. A year later, the chief constable reported on the force policy regarding treatment of rape victims and informed the authority that the recommendations of the review had now been put into effect. Only one reference was found to the treatment of victims of rape which was not a report from the chief constable. This was in a meeting of the police authority which noted a motion passed by one of the county councils expressing concern over the number of reported rapes, and requesting that the police authority look at the way victims of such offences are treated and suggesting they look at the possibility of providing special facilities. There was no record of any response to this by the police authority.

The investigation of child abuse was mentioned only briefly in the minutes; in 1987 the chief constable gave notice of a presentation to be made at the next police authority meeting on the force procedures for the investigation of child abuse and liaison with the other involved agencies. No references were found to force policy on domestic violence in the period 1982-90.

There were a number of references to civilianisation in the minutes of the police authority. Most of the discussions concerning civilianisation took place at meetings of the FGPC which then reported to the full police authority. The references usually consisted of a report from the chief constable to this sub-committee, which was then passed on to the full police authority as a report of the sub-committee. The first reference was from 1984 when the chief constable responded to a report by the Audit Inpectorate of the Department of the Environment comparing levels of civilianisation in ten forces, including force A. The report recorded that the chief constable would consider scope for further civilianisation within the force. A further report by the chief constable explained to the sub-committee that in response to the Home Office circular 114/83 there would be a wide-ranging force structure review, to include an examination of the scope for further civilianisation. The police authority was subsequently to support all the recommendations arising from this review. There was a considerable amount of detail given to the police authority concerning the nature and location of posts under consideration. One example is a chief constable's report to the sub-committee giving details of a review of police driver training, and recommending the civilianisation of some posts. A later development in the area was the introduction of administrative support units based at divisional level dealing largely with matters of file processing for court. These were to be staffed mainly by civilians. The sub-committee was asked to approve the recruitment of a number of extra civilian staff for employment in these units, to which it duly agreed. During the fieldwork, a chief constable's report to the sub-committee outlined his intention of undertaking a job evaluation project within the force with the aim of developing a career structure for civilian staff, and to improve recruitment and retention.

The general pattern thus appeared to be that the FGPC met a week or so before the full police authority. On matters of policy, the chief constable (usually) or the clerk (sometimes) presented what were often quite detailed reports to the sub-committee, often with recommendations. The sub-committee would accept the recommendations, and present them in their report to the full police authority who then, without fail, voted to accept the report and recommendations. No instance was found of the sub-committee or the police authority disagreeing or querying recommendations from the chief constable or the clerk. The overall impression was that there had been very little controversy at the police authority in the last ten years. One exception concerned some police public order action during 1986, which resulted in a lot of questions by members at the next meeting of the police authority. One Labour member in particular was highly critical of the police action. Another significant event documented in the minutes shows how the police authority defined its own role. At a meeting of the FGPC, a councillor had put forward a motion requesting that the force appoint a non-white police officer to a sub-division in which there was a significant ethnic minority population compared to the rest of the force area. The result was that the sub-committee report recommended that the police authority reaffirm its policy on equal opportunities. Significantly, the authority stated that it should not approve the councillor's motion in his words, because the staffing of a sub-division was an 'operational matter' for the chief constable, and the deployment of police officers was not a matter for discussion by the police authority.

A researcher attended a meeting of the police authority in order to supplement the information collected from the minutes. After the impression of passive non-interference given by analysis of the minutes, it was surprising to find that the meeting was lively and controversial. This was mainly due to a vociferous minority of Labour councillors (one in particular) who raised a number of concerns, and at times were openly critical of the police force. It was interesting to note that the magistrates on the police authority made few contributions to the meeting. The chief constable was unable to attend the meeting and so it was the deputy chief constable who provided the senior police representation. The meeting opened with the formality of re-electing the chair and the vice-chair (who were both elected unopposed).

The report of the buildings sub-committee passed without comment and then the meeting moved on to consider the report of the FGPC. This raised the subject of local consultation arrangements in the force area, which brought strong comment from two Labour councillors, one of whom turned out to be by far the most vocal member of the police authority. He argued that there needed to be far more discussion of policing issues, and that the level of discussion at the police authority was 'laughable' and 'superficial'. The 'self-congratulatory and mutual backslapping' nature of police authority meetings, along with the use of top-down presentations by the chief constable, did not in his view fulfil the proper role of a police authority. Another Labour councillor criticised the 'cosy arrangements' which existed for local consultation in the force area, and directly asked the deputy chief constable whether the force was complying with section 106 of PACE and Home Office best practice recommendations. The deputy chief defended the force arrangements by pointing out that most districts within the area had actively opposed the setting up of new formal mechanisms of consultation, and these could not be forced upon them. He went on to outline some of the other ways in which the force consulted the community, including CPPs, and the work of force CPOs with agencies outside the police.

The next item on the agenda concerned the regional crime squad, and again drew strong comment from the particularly vocal councillor. He said that there was danger of a national police force developing through stealth, and attacked the policy-making powers of ACPO saying, 'Who the hell are ACPO? They're not the Home Office and they're not Parliament!'. The deputy chief constable replied that the chief constable had publicly stated his support for a locally-accountable police structure, and opposed the notion of an operational nationwide crime squad. The next item on the agenda called for the police authority to approve the chief constable's attendance at a conference in Korea. The same councillor demanded to know how much it would cost to send representatives to such conferences, and asked for information about for the number of such visits, where they were, and the purpose of attendance. The deputy chief promised to make such information available. The next item drew praise from even the more critical members, being a draft statement of intent on equal opportunities policy in the force. One councillor outlined that the force needed to recruit more ethnic minority officers (a point accepted by the deputy chief), and asked for assurance that statements of intent would be followed up throughout the organisation. There followed quite a detailed discussion of the equal opportunities policy.

The central part of the meeting was taken up with a discussion of the chief constable's quarterly report which included details of recorded crime trends over the previous months. The deputy chief presented the report, and highlighted the increased crime figures, and also said that there had been a major child abuse investigation in one of the sub-divisions which had been successfully carried out jointly with the local social services department. The vocal Labour councillor then made quite a dramatic attack on the police, starting with their use of 'bandit cars' to tempt car thieves, moving on to say that senior officers were 'aggressively complacent' about the levels of crime in the force area, and ending with strong criticism of the principle of NW as a 'selfish displacement mechanism'. This stream of criticism brought growls of discontent from the majority of the other members. This did not deter the councillor, who continued with criticism of the 'disgraceful' behaviour of the Police Federation who had 'howled down' the Home Secretary at their annual conference. The deputy chief constable looked somewhat irritated, but answered each of the points in turn.

Another councillor, a Conservative member, questioned whether the police authority had the correct structure for addressing criticisms of the police. It was important that all matters were discussed fully, but under the current system important subjects could fail to reach the agenda. He argued that he had heard no discussion of the use of 'bandit cars' prior to their introduction. The chair interjected at this point, and stated that the policy had been mentioned in papers submitted to both the buildings and the FGP sub-committees, and therefore had not been concealed by the police. She added that it was the fault of authority members if the matter had not been discussed properly.

The overall impression of the meeting was one of quite lively debate marked by quite strong criticism voiced by one Labour councillor in particular. A large part of the meeting appeared to be taken up by a bi-lateral debate between the deputy chief constable and this particular councillor. The senior police officer was quite willing to respond to the points which were raised, but the sounds of disapproval from many of the other councillors and magistrates suggested they felt the councillor had no right to raise such matters.

The third source of information about the workings of the police authority was semi-structured interviews with the secretary to the authority, the chair and the leading Labour critic who had been so vocal at the meeting. Attempts were made to arrange interviews with the chairs of the two sub-committees of the police authority. However, these attempts were unsuccessful, and both members gave the impression that they did not wish to be interviewed at all.

In relation the proper role of the police authority, there were contrasting views offered by the Labour spokesperson and the chair who appeared to represent the majority view on the police authority. The secretary to the police authority made the distinction between operational and other matters, describing the former as 'matters not requiring a decision'. He did not elaborate on what matters should be considered operational however, and said that although some members felt that certain issues could have been discussed more fully, this had rarely led to real controversy. The chair made it clear that she saw a limited role for the police authority in its relationship with the chief constable. She went to some length to describe the good relationship between the authority and the chief constable, and said that this had also been the case with previous chief constables. In fact, the only times when the majority of the police authority expressed opposition to the views of the chief constable was when he initiated lay visiting schemes and new structures for consultation with the community. There was considerable opposition to these moves, as many members argued that the public already had such a high degree of trust of the police that such measures were a waste of time.

At the time of the research, there was an on-going debate about the structure of the police authority. Two Conservative councillors who were new to the authority had supported reforming the committee structure, with an 'outputs' sub-committee scrutinising policy in more detail than the under the current arrangements. The chair and the chief constable favoured removing the committee structure altogether and having six public meetings of the full police authority per year in conjunction with police-led seminars with members of the police authority (to which the public and press would not be admitted).[4] The comments of the chair about these changes clearly illustrated her view of the proper role of a police authority. She argued that the those who wished to introduce a policy outputs committee 'wanted to demand the kind of control which is not for members'. When pressed on this she referred to the 'operational element' in the duties of a chief constable. She added that an outputs committee would include a measure of performance monitoring, and that 'performance-related matters are important, but are matters for the chief constable only'. The Audit Commission was later to produce a report saying that performance monitoring was an important area in which police authorities could make a contribution, and the citizens charter was to require local authorities to publish a range of performance indicators for the police.

The unofficial opposition spokesperson had a totally different view of the proper role of a police authority. He admitted that the current committee structure had problems, but argued that there was a 'much deeper malaise' relating to the attitudes of members. He said that the level of discussion was very poor, and that most things were 'nodded through' without any real debate. The deferential attitudes of most of the authority members had led to a strange state of affairs regarding the relationship with the chief constable: 'We've a paradoxical situation in which senior police officers are much more willing to discuss policing than are members of the authority'.

Following his vocal criticism of the police at the authority meeting, it was somewhat surprising to note the respect he expressed for the senior police officers in the force. He described the chief constable as 'very politically astute', and the deputy chief as, 'a highly competent senior officer who has a very good ear for what local politicians and people are saying they want from the police'. He described the senior management of the force as 'Benthamite' in that they were prepared to respond to social and political pressures. He also said that senior officers were extremely forthcoming with information when he asked for it. However, he added that the police had in the past derived some advantage from the rather passive nature of the police authority.

As regards the chosen policy areas of the study, both members interviewed gave similar (although very differently phrased) impressions of the police authority involvement. When asked about the police authority role in promoting crime prevention in the force area, the chair said that the main contribution had been in selecting the 'right chief constable' and then supporting his initiatives. When asked about the police authority's influence over crime prevention policy, the opposition spokesperson's view was it had had 'none whatsoever'. Regarding changes in force policy in the area of rape and domestic violence the chair gave a full account of what the force had done, and gave credit to the influence of women's groups in the major town in the force area in changing policy in the first two of these. She was not so well-informed on changes in policy on policing child abuse, making a rather vague reference to working with social services. She supported the policy of civilianisation from the viewpoint of getting more growth and putting officers back on the beat. The Labour councillor presented an image of extremely limited police authority influence in these areas, as in crime prevention, saying that changes were nodded through without substantive comment. This may well have been a slight overstatement, for it was difficult to imagine him refraining from making any comment at all. The interview took place after a police authority meeting at which there had been quite an extensive discussion of crime prevention. When this was pointed out he admitted that there had been some discussion, but argued that this was more than was usual. The substantive point he was trying to make was that the police authority made no coherent or coordinated attempt to influence policy. The policy changes that had taken place occurred independently of the police authority, and would have been the same had it not existed.

It is quite important to remember that this councillor was willing to exaggerate for effect. He himself said that the passive deference of the majority of police authority members brought about a reaction in him which made him perhaps more critical of the police than he would otherwise be. He said 'sometimes I become a caricature of myself'. Because most members refused to take their role seriously, it seemed that meetings had become something of a game to this member. For example, he clearly admired and respected the senior officers who attended the meeting, and yet was quite outspoken in his public criticisms of them. He recounted how the deputy chief constable decided to remove police horses from the sub-division covering his area, a decision with which he agreed. However, he publicly denounced the decision at a police authority meeting: 'Of course I made a big fuss and publicly objected, but in efficiency terms he was right, you couldn't justify a couple of horses'. It appeared that he rather enjoyed his 'bad boy' reputation on the police authority, and also that the senior officers rather enjoyed his contributions.

One interesting finding concerned the way in which agendas for police authority meetings were set. The secretary to the police authority explained how two or three weeks prior to full meetings, there was a meeting of the chief officers group, comprising the clerk, the deputy clerk (county solicitor), the treasurer and the architect. At this meeting there was discussion of the issues to go forward to meetings. It is important to note that there was no member representation on this body. Draft agendas were then circulated amongst other officers to obtain agreement to what was to go forward. The secretary estimated that the input to the agenda was about 50 per cent from the chief constable.

Police-community consultative committees
The history of police-community consultation in the area was an unusual one with the force itself responding to Home Office guidelines, but being opposed in this by its police authority which argued that the current arrangements (informal meetings between the local police commander and district councillors) were sufficient. The argument was that the public already had a high level of trust for the police force, and that the introduction of more formal consultation mechanisms would simply be a waste of time and resources.

However, section 106 of PACE made it a statutory requirement that police authorities should set up local consultative mechanisms. In the light of this, the police authority decreed that the existing crime prevention panels in the county would be made 'more representative' and deemed consultative committees. The Labour-controlled borough council of the main town in the force area took a different view. They wanted a more active consultative body, and set up a police and public safety committee as a sub-committee of the council. They appointed a full-time police adviser to service the committee, and requested that the police force treat it as a section 106 consultative committee. The police authority opposed this development, but were pursuaded by the police force to accept the arrangement. The committee included local borough councillors, and representatives of various community groups and interests. The Conservative borough councillors refused to take up their places on the committee because they saw it as an anti-police body. The local police commander also attended the local crime prevention panel which continued to meet regularly.

The 'police and public safety' committee was unique in the study (possibly unique to the UK) in that it was a sub-committee of a borough council with elected members, and at the same time was recognised as a consultative committee under section 106 of PACE. As a sub-committee of the borough council policy and finance committee, this was the only section 106 committee in the study with direct access to funds and to local authority decision-making structures. The police adviser to the committee was interviewed, and a meeting was attended by a researcher. The committee had existed for about four years at the time of the research. It had a membership which reflected the political balance on the borough council, with five Labour councillors, one SLD, one Independent and spaces for two Conservatives (not taken up). Additionally, there were co-opted members, including two police authority members (in an individual capacity), and representatives from the local chamber of commerce, the federation of residents and tenants, the trades council, the local council for voluntary service, and Women's Aid. In an attempt to obtain a broader representation on the committee, an observer status had been created which was open to any organisation in the town. At the meeting attended by a PSI researcher, there were ten observers present, including representatives from NW, victim support, the local rape crisis centre, the local 'ethnic minorities advice project', a gay community organisation, a civil liberties group, and the lay visitors panel.

The initial impression was that the committee was viewed positively by all who were involved, although perhaps for slightly different reasons. For example, the chief constable and the chair of the police authority, both described the committee as a useful device for defusing political problems. The chief constable described it as a 'safety valve', and the chair said that the police had been 'very clever' in cooperating with the committee so that its 'anti-police' stance would be undermined. However, the chief constable also said that the committee had 'got things done'. The local sub-divisional commanders also spoke very positively about the committee. It was compared favourably to other consultative committees which tended to be just 'talking shops', and the police said that they had 'worked closely' with the committee to bring about a number of improvements in the town. The sub-divisional commander referred to it as 'true consultation', and explained that he was happy to release a good deal of information to the committee because of the high trust conditions which existed. He contrasted it with the unquestioning and 'stifling' support of some members of the police authority, which although flattering, was of little practical use. The sub-divisional commander did view the committee as unrepresentative, mainly due to the refusal of the Conservative councillors to participate. This led to the committee being perceived as a left-wing body in the town, and a bias towards left-leaning organisations. Right-of-centre and independent bodies were under-represented on the committee. The police were very keen to mention this committee and their cooperation with it, and appeared proud of a number of achievements associated with the forum. In particular they mentioned changes in relation to the policing of domestic violence, and crime prevention initiatives. An important feature of the committee's success from the police viewpoint was that it had access to financial resources, and to council policy.

The police adviser supported the views of the committee outlined by local senior police officers. She explained that a central reason behind the police authority's agreement to recognise the body as a section 106 committee was the fact that the police thought such an arrangement would be helpful. She said the the police had been supportive from the start, and willingly attended committee meetings and provided information. The committee had been active in some of the chosen policy areas. The Women's Aid representative had strongly criticised the local police response to domestic violence. Representatives from the committee then met with senior police officers from the sub-division to discuss the possible improvements in the police response to the problem. Although the initial response from the police was rather defensive, they did agree to bring about changes. A referral card was produced which gave guidelines to police officers dealing with domestic disputes, and reminding them that if there was evidence of assault (ABH or GBH) then the usual response should be an arrest. The card also gave a telephone number for a helpline in the local housing department. The card was distributed amongst all local police officers - the police adviser had checked with some new probationers and found that they were in fact carrying them. Although she recognised that it was very difficult to change policing practices, she felt that the referral card and the greater emphasis on domestic violence constituted an important change in local police policy.

Whilst the issue of rape investigation was raised in some detail at the meeting we attended, the police adviser felt that much of the influence for change in this area of policy had come via the Home Office circulars and force headquarters. However, the committee had produced a number of initiatives in terms of crime prevention. It had carried out a project on racial harrassment, and produced recommendations for the police and the local housing department. The police had responded positively to nearly all the recommendations (unlike the council department). The committee had provided funds for a target-hardening programme for council houses, and set up a joint security survey carried out by the police and the technical services department. They had also persuaded the housing department to create a secure homes officer post, to be a permanent link between the housing department and police crime prevention specialists. The committee had also funded a public survey on community safety in 1988, and published an extensive report with recommendations for all local council departments and the local police.

The meeting of the committee attended by a researcher was long and, at times, heated. After the meeting, the sub-divisional commander explained that it had been an unusually divisive meeting. The main issues on the agenda concerned a report from the local police on their objectives for the coming year, the police response to rape and sexual assault, a discussion of the fear of crime, reported crime statistics for the previous year, and police advice to local licensees. The most controversial part of the meeting was when the police received strong criticism for the level of reported rapes (recorded in the local statistics) which were 'no-crimed'. It was suggested that unsympathetic or disbelieving attitudes on the part of male officers were causing genuine victims of sexual assault to retract their statements. The police response was a led by the detective chief inspector (DCI) who presented the sub-divisional statistics on rape and sexual assault, and a female detective who outlined policy on dealing with somebody reporting sexual assault. The Women's Aid representative and a female councillor were not satisfied with this and said they knew of a number of cases in which the victim was not interviewed by a female officer and was questioned aggressively by a male officer. The DCI said this was contrary to force policy, and asked that he be given details of these cases after the meeting so that he could investigate what had happened. There followed a strong attack from the woman councillor on police attitudes to women in general. She attacked the CID in particular for its 'macho' culture, and low female representation. The debate became quite heated, with the local sub-divisional commander describing some of the claims as 'outrageous'. Another female councillor dissociated herself from what she called 'blanket attacks' on the police as an organisation.

The researcher was able to talk informally to the local sub-divisional commanders and the DCI immediately after the meeting. They expressed considerable frustration with the way the discussion had developed. One senior officer pointed out that the verbal attacks on the police would be reported widely by the local radio and newspapers, with a negative effect on their public image. The DCI used strong language to question the usefulness of cooperating with the committee, when he felt that it was 'anti-police' and would attack them whatever they did. However, another senior officer was more positive, and described it as a 'good lively meeting'. Although they argued that most of the criticisms of the police with regard to rape victims were unfounded, they also said that they would check some of the claims about particular cases. One senior officer suggested that they should try to ensure that retraction statements in rape cases (as well as reporting statements) should be taken by a trained female officer. Thus, although the criticisms of the police had been expressed in a hostile manner, the reaction of senior officers was by no means a totally defensive one.

Other forms of local consultation

Force A took the interesting initiative of commissioning a major survey of public attitudes about policing. The findings did appear to have an important effect on policy development within the force. As noted above, the findings were the subject of personal presentations by the chief and deputy constable to all sections of the force. Territorial and functional commanders were asked to respond to the findings with specific recommendations of ways to improve quality of service in the areas raised by the survey. One of the central findings highlighted by senior officers was an expressed desire for the police to be involved in proactive prevention activity, rather than concentrate on law enforcement. This was cited by the deputy chief constable as an important contributary factor to the development of the new force policy on crime prevention, which included the setting up of a special community crime prevention department. Another finding from the survey was a perceived desire for more visible police presence. The force had decided on a number of ways of responding to this, one of which was to add a crest and 'POLICE' logo to unmarked police cars in the force's vehicle fleet. The force was also considering ways to respond to the main three dissatisfactions expressed in the survey. These were the lack of follow-up and failure to keep people informed of the progress of cases; slow response to requests for assistance and failure to explain delays; and finally, complaints about the physical appearance of police stations, waiting rooms and reception areas.

The use of such surveys was an interesting departure from the more common institutional ways of measuring public preferences about policing. Although a minority of members of the police authority criticised its introduction as by-passing the formal channels of influence through local representatives, senior police officers argued that it was a more direct way of tapping into the perceptions and needs of the public. A main aim of the survey was to explore differences between perceived levels of service for people who had experienced contact with the police in a 12 month period (crime victims, people who have had to produce driving documents, people who have reported incidents to the police) and those who had not. The survey did *not* include people who had been arrested or reported for an offence.

The force also had a network of CPPs, which operated in most of the force area as the section 106 committees. Contact was made with both CPPs in the two sub-divisions: a researcher attended a meeting of one and interviewed the chair of the other. The meeting was that of the CPP in the same sub-division as the police and public safety sub-committee. The panel had a membership of about 18, 12 of whom attended the meeting. The non-police reprentatives included a residents' association, NW, the Red Cross Society, and the Association of British Insurers. The meeting was very much led by the police, and as outlined by the sub-divisional commander, the atmosphere was highly supportive, almost deferential towards them. The main part of the meeting was taken up with a description by the CPO of various crime prevention projects which the police were undertaking. There was little discussion of these, and the main initiative to come from the group was the plan to hold a crime prevention stall at a local fair. The senior police officers saw attending meetings of the CPP as mainly a public relations exercise, with little relevance for substantive policing issues on the sub-division. The chair of the CPP in the other sub-division said that being made into a section 106 committee had made little difference to the panel. He said that the panel had become more active in recent years due to the activities of the local CPO who was seen as a dynamic character who wanted to involve the CPP. The kinds of initiative he mentioned included a property-marking scheme, providing a crime prevention stall at the town show, and obtaining sponsorship to produce a crime prevention advice leaflet.

The other kind of local 'representative' with whom contact was made in this force were NW coordinators. Both sub-divisions had NW coordinators working in the main police station; one was employed full-time by the police authority, and the other was a part-time post funded by the Employment Training scheme. There was an official policy of encouraging NW in the force, and the coordinators helped to set up schemes, arranging initial meetings and the distribution of information packs. The coordinators sent out monthly crime figures to contact people on each beat. There was a variable level of contact with local beat officers on both sub-divisions with some officers keeping regular contact with NW schemes but others were less inclined to do so. There was an answerphone on one sub-division for scheme contact-persons to call in with information for the police. Both of the coordinators were also involved in more general adminstration in the sub-divisional crime prevention departments. In sum, the police-NW contact was usually limited to the setting up stage (when schemes were addressed by the CPO and/or beat officers), or occasional meetings such as AGMs. Most contact involved the passing of information relating to local reported crimes from the police to the schemes.

Force B

An analysis of the minutes and reports of the police authority was undertaken for the period 1985-1990. The principal officer to the police authority was unwilling to provide files from previous years, on the grounds that most changes in the three specific areas of policy had occurred after 1985.

There was a good deal of material in the minutes on each of the chosen policy areas. A number of references were found to crime prevention in the period covered. Of these, most were reports from the chief constable, usually requesting financial support from the police authority for certain schemes. For example, in September 1986 the chief constable reported that he had established a design advisory service with the help of Urban Programme funding, but that funding was now running out. The report requested that the police authority agree to continue the funding of two architect liaison posts so that the scheme would remain on a force-wide basis. Although this appears to fit in with the pattern of post-hoc accountability, introducing the scheme before reporting to the police authority, there was also evidence of a more active contribution on crime prevention from the police authority. The minutes referred to a special meeting of the authority held in 1989 to discuss current crime prevention initiatives, and the overall strategy and philosophy behind them. As a result of this, the police authority established a crime prevention sub-committee to which district councils were asked to nominate representatives. The minutes of a meeting held in February 1989 recorded that 'members asked the chief constable about the various crime prevention initiatives and the strategy and philosophy being pursued by the force'. The chief's response was that a paper was being prepared for the AMA on the respective roles of police authorities and police forces in the field of crime prevention, which would be discussed at the next meeting.

There were fewer references in the minutes to development in policy on rape, domestic violence and child abuse. However, there had been some important developments of policy within this force, and the minutes did refer to them. For example, in April 1988 the minutes recorded that the members had been in contact with the Greater Manchester Police Authority who had outlined details of the St Mary's Centre (a hospital-based victim reception service for victims of sexual assault). The police authority decided that current arrangements in their force were adequate, but asked the chief constable to consider the implications of the Manchester initiative and report back. This is evidence of the authority providing an impetus for change in this area of policy. In July 1988, the authority considered the Home Office circular 52/88 on the investigation of child abuse. The chief constable was asked to report back about the current force procedures for investigating child abuse. The chief duly reported back at the next meeting in some detail about the procedures in place in the force. There was one mention of domestic violence when in 1989 the chief constable reported to the police authority that the force had set up an experimental domestic violence unit in a particular sub-division. The police authority agreed to support the pilot project until it had been evaluated, with a view to such units becoming a permanent feature of the force. The other mention of this general area of policy came in a discussion of an annual HMIC report which commended force B as a leading police force nationally in the development of initiatives on domestic violence and child abuse. The police authority called for additional specific funding from central government to recognise their progress in these 'sensitive' areas of policing.

There was a great deal of information in the minutes about the policy of civilianisation and staffing in general. Again, the minutes implied that the police authority was more than just a passive receiver of information. In 1986 there was a general discussion about staffing, and the chief constable reported that the main drive to civilianisation had already occurred, with over 100 police officer posts released during the previous six years. Interestingly, the chief noted that there was 'little scope for further improvement in this area'. The minutes recorded how a force review in 1986 concluded with the argument that force B was heavily under-staffed given its levels of population and recorded crime. In November 1986, the minutes recorded the concern of the police authority that police establishments were the sole basis for determining the police part of the Department of Environment RSG. The authority had a personnel sub-committee which appeared to take a close interest in the details of civilian employment in the force. For example, the minutes of a meeting in early 1987 recorded that the personnel sub-committee needed to give its express agreement before the force could employ ex-police officers in receipt of a pension in a civilian post. An entry from two years later showed that this was followed up, when it was recorded that the chief asked for permission to employ two medically-retired former police officers as control room assistants on the grounds of their police experience. In 1988 a report from the 114/83 sub-committee stated that an experimental ASU had been set up in two sub-divisions. The personnel sub-committee requested a full report on civilianisation, including number of posts civilianised, number of police officers returned to operational duties, and an assessment of the scope for further progress. This report was duly provided by the chief constable. In 1989, the personnel sub-committee responded to the Home Office circular 105/88 by again requesting a review of the scope for civilianisation in the force and suggesting a check-list of areas. The chief responded to this at the next meeting with a full report of the progress made in the force so far, and giving details of the next stage of the civilianisation programme. Thus, while the chief had reported in 1986 that there was little further scope for civilianisation, there remained a great deal of interest at the police authority in the further development in the civilianisation programme. This seems to have been largely initiated by Home Office circulars and perceived staffing shortages. Overall, the minutes gave the impression that the authority had significant influence in this area of policy.

The other source of information on the workings of the police authority came from interviews with the principal officer, the chair, the opposition spokesperson, and the chair of the crime prevention sub-committee. There was general agreement that the police authority should take as active a role as possible in policy development. However, both the principal officer and the chair of the police authority were aware of the dependency of the authority on information from the police in order to fulfil this role. The principal officer argued that the authority was more active in influencing policy than shire county police authorities, and felt that this was a feature of all metropolitan authorities. The chair also made this point, and argued that the reason for the greater activism was that in metropolitan authorities members came from metropolitan district councils which were unitary authorities with responsibility for the whole range of local government services. This, in his view, encouraged members to look at policing as one of a number of inter-connected services rather than something distinct, and thus they did not feel they could not be involved in developing policy. However, the ability of the police authority to influence policy was hampered by its lack of information and support. The principal officer said that the authority probably lacked the 'clout' to actually initiate changes in policy, because it had to formulate its view almost entirely on police-based information. A related point was that members did not have the necessary expertise in particular areas of policing policy. The chair alluded to this point when discussing an experimental specialist unit, and whether the police authority would decide to bring in force-wide units. He said that it was very difficult for them to see the options clearly, because certain initiatives take on a 'political' importance within the police organisation and based on their information it was 'difficult to obtain an objective view'.

All those interviewed described a good working relationship with the chief constable, usually put down to 'good sense' on all sides, and the length of time he had been in the post which had allowed local relationships to become well-established. The chair of the crime prevention sub-committee and the opposition spokesperson made reference to the operational independence of the chief constable. Both said that there was an 'operational' element in the chief's role into which the police authority should not encroach, although as outlined in Chapter 1, the definition of operational was not entirely clear.

As regards perceived influence over the specific policy areas, it was clear that the chair saw an important role for the police authority in the promotion of crime prevention. He felt that the lead agencies in crime prevention should be local authorities, because of the range of services that they provide. Additionally, he argued that it was part of the police authority's role to promote crime prevention initiatives to the general public and to other agencies. He said that in view of this, they had set up a joint crime prevention committee comprising police authority members and members of the constituent district councils in the force area. This was intended to promote crime prevention initiatives at the local level. He argued that although such schemes as Safer Cities may have beneficial effects in the short-term, their benefits last only as long as funding does, and that a longer term approach was needed. However, the chair of the joint crime prevention committee did not appear to have well-developed views on crime prevention. His main concern was with law enforcement, and he expressed extreme frustration at what he saw as over-lenient treatment of offenders, along with insufficient police staffing. He made some vague references to the crime prevention initiatives in the force area, but seemed dubious about their chances of having a real effect.

The police authority chair felt that the main change in force policy with regard to rape victims was the development of victim reception suites. He could not remember exactly from where the initiative had come, but his impression was that of a combination of senior police officers and interested members of the authority. His main concern was with the financial resources required to support such a policy. He also expressed strong concern about domestic violence, saying that the incidence was increasing and that each case was a potential murder. He was undecided as to whether or not the force should have specialist units, and was awaiting the evaluation of the one experimental unit which had been set up in one sub-division. He was, however, aware of the 'political' nature of such issues within the police organisation, and appeared unsure whether the police authority would have all options set before them in an unbiased manner so that they could make an informed choice. He felt that there had probably been initial opposition to the child protection units, but these were now generally accepted as a successful initiative.

The policy of civilianisation was supported, subject to capping restrictions on expenditure by central government. Perceived under-staffing was a strong theme on the police authority, and civilianisation was seen as one way of making the best use of available staff. The introduction of ASUs was supported cautiously, subject to the results of an evaluation. The chair said that the general introduction of ASUs would be discussed in the police authority because it had major resource implications. The opposition spokesperson recalled that a number of members had called into question the concentration of civilian posts at the force headquarters. They had been invited to visit the premises and see for themselves what the staff were doing, in order to convince them that these posts were necessary. This indicates that members did take more than a passing interest in the policy of civilianisation, and were prepared to raise questions on the force policy in this area.

Perhaps one of the most interesting references to the influence of the police authority in the area of civilianisation was made by the force personnel officer. He outlined that it was the police authority, not the chief constable, who had the ultimate authority over grading and salaries of civilian staff. In practice, the authority tended to accept the recommendations of the chief constable, but an important part of the personnel officer's job was to negotiate and bargain with members and smooth the path to agreement. It was by no means a foregone conclusion that the chief constable would always prevail. In the words of the personnel officer:

> ...on grading structures and so on, of civilians, they can and sometimes do oppose what the chief constable himself would think... Not everything goes to the police authority, but everything with financial implications must go to the police authority to get their support. *No matter what the view of the chief constable is, if they don't agree with those policies then they are not adopted. He can shout until he is blue in the face, but they are not adopted.* (emphasis added)

Police-community consultative committees

Force B also had a network of local consultative committees organised on a sub-divisional basis, and chaired by members of the police authority. They were called 'police-community forums'. Sub-divisional commanders in both sub-divisions visited were asked about the operation of these committees in their areas. Both commanders were sceptical about the usefuless of the forums; one said that the meetings were well-attended, but that little useful information in terms of criminal intelligence or indicators of dissatisfaction arose from them. It was usually left to the police to lead the meetings with inputs from the CPO, or a talk from the DI on local crime

249

trends, or a talk from another officer on a special subject such as road safety. The commander of the other sub-division said that he did not have a great deal of faith in the forums. He also made the point that unless the police put matters on the agenda, few substantive issues were raised. It was all 'top-down' with agenda items coming either from himself, or the chair. Matters raised by the members were usually complaints about the lack of police officers, or minor matters of nuisance. The quarterly meetings were sparsely attended. The meetings were held at various venues within each sub-division. The commander of one preferred the meetings to be held in high-crime 'problem' areas. He described a particular meeting, held on a problem estate, as 'the best meeting I've been to in the last two years' because 'we got a right slagging off the people'. He said that he welcomed real criticism for a change, and joked that the forum chair (from the police authority) could not leave the meeting quickly enough. He appeared to welcome the challenge of lively debate, describing how he had addressed a meeting of the local Labour party and come in for 'one and a half hours of fast bowling'. It was impossible to judge, however, to what extent he would have been prepared to alter local policing priorities in response to regular and formal meetings like this, though he felt that if forums had access to some financial resources, then they would have more influence in terms of affecting policy.

Other forms of local consultation

One of the police sub-divisions visited was in the main city in the force area. Some years previously, the city council had designated certain deprived areas of the city 'priority areas' and set up what were called 'Priority Area Teams' (PATs). There were two PATs in the sub-division visited and the sub-divisional commander was very enthusiastic about them. We interviewed the coordinator of one PAT, who was an officer of the city council. He explained that the initial idea of such teams had been to bring officer representatives and local representatives together to identify and address particular local problems. Each team had a small budget (£32,000) provided by the city council and the 'Inner City Partnership'. The teams operated as formal sub-committees of the city council and were chaired by councillors. The idea was to identify particular local problems and then bring pressure to bear on the relevant service committees of the city council to address them. A number of problems had arisen with the teams, one being that they tended to marginalise local issues, with the result that some people felt it was better to address the main service committees directly.

The coordinator described crime as the best example of a problem which needed to be addressed by a number of different agencies. He desribed the particular team in the sub-division visited, as it was based in a socially-deprived council estate with over 80 per cent unemployment, a high proportion of single mothers and young children, and high levels of recorded crime. He said that the fear of crime was much higher than other areas with similar crime rates. The PAT had first taken the form of a working party, with representatives from assistant director level in council service departments, and from the police the sub-divisional commander and his deputy. Below this there was a 'task group' consisting of front-line workers (teachers, social workers, health visitors and the permanent beat officer) which met monthly, and passed advice and recommendations to the working party.

The only initiative connected with the police input which was mentioned concerned the redesign of the estate. The local police arranged for the council to liaise with the design advisory service at the force HQ who were able to input extensive crime prevention advice. While the police were enthusiastic about their participation in this team, the coordinator was cautious about the success they had achieved. He identified two problems in particular in relation to the police involvement. First, the low status of community policing in general, and PBOs in particular, within the police organisation. He said that it was very difficult for the PBOs to make a substantial contribution when their role was somewhat marginalised from mainstream policing activities. They were too-often moved away from PBO duties 'for operational reasons,' and their relatively lowly position within the organisational hierarchy prevented them from effectively developing priorities and strategies for their job. The second, and perhaps related problem, concerned differences in organisational ideology regarding the notion of community development. The coordinator of the PAT said: 'I see it as empowering people to take control of and improve their lives but the police see it more in terms of controlling people'. Despite these reservations, the relationship between the police and the members of the committee appeared to be cordial and the PATs can be regarded as a significant form of local police-community consultation.

The sub-divisions also had CPPs. The CPO in one sub-division explained that they were in the process of setting up the CPP there and it had yet to undertake initiatives or activities. The other sub-divisional panel met monthly, and was attended by the sub-divisional commander (or his deputy) and the CPO. The CPO said that the CPP involved 'an awful lot of talking and very little activity'. Additionally, the CPP had a number of sub-committees which also met monthly so that the CPO was attending a committee meeting every week of the month. However, the CPPs were considered useful in developing external sponsorship for the force. There was increasing interest in outside organisations in sponsoring crime prevention activities but when this was done via the police force a lot of time was spent clearing this with headquarters. To avoid this, the police would often direct sponsorship through the panel, and make it a CPP initiative.

Force B took a much more active role in supporting NW than the other forces in the study. At each sub-division, a NW liaison officer was interviewed. These were civilian employees of the police authority helping to set up and coordinate the schemes in the sub-division. The officers provided a two-way channel of information between the police and scheme coordinators. They each stated that most of the schemes were set up as a result of public demand (rather than police-initiated). There was a considerable amount of direct contact between police officers and NW schemes at the setting-up stage. The chief inspector would address a meeting of the members, and another meeting would involve a crime prevention video and a talk by the CPO. After this, the contact was mainly through the liaison officer. But this was quite an organised affair. The liaison officer would receive details about crimes in each NW area from the constable responsible for crime-pattern analysis on the sub-division. Details of crimes would be passed on daily to a contact person in each scheme. Additionally, there was a monthly NW newspaper produced by the force and distributed free to all of the schemes. Each sub-division had a quarterly meeting of scheme coordinators. So while the contact and influence was definitely still one-way (from police to the schemes), the organisation and support was far more coordinated than in other forces.

Force C

It was not possible to carry out as thorough an analysis of minutes and reports of police committee meetings in force C as in the other forces. However, the secretary to the police committee did provide the relevant extracts and reports from the meetings over the previous two years in which any of the chosen policy areas had been raised in the course of the discussion.

There were four references to matters concerning crime prevention. All concerned details about two particular projects being undertaken by the force. One of these involved consideration of the installation of closed circuit television cameras (CCTV) in the city centre of the main city in the force area. The minutes recorded that the matter was raised by the police committee chair, who supported the concept, but raised concern about the lack of information given to the committee on the project, and also the civil liberties implications. The chief constable explained that the project had been recommended by a working group on public disorder in the city centre, and a report had been passed to the city council for discussion with a view to making an application to the Safer Cities project for financial support. It is interesting to note the record of the chief constable's additional comments: 'This was an operational matter on which he was prepared to submit a report but in respect of which the Police Committee had no right to direct action'. The debate over this issue was to carry on into future meetings. The minutes of a later meeting included quite a detailed report of the working party set up to examine the possibility of CCTV in the city centre. The accompanying report from the chief constable explained that the working party asked the city council and the police force to produce a full technical specification, and asked that the police committee take note of this.

There were also two references in the committee minutes to the crime prevention initiative called 'Operation Lifestyle'. This simply informed the police committee of what the initiative was and how it worked over the previous year. The second report explained that the force was intending to fund the scheme for another year. The minutes noted that the committee resolved to 'note' the report, and take steps to increasing member involvement in the scheme in the coming year.

The secretary to the police authority also found a number of minutes and reports referring to rape, domestic violence and child abuse. The main subject was in fact domestic violence. At the request of the chair, the police committee considered the creation of a specialist domestic violence unit, and asked for a report to be submitted from the chief constable on this matter. The chief constable responded with two fairly basic reports of about a page or so in length. The first of these outlined the fact that a force working party had been set up to examine the feasibility of specialist units to deal with child abuse and sexual offences. The second announced to the police committee that the decision had been taken to introduce specialist units, with a primary responsibility for dealing with child abuse and sexual offences (and liaising with social services in this task), but with additional responsibility for appropriate cases of domestic violence. The units were to be introduced in four towns within the force area. Again, the details in the reports were minimal. The police committee was not asked to agree or support the recommendations, but simply to note that the report had been made.

Bearing in mind the limited data available it nevertheless appears that there was little evidence of active police committee involvement in any of the chosen policy areas. In fact, the minutes provide evidence not only of the police committee being told about initiatives after the event, but also of the limited nature of this *post hoc* information. The quotation from the chief about 'operational matters' showed clearly his limited view as to the proper role of the police committee, which was supported by interviews with leading members of the committee.

A researcher was able to attended a meeting of the force C police committee during the period of the fieldwork. Notes from this meeting suggest little productive discussion of policing policy at police committee meetings. The first item to draw real comment concerned the reorganisation of regional crime squads, whereby the regional office would close and be transfered to a town in a neighbouring force. Some members asked questions about whether the new arrangements would cost more, whether the old office should have remained because it was near to the docks. Another member asked if this was a step towards regional police forces, and the chief constable said he had raised the same point in ACPO. Another item concerned vacancies in the force establishment. One member gave an example of two applicants he knew who had been turned down, even though he thought they were good candidates. The chief gave an account of the selection procedure, and the chief superintendent in charge of personnel matters explained that transfer applicants were not given preference. There followed a general discussion about the need for more women applicants, which became quite heated as Labour members stressed the importance of recruiting more women. The chief constable, suppported by some Conservative members stressed the importance of equal opportunities, and argued that treating all people equally constrained the employment of more women.

The next item was a discussion of police training, following a review of provincial forces training by the District Audit Service. The chief constable had submitted what he called 'the District Auditor's findings and recommendations' although it appeared to be a summary only along with a brief note of his own. The recommendations were for significant changes; the force had not performed well compared to some of the other forces studied by the auditors. The force personnel officer made some comments which largely overlooked the substantive points made in the report. A member asked whether officers had job descriptions, and on receiving a negative reply, asked how officers were trained. The chief gave a vague reply about training of recruits being mainly for patrol work, and thereafter for various specialisms.

The coordinator of the Safer Cities initiative in the main city of the force area had submitted a paper about the possible introduction of CCTV in the city centre. The chief and Conservative members appeared to support this move, and doubts raised by Labour members caused some annoyance to the chief constable who asked for his 'disappointment' with the police committee to be put on record. The police committee chair proposed that a representative group be established to manage the crime prevention response in the city centre.

There was a major item on crime statistics which showed huge increases since the previous year. There was no real discussion of the actual figures, although members had referred to the increases in a general way during other parts of the meeting. Members asked questions about the effect of all-day drinking on crime figures, and the incidence of arson. The final item concerned the force priorities for the following year. The chief constable had circulated a brief note which stressed the development of 'quality of service'.

A number of semi-structured interviews were carried out with the secretary to the police committee, the chair, the vice-chair, a Conservative member, a magistrate, and the chief executive of the county council (who was the clerk to the police committee). A strong theme running through all the interviews was that there was a significant difference between members of the police committee and the chief constable as to their proper respective roles. The secretary said that the new chair felt that the police committee should have more of a proactive role in developing policing policy, whereas the chief constable took a more traditional line. This was developed in some detail by the members of the police committee, in particular the chair. He gave a number of examples where the chief constable had unilaterally introduced substantial changes without any discussion with the police committee. Furthermore, the chief was often unwilling to provide full information after the event, resulting in the police committee having to request reports on aspects of policing (as was their statutory right under the 1964 Police Act). According to the chair, the chief constable frequently described issues as 'operational matters' in order to prevent discussion at police committee meetings. When the police committee wanted to discuss the introduction of CCTV in the force, the chief constable took legal advice on whether he could over-ride any veto. The chair said that 'the only effective veto we have is not buying anything'. The CCTV example was important because the chief was in favour of introducing it to the city centre, and would be able to have the equipment bought for him by either the Safer Cities programme, or the city council. In the view of the chair, this raised important constitutional implications in that the chief could obtain equipment from other sources even if the police committee and the county council were strongly opposed. The chair summed up what he saw as the chief's view of the police committee: 'I feel really that he sees the police committee as something of an irritation rather than a necessity'.

This overall impression was supported by the leading Conservative member who was interviewed. He said: 'I don't know what goes on elsewhere, I'm not in the ruling group, but I do feel the chief constable makes problems for himself by not being as open as he might be on a number of subjects... He seems to be quite inflexible'. The magistrate member interviewed also said that there were a number of issues on which the chief should have consulted with the police committee before taking action. The over-riding impression therefore, was one of a difficult relationship between the chief constable and his police committee. It was the only police authority in the study where there was an open and substantial difference between leading members and the chief constable about their respective roles under the 1964 Police Act. This difference came out strongly in discussions about police committee influence in the particular areas of policy in which we were interested.

Taking crime prevention first, the force had gone ahead with a number of initiatives including NW, 'Operation Lifestyle' which had significant implications in terms of finance and police time, and of course the disputed CCTV project. None of the members of the police committee that were interviewed could remember full discussions on any of these before the chief went ahead with his plans. The chair had strong views on who should be the leading agency in terms of crime prevention projects. He felt that the police were too isolated and unwilling to work with other agencies to be suitable for the role, and therefore suggested that it should be the responsibility of local authorities, with the chief executive's office being in charge of overall coordination of crime prevention policy. The chair saw the central government-inspired initiatives of Crime Concern and Safer Cities (both of which were set up in the force area) as ways of diluting the responsibilities of local government, and confusing responsibility for crime prevention. Both the chair and the opposition spokesperson were strong supporters of NW. The latter had argued that the force should support NW in a number of police committee meetings, but the chief constable was reluctant to be involved, although the reasons for this were unclear. Eventually, the force decided to set up pilot schemes of NW, much later than had been the case in other forces. The feeling was that this was a response to central government championing of NW rather than the matter being raised in the police committee. When the decision to launch NW was taken, there was no discussion with the police committee, the chief constable simply went ahead with his plans. It was a similar case with Operation Lifestyle; the opposition spokesperson had strong misgivings about whether the project worked and whether the police should be involved, but the project was simply launched and the committee informed after the event.

The chair mentioned one area in which the police committee actually wished to initiate a crime prevention policy. He said that the committee were looking at the possibility of starting a security patrol scheme to prevent vandalism of schools and other council premises. He predicted that the chief constable would be strongly opposed to this. It appears therefore, that the police committee had little practical influence on the development of crime prevention initiatives in the force area, and the policy-making process was summed up in the words of the opposition spokesperson: 'I think it was very much a question of the chief constable deciding it was going to happen, and it happened'.

The police committee had little input into the development of policing policy regarding the treatment of rape victims, domestic violence or the investigation of child abuse. The chair did raise the issue of domestic violence by calling for a report from the chief constable. His report announced the setting up of a working party to examine the feasibility of specialist units covering serious sexual offences, child abuse and 'appropriate' incidents of domestic violence. The chief constable later decided to introduce these units. This development may have been a response to the matter being raised by the police committee chair. However, he argued that the police were already looking to set up specialist child abuse units, and simply 'tacked on' responsibility for dealing with rape and domestic violence to these because the chief constable was opposed to a specialist domestic violence unit. The chair felt strongly that these crimes should not all be grouped together as the remit of one kind of specialist unit. The opposition spokesperson supported the view that initiatives in these areas were not really discussed at police authority level. He described the introduction of specially-trained 'victim liaison officers' to deal with sexual offence victims, and the employment of female police surgeons, as 'initiatives that have very largely been undertaken by the police, behind the screen of police operational activities'. Regarding child abuse, the secretary to the police committee could find no record of reports or discussions in the minutes. The chair said that his main source of information on the developments being undertaken in the force, in particular cooperation between the police and social workers, was the social services committee of the county council where matters were more fully discussed. The chair summed up the police committee's involvement in each of these areas by saying 'we were not involved in any way in the formulation of that policy'.

The secretary to the police committee commented that the committee had strongly supported the policy of civilianisation since the early 1980s. Both the chair and the opposition spokesperson appeared to see the primary benefits of civilianisation in terms of growth of operational capacity, rather than organisational effectiveness. A number of posts had been civilianised within the force, and they had broken new ground by employing a civilian director of finance and administration in 1988. The civilians were employees of the police committee, but in the view of the chair, it made little practical difference who was the employing authority for police civilians. In practice they came under the direction and control of the chief constable. However, there was evidence that the employing authority *was* of some practical significance in so far as the chief did not necessarily have the final word over matters of grading and pay. There was an example of the police committee view prevailing against that of the chief, in a dispute over the grade of the force finance and administration officer. However, there was also evidence of the chief's view prevailing against that of the authority. One example was the force scenes of crime officers (SOCOs) who had been on a very low grade for some time. The police committee chair thought that they should be regraded, and was backed up by the county council personnel department. But the chief constable opposed this and the SOCOs remained on a low grade.

Police community consultative committees

At the time of the research, force C had a network of 16 police-community liaison committees, each chaired by a member of the police committee. These were established as section 106 committees when PACE came into effect in January 1985. A report by the chief constable to the police committee in 1989 said that the committees had operated in the force with 'varying degrees of success', and announced that a review of the committees' functioning had been completed. During the fieldwork, a number of sources explained to us that the committees had been largely police-led, although the (then) new chair of the police committee attempted to galvanise their role by initiating a 'police authority support group' to provide administrative back-up to the committee meetings (by for example taking minutes and producing agendas). One sub-divisional commander made the familiar criticism that the consultative committee in her sub-division was poorly-attended by the public and that what she saw as fairly trivial issues such as noise or dog-dirt were frequently the main topic for discussion. She also described her relationship with the chair of the committee (a Labour councillor) as 'very difficult'. When the committees were first established, the public were not admitted to meetings. The chair of the police committee described the operation of the consultative committees as 'very unsuccessful' due to lack of both public support and police cooperation. It was at his request that the public were admitted to meetings. No examples were found of the local consultative committees participating in substantial policy changes in any of the chosen policy areas.

Other forms of local representation

The force launched a network of CPPs in 1986, which in 1988 was rationalised to one per sub-division. There was a great deal of variation in the kinds of things which the CPPs were doing. For example, on one sub-division the commander did not attend meetings but sent a sergeant instead. The panel consisted of local councillors and did very little in practical terms. At another sub-division the panel was encouraged by the previous commander, and it took an active role, setting up for example an inter-agency working group looking at city centre disorder. It also met with brewery representatives to discuss the safety of public houses. The panel had pressured the local council on the issue of better lighting for car-parks to deter autocrime, had developed a 'vehicle watch' scheme, and had organised a well-attended crime prevention seminar at the offices of the main local employer.

Neighbourhood watch came to the force late, due to initial opposition from the chief constable. However, it was eventually decided that the police would support its development. The main problem was the amount of police time that was taken up servicing the schemes. The beat officer and CPO on one of the sub-divisions visited explained how it was such a drain on police time. It was the the PBO who responded to a request to start a scheme. He would circulate questionnaires, collect and review them, organise initial meetings and address them, as well as try to provide each scheme on his beat with up-to-date information. This meant that the schemes were very police-dependent. Although it was not possible to interview local NW coordinators, the strong impression was that the police-public contacts as regards NW were somewhat marginal to the main policy-making process.

Force D

The analysis of the minutes and reports of police authority meetings showed that the documentation it received and produced was substantially less, for example, than force A. There was little on record regarding the three policy areas chosen for study.

There were four references to crime prevention policy in the minutes, three of which were reports from the chief constable. First, in the annual report of the chief constable for 1983 there was a mention of the fact that physical target-hardening measures were the central area of the community affairs department's work. Second, in 1984, there was a report to the police authority by two members who had visited one of the early NW schemes in Bristol. The report recommended that the chief constable support the NW principle, and introduce experimental arrangements. In 1986, a report by the chief constable gave cautious support to NW and announced that the force had employed a civilian coordinator to administer NW schemes in the force area. Finally, the chief constable recommended in his 1988 report report that the Community Affairs Department should have a chief superintendent post at its head to give it a voice in the force policy team.

No references were found relating specifically to the investigation of rape, or to child sexual abuse. Two references to the policing of domestic violence were found in the minutes. The first, in the annual report of the chief constable for 1988, mentioned that a specialist unit had been set up with responsibility for dealing with victims of domestic violence. The second, and more substantial mention, was again in a report by the chief constable, although this time it was entirely about domestic violence. The report (from 1989) explained that the county council had set up a domestic violence panel in 1987, on which the chief constable was included. The panel had published its recommendations for all local authority departments in 1988. The report to the police authority went on to list the actions taken by the police force in response to these recommendations. These included circulation of details of women's refuges throughout the force; a re-examination of procedures resulting in the issue of a force standing order clarifying the role of the police in dealing with domestic violence; and finally the establishment of a 'family support unit'. The report concluded with a statement accepting the fact that the police were often criticised for failure to deal effectively with cases of domestic violence. However, it added, the role of other agencies, notably the Crown Prosecution Service, was also important.

There were a small number of references in the minutes to the policy of civilianisation. Most of these were reports from the chief constable on staff reviews, and one was a mention of the 1986 HMIC report on the force, commending it on its progressive approach to civilianisation. Of course, there were a number of papers and reports relating to administrative matters and matters other than the three chosen policy areas. There was reference to two things in particular which appeared significant. First, in 1982, the chief constable submitted a report to the police authority on the general subject of public order. The report referred to the Scarman recommendations on arrangements for reinforcement and improved public order training, and in particular, public order equipment. The report mentioned the availability of baton rounds and CS gas from the Home Secretary and stated that officers from all ranks in the force supported such provision. There was reference to the need to provide such equipment with a view to the force being 'adequate and efficient'. The minutes noted that the police authority called a special meeting to discuss this, and also planned to make representations to the regional HMI. No further references to this issue were found in subsequent minutes.

The other significant area mentioned in police authority minutes concerned local consultation. In 1982, a report from the clerk to the police authority recommended the setting up of a working party to consider the Scarman report. The following month, circular 54/1982, proposing local consultation arrangements, was received from the Home Secretary. The police authority working party report was presented with the specific recommendations for consultative committees in the force area. These recommendations were accepted by the police authority later in the year, and the Police-Liaison Advisory Committees (PLACS) were set up from that date on. The minutes show that the police authority took an active role in this development.

The second source of information about the influence of the police authority was based on observation of a meeting by a PSI researcher. The principal officer to the authority remarked that the meeting in question was a good one to attend because it had a particularly long agenda. He said that it was not uncommon for police authority meetings to last only about 15 minutes, whereas the meeting attended lasted about 90 minutes. The agenda was very long, and the chair rapidly pushed through the early stages. There were only two references during the meeting to the chosen policy areas. One was a brief comment in the chief constable's report on crime figures that rape and sexual offences were the only category to have shown a fall in reported crimes over the previous six months. The second was a brief reference to the fact that 14 officers had been released to operational duties by civilianisation.

The first part of the meeting involved the presentation of a series of awards to officers for brave or distinguished conduct. Each of these drew warm applause from members of the authority. There followed the main business of the day, a report from the chief constable on the figures for the reported crime in the force area over the previous six months. The main theme was one of alarming rises in recorded crime - a 116 per cent rise in total crime, with a 91 per cent increase in offences involving the taking of a car without the owner's consent (TWOC). The chief said that the main problem was a 'hard core' of juvenile offenders being re-cycled through the criminal justice system, many of these offenders being in local authority care. This report drew many comments from the members. The magistrates made at least as many contributions to the discussion as did elected members. The main point made by the magistrates was that they were unable to give custodial sentences to many of these offenders, a large proportion of whom were below the age of 15. One magistrate commented that the police authority should try to exert influence at a higher level, and add to the pressure to change the law (presumably to allow custodial sentences for the under 15s). Another magistrate blamed declining parental standards for the increase in juvenile crime, a point taken up by a Labour member who talked at some length about the need for more discipline among young people. Another Labour member blamed the media for glamourising crime and fast cars, another appeared to think that the problem lay in changes to the legal system stating that 'if the law was today what it was ten years ago we wouldn't have this problem'. A magistrate argued that one contribution to indiscipline and crime was the inability of social workers to administer sanctions against children in care. A Conservative member blamed school regimes for young offenders, and congratulated the chief constable for addressing this through the schools liasion programme. The chief constable agreed that the problem of juvenile crime was an issue for national debate, and said that it would be helpful for the police authority raise the problems with the current situation at the national level. The chair responded with a commitment that he would draft a motion to go to the police committee of the ACC outlining the concern of the police authority about juvenile crime. This section of the meeting ended with the chair expressing his congratulations to the members of the police authority for their contributions to a 'lively debate' on rising crime levels.

The latter part of the meeting involved few contributions from the members of the police authority. There was a report from the chief constable about the regional crime squad contingency fund which was accepted without comment. The chief suggested that members should visit the regional forensic science laboratory and explained that forces were now to be charged for use of such services whereas previously the costs had been covered in the common police services budget. There followed an item about officers visiting EEC countries, and one councillor asked if language skills were an important factor in selection or promotion, to which the chief replied in the negative. The chief then raised the subject of equal opportunities, and explained that in response to Home Office guidelines, the force was intending to employ an equal opportunities officer with administrative support at an annual cost of £30,000. The Conservative spokesperson pointed out that the authority was financially-pressed, and would need to cut back on 'luxuries'. The chair interjected with a strong statement of the importance of equal opportunities and that such a post should not be seen as a 'luxury'. The final issue was a report from the chief constable about the force's organisation of court file processing, highlighting the growing burden of paperwork on operational officers over recent years. The report was somewhat vague, and simply said that the chief was looking at long-term solutions to the problems, and could eventually reverse the policy of previous years and devolve staff and responsibilities to division or sub-division. The report drew little comment except for congratulations from the Conservative spokesperson for releasing 14 officers to operational duties through civilianisation.

The observation of the above meeting confirmed the impression given by analysis of minutes and reports. The meeting was largely uncontroversial, and heavily dependent on the chief constable and his reports. There was little detailed debate of the subjects on the agenda, particularly that of juvenile crime. Much of the members' contribution to the discussion was at the level of general and sometimes vague comment. In addition to the atmosphere of support and congratulation to the chief constable, two further points were striking. First, the relatively vocal nature of the magistrate representation on the police authority, who made at least as many contributions as members. Second, the use of the police authority by the chief as a political lever, to campaign for changes in the law at national level through its motion to the ACC.

The final source of information about the role of the police authority was semi-structured interviews carried out with the principal officer, the chair, the opposition spokesperson, and the clerk to the authority (who was also the chief executive of the county council). A number of themes arose from these interviews. The first concerned the respective roles of the police authority and the chief constable. The police authority members and the principal officers all stressed the good relationship maintained with the chief constable and the lack of the kind of confrontation found in some metropolitan areas during the 1980s. The chair of the authority explained this in terms of the moderation and good sense of the Labour majority, but also on the fact that the police authority had chosen their chief constable themselves: 'The police authority has always made satisfactory appointments, and got the right results from them'.

The opposition spokesperson clearly felt that the authority was filling its proper role, which he described as 'working in consensus to support the chief constable'. In reply to a question about the respective legal responsibilities of the police authority and the chief constable, the chair strongly argued that the chief should not be allowed to hide behind the notion of 'operational matters'. He argued that the definition of operational matters was dependent on the calibre of the membership, and that the police authority did not allow the chief to bypass them on the pretext that operational matters do not concern them. He said that the chief was aware of this and therefore maximised information flows to avoid confrontation. The examples of police authority assertiveness which he gave included a dispute over the kinds of questions which PLAC members could ask of the police. A previous chief had argued that they could not stray into 'operational matters' and the chair had argued that if there was a local problem it should be referred to the county council who would take it up on the authority (which seems to call into question the whole purpose of PLACS). The other example was the argument over plastic bullets and CS gas, of which there were slightly different stories from the chair and the opposition spokesperson. The former saw this as a clear victory for the police authority. The chief constable had wanted the force to buy this equipment, and the police authority had strongly opposed this move. Leading members had met with the regional HMI to check that they would still be certified efficient for police grant purposes if they refused to agree to the chief constable's requests. It appears that the result was that the force did not buy in CS gas and plastic bullets. However, the opposition spokesperson underplayed the controversy saying:

> A: It was a bit of fun really. It didn't make any difference anyway since the chief could get them from the Home Office if he needed them.

> Q: So it wasn't really a case of the chief constable backing down in the face of police authority pressure. It was a case of there being no point in challenging the police authority because he knew he could get them if he wanted anyway.

> A: Exactly. In fact the chief constable told me so in private.

The chair and the opposition spokesperson both appeared to identify the police authority with the police force organisation. They repeatedly used the term 'we' to describe what the police force was doing in certain areas of policy.

The clerk (who was the chief executive of the county council) clearly had a different view as to the proper role of the police authority. He argued that external criticism of the police had too-often been equated with left-wing 'police-bashing', and argued that there needed to be a more informed and coherent public debate about policing. This was a general point, not made specifically with reference to his own county. However, he made it clear that he thought the level of information and debate could be a lot higher at the police authority in force D. He said that only a minority of members shared his view on the need for a more active contribution to the development of policing policy. Additionally, there had been some controversy surrounding the clerk's beliefs on the relationship of police to local government since he had become chief executive of the authority. He was relatively new in the job at the time of the research, and said he had 'ruffled feathers' by expecting the chief constable to attend management team meetings along with other local authority chief officers. It was clear that there was a difference of opinion with the chief constable here, who saw himself as more independent of the local authority (in terms of policy-making) than other public services. On the other hand the chief executive felt that policing should not be viewed as a wholly separate entity from the county council. Although the police authority chair did not mention this disagreement, the opposition spokesperson did, and stated that the police authority supported the chief constable's position.

In terms of the contribution policy-making, the interviews confirmed the impression given by other sources. This was that the police authority had contributed little to the development of policing policy in the areas of crime prevention, civilianisation, or the investigation of crimes against women and children. Taking crime prevention first, the police authority members were asked about who should take the lead in crime prevention matters. The chair said that crime prevention was 'a very important role' for the police force, and in view of this the police authority needed to 'know what is going on in the force area'. The view underlying this clearly does not see a proactive role for the police authority as an initiator of crime prevention policy. Despite this, the chair was critical of the decision to set up a Safer Cities project in the main city in the force area because 'the money could have been better directed through the police authority'. One area of crime prevention where the police authority did appear to have been proactive though was that of NW schemes, and the chair expressed strong support for the NW concept. He explained that a visit by members to an early scheme in the West country led to pressure being put on the chief constable to set up NW in this force area. The opposition spokesperson made a number of general statements giving broad support to the idea of crime prevention, and the need to involve other agencies because 'the police cannot do it all themselves'.

In terms of new police responses to rape, domestic violence and child abuse, the chair and opposition spokesperson were both very proud of the efforts made by the force to improve policy. They each described what the force was doing (using the term 'we') in glowing terms. However, there was a tendency to exaggerate achievements. For example, there were references to 'specialist teams' for the investigation of rape, and similarly specialist units dealing with domestic violence and also dedicated child abuse teams. In fact, research in the force showed that only one specialist team had been set up in the main conurbation, with terms of reference including all three areas of policy, but which in practice dealt almost exclusively with minor child physical abuse cases. The police authority contribution to the development of policy in this area appears to have been in providing resources for new training and the two rape suites set up in the force area. The main impetus for the development in responses to domestic violence appears to have come from another committee of the county council, the policy and general purposes committee, who took the initiative of setting up a domestic violence panel and arranging a large conference on the subject (which was addressed by the chief constable). The county council women's officer said that the police authority had a negligible role in this development. At the time of the research, there was a public disagreement between the police force and the county council social services department over the investigation of allegations of child sexual abuse in the area. Despite this, neither member could remember the topic of child abuse being raised at police authority meetings. The opposition spokesperson said specifically that the matter had not been debated in the police authority, and was 'best left to social services'. However, he supported the chief constable's position in the dispute.

The comments of the chair indicated strong support for the policy of civilianisation, but also clearly implied that the lead was coming from within the police force. The support for the policy was based mainly in the desire to get more police officers out on the beat (released by putting civilians into the organisation), and also in the idea of receiving establishment increases from the Home Office (who had tied increases in police officer establishment with the policy of civilianisation). The opposition spokesperson made some very general comments in support of civilianisation, claiming that the force was very advanced in this respect compared to other forces. He also saw the policy as being a way of achieving increases in authorised establishment of police officers. He said that the decision of that year to increase civilian establishment (and not bid for more police officers) was justified to the police authority as a way of strengthening their case for more officers the following year.

Another important theme to come out of the interviews concerned the way that issues were put on the agenda for police authority meetings. There was a 'pre-agenda' meeting before each of the full police authority meetings attended by the chair, the vice-chair, the opposition spokesperson, the chief constable, the force administrative officer (who drew up the 'pre-agenda' agenda) and the clerk (the chief executive of the county council). It did appear that this meeting was very important and that matters were often effectively decided there. For example, the principal officer explained how, when the ruling Labour group had an overall majority, the chief knew that discussions with the Labour chair would effectively tell him what the police authority would support. Now that the opposition position had been strengthened there would be a need for more consultation between Labour and the opposition to ensure continued cooperation. It should be noted that the agenda to the pre-agenda meeting was drawn up by the force administrative officer who was a civilian member of the chief constable's command team. A comment by the clerk seemed to imply his belief that the agenda was too police-dominated when he described his role as 'a gentle counterbalance to the chief constable': in other words, he saw himself as an alternative source of advice and information to the police authority.

Police-community consultative committees

As was outlined above, the police authority developed a network of Police-Liaison Advisory Committees in 1983, as a response to the Scarman Report. At the time of the research, there were 15 such committees in the force area. The authority set up a working party to respond to the recommendations, and drew up a constitution and terms of reference for the committees. The constitution laid down that the committees' function was to be advisory, that they were to be organised on a sub-divisional basis, chaired by a member of the police authority, and to meet on a quarterly basis. The constitution laid down that the chairs would be allowed to admit the public to meetings 'after appropriate consultations'. There was a maximum membership of 15 people, including a 'core' membership comprising the chair, one district councillor per district in the sub-division, one representative of parish councils, and one representative from the local trades council. The police representative was to be the sub-divisional commander. Each committee was to co-opt other members as appropriate, and in cases where representatives from the Afro-Caribbean or Asian communities was desired, such representatives were to be nominated by the 'Afro-Caribbean and Asian Forum', a local organisation. Membership was to be reviewed annually by the core membership.

The police authority funded a full-time secretary to administer the PLACS. This person provided each committee with information about its sub-division, and also produced reports about the functioning of each committee during the period 1983-88. This included details of the frequency at which certain topics had been raised for discussion and the papers for the two relevant sub-divisions were made available to the research team. Each paper produced for the committees provided basic information about the organisation and resourcing of policing. It gave the address and telephone number of the sub-divisional headquarters, the authorised establishment of force D, the population covered, and the division of the county into divisions and sub-divisions. There was a breakdown of sub-divisional police staff by rank, and details about the usual working hours and the shift system. There followed some background information about policing the sub-division, including population details, main towns, and the average number of operational officers on duty in the sub-division at one time.

The paper finished with a section outlining the way that emergency and other calls to the police are dealt with. The reports on the activity of the two committees over a five year period are very similar. They had each held 25 meetings in the period, the majority of which had been committee meetings only. The dates and venues of the public meetings were listed, and average attendance of committee members and the public (at public meetings). This latter figure was quite high, in both cases over 70. The membership of the committees was outlined, and then the frequency with which subjects were raised for discussion. During the five year period, on one sub-division the top three subjects (by frequency of mention) were public order (14), traffic problems and the relationship between young people and the police. At the other sub-division, the list was the same, except equal top was the issue of community policing and local beat officers (for example, requests for more frequent patrols or additional officers) which was raised on eight occasions. As regards the chosen policy areas covered in this study, 'crime prevention matters' were raised in both committees (on five and three occasions respectively), and 'rape and the treatment of rape victims' was raised at one meeting of each committee.

An interview was conducted with the secretary to the PLACs who was a committed and enthusiastic man with clear views as to the role of these committees in the county. He saw their primary role as to inform the public about the nature of policing and resources. In his view, the main source of criticism of the police was the ignorance of the public about policing problems, and about the resources available. This view of the purpose of local consultation was supported by the nature of the information papers he provided for each committee. He was strongly supportive of the police, and equated criticism of policing policy with what he called 'politicisation'. When asked if some committees were more active than others he responded firmly that they were all very much against the 'politicisation' of the police.

It was not possible to attend any PLAC meetings, but the sub-divisional commanders were asked about their experience and views of the operation of the committees. Both felt that the committees concentrated on trivial matters such as cycling without lights, litter, or dogs fouling footpaths, and rarely discussed serious crime. In the words of one commander the PLACS were 'helpful but also frustrating'. The other commander described an average committee meeting as a 'friendly, backslapping and not very meaningful exercise'. The purpose of the committees was seen as a way of explaining the difficulties of policing to the public to secure their support. This was summed up by one commander when he summarised the purpose as 'to explain the demands upon us and ask them not to blame us for increasing crime rates'. Both commanders saw a lack of knowledge about policing as a key problem for the committees. One of the sub-divisional commanders complained that there was no 'real criticism' because of this lack of expertise, and that other forums for consultation with the community were more useful.

Little evidence was found as to the substantive effects of PLACs on local policing priorities. However, two specific examples of effects were reported. The PLACs' secretary explained that one committee had complained that dog-owners were allowing their animals to foul a children's playing field in the area. The local beat officer had responded by asking dog-walkers to keep their pets off the playing area. The second example came from a chief inspector on one sub-division. He said that the local PLAC had repeatedly complained about men importuning in a particular public toilet. The complaints reached such a level that the police allotted a small group of officers to observe the toilets, and as a result arrested 30 men, most of whom were subsequently convicted of indecency offences. The police made representations to the local council who closed down the toilets. The chief inspector was amused that such matters appeared to concern local residents more than the growing incidence of armed robbery in the area.

Other forms of local consultation

As well as the PLACS, there was contact with the public through a network of CPPs and NW schemes. Interviews were conducted with representatives of the CPP at each sub-division. Both gave the impression of low-level activity, highly dependent on input from the local police. Examples of the kinds of initiative that they had run were a property-marking campaign (which was rather unsuccessful) and setting up a crime prevention stall at a bank holiday show. One of the CPPs had been told by the local CPO that the main problem in the area was autocrime, and so had nominated a few members to gather information about various aspects of autocrime prevention. One of the representatives explained that the CPP was populated by community-minded 'committee-types' who tended to be involved in a number of panels and committees, and therefore had little time to devote to crime prevention work.

Interviews with NW coordinators suggested that there was a lot of variation in activity between schemes. Contact with the police was low-level, usually with the local CPO or beat officer at the initial stage of setting up the scheme. One of the schemes appeared to be quite active, with an area committee holding regular meetings and organising the distribution of property-marking pens, and a newsletter with information about local crime problems. The other scheme was less active, and had simply held one or two social evenings to enable neighbours to get to know one another better.

On one of the sub-divisions there was a relatively large ethnic minority population. The chief inspector who was deputy sub-divisional commander explained that he viewed forums other than the PLAC as much more useful in terms of consultation. These included meetings with the local Afro-Caribbean and Asian Forum, with youth and community groups, and other *ad hoc* meetings. For example, occasionally local district councillors would be invited to travel in a patrol car on a Friday evening shift to see 'policing at the sharp end'. The same chief inspector saw general complaints from the public as having an effect on policy. He argued that there were a lot of complaints about street trading of cannabis which had been raised by the PLAC, by local councillors, and by the local press. He made it clear that he saw this as a low-priority problem, saying that 'a lot of people think it should be legalised'. In his view, this meant that a disproportionate amount of police time was spent combatting cannabis trading, rather than tackling the more serious problems (in his view) such as house burglary.

SUMMARY AND CONCLUSIONS

Of all the Government's proposals to reform the police in the 1990s, the planned changes to the role of police authorities drew some of the heaviest criticism. Not only were these proposals unwise, critics claimed, they were 'undemocratic'. This, it was claimed, was because the proposals would constrain the already-weakened position of local councillors over policing policies, and further increase central control over the police service. This concluding section summarises the findings about the nature and extent of the practical influence of local representatives over police policy-making. It considers which factors help to determine this influence, and what implications this might have for suggested reforms.

Police authorities

Nature and extent of influence over policy

Previous research highlighted the relatively weak position of police authorities in relation to chief constables and the Home Office. The evidence in this and previous chapters does show how the impetus for important and specific changes came largely from other parties in the system. However, this is not to say that all police authorities exerted no influence at all. In the extent and nature of this influence, there were significant differences between the four police authorities covered by the study.

The police authority for force A had little *effective influence* on the development of policy in the chosen areas. This was largely due to the lack of *activism* over these areas of policy. Paradoxically, on the only occasions when the police authority had tried to assert itself as a body, this was to prevent the chief constable from developing community consultative committees, to oppose (initially) the police cooperation with the police and public safety committee, and to oppose the introduction of the lay visitors scheme. All these attempts were unsuccessful. The level of *information* which was provided by the police appeared to be high. Too high, in fact, for the liking of many police authority members who felt that the chief constable was wasting his time providing so much information for them. The reports provided by the chief constable were numerous and thorough, and there was a good deal of material on the chosen policy areas relative to other forces. This arose despite the strongly supportive, almost deferential, *attitudes* of the majority of authority members towards the police. Both the minutes and the interview with the chair illustrated how the police authority circumscribed its own role. There was an at times vociferous minority of members on the police authority who were prepared to criticise the police quite strongly. The constrasting attitudes of these members did not detract from the chief constable's willingness to give information – indeed they may have encouraged it.

The joint board police authority of force B was the most active and influential of all the four covered by the study. This was initially suggested by its particular committee structure, with sub-committees devoted to discussion of important policy areas, such as the 114/83 sub-committee and the crime prevention standing committee. It was also suggested by the minutes of the police authority, which recorded a number of areas of *effective influence*.

In the chosen policy areas, the interventions of the police authority appeared to be qualitatively different from those of the other authorities in the study. First, it was the police authority which often took the initiative in calling for a report from the chief constable. It was not the norm that reports from the chief simply appeared, as was the case in force A. Second, the information requested was of a more comprehensive nature than a few factual details about what the force was doing. In the field of crime prevention, the police authority asked not only for details of current initiatives, but also for an account of the force's overall strategy and philosophy of approach. It was the police authority that had been in contact with the Greater Manchester Police Authority and drew attention to the St Mary's Centre development, an example which was later followed by the force. The chief was asked to report on the implications of the Manchester initiative for force B. The personnel sub-committee needed to give its approval before the chief could employ retired police officers on pension as civilians in the force, and there was evidence that the chief *did* seek such approval. It is not intended to suggest that the police authority was actively formulating policy and giving directions to the chief constable. Rather, the influence was in the form of advice and consultation. Indeed, the principal officer argued that, if it was decided that detailed policy making was the proper role of members, the police authority in its current form would not be a suitable vehicle for this. Even so, there was a significant influence exerted by the police authority in the particular areas which formed the focus of the study.

Not surprisingly, the quantity and quality of *information* available to the police authority was relatively high. The minutes recorded quite detailed reports from the chief constable in response to enquiries about force policy. The detailed requests for information on the whole received detailed replies. The *attitudes* of the members interviewed suggested strong support for the chief constable and a wish to disassociate this police authority from the radical metropolitan authorities of the early 1980s. The argument was that even before the introduction of the joint board, the local Labour Party was dominated by 'moderates', and there was not the same history of conflict between the police authority and its chief constable as had been the case in other metropolitan areas. It was important that at the time of the research, the chief constable was a senior figure who had been in post for many years, allowing established relationships to develop.

Force C police committee was the only police authority covered by the study to have a persistently difficult relationship with its chief constable. The evidence suggested that it had no *effective influence* at all on policy, both in the chosen policy areas and in general. However, there was evidence of *activism* over policy, often initiated by the chair. The kind of influence which he had in mind appeared to be of a broader kind than any attempted influence in other areas. This met with total opposition from the chief constable, who had a completely different view from all members about the proper role of the police authority. The term 'operational matters', it seemed, was used regularly not only to avoid prior consultation, but also to avoid informing the police committee of developments. This was reflected in the level of *information*, available to the police authority, which was by a long way the lowest of all the authorities studied. While there was little evidence in other force areas of proactive police authority input into policy, the analysis of reports and minutes of meetings showed that chief constables were prepared to give what were sometimes quite detailed accounts and explanations of what their forces were doing. This was not the case in force C. The chief appeared to oppose even a post-hoc (or 'explanatory') accountability. On one occasion, for example, the police committee found out about quite important policy developments (for example, CCTV) by chance. The chief had to be pushed to provide information about policy, and when he did, the information was lacking in substance. Not surprisingly, this led to somewhat frustrated *attitudes* on the part of members of the committee. The feeling that the police authority was being deliberately prevented from playing its proper role was shared by Labour and Conservative members.

In force D, there was little evidence that the police authority had much *effective influence* in any of the chosen policy areas, apart from a minor influence over the starting up of NW schemes in the force. There was evidence of some local authority influence leading to the adoption of written force guidelines on domestic violence, the initiator in this case being the policy and general purposes committee of the county council. There was little evidence of effective police authority influence over most other areas of policy. There were two exceptions to this, the first being the opposition to the force purchasing baton rounds. The chair's portrayal of this as a victory for the police authority may have been an overstatement, but there seems to have been some influence here as the chief did not in the event purchase the equipment. The other area in which the police authority had effective influence was in developing the community consultative committees (although this later became a statutory requirement on police authorities).

As well as there being little effective influence, there was little *activism* on the part of the police authority: there were few attempts to influence policy in a significant way. The chair tried to imply that this was a proactive police authority. However, from the evidence of minutes, the observation of a meeting, and interviews with members, the police authority did not appear to see its role in terms of attempting to influence policy in any substantive way. The main contribution which it had made to policy development was selecting the chief constable, and giving him full support. It was certainly not the case that the chief was circumventing or over-riding the attempt of the authority to influence policy.

The only explicit statement made by the chair in relation to one of the chosen policy areas, was that the police authority needed to be informed of what the chief was doing. This post-hoc accountability was dependent upon the chief keeping his authority informed of developments in his force. However, it appeared that the level of *information* available to the police authority was not as high as in the other force areas studied (with the exception of force C). The reports to the police authority were brief and not designed to promote detailed discussion. The level of debate and information at the observed meeting was poor to say the least (and this, apparently, was an unusually lengthy and productive meeting). Finally, both the chair and the opposition spokesperson appeared to be unclear about what the force was actually doing in some areas of policy. They both claimed that the force had developed specialist units in functions where no such units existed.

Finally, the *attitudes* of police authority members were strongly supportive of the chief constable. This is not surprising, as they clearly saw him as 'their man'. They had selected him and consequently any criticism of him was viewed as self-damning . Although the chair argued that the police authority would never allow a chief constable to bypass the authority on 'operational' grounds, both he and the opposition member interviewed clearly identified the police authority with the police organisation itself, using the term 'we' with some pride to refer to developments introduced by the police force.

Determinants of influence

The above results show great variations in the amount and the type of activism and influence exerted by police authorities over local policing policy. These differences may be explained by reference to a combination of factors, the most important of which include: statutory powers; the nature of the police authority; the local political situation; self-imposed limits; size and structure of the authority; and the available information and expertise.

* *Statutory powers* – the evidence from the four force areas confirmed that statutory powers are an important determinant of what a police authority can influence. The only one of the three specific policy areas studied in which police authorities had some clear statutory powers was that of civilianisation. In some important ways, each of the forces exerted a significant influence. Although the chief constable had the overall direction and control of the force, it was the police authority (or

the local authority) who employed the civilians. Thus, should there be a disagreement over matters such as grading, or employing people in receipt of a pension, the police authority could (and in some cases did) successfully prevail against the chief constable. Contrary to Reiner's (1993:17) argument that chief constables 'are not bound to take any notice of the views of the authority', where police authorities do have (limited) statutory powers, the chief cannot necessarily overturn these.

- *Police authority type* – it is interesting to note that the most influential and active police authority in the study was the joint board in force B. This is contrary to the predictions of authors such as Loveday (1987:99) who argued that 'the joint boards exhibit structural weaknesses which must limit their ability to fulfil even those limited statutory duties placed upon them'. Loveday argued that single county police authorities have a more 'corporate' nature than joint boards which had to try to balance disparate district interests. Lustgarten (1986) argued that single county police authorities were more effective because elected members would often sit on a number of other local service committees. This implies that policing would be more closely tied with the rest of the local authority business, as one of several locally-run services. There were mixed findings about the two single county police authorities in the study. For different reasons, neither was particularly effective. In force C, there was a more concerted attempt to influence policy, but this appeared to be strongly related to the approach of the chair rather than the type of authority. In any case, these attempts were largely unsuccessful. In the other single county authority (force D), there was little evidence of activism, or of a closer connection with the local authority as a whole. In fact, the police authority supported the chief in his view of the police as highly distinct from other local services.

- *Political complexion* – during the 1980s, high levels of police authority activism were associated with (radical) Labour authorities. There is limited support from this study that Labour authorities may tend to be more active. Thus, for example, the most influential police authority in force B was dominated by Labour members, and the pressure for a more active role in force A's authority came largely from Labour members. However, in force C, Labour members' activism was largely ignored by the chief constable. Furthermore, the police authority in force D was also dominated by Labour and there was little evidence of attempted or effective influence.

- *Self-limitation* – this was a particularly strong constraint on the influence of the force A police authority. Here, the chief constable went to some lengths to encourage a more active input, but to no avail. This was also the case in force D, where despite the chair's contention that they were an active police authority there was little evidence of attempted or effective influence over policy. In these forces, leading members of the police authority appeared to assume quite a narrow role for the police authority.

• *Size and structure* – the police authorities in forces A, B and D had 27-30 members, and that in force C had 21 members, and covered large areas with many different communities within them. Police authorities were not conducive to detailed consideration of policy matters at the level of the full committee. Indeed, it is reasonable to argue that the 1964 Act did not design them with proactive policy-framing in mind. As was suggested in Chapter 1, the notion of policing policy is a relatively recent development. It seems likely therefore the framers of the 1964 Act probably only had a retrospective 'explanatory' kind of accountability in mind. Force B's police authority may have been more able to discuss policy in detail with its specialist policy sub-committees. These permitted a more detailed consideration of developments. But even these did not in any way proactively frame and develop policy. That remained the job of the chief constable.

• *Information and expertise* – Lustgarten (1986) argued that police authorities were dependent on the information provided by their police in order to make any informed criticisms. Officers to the police authorities in forces B and D explicitly stated that objective criticism or advice was difficult in light of this dependency on the police for information. The levels of information provided by the four police forces varied, with forces A and B being relatively free with information, and forces C and D less forthcoming. In addition to the levels of information available, how the available information was used was also important. It seemed, for example, that many members of force A's police authority had little knowledge about policing matters. Consequently, even though the chief provided a lot of information, he rarely received useful responses from the authority.

Although police authorities can have influence, it is important to consider what kind of influence this is, and indeed could be. Many commentators on the left appear to assume evidence of conflict or even confrontation with chief constables to be a necessary condition of a police authority doing an effective job. This overlooks one of the major functions of police authorities, which is its legal responsibility to select the chief constable. Although such appointments are subject to the approval of the

Home Secretary, this approval has in practice rarely been withheld (Derbyshire being the notable exception). Police authorities, understandably therefore, consider themselves to be responsible not only for the appointment, but also in some senses for the performance of the appointee. In areas of relative political stability, it is therefore unrealistic to expect a police authority to actively seek to criticise or undermine its chief officer. Such criticism would surely reflect on their judgement in recruiting him.

Other forms of consultation

On the whole, local consultative committees, CPPs, and NW schemes had little substantive input into local policing policy. The notable exception to this rule was the police and public safety sub-committee in one sub-division in force A, which was substantially different from any other section 106 committee in the study. It had an important influence on two out of the three chosen policy areas locally, as well as a reported influence over the character of policing generally in that sub-division. This was despite the unrepresentative nature of the committee, and the inclusion of a number of organisations which were strongly critical of the police.

A number of important features distinguished this committee from the other community consultative committees covered in the study. First, there was a relatively high level of information about policing in general, and local policy in particular, available to the committee. Inevitably, much of this information came from the police, but it was at a level of far greater detail than was the case in other committees (for example, detailed information about the number of alleged rapes no-crimed locally and force procedures on rape victims, rather than statistics about staffing). The information given by the police was processed and supplemented by an full-time independent police adviser. Thus, this was not a police-dominated forum. Second, the membership did not exclude representatives of some groups with traditionally difficult relationships with the police. Thus, the committee provided an opportunity for dialogue with some groups which did not exist in other areas. Third, and crucially from the local police viewpoint, the committee actually achieved things in terms of practical action. This was because it was a sub-committee of the borough council, with access to financial resources and to the council decision-making process.

Force A also provided an example of one other way in which public views and perceptions had an input into policing policy. This was via the public attitude survey commissioned by the police force during the research. This was an attempt to tap the views on policing and community safety of a 'representative' sample of people in the force area. Senior officers were extremely committed to the concept of the survey and, at the time of the research, the results appeared to be having a significant influence on policy. For example, the finding that respondents wanted preventive policing enhanced added impetus to the development of the upgraded community crime prevention department. Senior officers requested that all sections of the force staff respond to the survey results with proposals for improvements in policy and practice. In this sense, the survey appeared to represent a novel experiment by the force in measuring and responding to the perceptions and views of the public. It is possible that this was partly a response to the lack of useful input by the police authority, reinforcing the view that such authorities were, at least in part, the architects of their own ineffectiveness.

Notes

1. The Local Government Act 1985 increased it again, this time to the 'symbolic' figure of 51 per cent.

2. 613 HC Deb. 5s. c.1239-1303

3. As a result of his research, Morgan (1992) concludes that the 'Home Office guidelines, which with minor amendments and some change of emphasis were updated in 1985 (HO 2/85 – issued after PACE came into force) and 1989 (HO 62/1989, issued after our research and a Home Office review of arrangements had been conducted) were seen by most councillors and senior police officers not as advice but as instructions.

4. The police authority eventually voted for this option after an initial vote had split the authority 50:50 and the chair exercised her casting vote in favour of the option she preferred, much to the outrage of the vocal Labour councillor.

6 Conclusions

The purpose of this study is to explore democracy by analysing how and why policing policy has changed in recent years. In approaching this task, the study is concerned both with the actual institutions and processes involved in decision making, and with democratic ideals. Although a preliminary attempt was made in the first chapter to establish a framework of analysis for deciding whether a set of institutions and processes are democratic, such a framework will only be useful to the extent that it can be applied to a specific and concrete case such as the shaping of policing policy. On the one hand, actual institutions and processes need to be evaluated by reference to a democratic ideal, or to a more elaborated set of standards or criteria. On the other hand, the pertinence and usefulness of the standards themselves need to be evaluated in the light of the results produced by applying them to a concrete and specific case. Hence, exploring democracy involves an interaction between actual processes of change and the framework of analysis used to evaluate them.

The strategy adopted was to focus, not on 'political' institutions, but on one of the central public services – the police – within the modern state. Democratic theory evolved at a time when the functions of the state were far more limited than they are today. In eighteenth century England, government expenditure accounted for about 5 per cent of gross national product, compared with about 50 per cent in the 1980s. In order to be applicable to modern conditions, the idea of democracy needs to be extended and developed so as to apply not just to central government institutions, but more widely to the whole apparatus of the service-delivery state.

For practical reasons, any study in this field must concentrate on a limited number of chosen areas of policy. Nevertheless, the three areas of policy chosen in this case cover such a wide range that they might be expected to highlight some of the main contrasts in the policy-making process. They include one of the three central policing functions (crime prevention) as these were defined by the founders of the modern police in England; a field in which the sphere of formal regulation is expanding in response to fundamental changes in the wider society (the police response to rape, domestic violence, and child abuse); and an aspect of the internal organisation of the police that has an important influence on service delivery and value for money (civilianisation).

As set out in Chapter 1, an apparent limitation of the focus on change is that this cannot explain why certain aspects of policing have remained the same. Yet in practice the changes in the response to rape, domestic violence, and child abuse turn out to be much more far-reaching than in the field of crime prevention, where, in spite of a kaleidoscope of new initiatives, it seems that 'plus ça change, plus c'est la même chose'. Hence, the findings allow us to probe the reasons for the failure to address the crime prevention task in a convincing way, as well as the causes of more positive change in other fields.

THE EXTENT AND NATURE OF CHANGE

The evidence of a change in policy and practice over the 1980s was perhaps strongest in the case of the response to rape, domestic violence, and child abuse. During that period, a number of concrete initiatives had been taken in the four study forces.

- All four had introduced specialist teams of some sort. Two forces had created a team on each division, one had designated individual women officers as victim liaison officers on each sub-division, and planned to introduce a specialist child abuse team, while the fourth had established a central 'family support unit'. Most of these teams were concerned primarily with child abuse, although in three of the four forces they were also involved in cases of rape and sexual assault.

- Two of the four forces had introduced victim examination suites.

- There had been a large increase in the amount of training given both to specialist officers and to others in dealing with victims of rape and child abuse.

- Detailed written guidelines had been introduced in all four forces, although they were fuller in some forces than others.

- New inter-agency structures had been put in place, most significantly those supporting joint investigations of child abuse by the police and social services.

- All four forces had by 1990 recruited and inducted female police surgeons, and had introduced procedures that allowed female victims to choose to be examined by them.

- With varying degrees of success, all four forces had made efforts to ensure that victims of rape and sexual assault, and of child abuse, would be given sensitive consideration and continuing support.

- In all four forces, there had been an increase over the 1980s in the proportion of women police officers.

Whereas there had been substantial changes of policy in the response to rape and to child abuse, changes in the response to domestic violence were comparatively slight. Although this research did not include observation of policing on the ground, there was good evidence that policy changes had been accompanied by some substantial changes in the actual pattern and style of policing. For example, specialist officers, and others who had received special training, seemed to be sympathetic to rape victims; in many cases they volunteered that a few years earlier police officers had generally had negative attitudes towards rape victims, and had treated them badly; they strongly disapproved of those earlier attitudes, and saw their own approach as entirely different.

Although there had been substantial change in all four forces in the response to rape and to child abuse, structures and policies varied in detail between them, and implementation was patchy in some cases.

The history of policy development on the civilianisation of posts formerly held by police officers is a longer one. Although there had been a few civilians in the police forces since their establishment in the nineteenth century, a rapid expansion occurred between 1945 and 1975, and this was encouraged by official pronouncements, starting with the report of the Oaksey committee in 1949. However, central government has followed a stop-go policy in this as in other fields. Home Office circulars in 1975 and 1976 reversed the earlier policy by calling for reductions in civilian staff. This was followed by actual declines in the proportion of civilian staff in police forces throughout England and Wales, and specifically within the four study forces. It was the Home Office Circular of 1983 on *Manpower, Effectiveness and Efficiency in the Police Service* that explicitly reversed the policy again, and this was followed from 1985 by increases in the proportion of civilian staff in the service, which by 1993 had climbed back to the peak earlier scaled in 1975.

There is evidence of a fairly strong drive towards civilianisation in the latter half of the 1980s in the four study forces.

- The number of civilians employed increased both in absolute terms and as a proportion of an expanding total staff in all four forces.

- Home Office circular 105 of 1988 included a check-list of functions deemed suitable for civilianisation, referred to as 'key posts'. The percentage of key posts that were held by civilians increased considerably in all four study forces between 1987 and 1990. By 1990 the highest figure reached was 75.3 per cent in force A, whereas the lowest was 67 per cent in force B.

- During the 1980s, administrative support units, staffed partly by civilians, were established in two of the four study forces to deal with preparation of case files and other paperwork. This followed recommendations by the Home Office and the Audit Commission.

- In circular 114 of 1983, the Home Office made it clear that an increase in police officer establishment would not normally be approved unless the force was making progress towards civilianisation. Within all four study forces it became clear from interviews with senior officers that this was an effective lever that had caused them to look again at their civilianisation plans.

- Home Office circular 105 of 1988 made more detailed recommendations on staffing reviews and identified key posts for civilianisation. In addition, it drew attention to the need for career structures for civilian staff.

- According to Home Office statistics, considerable numbers of police officers were 'released' from posts not requiring police powers or training by civilianisation in each of the four study forces in the period 1985-1990. Whether there was actually an increase in the number of police officers engaged in functions for which police powers or training are required is nevertheless open to question (see below).

- In broad terms, the policy of civilianisation was supported by the most senior officers in all four study forces. They did not believe that the scope for civilianisation had yet been exhausted.

- In the second half of the 1980s, all four forces had introduced procedures for designating posts for civilianisation, and for putting this into effect. In two of the forces, this was through centrally organised staff reviews, whereas at the other two it was through systems whereby local commanders bid for staff and other resources.

- All four forces had a personnel department for civilian staff headed by a civilian.

- All had a civilian in charge of administration and finance, and in certain cases this post was very senior and influential.

It may be thought that the growth in the number of civilians within police forces might influence the styles of management used when dealing with police officers, and the culture of working groups. Effects of this kind seem more likely to the extent that there are civilians in more senior or expert posts, and to the extent that civilian staff generally have opportunities for training and advancement. However, it has not been possible to establish from the present research whether civilianisation has had an influence of this kind on the police organisation as a whole.

The conclusion that there was a substantial move towards civilianisation in the study forces has to be qualified in two ways. Although the increase in the number of civilian staff was real, this change never meant that police officers were *replaced*. Civilianisation always meant growth. For senior police officers, the first priority was probably to maintain or increase the number of police officers in the organisation. The price for doing this was that they had to bring about a greater increase in the number of civilians.

Again, although the Home Office has counted the number of police officers 'released' by civilianisation for 'proper' police duties, there is no clear evidence that the number or proportion of police officers engaged in 'proper' police work has actually increased. The problem is that the police officers who are 'released' from one administrative post may be redeployed to another; and new growth in the number of police officers may expand the number of administrative as well as 'proper police' posts held by police officers. A report by the National Audit Office (1991) has suggested that although more than 3,000 posts were civilianised between 1985 and 1989, the proportion of police officers classed as 'operational patrol' remained constant at around 55 per cent.

The story of policy change in the field of crime prevention is considerably more complex than in either of the other two cases. There are a number of reasons for that greater complexity. First, crime prevention is potentially a large and varied field of activity, yet it is one that is still at an early stage of development. At the present stage, there are many different, often contrasting and uncoordinated initiatives; and there is no well-established body of knowledge, or widely-shared set of assumptions, about what does and does not work. Second, crime prevention was in the nineteenth century said to be one of the three basic functions of the police (along with maintaining public tranquillity and upholding the law). It was for long assumed that the police could exercise this function through uniform patrol. In modern conditions, however, neither uniform foot patrol nor vehicle patrol is an effective or efficient method of crime prevention. The process of policy change therefore involves finding new methods of crime prevention that the police can implement either on their own or in collaboration with other agencies. This cannot be a linear process of development. It involves the creation of new forms of social action and organisational structures. Third, the question of what the role of the police (as opposed to other agencies) should be in crime prevention has remained unresolved. Fourth, far from clarifying these complexities, government has tended to cloud the waters further by dividing responsibility between departments of central government and by creating new agencies. For example, the Department of the Environment and the Home Office in the 1980s launched fairly similar initiatives to reduce crime on inner city housing estates (the Priority Estates Programme (PEP) was launched by the DoE, whereas the Safer Cities Programme was launched by the Home Office); at the same time, the Home Office funded crime reduction initiatives on housing estates run by the Safe Neighbourhoods Unit of the non profit-making NACRO (although the Safe Neighbourhoods Unit was later floated off as a separate organisation); and it established another semi-autonomous and semi-governmental but apparently voluntary organisation, Crime Concern, which also launched some crime reduction programmes on housing estates (among other things). One purpose of all this was to avoid giving budgets or statutory responsibility for crime prevention to local authorities. Another consequence, however, was that the nature of the police responsibility for crime prevention became increasingly obscure.

In this field, therefore, changes in policing policy are an aspect of wider changes in crime prevention policies implemented by a medley of governmental, semi-governmental, and non-governmental organisations. Although, taking account of the many relevant initiatives, policy developments, and organisations, there was a huge increase over the 1980s in the attention given to crime prevention overall, changes in *policing* policy in the field were fairly superficial. The following is a summary of the evidence for limited policy change in the four study forces.

- All of the forces had specialist crime prevention officers and central departments. In one (force B) the central crime prevention department was larger and better funded than in the others, and some growth in the size and prestige of this department had occurred over the 1980s. The chief constable had made great play in public of the emphasis he placed on crime prevention, and that was reflected in the high profile of some of the force's crime prevention activities. A restructuring of staff concerned with crime prevention had been carried through in two of the other forces. The objectives were to devolve responsibility for crime prevention activity to officers based at divisions or sub-divisions, but create a channel of communication or line of management between them and the central crime prevention department.

- The 1980s saw the introduction and rapid proliferation of neighbourhood watch schemes throughout the country, though not evenly across types of neighbourhood. Although this was not strictly a change in policing policy, considerable policing resources were devoted to servicing these schemes.

- All of the four study forces had introduced new policies for dealing with burglar alarms following recommendations made by ACPO in 1989. The new ACPO policy shifts responsibility away from the police and towards central alarm stations in the first instance: for example, it is these alarm stations that contact keyholders to check whether an alarm call is genuine. The guidelines also state that wherever there are seven or more false calls in any 12 month period from a single alarm source, the police should withdraw response for a minimum of 12 months or until they are satisfied that the fault has been rectified. The new policies introduced by the study forces should have had the effect of reducing the amount of police time wasted by false calls.

- A wide variety of special projects with crime prevention objectives were introduced or supported by the police over the 1980s. All of the four study forces had started to offer advice to local authorities, architects, and building developers about the crime prevention implications of design features, some within the framework of the *Secured by Design* initiative. All of the four forces had become involved in social crime prevention schemes of one kind or another: 'crime theatre' schemes (by which children were encouraged to develop short plays with a crime prevention theme); training schemes for young people; organised activities for young people during the summer holidays. Schools visits took place in all four areas, but in one (force C) the schools liaison programme was reshaped in the latter half of the 1980s. Force B had introduced the policy of dedicating one police officer in each sub-division to analysing the local crime patterns and presenting the information to management and operational officers. There was some police support for crime prevention panels in each of the four areas, and in one there was evidence of an effort to stimulate this kind of activity. There were various other more specific initiatives such as the crime prevention 'theme of the month' in force D, the 'light against crime' campaign in the same area to encourage householders to reduce crime by increasing the level of lighting around their properties, an autocrime prevention initiative in the same area, and the 'coalition against crime' in force B, in which a committee of business people and others were intended to launch crime prevention initiatives, although examples of specific initiatives that had been launched in this way were scarce.

- The police had been involved in a number of local initiatives launched within the framework of the Safer Cities Programme. For example, force C was involved in a target-hardening and property-marking scheme in a particular area of the city, and in a project against obscene telephone calls, both launched by the local Safer Cities Programme. Again, in force D area there was police involvement in many aspects of Safer Cities work. For example, a burglary project was coordinated by a seconded police inspector, a sub-divisional crime prevention officer carried out security surveys and provided advice for a target-hardening programme, and the police were represented on working groups set up to examine racial harassment and women's safety.

- In force B area, multi-agency crime prevention initiatives were established in each local authority area, led by a co-ordinator and steering group. There was evidence that the police had played an important role in these initiatives, although it was not clear that the schemes had taken effective action to counter crime problems as opposed to collating information and identifying what the problems were.

- Force C had taken a leading role in setting up a working party on inner-city disorder, which had come up with various actions, such as reducing the sale of half-price drinks, detailed instructions to doorstaff at pubs and clubs, and afternoon closure of pubs on days before Christmas when there had previously been trouble. The working party had recommended that closed circuit television be installed in the central city area, although at the time of the research this proposal was still the subject of controversy.

In spite of these developments, there was evidence of a wider failure by the police to make substantive changes towards introducing effective crime prevention policies.

- Except in force B, crime prevention departments remained small and had not grown. Staff with specific crime prevention responsibilities still amounted to only around 1 per cent of the total by the end of the 1980s.

Contrary to Reiner's (1992:99) statement that they had become 'the belles of the ball', their status remained low.

- There was much rhetoric during the 1980s in support of 'community policing' and 'community-based crime prevention', but there was no clear line of development in putting such ideas into practice. Any police contribution to community-based crime prevention schemes was minor.

- Although there was a huge growth of NW schemes, the police rapidly came to realise that they could not support these schemes adequately. Because of inadequate support, and for other reasons, the NW idea was not fully implemented. There is little evidence for the effectiveness of NW as it emerged in Britain in the 1980s.

- There was a continual lack of clarity in the structures within police forces for dealing with crime prevention. Changes tended to make matters worse. In several of the study forces, specialist crime prevention officers came to have a dual responsibility to the local commander and to a central crime prevention department.

- There was generally a lack of resources and expertise within the study forces to support proactive crime prevention. For example, the amount of impact that could be made by architectural liaison officers in their very small numbers must have been minimal in relation to the enormous task of re-designing the built environment. Also, their level of expertise must have been low compared to that of a professional architect who would have had seven years' full-time training.

- Social crime prevention projects initiated by the police had tenuous links with concrete crime prevention objectives. They can be regarded as good public relations for the police rather than hard-nosed schemes to reduce crime.

- Whatever the role of the police in crime prevention should finally be, it is clear that since they record crime and process criminal investigations the police are in a better position than anyone else to analyse the patterns of crime and draw conclusions about possible actions to prevent it. Yet, on the whole, the study forces had failed to develop detailed crime pattern analysis. For the most part, they had not even begun to take an analytical approach to the development of crime prevention strategy.

- For the most part, multi-agency crime prevention involving the police was not a reality. At best, there were initiatives where the police cooperated with one other agency. The other agencies involved tended to perceive the police as wanting to direct any initiative in which they were involved, and this attitude was unpopular. There was little evidence of concrete policy initiatives embodying a major transformation away from narrow target-hardening initiatives and towards the multi-agency approach.

• Although more resources were devoted to crime prevention in force B than elsewhere, most crime prevention initiatives by that force lacked substance and were largely exercises in public relations.

• None of the crime prevention activity by the study forces was adequately evaluated. There was little or no evidence that it was effective.

INFLUENCES ON POLICING POLICY

The findings on policy change in the three areas covered by the study are therefore mixed. They show a major change in policy and practice in the response to rape and child abuse, and a smaller change in the response to domestic violence. Even allowing for patchy implementation of new policies, this probably led to substantive change in the style and pattern of policing on the ground. There has also been real change in the employment of civilians within the police force, both in terms of their numbers and proportion of total staff, and in terms of the range of tasks they undertake. However, it is not clear that this has caused any more fundamental change in the nature of the police organisation. Also, the policy has been implemented defensively by chief constables, as part of a package of growth that allowed them to maintain and increase the numbers of police officers in their organisations. It is not clear that the amount of 'proper police work' carried out has increased as a result of civilianisation. In the case of crime prevention, the police have mounted many small initiatives and have participated to some extent in the plethora of schemes originating from elsewhere, and they have provided some limited support to the huge number of neighbourhood watch groups that grew up in the 1980s. But there has been no major change in the police role in crime prevention, or in the amount of resources they devote to it. At a time when crime prevention has come to assume greatly increasing importance in public policy, the police have largely failed to establish a credible role for themselves in this field.

This section analyses the influences leading to policy change in certain areas, and the constraints that have prevented constructive change in others. That prepares the way for an evaluation in the final section of the institutions and processes leading to change or stability in the light of the democratic ideals set out in Chapter 1.

Central government

The Home Office clearly had a strong influence on the development of policy in all three areas, and in the case of crime prevention there was also an influence from the Department of the Environment and, at one period, from the Prime Minister's office. In all three policy areas, Home Office circulars were a central element of policy change. Although the researchers did not have privileged access to Home Office files, it was not difficult to trace the origins of these circulars, and a considerable body of information was collected about the process of consultation that took place before they were issued in their final form. A number of conclusions can be drawn.

First, none of the circulars, and none of the policy changes of which they were a central element, arose from the concerns or interests of ministers. The impetus for the development of crime prevention policy came from a new Permanent Under Secretary in the Home Office, and grew out of research and analysis carried out by the Home Office Research and Planning Unit. Thereafter officials awaited favourable political conditions to float their proposals. It was officials who took the initiative in drafting the Home Office circulars on rape (of 1982 and 1986), on child abuse (of 1988) and on domestic violence (of 1990). In several of these cases, officials were responding to stimuli from pressure groups (the Women's National Commission Report) or events (development of new approaches to policing crimes against women and children in the Metropolitan Police); or events gained acceptance for a circular already drafted (the Cleveland controversy). The reversal of policy on civilianisation in 1983 may seem to be the exception, in that it grew out of the government's Financial Management Initiative (FMI), which had originated with ministers. However, such an analysis would be misleading. What is most remarkable is that the Home Office had avoided applying FMI to the police for four years after the Conservative Government came to power. At a time when other public services were being squeezed, no questions were asked about the efficiency of the police, and greatly increased amounts of money were thrown at them. The reversal that occurred in 1983 was not the result of a ministerial decision, but as Sir Clive Whitmore publicly testified to the Public Accounts Committee, was a response to pressure by Treasury officials.

Second, although ministers did not initiate any of the policies, they were involved in their further development at a later stage in two cases. At the 1987 election (*after* the first circular on crime prevention) the Conservatives made a manifesto promise to put more resources into crime prevention, and the new Home Secretary, Douglas Hurd, decided to pursue this as a major plank of policy. John Patten was put in charge of developing a 'total response' to crime, and a Ministerial Group on Crime Prevention was set up to coordinate action between government departments. Similarly, *after* officials had started to take initiatives on the response to crimes against women and children (including drafting circulars) a Ministerial Group on Women was formed with John Patten as chair. However, there was little evidence that either of these groups had exerted any specific influence on the development of policy, except to give extra weight to it.

Third, the circulars tended to be the product of a wide range of influences, because each one emerged in its final form only after a considerable amount of consultation with bodies outside the Home Office. Information about the consultative process is incomplete because ACPO declined to cooperate with this research. However, it seems certain that ACPO was formally consulted in every case. The first crime prevention circular was also discussed in draft with the local authority associations, and with individual local authorities. The second was sent to about 30 organisations, including the police staff associations, the local authority associations, the Association of Chief Officers of Probation, the Fire Unions, NACRO, and Crime Concern, although the comments did not lead to major changes. The 1983 circular on *Manpower, Effectiveness and Efficiency in the Police Service* was discussed in draft by the Tripartite Forum, which includes representatives of the Home Office, ACPO, and the local authority associations. The second on *Civilian Staff in the Police Service* (105/88) was discussed by the Police Advisory Board, which includes in addition representatives of the Superintendents' Association and Police Federation. In addition it was sent in draft to trade unions representing civilians in the police service (principally NALGO). The influence of bodies outside the Home Office was marked in the case of the various circulars on the response to crimes against women and children. In several cases, Home Office officials felt they should respond to events or outside pressures, but initially lacked the knowledge and expertise needed to draft guidance; they therefore looked to people and organisations with experience and ideas, notably to those leading new initiatives within the Metropolitan Police. Also, ACPO was very influential in several cases: in fact, it was virtually the joint author of the circulars on rape and on child abuse. The draft circular on child abuse was also circulated to police staff associations. The role of outside pressure groups had been to stimulate activity in these areas; they did not have an input into the detailed drafting of circulars.

Fourth, in some of these cases central government acted on its own initiative in launching these policy changes, whereas in others it responded to outside pressures or to a sea change in the wider society. The development of crime prevention and civilianisation were proactive, whereas the reforms in the response to crimes against women and children were more responsive. Nevertheless, the original initiative to develop guidance on investigating child abuse was begun by the Home Office before there was obvious or specific outside pressure; the Cleveland controversy broke after the circular had been drafted.

Her Majesty's Inspectorate of Constabulary

During the 1980s, the role of HMIC was extended and its resources were strengthened. The most notable developments were the decision to publish reports of inspections of individual forces from 1988; a more systematic and thorough approach to the collection and analysis of information about police forces, in line with the development of measures of performance by the Audit Commission; and the appointment of younger men to the inspectorate, which had previously consisted exclusively of men who had completed full careers as chief constables. Because of these changes, HMIC has tended to become more influential in general terms. Yet the Inspectorate played no part in initiating any of the policy changes considered in this study. Also, it played no significant part in the further development of policy in the fields of crime prevention and the response to crimes against women and children. HMIC did, however, have an important influence in keeping up the pressure for civilianisation once the 1983 circular had been issued. Individual inspections would always consider whether civilianisation was proceeding as fast as it should be. However, this role was limited to policy implementation.

Reiner (1991) has argued that the strengthened role of HMIC is an aspect of increasing central control over policing. These findings suggest that this argument is an over-simplification. The strengthened role of HMIC may have led to a more even implementation of policy (although even so, implementation often remains patchy, as argued below). It has not, however, led to any increase in central control over the process of policy making.

The Association of Chief Police Officers

ACPO is the body through which chief officers can express a collective view. (Besides chief constables, chief officers include assistant chief constables in provincial forces and those at the rank of commander and above in the Metropolitan Police.) In formal terms it is merely a staff association, except that the taxpayer foots the bill for its secretariat, conferences, and other expenses. In practice it can be argued that it is the emergent network of a national police organisation. The clearest evidence of this is the Association's role in setting up the National Reporting Centre which coordinates the response to major public disorder across all police forces. ACPO has an extensive structure of committees and sub-committees (always made up of chief officers) on areas of policy such as crime prevention or drugs. The members of the committees, and the dates and agendas of their meetings, remain outside the public domain. ACPO does, however, hold several conferences each year, to which the press are invited.

ACPO certainly had an important influence on the development of policy in the areas covered in this study, but that influence did not always dominate, and it seems that ACPO suffered some important defeats. Most notably, ACPO was clearly opposed to further civilianisation in the 1970s. Although its view prevailed for a while, and may have helped bring about a reverse of Home Office policy between 1975 and 1983, ACPO gave in when officials decided to apply the Financial Management Initiative to the police. Further, in order to reduce the influence of local authorities over the growing number of civilian staff in the police service, ACPO argued in the early 1980s for a national civilian service. This would have avoided the present situation in which police civilians are employed by local authorities (or police authorities). However, this proposal was not adopted, and ACPO had to give ground. As pointed out earlier, however, the chief officers perhaps won the most important battle in ensuring that civilianisation would always be interpreted as growth, and would never lead to a reduction in the number of police officers employed.

In the case of the initiatives in responding to crimes against women and children, ACPO was not among the initiators of change, but it was closely involved from an early stage in the formulation of detailed policy through the drafting of circulars.

The analysis of ACPO's influence is most interesting and problematic in the case of crime prevention. The chief officers as a body were certainly not among those who initiated the move towards placing a greater emphasis on crime prevention, although a couple of individual chief constables were influential in that way. ACPO was consulted about the two crime prevention circulars, but there is no evidence that its advice led to any important changes. After the new emphasis on crime prevention was well established, ACPO's crime prevention sub-committee produced a paper outlining a model for a community crime prevention department, and this model was an important influence on one of the four forces covered by this study. The same committee also set out a national 'burglar alarm policy' which strongly influenced all of the four forces studied. In both cases, these models were based on the arrangements in one force headed by a chief constable who had become known as a crusader on behalf of crime prevention.

In spite of these limited and specific influences, it can be argued that ACPO tended to prevent the police service from finding its mission in the field of crime prevention. It had the choice of jumping in one of two ways. One choice would be to argue that the police should be the lead agency in crime prevention, and to put forward ambitious plans for developing new methods and structures for dealing with crime prevention. The other choice would be to argue that some other body should take the lead (for example, local authorities, or a new national agency) and to define a role for the police in a crime prevention effort directed by this other organisation. Although this is difficult to reconstruct, it seems likely that ACPO failed to make a choice between these alternatives, and adopted spoiling tactics. Because of its general hostility to local authorities, the government would have been reluctant to give them a new statutory responsibility for crime prevention, or the funds needed to discharge such a responsibility. However, an additional factor may well have been ACPO's hostility to the idea. It would have seen crime prevention as a source of new funding, and would have been reluctant to see those funds going elsewhere. At the same time, most senior police officers interviewed as part of this study would be extremely reluctant to take on the main responsibility for crime prevention: they lack the appetite and expertise for such a task, they see the need for the active participation of other organisations, and they understand that those organisations would generally not accept police leadership. Hence, in the words of a chief superintendent in force C, 'the partnership approach is a response to pressure from the police'. It is plausible to suggest, although it cannot be proved, that this particular fudge is largely the product of ACPO influence in blocking more imaginative proposals in which other organisations would take the lead, while failing to take the lead itself.

The local authority associations

The level of influence of the local authority associations on changes in policing policy has been mixed. The associations had a strong influence on circular 114 of 1983 on *Manpower, Effectiveness and Efficiency in the Police Service*, and one of them (the Association of County Councils) caused circular 115 of 1988 on *Civilians Staff in the Police Service* to be revised. They cautioned against new initiatives to deal with crimes against women and children, particularly the creation of specialist units, without specific additional funds to cover them. Most interesting, however, was their attempt to influence the development of crime prevention policy. The Association of Metropolitan Authorities set up a working party in 1988 to examine the local authority role in crime prevention, which recommended that the major responsibilities should be divided between three tiers (central government, county councils, and district councils); that county and district councillors working together should draw up general strategies and more specific plans; and that crime prevention should be resourced by a specific grant from central government. So far these recommendations have been ignored, possibly in part because of representations from ACPO (see above).

Staff associations and trade unions

The Police Federation is a natural opponent of civilianisation, and has consistently argued against it or tried to slow it down. For example, in July 1981, the Federation submitted a paper to the Police Advisory Board which expressed concern at the growth of the civilian element in the police service in the climate of industrial militancy. Perhaps because of its known opposition, the Federation was not asked to comment on the draft circular of 1983, which was only submitted to the Tripartite Forum (see above). It was given the opportunity to comment (as a member of the Police Advisory Board) on the later circular of 1988 on civilianisation. However, the objections that it submitted in response (mainly to the civilianisation of specific posts) were brushed aside.

The Federation supported the development of improved training packages for investigating serious sexual offences and the setting up of specialist units. The Federation did not play a part in initiating interest in the field, but followed the lead of the report of the Women's National Commission on *Violence Against Women*. The initiatives suggested by that report were seen as being in the interests of Federation members, because they would help to attract resources to the police service, and would tend to enhance the level of skill and training required by police officers, and raise them in the esteem of the public. By contrast, the Police Federation seems not to have played a significant role in debate about crime prevention policy, perhaps because the role of the police in this field seems either unclear, or if clear, mundane.

The National and Local Government Officers' union (NALGO – now part of Unison), which at the time of the research had 25,000 members in British police forces, influenced policy through its role in collective bargaining over pay and conditions for local authority staff, including civilians in the police service. Although (in contrast to the Police Federation) it was a natural supporter of civilianisation, it was not formally asked to comment on the circular of 1983. However, as well as members of the Police Advisory Board, it was asked to comment on the later draft circular of 1988 on civilianisation. It is not possible to trace any specific influence of the views NALGO expressed on civilianisation, however. The union did not appear to have had any influence on policy change in the fields of crime prevention or the response to crimes against women and children.

The Audit Commission and the National Audit Office
From 1986, the Audit Commission began working on improving value for money in the police service; it produced audit guides for use in forces, and a series of published papers on police management topics. Subsequently the Commission was given responsibility by the government for developing a set of performance indicators for the police service. By that time, a close relationship had developed between the Audit Commission and HMIC, so that the subjects for the Commission's police papers and, later, the performance indicators arose from a close interaction between the Commission and the Inspectorate (as well as with senior officers within the police service).

The Audit Commission's 1988 paper *Administrative Support for Operational Police Officers* appears to have been an important influence in stimulating the development of civilian administrative support units within police forces. Otherwise, the Commission appears not to have had a direct influence on the policy of civilianisation.

The National Audit Office (a body that certifies the accounts of government departments and a range of other public bodies) in 1991 published a report on value for money in the police service, which examined civilianisation in that context and criticised the effectiveness with which the policy had been pursued. This provided useful ammunition for the House of Commons Public Accounts Committee (see below).

Parliament
There were not enough resources within the present study to carry out a systematic analysis of all questions and debates in Parliament touching on the three chosen areas of policing policy. Instead the problem was approached the other way about by asking participants in the policy-making process whether they had taken note of parliamentary debates or answers, and by carrying out a few interviews with MPs. Although they are not exhaustive, the findings firmly establish the conclusion that Parliament had only a very limited effect on policy change in the three chosen areas. The clearest example of a specific influence was provided by the 1991 report of the House of Commons Public Accounts Committee on value for money in provincial police forces. The committee strongly criticised the inability of the Home Office to exert direct control over the progress of civilianisation, and more generally felt there was a lack of control by central government over police expenditure, more than 70 per cent of which came

from central taxation. Although this kind of criticism may prove to be influential in the 1990s, it is notable that Parliament only got round to discussing the subject about eight years after it had been highlighted within the Home Office. There is no evidence that Parliament had any influence on civilianisation in the 1980s, or on the drive towards value for money in the police service that took place then.

In order to investigate possible Parliamentary influence on the response to crimes against women and children, an interview was carried out with the late Jo Richardson MP, who had campaigned for many years on women's issues. However, she made no strong claims about her own influence, or that of other members, on policy developments in the 1980s. She had earlier been instrumental in making it possible for a woman to get a court injunction requiring a man to stay away from her, and had played a role in the establishment of the Ministerial Group on Women's Issues. However, that group was not a major influence on changes in policing policy. Officials in the Home Office who had been responsible for drafting circulars mentioned parliamentary questions as something that might, in principle, draw their attention to a particular problem; but they did not in fact cite parliamentary questions as the stimulus for the development of any of the relevant circulars.

In the case of crime prevention, the field of possible parliamentary influence is so wide that it would be impossible to monitor. Many parliamentary debates touch on rising crime and what is to be done about it in a general way, but there was not the slightest indication from interviews with participants in the policy-making process that these had been influential or even noticed. During the latter part of the 1980s the Labour Party had begun to develop its 'new realist' approach to crime, which advocates a combination of firm law enforcement and practical crime prevention. There was no indication in the 1980s that the Labour Party's stance had encouraged the government to embrace crime prevention with more enthusiasm. Its main effect in the 1990s has been to drive the Conservative government back to get-tough policies of stiffer penalties and specifically higher rates of imprisonment.

Local representatives
In general the police authorities in the four study areas had little or no influence on policy change in civilianisation, the response to crimes against women and children, or crime prevention. There were, however, important differences between the police authorities in the four areas. Two of them (A and C) had no effective influence, but for contrasting reasons. In area A, the authority circumscribed its own role. It adopted an attitude of

exaggerated deference towards the chief constable, never tried to exert an influence, and complained that it was provided with too much information. In area C, by contrast, the Labour-led authority under a young and active chair tried hard to have an influence but was met with total opposition from the chief constable. The authority had a very low level of information, since the chief constable not only took action without consulting it, but also frequently refused to provide information about what had been done after the event. As well as being deaf to the majority on the authority, the chief constable also refused to bow to Conservative demands that NW schemes should be supported.

Like the one in area A, the authority in area D circumscribed its own role, was strongly supportive of the chief constable, and had little effective influence, although it did have some. The authority in area B was more active and influential than the others. It took the initiative in calling for reports, and knew how to ask for useful information, which was generally provided. It strongly supported the chief constable.

It has been suggested (Loveday, 1987) that the joint boards created on the abolition of the metropolitan counties are likely to be more impotent than single-county police authorities. However, among the four authorities studied here, by far the most active and influential was the one joint board, which was in area B.

The findings cast some light on the reasons for the lack of influence of police authorities. One important factor seems to be their circumscribed legal powers. Although an amenable chief constable will not stand on legal niceties, an unhelpful one has plenty of legal arguments on his side. Also it is significant that in several areas police authorities did insist on having their way on the grading of civilian staff and won because their statutory powers were unassailable in that field. Differences between the police authorities are not explained by which party was in power, but they may have been related to the political complexion of the ruling group within that party. Thus, a moderate Labour ruling group was the most influential one. The approach of the chief constable was important in determining how influential the authority was allowed to be, although where it had the relevant powers the authority might win in any case. The way the authority defined its own role seemed to be extremely important. Finally, having sub-committees on specific areas of policy probably helped an authority to be more effective and influential. Taken together these findings suggest that bodies with statutory powers similar to those of the present police authorities could be considerably more influential than the present ones generally are. Increasing their statutory powers would be a necessary but by no means sufficient condition of making them more influential.

Other local representative bodies, such as police consultative committees, crime prevention panels, and NW groups, made no discernible input into local policing policy. This confirms the results of previous research (Morgan, 1989). In area A, however, a police and public safety committee covering one major town had been active and influential. Among the reasons for its success were that it had the services of a full-time adviser, who analysed information regularly produced by the police; that it included members of groups that often have difficult relations with the police; and that it had achieved results, because it was a sub-committee of the borough council with access to resources and to the council decision-making process.

Pressure groups and voluntary organisations

Women's groups had an important influence in stimulating policy change in the police response to rape and (less successfully) to domestic violence. Among these the most important were the Women's Aid Federation and Women Against Rape, which in 1985 published a report *Ask Any Woman* (Hall, 1985) that suggested detailed requirements for police procedures in the investigation of rape. These organisations were building on a body of research and analysis that had been accumulating for more than a decade. They had modest contacts with the police at the local level, and their main influence was through the national publicity given to their reports. The crucial influence on the Home Office when it introduced its second circular, however, was the report published in 1986 of the working party set up by the Women's National Commission. This was a governmental advisory group rather than a pressure group completely outside government, and it may have been particularly influential for that reason.

Much the largest voluntary organisation with relevant interests is Victim Support, which was started in the early 1970s, and by the late 1980s encompassed 400 local victim support schemes. The main purpose of the organisation is to provide support to victims of all crimes, but in recent years some of its volunteers have been trained to support victims of sexual offences specifically. The emphasis has therefore always been on providing a service rather than lobbying, and contacts with the police have always been close because people have to be referred to Victim Support by the police. Victim Support may have been part of the attitude shift towards emphasising the needs of the victim rather than those of justice in the abstract, but it was not a force behind the specific policy changes in the 1980s. However, more recently (in 1992) Victim Support published a report of a national inter-agency working party on domestic violence, which made specific recommendations for all agencies, including the police.

NACRO (the National Association for the Care and Resettlement of Offenders) had an important influence on the development of crime prevention policy in the 1980s. From the late 1970s, with the establishment of its Crime Prevention Unit and Safe Neighbourhoods Unit, NACRO became involved in crime prevention initiatives, particularly on 'problem estates'. A seminar it organised in 1982 had what a senior Home Office official described as a 'really quite critical' influence on the development of thinking about crime prevention within the Home Office. Later its crime prevention initiatives became a source of practical knowledge, and its former staff moved on to newer parts of the growing crime prevention industry.

Pressure groups and voluntary organisations had no influence on the development of thinking about civilianisation in the 1980s. More recently, 'New Right' think-tanks such as the Adam Smith Institute have started to turn their attention to the police, but their influence lies more behind more recent developments such as parts of the Police and Magistrates' Courts Bill, and not behind the changes in the 1980s and early 1990s that are under discussion here.

The media

The influence of the mass media on policy change tends to be pervasive and difficult to pin down but, perhaps surprisingly, some useful conclusions can be drawn from the examples analysed in this study. In the case of the response to rape, there was widespread agreement that a particular television programme transmitted in 1982 had had a decisive influence on changes in the investigation of rape. This was the famous programme in the series by Roger Graef filmed in the Thames Valley Police, which showed a woman who alleged that she had been raped being interviewed by two disbelieving CID officers. The impact of the programme was so great that it caused a massive public reaction. The Home Office felt obliged to issue a circular that year on rape investigation, although it had to be couched in vague terms because officials had not had time to develop examples or precepts of good practice. This programme was spontaneously mentioned about eight years after its transmission by many of those interviewed about policy change in rape investigation both inside and outside the police forces.

Later, in 1986, television and newspaper reporting of the controversy about alleged child abuse in Cleveland again had a strong impact. The Home Office had already drafted a circular, but the media coverage ensured that the police in the words of one senior official 'were screaming for it' and enforced acceptance of its recommendations.

It is not possible to point to any specific media coverage that had a comparable effect in the case of crime prevention, and still less, of course, in the case of civilianisation. As an aspect of the internal organisation of the police, civilianisation is obviously not a subject with mass appeal. The case of crime prevention, and its contrast with rape, is more revealing, however. What was wrong with the police investigation of rape could be devastatingly revealed by simply filming a single case. The whole pattern was encapsulated in the individual drama. The failure to find effective means of preventing crime could not possibly be dramatised in any comparable way. Worse, the only neat and dramatic response that can be found for rising crime is catching and punishing an exemplary criminal. Crime prevention schemes are merely the fodder of outstandingly boring documentaries.

Individual police forces

Although chief constables had an important influence as a collective, through ACPO, there was also evidence that each individual chief constable had a specific influence on policy change within his own force. The clearest illustration is in the field of crime prevention, in which the chief constable of force B considered himself to be a pioneer. The central crime prevention department was considerably larger in force B than elsewhere, and the model structure for such a department that was adopted by ACPO was on the pattern of force B. Similarly, ACPO's burglar alarm policy was force B's policy writ large. This was not necessarily a good model of policy development, however. There was a strong view both within force B, and in other forces, that much of its crime prevention activity was lacking in substance. Indeed, as in other forces, the results of these schemes were never properly evaluated.

Again, although all chief constables gave some support to NW, they did so at different times, and with varying degrees of enthusiasm. The extreme case of reluctance was force C, where the chief constable resisted until very late, then mounted an 'experimental' scheme, then extended support for NW more widely even though the evaluation of the experiment was unfavourable, then partially withdrew support when he became alarmed at the amount of resources consumed.

Policy change on the investigation of child abuse was fairly consistent across the four forces studied, but the same was not true of the response to rape, or to domestic violence. Although all of the forces had done something, there were wide variations in what they had done. In particular, there was no general pattern with regard to specialist units or the breadth of their responsibilities.

There were fairly important differences, too, between timing and rate of civilianisation in the four forces, and the differences became much greater at the level of particular functions, some of which had been completely civilianised in one force, half in another, and not at all in a third.

In general, these differences between individual forces could be traced to the views of the chief constables, or to internal history and politics. They had nothing to do with patterns of demand in the area, the views of local people, or the positions adopted by the police authority or local consultative committees.

Cultural shift

So far the analysis has considered the influence of various organisations, institutions, or groups on change in policing policy. However, an account in those terms clearly lacks something. This is particularly clear in the case of the response to crimes against women and children. It is possible to point to organisations such as Women Against Rape, the Women's Aid Federation, and the Women's National Commission that had an influence; but it seems unlikely that these small, ill-funded, and essentially rather marginal organisations were the major cause of change. After all, many larger and better-funded pressure groups or national commissions have failed to achieve any of their objectives over long periods.

It is plain that the change in policing policy in this field is an aspect of a much wider and deeper cultural shift. The case study of policing policy on the response to rape provides a particularly striking illustration of this. The two CID officers featured in the Thames Valley film were apparently comfortable with their own behaviour at the time that they interviewed the alleged rape victim. They knew that they were being filmed, and that the film might be transmitted to millions, yet they appeared to make no attempt to behave in a way that others would find acceptable. This strongly suggests that they saw their behaviour as normal and correct in the circumstances, and were unable to grasp that others would see it differently. When the film was transmitted, the response on the part of a large number of viewers (men as well as women) was shock and outrage. That was an immediate and spontaneous response, not the result of deliberation or analysis. Those facts demonstrate a radical disjuncture between the way the CID officers saw the interview and the way many viewers saw it. It can only be explained on the assumption that a major cultural shift was taking place, and had opened up a fissure between the CID officers, still rooted in an old tradition, and many viewers who had shifted to a new one.

It would be superficial to say that the Thames Valley film caused the change of policing policy. It was the flashgun that momentarily illuminated the clash of perceptions, assumptions, and values between the police and many of their customers. The fundamental cause of change, however, was the underlying cultural shift. The activities of the organisations described in the last section were a part of that shift and no doubt contributed to it; but they were themselves partly a product of the underlying shift that was taking place.

This kind of analysis is based on the assumption that culture develops to some extent according to a logic of its own. Although the shift in the way that rape victims are perceived can be represented in crude Marxist terms as a consequence merely of a change in the balance of power (in this case between men and women), that would be much less true of the cultural shift that underlies the increasing emphasis on crime prevention. This is akin to the 'paradigm shift' that Kuhn (1970) argued lies at the heart of scientific revolutions. The paradigm, in this case, is the idea that the only proper response to crime is punishment, and that the threefold purpose of punishment is retribution, deterrence, and reform. Social scientists have found it increasingly difficult to reconcile their findings with such a paradigm, and accordingly a shift of paradigm is in progress. There is an increasing body of evidence to show that the individual who is punished is not deterred but becomes more likely to reoffend as a result. Imprisonment at thinkable levels does not incapacitate more than an insignificant fraction of offenders. There is little or no evidence that a high rate of conviction or severity of punishment causes a reduction in the overall crime rate. And punishment by the state does not reform people: to quote the 1988 White Paper, 'imprisonment is an expensive way of making bad people worse'.

The paradigm shift that is taking place involves separating what have been thought of as the inter-related functions of punishment, and using different means to achieve the different objectives. The ritual or symbolic function of punishment as retribution is important, and cannot be abandoned, although restitution can in some cases be added to it. Yet these symbolic acts cannot achieve the objective of reducing the aggregate level of crime. The growth of interest in crime prevention arises directly from this. Practical methods of reducing crime that are completely unconnected with punishment or even law enforcement must be found.

At a more detailed level, of course, the growth of interest in crime prevention arose from the results of research by the Home Office Research and Planning Unit on methods of reducing opportunities for crime in specific situations, but the basic idea is much broader than that. It arises from a paradigm shift that allows us to see the reduction of crime as a separate objective from the punishment of offenders.

This analysis helps to explain why crime prevention policy has changed less than in each of the other areas studied. Essentially it is because the shift in this case affects the paradigm used by specialists in the field, and has had comparatively little influence on popular culture. There is, as it were, a coterie that is trying to develop new remedies on a scientific basis while the mass of the people still rely on herbal folk medicines. Politicians of all parties find it easy and convenient to appeal to the old way of thinking. Consequently, the paradigm shift that would truly put crime prevention policy at the centre of the stage has not been accomplished.

CRITERIA OF DEMOCRACY REVISITED

It is now time to return to the seven criteria of democracy suggested in Chapter 1. If this framework of analysis can usefully be applied to the results on policy change in the police service, then it should be possible to say how far and in what ways British policing is democratic.

Equity

The concept of equity does not seem to be relevant to the process of civilianisation, but it does have immediate application to the other two cases. The whole shift of policy on the response to rape, domestic violence, and child abuse can be represented as an attempt to equalise the treatment of different sorts of victim, and to open up access to justice to certain disadvantaged groups. It can also be represented as an extension of formal control to what was hitherto a largely private domain, but equity is the motive and justification for such an extension. In principle, the growth of crime prevention can also be justified on the basis of equity. First, many types of crime, and statistically the majority of all crimes, affect the weaker and poorer sections of society disproportionately, so crime prevention, if effective, would tend to redress the balance in their favour. Second, crime prevention activity can be targeted on disadvantaged groups, and in fact much of it has been (crime prevention on 'problem' housing estates) although some of it has not (NW). Third, the paradigm shift that leads towards an increasing emphasis on crime prevention as opposed to law enforcement and retribution is broadly in line with the principle of equity. Offenders who are caught and punished tend very strongly to be poor, weak, and disadvantaged. Shifting the emphasis to crime prevention should help potential victims of crime while reducing the degree to which weak and inadequate people are stigmatised by the criminal justice system. It has been argued above, however, that the shift towards crime prevention has yet to be effectively accomplished. To the extent that that is true, the trend of policy has failed to follow the principle of equity.

Delivery of service

All three cases of policy change move towards delivering an appropriate service more effectively and efficiently to the public. In the case of civilianisation, that is the dominant theme of the change of policy. It is not possible to say unequivocally that civilianisation has, in fact, led to an improvement in service delivery. An equally plausible interpretation is that the main objective of civilianisation for chief constables is to maintain or increase the number of police officers in their organisations. There may have been an expansion of tasks carried out by civilians without any consequential increase in the number of police officers doing 'operational' work. However, as outlined in Chapter 4, demands upon the police service would have increased whether or not forces had civilianised. It thus seems reasonable to argue that civilianisation most likely prevented a sharper decline in service levels in the face of such demands upon police resources.

There is clear evidence of a major improvement in the service delivered to women and children as victims of rape and sexual abuse. Without confusing changes in policy with changes in practice, it seems clear that in general, rape and child abuse are now dealt with in a completely different manner than was the case 10 years ago. However, the police response to domestic assault has shown less evidence of change. The changes in the study forces were confined to local initiatives.

There has been a marked increase in the profile of crime prevention as measured by the rhetoric of chief officers and Home Office circulars. However, in terms of major developments in the crime prevention role of the police, there remains little evidence of a significant shift. The ambiguity of the police role in crime prevention is compounded by the lack of evaluation of activities, making it difficult to measure the extent to which service delivery has improved.

Responsiveness

In general, the developments in policing policy examined in this study cannot be represented as a response to views expressed by police authorities or by others at the local level. In all three fields considered in this study, policing policy has, however, been responsive to advice and direction from the Home Office. Some have argued – for example, the House of Commons Public Accounts Committee – that since central government pays over 70 per cent of the bill for policing, this is the appropriate kind of responsiveness. However, as observed by Reiner (1991), this opens up a serious gap in the system of accountability, as the Home Secretary does not have statutory responsibility for most matters affecting provincial police forces and therefore cannot be held accountable for them in Parliament. In practice, Parliament had little influence on the developments in policing policy considered in this study.

The findings suggest that police authorities lack influence both because their statutory powers are limited and because in many cases they circumscribe their own activities and do much less than they could. The level of knowledge and interest among police authority members is often low, and the standard of debate is frequently poor.

Two kinds of reform can be suggested. First reform which aims to increase the influence of local police authorities. For example, police authorities could be given the statutory power to determine broad policy priorities, though this would not be a sufficient condition to increasing their practical influence. In addition, and as was recognised by leading members in at least two police authorities, they simply did not have the expertise or the information to give them the 'clout' to initiate change proactively. Thus, it would also be necessary to impose a duty on chief constables to provide regular information on a range of matters. Further reforms would be required to enhance the status, seniority, and knowledge base of the clerks to the authorities. This supports the recommendations of some other authors, for example Loveday (1994:29) who suggested that 'if [a] police authority is to act independently of the police force, then it will also need a secretariat, with sufficient resources to cost police proposals, identify local priorities and liaise with local communities'.

Finally, given the degree of influence now exercised from the centre, further reform is needed to make the Home Office answerable to Parliament for the use of its very considerable powers in relation to provincial police forces. This would appear to be a prerequisite of an enhanced form of responsiveness.

Distribution of power

In all three areas considered, the Home Office played the leading role in policy making, although there was also a considerable degree of consultation with the other participants. This process of consultation usually appeared to be a genuine effort on the part of officials to gather reactions to proposed changes from interested parties. On occasion, the Home Office was prepared to withdraw proposals and revise them in response to comments received from other bodies. Furthermore, it seems that officials took account of the expected reactions of other parties in the policy-making process before drafting circular advice, so that there was (on occasion) an exercise of power even where there was no detectable conflict. In this sense, although the Home Office was clearly the central influence, the distribution of power was not as concentrated or as absolute as is sometimes implied.

The Home Office appeared to have considerable influence in determining the broad direction of policy, but a lot less influence over the details of implementation. In the case of civilianisation, for example, it can be argued that the police actually achieved most of what they wanted (growth of police officer numbers). In the case of crime prevention, it can be argued that the police successfully forestalled a possible attempt to shift more of the responsibility to another agency, and that this has been a major block to the development of policy. The changes in the handling of crimes against women and children can most plausibly be seen as a response by all participants to a major cultural shift. Power relations were less important because all participants supported the broad trend of policy, with the exception of the local authority associations, which were cautious about the resource implications.

As was suggested in Chapter 1, it is important that the 'democratic criteria' be considered as overlapping and inter-dependent. Thus, for example, in two of the chosen policy areas at least, the criteria of distribution of power and effective service delivery cannot be properly viewed entirely independently. For example, a central criticism made by the members of the House of Commons Public Accounts Committee, was that the Home Office had encouraged forces to civilianise, but had little direct control of the increasing costs of provincial forces. In other words, there was an *insufficient* concentration of power in the hands of the Home Office under the present arrangements. In the field of crime prevention, Home Office officials argued that they had deliberately avoided giving clear responsibility to a single body in order to keep all the 'players on board'. However, as Chapter 2 illustrates, this dispersal of power was a barrier to the development of an effective crime prevention strategy. In this instance, the distribution of power appeared to be in conflict with the criterion of effective service delivery.

Information
There has hitherto been a serious shortage of information on funding, expenditure, activity, and outputs. The amount of information available to police authorities varied widely between one authority and another. The experience in force A – where detailed information was provided – showed that provision of information alone was insufficient to lead to an effective contribution from police authority members. However, it seems that information about what the police are doing and how they do it is a crucial precondition to effective functioning of other democratic criteria.

However, it was not generally the case that a representative body could engage in a continuing dialogue with the professional police managers so as to become better informed and to elicit relevant information. The present Government's policy is to develop standard measures of performance and to require police forces to provide regular information to police authorities and central government based on these indicators of performance. It is a policy that should lead to improvements in this area, although there will still be a considerable emphasis on the ability and the will of police authorities to use this information as a basis for starting to build a more productive relationship with their chief constables.

Redress

The findings of this study show that policing policy can be reversed in line with a deep shift in culture or public opinion, although they also show that it was not elected representatives who acted as the channel through which the new opinions were expressed.

In Chapter 1, two other notions of redress were also rehearsed. The first was the possibility of removing an incompetent or malevolent police management. The second was the opportunity for individuals who have been wronged by the police to have their complaints investigated, and to gain compensation, if upheld. There is no specific information on either of these points from the present study. No chief constable has been removed since the Second World War, although some have moved on following difficulties. Recent research on complaints investigation (Maguire and Corbett, 1991) suggests that many complainants remain dissatisfied, but that prospects for improving the system may not be good.

Participation

In general, the style of policy making in the three areas studied did not involve active participation by the wider public or their representatives, at least in any direct sense. Developments which were intended to enhance wider participation in discussions over policing policy, on the whole, failed in this objective. Both section 106 committees and crime prevention panels were almost without exception unrepresentative and marginal to the policy-making process. There was no influence by the wider public in the case of civilianisation, and very little in the case of crime prevention. The growing emphasis on crime prevention arose from paradigm shift among highly informed people only. The greatest level of participation was in changing the response to crimes against women and children. This 'participation', however, largely by-passed the formal institutions of local and national representation. Pressure groups concerned with women's issues were an important influence on the national debate to which Home Office officials responded by developing circular advice. The voices of the pressure groups were heard because they were in tune with a wider cultural shift.

The findings of this study therefore confirm that participation, particularly in the formal democratic mechanisms, was less important than other democratic criteria in leading to change. Consequently, they also call into question the possibility that participation might form a central plank in some future system of 'democratic' control of policing.

THE BALANCE SHEET

One of the main conclusions of PSI's programme of research on *Police and People in London* carried out between 1980 and 1983 was that the style and pattern of policing on the ground is determined largely by the immediate demands that are made on police officers, by the way police officers perceive these demands, by the goals, satisfactions and frustrations that are built into the job, by the internal logic of the encounters between police officers and members of the public, and by the internal dynamics of the police organisation. It was concluded that, by contrast, organisations outside the police force, such as Parliament or police authorities, had comparatively little influence, and that attempts to control police behaviour through systems of rules tended to be ineffective.

There was an element of deliberate exaggeration in those conclusions. In an attempt to redress the balance, the purpose of the present study was to look in detail at change in the police service and to consider whether and how far it is a response to democratic influences originating from the wider society.

The study concentrated on three chosen areas of policy in which important changes were thought to have occurred. The findings confirm that substantial changes took place over the 1980s in the style and pattern of responding to crimes against women and children. Also, a long process of internal reorganisation continued as the pace of civilianisation picked up again in the second half of the 1980s. On the other hand, changes in police activity in the field of crime prevention were relatively superficial, even though this looks to most observers like the first priority for major policy change.

Where the change in the style and pattern of policing has been clearest – in the handling of crimes against women and children – this was a response to a deep cultural shift in society at large. The change has occurred because police officers, under pressure, have come to see things differently: there has been a cultural shift within the police service, too. This is entirely in accord with the conclusion from the earlier PSI research that only internalised principles of conduct have a consistent effect on behaviour. On the other hand, the shift was partly accomplished by the development of new codes of conduct (most notably for the investigation of child abuse), by associated training programmes, and by a consistent approach by management to the application of the new standards. So in the context of a cultural shift, rules were critically important in bringing about a change in police behaviour.

The foregoing analysis suggests that British policing currently meets or partially meets a number of democratic criteria. Two of the policy changes upon which this study has concentrated can be justified with reference to the principle of equity. All three policy changes have been aimed at, with varying degrees of success, an improved delivery of service. The levels of information about the inputs and outputs of policing have been improved in recent years, even though there is much room for further progress. Finally, even though the Home Office is clearly the most influential player, power is perhaps more dispersed in the system than other studies have allowed. However, the formal democratic institutions that are supposed to frame policing – police authorities, consultative committees, Parliament – do not appear to have played an important role in the development of policy. The criteria of responsiveness and participation have featured little in the process of policy change in the three areas studied. This confirms the argument put forward in Chapter 1 that democracy is not only or primarily about governmental institutions, but more generally about the openness of a society and its capacity to respond flexibly to new demands and pressures. The change in the police response to rape came about largely without any active participation by police authorities, or by other local or national representatives. It seems that the distribution of power does not always depend on active participation in formal democratic institutions.

Much recent debate has been critical of an alleged tendency towards increased centralisation of decision making about policing. The analysis put forward in this study is rather different. It starts from the observation that nearly three-quarters of the cost of policing is met by central government. It is most unlikely that the share of the costs met by local taxation will increase: it is more likely to decline. In those circumstances, central government certainly has a duty to get a better deal for the taxpayer by improving the efficiency of service delivery. The four police authorities included in this study had made no substantial effort to put pressure on their police forces to improve the efficiency of service delivery. That reinforces the need for central government to do so.

Criticism of centralisation has particularly highlighted disputes over the supply of equipment for dealing with public disorder (CS gas and baton rounds). Police authorities have not ultimately succeeded against the wishes of central government in denying chief constables access to equipment of this kind. Yet the argument of the Appeal Court in the crucial case (*R v Secretary of State for the Home Department, ex p Northumbria Police Authority* [1988] 2 WLR 590) was that the Home Secretary had the power to do what was necessary to preserve the Queen's peace, and implicitly the case was concerned with public disorder that would transcend local police boundaries. There does not seem to be anything antidemocratic about central government making provision for dealing with major public disorder that is not restricted to one police force area.

These arguments suggest that central government is bound to have the major share of responsibility for improving efficiency of service delivery and value for money for expenditure on policing, and for ensuring that the police can deal with large-scale outbreaks of public disorder. Any suggestion that these responsibilities can be decentralised to police authorities is unrealistic. However, this does highlight an important weakness in the present structure of accountability. The true extent of the Home Secretary's responsibility for provincial police forces is not fully recognised by the present arrangements. For example, although the Home Office is in fact trying to improve the effectiveness and efficiency of provincial police forces, the Home Secretary is not answerable to Parliament for the service they deliver. The main problem with the fudge enshrined in the 1964 Police Act is that it fails to make the Home Secretary adequately answerable for the powers that, in practice, he exercises.

The findings on police authorities and consultative committees suggest that it is very hard to create a forum in which useful discussion of policing policy will take place. The main counter-example in this study was a police and public safety committee that covered one major town within one of the four police force areas studied. Three reasons can be suggested for the success of this committee. First, it included both natural opponents and natural supporters of the police among its members. Second, it was serviced by a full-time official who made good use of the substantial amount of information supplied by the police. Third, the committee covered a town with a strong sense of identity and was therefore at a scale intermediate between the much less successful police authority on the one hand and consultative committees on the other. This example suggests that there is scope for some aspects of policing policy to be determined by local representative bodies, but that neither police authorities nor consultative committees (in their current forms) are the appropriate model. They are at the wrong scale, they are not adequately serviced by professional advisers, they do not adequately represent groups that come into conflict with the police, and their members have too little awareness, knowledge, or motivation.

It would be useful to compare policing with some other public service, such as health or education, in terms of democratic responsiveness and accountability. That was beyond the scope of the present study. The broad impression gained from the findings is that policing is democratic on a number of criteria. However, as outlined above the most important criteria have not included those of participation or responsiveness to elected bodies. This is not to suggest that these elements of democracy have no importance. The argument is, that if changes in policing are to be described as democratic, it is largely in spite of the lack of participation rather than because of it. The police authorities had little influence over the policy changes considered in this study; in the rare instances where they were relatively active, they tended to articulate points of view that had earlier been developed at a national level, rather than reflect the particular conditions or concerns that existed at the local level. The strategy implicit in the Police and Magistrates' Courts Bill is to try to make police authorities more effective by establishing measures of police performance, giving the authorities responsibility for improving standards on these measures, and appointing more experienced people to them (although defining what counts as relevant experience turns out to be very difficult). Measures of this kind may help, but it seems likely that police authorities for whole police forces at the present scale will at best provide retrospective accountability rather than act as a decision making forum. As suggested above, more active discussion of policing policy seems more likely at the level of a city or town (at a substantially smaller scale than the present police forces).

The conclusion that emerges most strongly from the findings of this study is that the police can only continue to behave in ways that people find unacceptable if their behaviour largely remains hidden. Just one film of a CID interview with a rape victim was enough to tip the balance against a whole tradition of dealing with this kind of case. The decision by Peter Imbert, then Chief Constable of the Thames Valley Police, to allow that series of television documentaries to be made was probably more important in making police governance democratic than the whole apparatus established by the 1964 Act. Similarly, police corruption and oppressive behaviour which have surfaced through the highlighting of miscarriages of justice in recent years can only continue in the dark. It has not been the bodies concerned with the governance of police, such as police authorities or the Home Office, that have brought these matters to light. This does not mean that the formal democratic institutions are unimportant in the governance of the police. Their influence, however, is circumscribed in several important ways, and it is clear that their role is one that could and, arguably, should be enhanced. The results of this research suggest, though, that consideration of the potential influence of the formal institutions must take into account the very real limits of their role. Consequently, any analysis of the relationship between democracy and policing must focus more broadly on a variety of other means of influence and control. In particular, policy makers should also concentrate on openness, information, and the opportunity for people to see, as directly as possible, what the police do and how they do it.

Bibliography

ACC and AMA (1993) Association of County Councils and Association of Metropolitan Authorities Joint Conference, *Control of the Police: Democracy at Risk* London, 21 July 1993

Adam Smith Institute (1983) *The Omega File: Local Government Policy* London: Adam Smith Institute

Adler, Z. (1987) *Rape on Trial* London: RKP

Alderson, J. (1979) *Policing Freedom* Plymouth: McDonald and Evans

Allen, R.J. (1976) The police and substantive rulemaking: reconciling principle and expediency *University of Pennsylvania Law Review* November, 62-117

Alinsky, S. (1969) *Rules for Radicals* New York: Random House

Arendt, H. (1963) *On Revolution* New York: Viking Press

Association of Chief Police Officers (1988) *Civilian Staff in the Police Service: Career Structures and other Contemporary Issues* London: ACPO

Association of Chief Police Officers (1993) *Your Police: the Facts* ACPO Factsheet May 1993 London: ACPO

Ascher, K. (1987) *The Politics of Privatisation* London: Macmillan

Audit Commission (1988) *Administrative Support for Operational Police Officers* Police Paper No.5 London: Audit Commission

Audit Commission (1990a) *Effective Policing – Performance Review in Police Forces* Police Paper No.8. London: HMSO

Audit Commission (1990b) *We Can't Go On Meeting Like This: The Changing Role of Local Authority Members* Management Paper No.8 London: Audit Commission

Audit Commission (1991) *Pounds and Coppers: the financing of provincial police forces* Police Paper No.10 London: Audit Commission

Bachrach, P. (1969) *The Theory of Democratic Elitism: A Critique* Boston: Little, Brown and Co

Bachrach, P. and Baratz, M. (1962) The two faces of power *American Political Science Review* 56(4), 942-52

Barr, R. and Pease, K. (1990) Crime placement, displacement and deflection. In N. Morris and M. Tonry, (eds) *Crime and Justice: A Review of Research* Vol.12, Chicago: University of Chicago Press

Bayley, D. (1991) Policing democracy, unpublished paper

Bell, S. (1988) *When Salem Came to the Boro: The True Story of the Cleveland Child Abuse Crisis* London: Pan

Bennett, T.H. (1990) *Evaluating Neighbourhood Watch* Aldershot: Gower

Berelson, B., Lazarfeld, P.F. and McPhee, W. (1954) *Voting* Chicago: University of Chicago Press

Berger, V. (1977) Trial, women's tribulation: Rape cases in the court room, *Columbia Law Review* Volume 77:1

Binney, V., Harkell, G. and Nixon, J. (1981) *Leaving Violent Men: A Study of Refuges and Housing for Battered Women* Leeds: Women's Aid Federation England

Bottoms, A.E. (1990) Crime prevention facing the 1990s *Policing and Society* Vol.1 No.1 pp.3-22

Brogden, M. (1982) *The Police: Autonomy and Consent* London: Academic Press

Brown, D. and Iles, S. (1985) *Community Constables: A study of a policing initiative* Research and Planning Unit Paper 30 London: Home Office

Burrows, J. and Lewis, H. (1988) *Directing Patrolwork: A study of uniformed policing* Home Office Research Study No.99 London: HMSO

Butler-Sloss (1989) *Report of the Inquiry into Child Abuse in Cleveland 1987* Cmnd 412 London: HMSO 1988

Campbell, B. (1988) *Unofficial Secrets: Child Sexual Abuse – The Cleveland Case* London: Virago

Carter, A. (1988) *The Politics of Women's Rights* Harlow: Longman

Chambers, G. and Millar, A. (1983) *Investigating Sexual Assault* Scottish Office Central Research Unit Edinburgh: HMSO

Chatterton, M. and Rogers, M. (1989) Focused Policing. In, R. Morgan and D. Smith (eds) *Coming to Terms With Policing* London: Routledge

Clarke, R.V.G. (1981) The Prospects for Controlling Crime *Research Bulletin* No.12 London: Home Office

Clarke, R.V.G. (ed) (1992) *Situational Crime Prevention* New York: Harrow and Heston

Clarke, R.V.G. and Hough, M. *Crime and Police Effectiveness* Home Office Research Study No. 79 London: HMSO

Clarke, R.V.G. and Mayhew, P. (eds) (1980) *Designing Out Crime* London: HMSO

Coleman, A. (1985) *Utopia on Trial* London: Hilary Shipman

Coote, A. and Campbell, B. (1987) *Sweet Freedom: The Struggle for Women's Liberation* 2nd edition, Oxford: Blackwell

Corcoran P. (1983) The limits of democratic theory, in Duncan G. (ed) *Democratic Theory and Practice* Cambridge: Cambridge University Press

Critchley, T.A. (1978) *A History of the Police in England and Wales* London: Constable

Dahl, R. (1961) *Who Governs? Democracy and Power in an American City* New Haven and London: Yale University Press

Dale, B. and Hayward, S. (1984) Quality circle failures in UK manufacturing companies *Omega* 12:5, 475-484

Day, P. and Klein, R. (1987) *Accountabilities* London: Tavistock

Department of Employment (1974) *Women and Work: A Statistical Survey* Manpower Paper No.9 London: HMSO

Department of the Environment (1983) *Civilianisation and Overtime in Police Forces* Department of the Environment Audit Inspectorate

Dobash, R.E. and Dobash, R.P. (1970) *Violence Against Wives* New York: The Free Press

Dobash, R.E. and Dobash, R.P. (1992) *Women, Violence and Social Change* London: Routledge

Downs, A. (1957) *An Economic Theory of Democracy* New York: Harper and Row

Edwards, S. (1989) *Policing 'Domestic' Violence: Women, Law and the State* London: Sage

Emsley, C. (1983) *Policing and its Context, 1750-1870* London: Macmillan

Evans, T. (1991) The need for change. In T. Evans (ed) *An Arresting Idea: The Management of Police Services in Modern Britain* London: Adam Smith Institute

Feldman, D. (1990) Regulating treatment of suspects in police stations: judicial interpretations of detention provisions in the Police and Criminal Evidence Act 1984 *Criminal Law Review*, 452-471

Fox, A. (1985) *Man Mismanagement* (2nd edition) London: Hutchinson

Fukuyama, F. (1989) The end of history? *The National Interest* No.16, 1-18

Gelsthorpe, L. and Morris, A. (1990) *Feminist Perspectives in Criminology* Milton Keynes: Open University Press

Gladstone, F.J. (1980) *Coordinating Crime Prevention Efforts* Home Office Research Study No.62 London: HMSO

Graef, R. (1989) *Talking Blues* London: Fontana

Hall, S. (1980) Reformism and the legislation of consent. In National Deviancy Conference (eds) *Permissiveness and Control. The fate of sixties legislation* Basingstoke: Macmillan

Hall, R. (1985) *Ask Any Woman: A London Inquiry into Rape and Sexual Assault* London: Falling Wall Press

Hanmer, J., Radford, J. and Stanko, E.A. (1989) *Women, Policing and Male Violence* London: Routledge

Harvey, L., Grimshaw, P. and Pease, K. (1989) Crime prevention delivery: the work of crime prevention officers. In Morgan and Smith (eds) *Coming to Terms with Policing* London: Routledge

Heald, D. and Morris, G (1984) Why public sector unions are on the defensive. *Personnel Management*, May

Hennessy, P. (1989) *Whitehall* London: Secker and Warburg

Hibberd, M. (1985) *The Colville Crime Survey* London: Police Foundation

Highmore, S. (1993) *The Integration of Police Officers and Civilian Staff. A study of internal service quality* Home Office: Police Reseach Group

Hirst, P. (1988) Representative democracy and its limits *The Political Quarterly*, 59: 190-205

Hodgson, G. (1984) *The Democratic Economy* Harmondsworth: Penguin

Holdaway, S. (1984) *Inside the British Police* Oxford: Blackwell

Holtom, C. and Raynor, P. (1988) Origins of victims support philosophy and practice. In J. Pointing and M Maguire *Victims of Crime: A New Deal?* Milton Keynes: Open University Press

Home Office (1967) *Police Manpower, Equipment and Efficiency* London: HMSO

22222222222222222

222 2 222 2 22 2 2 2222

2222222222

Home Office (1971) *Crime Prevention Panels* Home Office Circular 48/1971 London: Home Office

Home Office (1983) *Manpower, Effectiveness, and Efficiency in the Police Service* Circular 114/83 London: Home Office

Home Office and others (1984) *Crime Prevention* Home Office circular 8/1984 London: Home Office

Home Office (1986) *Violence Against Women* Home Office circular 69/1986 London: Home Office

Home Office (1988) *Practical Ways to Crack Crime* London: Home Office

Home Office (1988) *The Investigation of Child Sexual Abuse* Home Office circular 52/1988 London: Home Office

Home Office (1988) *Civilians in the Police Service* Home Office circular 105/1988 London: Home Office

Home Office and others (1990) *Partnership and Crime Prevention* Home Office circular 44/1990 London: Home Office

Home Office (1993) *Police Reform: a Police Service for the Twenty-First Century* Cm 2281 London: HMSO

Hope, T. (1985) *Implementing Crime Prevention Measures* Home Office Research Study No.86 HMSO

Hope, T. and Murphy, D.J.I. (1983) Problems of implementing crime prevention: the experience of a demonstration project. *Howard Journal of Criminal Justice.* 22, pp.38-50

Hope, T. and Shaw, M. (eds) (1988) *Communities and Crime Reduction* London: HMSO

Horton, C. and Smith, D.J. (1988) *Evaluating Police Work: An Action Research Project* London: Policy Studies Institute

Hough, J.M. and Mayhew, P. (1985) *Taking Account of Crime: Key Findings from the 1984 British Crime Survey* London: HMSO

House of Commons (1957-8) Select Committee on Estimates, *First Report* 1957-58

House of Commons Expenditure Committee (1977) *Selected Public Expenditure Programmes, chapter 4: The Employment of Civilians for Police Purposes: Ninth Report*, Session 1976-77 London: HMSO

House of Commons Committee of Public Accounts, (1991) *Promoting Value for Money in Provincial Police Forces: Eighth Report* London: HMSO

Husain, S. (1988) Neighbourhood Watch in England and Wales: a locational analysis *Crime Prevention Unit Paper* No.12 London: Home Office

Irving, B., Bird, C., Hibberd, M. and Willmore, J. (1989) *Neighbourhood Policing: The natural history of a policing experiment* London: Police Foundation

Jefferson, T. (1990) *The Case Against Paramilitary Policing* Milton Keynes: Open University Press

Jefferson, T. and Grimshaw, R. (1984) *Controlling the Constable* London: Frederick Muller/The Cobden Trust

Jeffrey, C.R. (1971) *Crime Prevention through Environmental Design* California: Sage

Johnston, L. (1987) Controlling policework: problems of organisational reform in large public bureaucracies, *Work, Employment and Society* 2:1

Johnston, V., Shapland, J. and Wiles, P. (1993) *Developing Police Crime Prevention: Management and Organisational Change* Police Research Group Crime Prevention Unit Series paper No. 41, London: Home Office Police Department

Katz, S. and Mazur, M. (1979) *Understanding the Rape Victim* John Wiley and Sons

Kelly, L. and Regan, L. (1990) Flawed protection, *Social Work Today*, 19 April

Kinsey, R. (1984) *The Merseyside Crime Survey* First Report, Merseyside Metropolitan Council

Kinsey, R., Lea, J. and Young, J. (1986) *Losing the Fight Against Crime* Oxford: Basil Blackwell

Kuhn, T.S. (1970) *The Structure of Scientific Revolutions* Second edition. Chicago: University of Chicago Press

Laycock, G. and Heal, K. (1989) Crime prevention: The British experience. In D.J. Evans and D.T. Herbert (eds) *The Geography of Crime* London: Routledge

LeBon, G. (1960 [1895]) *The Crowd* New York: Viking

Levens B. and Dutton D. *The Social Service Role of the Police: Domestic Crisis Intervention* Ministry of Supply and Services (Canada 1980)

Lloyd, C. (1985) National riot police: Britain's third force?. In B. Fine and R. Milllar (eds) *Policing the Miners' Strike* London: Lawrence and Wishart

Loveday, B. (1987) Joint boards for police in Metropolitan areas – A preliminary assessment *Local Government Studies* 13:3, 85-101

Loveday, B. (1990) Joint boards and the local accountability of police in the metropolitan areas *Local Government Studies* 16:2 March/April, 37-53

Loveday, B. (1991) The new police authorities *Policing and Society* 1:3, 193-212

Loveday, B. (1993a) Civilian staff in the police service *Policing* Summer

Loveday, B. (1993b) The local accountability of police in England and Wales: future prospects. In R. Reiner and S. Spencer (eds) *Accountable Policing.* London: Institute for Public Policy Research

Loveday, B. (1994) Police reform. Problems of accountability and the measurement of police effectiveness. Institute of Public Policy, Department of Management, University of Central England

Lukes, S. (1974) *Power: A Radical View* London: Macmillan

Lustgarten, L. (1986) *The Governance of Police* London: Sweet and Maxwell

McBarnet, D. (1981) *Conviction* London: Macmillan

McConville, M. and Shepherd, D. (1992) *Watching Police, Watching Communities* London: Routledge

McCrudden, C., Smith, D.J. and Brown, C. (1991) *Racial Justice at Work: The Enforcement of the Race Relations Act 1976 in Employment* London: Policy Studies Institute

Maguire, M. and Corbett, C. (1987) *The Effects of Crime and the Work of Victims Support Schemes* Aldershot: Gower

Maguire, M. and Corbett, C. (1991) *A Study of the Police Complaints System* London: HMSO

Marginson, P. (1988) *Beyond the Workplace* Oxford: Blackwell

Manwaring-White, S. (1983) *The Policing Revolution. Police technology, democracy and liberty in Britain* Brighton: Harvester Press

Marshall, G. (1965) *Police and Government* London: Methuen

Marshall, G. (1978) Police accountability revisited. In, D. Butler and A.H. Halsey, (eds) *Policy and Politics* London: Macmillan

Matthews, R. (1990) Developing more effective strategies for curbing prostitution *Security Journal* 1:182-87

Mawby, R. and Gill, M. (1987) *Crime Victims* London: Tavistock

Metropolitan Police Service (1992) *Response to the Home Office Inquiry into police responsibilities and rewards* London: Metropolitan Police Service

Metropolitan Police and the London Borough of Bexley (1987) *Child Sexual Abuse Joint Investigative Project: Final report* London: HMSO

Michels, R. (1958) *Political Parties: A Sociological Examination of the Oligarchical Tendencies of Modern Democracy* Glencoe: The Free Press

Mill, J. S. (1910) *Representative Government* London: Everyman

Millward, N (1994) *The New Industrial Relations* London: PSI

Morgan, J. and Zedner, L. (1991) *Child Victims* Oxford: Oxford University Press

Morgan, R. (1987) The local determinants of policing policy. In P. Willmott (ed) *Policing and the Community* London: Policy Studies Institute

Morgan, R. (1989) Policing by consent: legitimating the doctrine. In R. Morgan and D.J. Smith (eds) *Coming to Terms with Policing* London: Routledge

Morgan, R. (1992) Talking About Policing. In D. Downes (ed) *Unravelling Criminal Justice* London: Macmillan

Morgan, R. and Maggs, C. (1985). Called to Account? The Implications of Consultative Groups for Police *Policing* 1: 87-95

Morgan, R. and Swift, P. (1987) The future of police authorities: members' views *Public Administration* 65:3 259-276

Mosca, G (1939) *The Ruling Class* New York: McGraw-Hill

Muir, K.W. (1977) *Police: Streetcorner Politicians* Chicago: University of Chicago Press

National Audit Office (1991) *Promoting Value for Money in Provincial Police Forces* London: HMSO

Nelken, D. (1985) Community involvement in crime control *Current Legal Problems*, 38, 239-267

Newburn, T. (1991) *Permission and Regulation: Law and Morals in Post-War Britain* London: Routledge

Oaksey, Lord (1949) *Police Conditions of Service* London: Home Office

Osborn, S. (1982) Crime and public housing: Community planning approach to tackling crime. In M. Hough and P. Mayhew (eds) *Crime and Public Housing* Research and Planning Unit Paper No.6 London: Home Office

Pahl, J. (1982) Police response to battered women *Journal of Social Welfare Law* November, 337-43

Pareto, V. (1935) *The Mind and Society* New York: McGraw-Hill

Parnas, R.I. (1972) The police response to domestic disturbance. In L. Radzinowitz and M.E. Wolfgang (eds) *The Criminal in the Arms of the Law* New York: Basic Books

Parrett L. (1992) *Past, Present and Future Roles of Civilians in the Police Service* Home Office: Police Research Group

Parton, N. (1985) *The Politics of Child Abuse* London: Macmillan

Pateman, C. (1970) *Participation and Democratic Theory.* Cambridge: Cambridge University Press

Pease, K. (1991) The Kirkholt project: preventing burglary on a British public housing estate *Security Journal* 2:73-77

Pease, K. (1994) Crime Prevention. In M. Maguire, R. Morgan and R. Reiner (eds) *The Oxford Handbook of Criminology* Oxford: Oxford University Press

Pizzey, E. (1974) *Scream Quietly or the Neighbours will Hear* Harmonsworth: Penguin

Police Foundation (1981) *Newark Foot Patrol Experiment* Washington: Police Foundation

Polsby, N. (1963) *Community Power and Political Theory* New Haven and London: Yale University Press

Powell, E. (1969) *Freedom and Reality*. London: Batsford

Punch, M. (1979) The Secret Social service. In S. Holdaway (ed) *The British Police* London: Edward Arnold

Rape Research and Counselling Project (1981) Submission to the Criminal Law Revision Committee, November

Raphael, D.D. (1976) *Problems of Political Philosophy* (revised edition) London: Macmillan

Reiner, R. (1991) *Chief Constables* Oxford: Oxford University Press

Reiner, R. (1992) *The Politics of the Police* Hemel Hemstead: Harvester Wheatsheaf. Second Edition

Reiner, R. (1993) Police Accountability: Principles, patterns and practices. In, R. Reiner and S. Spencer (eds) *Accountable Policing: Effectiveness, Empowerment and Equity* London: Institute for Public Policy Research

Richardson, A. (1983) *Participation* London: Routledge and Kegan Paul

Rock, P. (1988) Crime reduction initiatives on problem estates. In T. Hope and M. Shaw (eds) *Communities and Crime Reduction* London: HMSO

Rock, P. (1990) *Helping Victims of Crime* Oxford: Oxford University Press

Rose, R. (1980) *Do parties make a difference?* London: Macmillan

Rosenbaum, D.P. (1988) Community crime prevention: A review and synthesis of the literature *Justice Quarterly* Vol.5 No.3 pp. 323-396

Royal Commission on the Police (1960) *Interim Report* Cmnd 1222, London: HMSO

Royal Commission on the Police (1962) *Final Report* Cmnd 1728, London: HMSO,

Sanders, A. (1993) Controlling the discretion of the individual officer. In R. Reiner and S. Spencer (eds) *Accountable Policing* London: Institute for Public Policy Research

Sartori, G. (1962) *Democratic Theory* Detroit: Wayne State University Press

Scarman, Lord (1982) *The Brixton Disorders 10-12 April 1981: Report of an Inquiry by Lord Scarman* London: HMSO

Schumpeter, J.A. (1961) *Capitalism, Socialism and Democracy* London: Allen and Unwin

Seebhohm, Lord (1968) *Report of the Committee on Local Authority and Allied Personal Services* Cmnd.3703 London: HMSO

Shapland, J., Willmore, J. and Duff, P. (1985) *Victims in the Criminal Justice System* Aldershot: Gower

Shapland, J., Wiles, P. and Leek, M. (1990) *Policing in Sussex: a report of a survey* University of Sheffield/Sussex Police

Sheehy, Sir Patrick (1993) *Inquiry into Police Responsibility and Rewards*, CM2280.1 London: HMSO

Sherman, L. and Berk, R. (1983) The Minneapolis Domestic Violence Experiment, *Police Foundation Reports*, July

Sherman, L. and others (1992) The variable effects of arrest on criminal careers: the Milwaukee Domestic Violence Experiment *The Journal of Criminal Law and Criminology* 83:1 Spring

Sinclair, I. and Miller, C. (1984) *Measures of Police Effectiveness and Efficiency* Home Office Research and Planning Unit Paper 25. London: Home Office

Small, S. (1983) *Police and People in London: II A Group of Young Black People* London: Policy Studies Institute

Smith, D.J. (1983a) *Police and People in London: I A Survey of Londoners*. London: Policy Studies Institute

Smith, D.J. (1983b) *Police and People in London: III A Survey of Police Officers* London: Policy Studies Institute

Smith, D.J. (1986) The Framework of Law and Policing Practice. In, J. Benyon and C. Bourn (eds) *The Police: Powers, Procedures and Proprieties* Oxford: Pergamon Press

Smith, D.J. (in press) Youth crime and conduct disorders: time trends, patterns, and causal explanations. In M. Rutter and D.J. Smith (eds) *Psychosocial Disorders in Young People: Time Trends and Their Causes* London: Wiley

Smith, D.J. and Gray, J. (1983) *Police and People in London: IV The Police in Action* London: Policy Studies Institute

Smith, L.J.F. (1989a) *Concerns About Rape* Home Office Research Study No.106 London: HMSO

Smith, L.J.F. (1989b) *Domestic Violence* Home Office Research Study No.107 London: HMSO

Spencer, S. (1985) *Called to Account: The Case for Police Accountability in England and Wales* London: NCCL

Stanko, E.A. (1988) Hidden violence against women. In J. Pointing and M. Maguire *Victims of Crime: A New Deal?* Milton Keynes: Open University Press

Stratta, E. (1990) A lack of consultation? *Policing* 6: Autumn, 523-549

Tullock, G. (1976) *The Vote Motive* London: Institute of Economic Affairs

Victim Support (1992) *Domestic Violence: report of a national inter-agency working party*

Waddington, P.A.J. (1991) *The Strong Arm of the Law* Oxford: Oxford University Press

Weatheritt, M. (1986) *Innovations in Policing* Beckenham: Croom Helm

Weatheritt, M. (1993) Measuring Police Performance: Accounting or Accountability? In R. Reiner and S. Spencer *Accountable Policing: Effectiveness, Empowerment and Equity*, Institute of Public Policy Research

Weber, M. (1964) *The Theory of Economic and Social Organisation* Glencoe: Free Press

Weeks, J. (1981) *Sex, Politics and Society: The Regulation of Sexuality since 1800* London: Longman

Whitaker, B. (1982) *The Police in Society* London: Eyre Methuen

Willmott, P. (1987) *Policing and the Community* London: Policy Studies Institute

Wilson, J.Q. (1975) *Thinking About Crime* New York: Vintage Books

Wolin, S. (1960) *Politics and Vision* London: George Allen and Unwin

Women's National Commission (1985) *Violence Against Women* London: Cabinet Office

Index

*R v Metropolitan Police
Commissioner, ex p Blackburn*, 13,
15
*R v Secretary of State for the Home
Department, ex p Northumbria
Police Authority*, 16-17, 310
Ralphs, Lady, 145
Rantzen, Esther, 116
rape, 7, 10, 232, 245, 248, 253, 256,
260, 273, 279, 281, 298 299-300
Crisis, 111, 113, 123, 127, 129,
148, 160
domestic violence and sexual
assault, 110-14, 130-3
Research and Counselling Project,
111
trauma syndrome (RTS), 121-2, 125
Raphael, D.D., 38
Raynor, P., 148
Regan, L., 115
Reiner, Robert, 1, 3, 6, 17, 20, 24,
27-8, 50-1, 55, 222-3, 275, 287, 291,
304
Report on social services (Seebohm),
42
Representative Government, 38
Republic, The, 37-8
Revenue Support Grant (RSG), 19,
172, 174, 181-2, 195, 225, 246
Richardson, A., 42
Richardson, Jo, 150-1, 296
Rights of Women, 146-8
Rock, P., 102, 165
Rogers, M., 54
Rosenbaum, D.P., 59
Rousseau, Jean Jacques, 38
Royal Commission on the Police 1962,
26, 169-70, 220
Rumbold, Angela, 150

Safe Neighbourhoods Unit, 101-2,
284, 299
Safer Cities Programme, 55, 57, 76,
79-84, 85, 87-8, 92, 94-5, 99-101,
103, 248, 254-6, 265, 284, 286
St. Marys Centre, 120, 144, 157, 245,
272
Sanders, A., 24

Sartori, G., 40
Scarman Report, 22, 223-4, 226, 228,
230, 260-1, 267
scenes of crime officers (SOCOs), 180,
183-4, 195, 258
Schools Liaison Officer (SLO), 59-60,
71, 73, 285
Schumpeter, Joseph, 38-40, 45
Secured by Design, 69-71, 93, 285
Seebohm, Lord, 42
Select Committee on Estimates Report,
168, 170
SEUs *see* special enquiry units
sexual assault *see* domestic violence
and rape
Shapland, J., 110, 211
Shaw, M., 57
Sheehy Inquiry, 2, 25, 31, 58, 183
Shepherd, D., 54
Sherman, L., 112-13
Sinclair, I., 25
SLO *see* Schools Liaison Officer
Smith, D.J., 4-6, 10, 33, 51, 112, 129
Smith, L.J.F., 129, 141, 150
Smith, Tim, 201
special enquiry units (SEUs), 118, 136
Spencer, S., 28, 219
staff associations and policing policy,
294-5
Stafford Crime Prevention Centre, 53
Stanbury v. Exeter Corporation, 13
Standing Spending Assessment (SSA),
174, 181-2
Stanko, E. A., 154
Stern, Vivien, 102
Stratta, E., 22-3
Straw, Jack, 27-8
Superintendents' Association, 190,
193, 206, 290
Swift, P., 18

Thames Valley Police television
documentary, 111, 130, 138, 152,
160, 163, 299, 301, 311
'Theme of the month' scheme, 75-6
trade union(s), 12, 294-5
Traffic and Operation Support
Department, 59